The
MECHANISM
DEMANDS A
MYSTICISM

An Exploration of Spirit,
Matter and Physics

Thomas G. Brophy

MEDICINE BEAR PUBLISHING
BLUE HILL, ME

The Mechanism Demands A Mysticism:
An Exploration of Spirit, Matter and Physics
by
Thomas G. Brophy

Published in 1999
Copyright © 1996, 1997, 1998 Thomas G. Brophy
All rights reserved. No part of this book may be reproduced, stored in a mechanical retrieval system, or transmitted in any form by electronic, video, laser, mechanical, photocopying, recording means or otherwise, in part or in whole, without written consent of the publisher.
02 01 00 99   0 9 8 7 6 5 4 3 2 1

Published by
MEDICINE BEAR PUBLISHING
PO BOX 1075
BLUE HILL, ME 04614

Library of Congress Cataloging in Publication Data
Brophy, Thomas G., 1960 -
    The mechanism demands a mysticism / Thomas G. Brophy.
        p.   cm.
    Includes bibliographical references and index.
    ISBN 1-891850-12-1 (pbk.)
    1. Science-philosophy.   2. Physics - philosophy.   3. Hylozoism.
        I. Title.
BD646.B76   1999
110—dc21
                                                99-17722
                                                    CIP
ISBN 1-891850-12-1
            Printed in the USA

Contents

Acknowledgments .... *vii*
About the Cover .... *viii*

Introduction .... *ix*
   A Dialogue .... *ix*
   A Note On Terminology.. *x*
   Holographic Paradigm?... *xiii*
   A Note On History... *xv*
   A Note On Transformation, and an Exercise .... *xvi*

PART I: BOUNDARIES OF THE KNOWN 1

1. Scientists—A Priesthood in Crisis........................... 3
   The Present Crisis of Science 4
   Crises of Being..11

2. Transcendent Experience 15
   The Role of Transcendent Experience 15
   Examples of Transcendent Experience 18
   Transcendent Experience in Psychology and Psychiatry 23
   Effect of Rejecting Transcendent Experience................................27

3. The Views of the Founders.................................... 31
   The Founders Became Hylozoists..32
   Einstein's "Mistake" 42

4: The Present Concensus.. 45
   "There Are No Phenomena…That There Is Deep Mystery About" .45
   Paradigmatic Inertia 54
   Ode to Giordano Bruno..55

PART II: THE FACT OF MATTER 57

5. Matter in Motion 59
Dynamics 60
Tides 61
Newton's Apple 63
Some Asides About Tides 63
Newton's Laws, Maxwell's Demons, and Boltzmann's Demise 65
Simple Electricity and Magnetism Begets Light and Relativity 71
Sneaking Up On the Nature of Atoms 76

6. The Stochastic Universe 77
A Theory Of Everything? 78
Failures of Classical Physics 80
The Ultraviolet Catastrophe 81
Those Troublesome Atoms 86
Wave-Particle Paradox? 89
"Uncertainty" or Complementarity? 91
Einstein Loses in Brussels 93
The Hylostochastic Paradigm 94
Back to the Breeze 95
Proof of Nonlocality 97
Beyond the Breeze 99

7. The Butterfly Effect 103
The Paradigmatic Crisis 104
Back to Matter for Now 105
The Sensitive Universe 106
A Need to Know 109
Nonlinear Weather Is Unpredictable 109
The Butterfly Effect 113
Strange Attractors 114
Fractal Nature 116
Deterministic Chaos 118
A Mathematician on Mathematicians 119
"Complexity Theory" 120
Paradigms Completed, and Lacking 124

PART III: THE EFFECT OF SPIRIT 127

8. The Creative Universe 129
Layers of Reality 130
Spirit and Matter 131
The Hylozoic Paradigm—Planckian Butterflies 132
Prana, Lifetrons, and Subtle Realms 133
Different Religions and the Hylozoic Paradigm 136
The Dreaded Dualism 140
Proofs Of Materialism Are Still Wrong 142
Planckian Butterflies In Action 145

9. Life in the Valleys 149
An Earthquake Triggers an Inner Quake 150
Predicting the Next Great Tokyo Earthquake? 154
Sensitive Earthquakes: A Link to Planckian Butterflies? 158
Volcanoes 161
The Weather 163
The "Clockwork" Motions of the Planets 166
"Just Because We Can't Predict Tornadoes Doesn't Mean the World Isn't Round." 169
Just Turn Off the Terminals and See What Happens 171
Nature Spirits 173

10. Consciousness Not Explained 175
Some Facts about the Brain 175
Cognitive Models—Open or Closed? 176
Computer Fear 179
Dennett's Wrong Axiom 182
Evidence for Larger Models 184
A Note on the Mechanism 189
The Decision 190

11. The Lives of Planets 197
Formation of Earth 200
The Collapse 202
The Turbulence 204
The Solar Nebula Thought Experiment 205
The Lives 210
The Seventh Makham of Andalusian Sufism 215

PART IV: FREEDOM FROM THE KNOWN 219

12. From Superstition to Intuition 221
East and West.. *223*
Barriers to Intuition *227*
Democracy of the Transcendent... *228*
The Dark Side *229*
A Responsibility to Investigate... *235*

13: Intelligence—Allowing Spirit into Matter 237
Horses' Teeth.. *238*
A Kogi Message from the Past... *240*
The Ageless Wisdom *248*
A Plausible Avatar... *254*
A Sublime Dream... *266*
Two Different Masters *270*
Hylozoic What?.. *272*

14. Frauds, Fools, Magicians, Messiahs, and Us......275
Time Travel As Example... *276*
Spiritual Abduction?... *278*
Plant Behavior? *286*
Debunking Debunkers *292*
Example: A Rumor of Fraud.. *294*
Anti Antinomian Authorities (The Inflationary Guru Problem)..... *298*
*De-Glamourized Teachers, Intuition, and Four Signs of Ego
Inflation* *305*

15. Freedom from the Known—Science as Partner 311
Experimental Certainty?... *313*
Mystical Physiology *314*
An Historical "Pack of Tricks," Benignly *321*
Experimental Tests Exist But Are Not Accepted........................ *324*
Waking Up... *329*
Hylozoic Astronomy.. *331*
"New Science" Is Reconnection with the Ageless Wisdom.......... *333*

Endnotes.. *336*
Index *356*

Acknowledgements

While researching, writing and developing the ideas for this book, I benefited from interactions with many wonderful souls. A complete list of all to whom I am indebted would be impossible. I thank Yem Sue Fong, Charles Robert, Ashuan Seow, Zoe Zimmerman, John Williamson, Marjorie Fox, Misae Nishikura, Richard Moss, Jacquie Small, and specially James T. and June H. Brophy for their intellectual support and emotional encouragement; while some of them did not even know I was writing this book, their humanity made it possible.

I thank Freeman Dyson for taking the time to encourage some of my early work, Paul Rosen for being an excellent and dedicated partner on some early career scientific papers, and Larry Esposito for enabling my dissertation work.

Michael Toms, Jacqueline Small, Thomas Moore, Hiroshi Motoyama, Stanley Krippner, Gaetan Chevalier and Doug Robert provided encouraging, informative and indispensable comments on the text.

Tony Stubbs and Wendy Ruiz provided professional copyediting and proof reading, respectively. Marjorie Fox provided indispensable general consulting.

I thank Paul Diamond, and USWEST, for allowing me flexible work schedules while I completed researches related to this book. I thank Hiroshi Motoyama, and Tamamitsu Shinto Shrine, for supporting two months on a "Motoyama-Bentov" fellowship. My students at the California Institute for Human Science provided inspiration by their will to uncover the truth with humanity and conviction.

I thank Jonathon Ray Spinney, of Medicine Bear, for publishing the book.

Finally I thank all serious physicists past and present, even those who may vigorously disagree with this book, for at least they seek the truth.

About the Cover

The cover picture was taken on April 1, 1995 with the Hubble Space Telescope Wide Field and Planetary Camera 2. It shows a nearby star-forming region 7,000 light-years away from Earth in the constellation Serpens. The size of the region shown is equivalent to many of our whole solar systems. Bright light shining from hot massive nearby stars, out of the photo, is boiling off the gas of this molecular cloud, revealing small dense clumps which contain nascent stars. Those clumps are probably birthing planetary systems similar to our own. This image stunned professional astronomers and lay people alike by revealing the complexity, beauty, and I would say "aliveness" that accompanies the birth of suns. As a released NASA, HST image, this photo is U.S. "public domain". Versions of it are popular in many major scientific centers, such as the Beckman Center of the National Academy of Sciences at U.C. Irvine.

Introduction

Physics does not prove mysticism. However, considered fully and passionately, physics nearly demands a mysticism. This was noted by Prince Louis De Broglie, one of the great founders of modern physics, who said "the mechanism demands a mysticism" in the 1920s. A tragedy is that now, seventy years later, our scientific and cultural communities still do not acknowledge it.

A Dialogue

In a series of dialogues during many years, an influential philosopher and teacher met with an influential quantum physics professor. They struggled together to identify what it is, fundamentally, that a human *is*—what they themselves were, in an immediate, tangible, and very relevant sense. Reviewing their dialogues, one senses that they came close, perhaps would contact, and then recede from, only to approach again, a very important fact of existence. And yet, even after years of such pursuit, physicist David Bohm returned earnestly to the question, to philosopher J. Krishnamurti, "But this is a difficult problem, you see, how mind is able to act in matter?"

After spending much of their lives in seemingly disparate fields, these two felt an immediate rapport when they met. In their dialogues, one senses that Krishnamurti was in touch with something that he wanted, even somehow needed, to communicate and that Bohm was also beginning to sense Krishnamurti's territory. Bohm also had a whole new set of tools with which to build signs to Krishnamurti's territory—the tools of physics. One senses Bohm's awe at his realization that that territory is beyond physics, beyond matter, beyond the brain, and beyond control, but in a tangible and important way as real as the matter he'd studied with his physics. The two inquirers always returned to the same core question: "how is mind [an aspect of nonmatter] able to act in matter?" The questions are always fresh. "This is a difficult problem, you see."

We may have a flash of insight, a deep meditative experience, an insight to mystical states, even a transformational crisis, and when we return to ordinary reality it's still a difficult problem. How is nonmatter able to act in matter? Krishnamurti, Bohm and many others have emphasized, this is not merely an academic question. It is a raging conflict—within ourselves, among our relationships, our societies, nations, even in nature, perhaps for the whole planet and beyond—the source of dualities of suffering and joy, the origin of relentless circles of life and death in the human, animal, and plant kingdoms.

And in the following book, we are going to resolve all those problems. If that statement gave you the impulse to jettison this book, good! Our intent will be only to try and share some of the struggle that the two explorers described above exemplified. To pretend to more—to have solutions—would be foolish at best.

This book *is* about one small, but fundamental, aspect of those perennial problems, as expressed in three questions. From what we in our scientific/intellectual culture, after tremendous and ingenuous effort, now know about the mechanics of how matter works, is matter open to the influence of nonmatter, or not? And if matter is open to such influence, how much so? And what does this mean for how we might go about living in the world? The first two questions are objective—as much as objectivity is possible. The third question is necessarily subjective. This distinction between subjective opinions and objective knowledge is important. Many who explore these questions jumble together the two and some of the subjective stuff necessarily ends up wrong in some sense. Then others who for subjective reasons of their own want to discredit the whole topic, have a tool to do so.

In this book, I try to make a careful distinction between the subjective and objective parts. As you think critically about the book, keep this in mind. Don't discard the important objective conclusions even if something subjective irritates you. Do your own subjective part—sell your own Antarctic ice—if you like. But be clear about the objective information about how things actually work, and especially be clear about whether this perspective really is leading, or could lead, us toward a new paradigm for relating to the world.

A Note on Terminology

This book is about the scientific basis for a paradigm shift. Since Thomas Kuhn's *The Structure of Scientific Revolutions,* the word paradigm has entered the household lexicon. The concept of paradigm taps such power and imagination that it is tempting to use it for any profound theory. The word is often overused for essentially minor concepts and models. The topic of this book however deserves the word paradigm.

We are all aware that our world is careening through changes at rates previously unimagined. It is likely that this process is not only change but transformation. Accompanying that transformation, in the world of ideas, intellect and science, is a paradigm shift. The shift is in some ways gradual and in some ways immediate, in some ways subtle and in some ways like a ton of bricks. Many are aware of the shift and have written about aspects of it. Books about "Quantum Questions," "Quantum Medicine," "Chaos," the "Holographic Model of the Universe," and even "Quantum Politics" are talking about aspects of the shift.

No satisfactory name for the new paradigm has emerged. The term "new science" is loosely used, but it is often not clear what the real difference between the new and old sciences is. This lack of clear terminology adds to the general lack of clarity that is sometimes exploited by those who would peddle nearly anything "New Age" to a gullible market. This book attempts to define clearly the difference between the new paradigm and the old paradigm, to help us to know for ourselves which paradigm we are in and which we want to be in. For that purpose, I've proposed a name. The paradigm shift has a life of its own and will be lived regardless of the language we use to describe it. The ideas in this book are meant to clarify our understanding of the shift. The concepts offered are independent of whether the name I propose sticks, but I think it's a good name.

Hylozoism comes from the Greek roots "hylo" meaning matter, and "zo" meaning life. Hylozoism is the belief that matter is alive, that nonmaterial influences infuse matter (matter which need not necessarily be so infused) making it alive. In the hylozoic paradigm, life is the interplay of spirit and matter. But this is not the same as "vitalism." In vitalism, living things are said to be specially alive, whereas inorganic matter is dead. The hylozoic paradigm is the realization and acceptance that matter functions in a way that is open to the influence of spirit, and that spirit is both quite real and quite nonmaterial. Matter is quarks, electrons, protons, atoms, molecules, electromagnetic fields, light and gravity, with everything described by the equations of physics. Spirit is nonmaterial, and spirit can affect matter. How it does this is the subject of this book.

We can further understand the unfamiliar word "hylozoism" by considering what it is not. What is the opposite of hylozoism? To answer this, I am going to coin two new words. Many will recognize the concepts behind these words as nothing new; indeed there is no new physics anywhere in this book. The reason for two new words is that the old labels have gathered confusing baggage beyond their useful meanings. Also these words, together with hylozoic, form a family which I think clearly contain the basic concepts and bring to focus the different possible paradigms.

First, consider "hylostochastism," combining the Greek "stochastic," random, with "hylo" for matter. In the hylostochastic paradigm the unknowable, immeasurable and indeterminate events in nature, in matter, are believed to be actuated by purely random (stochastic) processes. In hylostochastism nature, matter is therefore partially deterministic and partially random and meaningless (meaningless to the extent that events can have no meaning other than the demonstration of randomness or the deterministic propagation of past material influences). Hylostochastism is the standard model, orthodoxy or "party line," of science today. It is based on the so-called "Copenhagen interpretation"[1] of quantum mechanics.

Our second coined word is "hylostatic," using the Greek-derived "static"—standing still, unchanging. Hylostatism is the paradigm of the mechanistic or Cartesian scientific worldview. In the hylostatic paradigm, matter—the whole world—is believed to be static and unchanging in a four-dimensional sense. In the hylostatic paradigm, the world is believed to be a great machine like an 18th-century French wind-up parlor amusement. The equations that govern the functioning of matter are considered to be infinitely precise, constant and time-reversible. So, in four dimensions, the material world is a static, unchanging object. The moving three-dimensional world we see can be described in the hylostatic paradigm as simply a progression of cross-sections moving through the fixed four-dimensional[2] object-world. The hylostatic worldview is only deterministic.[3]

We will see how, as far as scientists now know, the material world is either hylozoic or hylostochastic; it cannot be hylostatic as was the Cartesian/Newtonian world. The hylostatic description is an adequate partial description of the way things are. But the four-dimensional object-world is neither fixed, nor infinite, nor even fully determined. Nearly every scientist now agrees (or would agree if they study the facts) that it is an objective fact that the world is not (completely) hylostatic. The remaining question to be investigated then is whether the world is hylozoic or hylostochastic. And this question has not been seriously investigated by the scientific community.[4] The largely-held opinion, however, is that the world is somehow obviously or without question, hylostochastic—at least that seems the only explanation for the otherwise bizarre attitudes of many scientists toward even considering the question. Further, the common belief seems to be that the world is hylostochastic in such a way that anything that occurs in our environment and in ourselves is no different from hylostatic—that the nondeterministic parts of events are so small as to be irrelevant. This book shows that the belief in hylostochastism is far from obviously or unquestionably true, and that there is more evidence that it is wrong than there is evidence that it is right. Also, it will be argued that the nondeterministic aspect of events is very relevant.

Holographic Paradigm?

The rest of this section uses some names, terminology and concepts that will be unfamiliar to many readers. This section is meant mainly to decondition those who are already familiar with these terms so that they can read the rest of the book less encumbered—so this section can be skipped, without loss, if you find yourself unfamiliar.

Some have used the word "holographic" for the new paradigm. This label arose from a mixture of Karl Pribram's (and other brain-psychology researchers') insights into brain function models, and the implicate/explicate order quantum mechanical interpretations of David Bohm, and Ken Wilber's syntheses of Western and Buddhist psychologies. This label has not found broad usage however, I think for two good reasons.

First, it does not make sense to me to name the new paradigm, the paradigm which is supposed to reenchant the world by making clear the existence of subtle realms that interact with matter—a most emphatically *not* mechanistic paradigm—to name it after a specific sort of machine, the holograph! The holograph is an exciting, beautiful, insight-producing, and complicated sort of machine, but a machine nonetheless. It is not a good name for the paradigm which will replace mechanism.

Second, while the goal of synthesizing all the way from matter, through life, through various psychological levels, through mystical states, through spiritual realms, and including cosmic unity, is a worthy goal; to put all these things in the same bin, labeled holographic, seems a little premature. The emphasis on unity in the descriptions of the holographic paradigm, which is the reason for the label *holo*-graphic, is undoubtedly correct in the final analysis (irony intended). But in Wilber's own syntheses, the true Unity level is several levels removed from any ordinary psychological states, and several levels removed from anything presently considered in science. Most of us are still wondering, as were Bohm and Krishnamurti, whether anything nonmaterial (Bohm's and Krishnamurti's "mind," or "spirit" as it is used in this book) can indeed affect matter. The doctrine of unity, oddly, has been used to justify almost any dogma or personal stance, from Marxism to "Taoist anarchy," and even a solipsistic admixture of metaphors called "chaos linguistics"—which advocates an attitude something like, "all is one, and language is separative, so language is necessarily meaningless, so anything anyone else says is meaningless, so anything I say or do is as meaningful as can be."

The focus of this book is several paces back from the unity level, and asks the questions: "How does matter really work? What is the most accurate scientific paradigm for how matter works?" As we shall see, this will carry us quite far—up through much of biology and perhaps even ordinary psychological states—and the hylozoic paradigm for matter will open the gates to investigating the spiritual, mystical, and even unitive levels, but it certainly will not explain these larger realms.

Readers familiar with David Bohm's ground-breaking implicate-explicate order interpretation of quantum mechanics will notice that the following descriptions of the hylozoic paradigm are quite different. Bohm's models of the implicate order are essentially a subset of the hylozoic paradigm. His models may be right, but we don't even need to get that specific in order to appreciate the magnitude of the paradigm shift. Also, the emphasis on the "frequency realm" is a valid way, but only one way to approach the issue. Some people love to think in terms of Fourier transforms and some people don't. If you don't, if you like to think in terms of real geometric objects and spatial-temporal events, you can get to the same conclusions as by emphasizing the wavelike description of things, and that is the sort of development method used in this book.

A Note on History

Some mention of historical developments and historical progressions are given in the book. The historical presentation is not meant to be exhaustive or even comprehensive. Its purpose is to include a little bit of context for the ideas presented. If the history presented resonates with the reader's own sense and knowledge of history, then it can help bolster the subjective arguments for the ideas presented.

A number of excellent books on the history of scientific ideas, some even by historians, are available. Some popular science history books, in order to advance a specific point of view, present a rather patronizing linear progression of ideas. Personally, the more I try to develop a concrete, linear, or progressive history of ideas—a history of which I am not skeptical—the further I find that ideational progression is more spiral than linear, more like a twisted mobius strip of ideas, or even a tortuous multidimensional Klien surface, if not a completely turbulent froth.

If one digs to find proponents of any given philosophical stance, it is not difficult to find some obscure medieval monk, or some not-so-obscure ancient Greek, or a Vedantic sage (of any age), or a Tibetan Buddhist of the Golden Age (the European Dark Age), or an ancient Chinese, or a Kogi Indian, or a Gnostic Christian, or an Aztec astronomer, who has lived by precisely that stance. So I suggest that one could invent any linear historical progression of ideas and then find references to document it. The philosophical or scientific ideas of the politically or economically or militarily powerful portions of a given culture however may indeed have a specific lineage and that, I guess, is what we are implicitly talking about when we talk about "The History of Ideas." Some of the most powerful people, however, have held some of the most fantastic, bizarre and wrong ideas (as we'll see, this includes some of the most powerful scientists). So a progression of the history of the ideas of powerful people clearly has little to do with our first focus in this book—a clear analysis of what we *demonstrably* know about the objective science of how matter, the world, works and what this demonstrable knowledge may mean for our understanding of what we are and how we can interact with that which we know. As for the second focus, a subjective look at what this means for our culture, its progression and how one might want to interact with this progression, this second task can benefit much from the history of the ideas of various powerful cultural elites.

A Note on Transformation, and an Exercise

Finally, the intellectual movement toward the hylozoic paradigm is only one aspect of a great journey of transformation. Something—an unusually large and rapid change—seems to be going on in the world. It is occurring on many levels in many ways—cultural, spiritual and personal, even economic and political as well as scientific. It is not at all obvious which, if any, of these aspects or levels of change causes the others. On a personal level, one's acceptance of the hylozoic paradigm for understanding the scientific and material worlds seems to be only part of a multi-aspect personal change. As we go on this journey, we benefit from whatever maps we can find, no matter how partial or sketchy. And so, as part of the secondary theme in this book, I try to point out a few maps and sketch perhaps a tiny bit of the new terrain.

To see if this book is for you, try the following exercise. Slow down your thoughts and relax for a moment. Look at or visualize the weather or anything moving in the environment (rapid creeks and thunderstorms are perfect). Ask yourself, very sincerely, what is it, really, in the most basic sense that is happening. Sense whatever is going on in yourself, your body, your emotions and especially your thoughts as you experience and question what you are looking at. End of exercise.

If you sensed, thought, or felt—even for an instant—that anything extraordinary or beyond the surface appearance of things might be happening, this book is for you. If you wanted to do the exercise but couldn't because your mind was racing, you might as well let your mind race through this book as any other. If you lapsed into spontaneous samadhi, take a rest and then write your own book. If nothing at all subtle happened, and if you have no interest in the exercise—if everything seems hunky-dory and you're certain that you understand everything worth understanding—don't read this book (and please don't write a review of it either).

PART I:

BOUNDARIES OF THE KNOWN

1. Scientists—A Priesthood in Crisis

On a humid summer evening in the ancient city of Kyoto, we kneeled Japanese-style on straw tatami mats, sipping sake in a traditional banquet room. I'd walked there, through the forested temple district, at sunset. The stone and wooden buddhas, demons, spirits and bodhissatvas, the exquisitely tended gardens, the semi-wild monkeys in the semi-wild forest, all seemed to be speaking to me—subtle invitations to a heresy that I couldn't quite discern.

Inside at the banquet, the communications became clear. We were a group of astronomers and astrophysicists, gathered in Kyoto for an International Astronomical Union conference. Our concern was the scientific understanding of the formation and evolution of the solar system. We had managed to get governments and universities to send us to Kyoto, ironically a traditional center of the study of Buddhist cosmology.

As an apprentice geisha in traditional kimono delicately served us, I interpreted for my neighbors at the banquet who could only speak English. On my right, a "cosmogeochemist" with the National Aeronautics and Space Administration was well into a bottle of sake. "You know, this is why we do it," he said to me. "Science. Astronomy. It's not because we like to write computer programs or do chemistry experiments. We don't make a lot of money. We do it so that we can go to banquets like this ... we do it because we're a sort of modern priesthood."

When I heard that, I entered one of those moments of clarity, when we are in and of a situation and we are simultaneously aware of a deeper connection occurring in ourselves. For the cosmogeochemist was right. That had become the reason why I continued to do research astronomy, though not why I went into it in the first place. Indeed, the motives of the fundamental scientific research community as a whole suddenly appeared suspect.

Is science the quest for the truth about how the world works? Or, is it the development of technology for the making of conveniences or weapons? Might it be only the assertion of authority and power by a self-appointed intellectual elite? The lifelike ancient stone demons and buddhas across the street seemed silently to question us scientists at the banquet.

The discussions that follow are based on the premise that fundamental science is, or at least should be, the search for truth[5] about how things work. Technology, engineering, medicine and applied sciences have their own motivations; they use the tools that fundamental science creates. Fundamental science infuses our belief structures—how we understand what our environment is, how it works, what *we* are, how *we* work.

The Present Crisis of Science

Much of fundamental science today is in a state of crisis. We'll consider symptoms of this crisis below. But first an anecdote points to what I think is a cause of the crisis.

A Ph.D. classmate passed his difficult comprehensive exams and stood before a committee of physics professors to ask permission for his chosen dissertation topic. He proposed to study the foundations and meaning of quantum theory. In the midst of the proposal, a professor known for his technical brilliance and intimidating style interjected to comment, "I want you to know that I consider the study of the meaning of quantum theory in the same league as the study of UFOs and ESP." Now, some New Agers might think that was a compliment, but everyone present knew it meant that the student was sticking his nose where it wasn't wanted and he was going to be told as much. Every trained scientist knows that there is a class of issues that are taboo. Even to mention these issues causes shivers of revulsion, or automatic ridicule. These topics are even spoken of as "dangerous."[6]

My classmate was, in effect, proposing to make some eyeglasses to see if the emperor of the scientific paradigm really was wearing clothes. He was being told unabashedly that the glasses had been around for awhile, but they were in a sort of Pandora's box and only kooks and crackpots would go near Pandora's box. A major source of the paradoxical despair in science today is that growing numbers of perfectly sensible people know quite clearly that this particular emperor is quite naked. But the emperor's priests and generals insist on continuing as if the myth were intact.

The symptoms of crisis apparent within the scientific community are many. A physicist writes, "... evidence of low morale in the entire scientific community has been building steadily lately. The malaise is all around us ... in a few more years, physics will be like ancient Latin and Greek, a dead language. The uses of physics will never die, for they are profitable. But true physics, 'natural philosophy,' the search for natural truth and understanding, is ill, perhaps mortally."[7]

Struggling to find the reasons for this, he continues, "Somewhere near the center [of the reason] lie such ancient sins as ego, narrow-mindedness, and self-centeredness [of scientists] ... an egotistical failure to listen and take seriously other nonscientific points of view." An eminent mathematical physicist who has had his scientific papers vandalized and cut out of journals to prevent their use laments, "The main [intention of many scientists] is no longer to convince other scientists that your controversial ideas represent physical reality, but to get ahead of the competition using whatever means are available."[8]

The scandal surrounding Nobel prize winning molecular biologist David Baltimore's defense of fraudulent data was well publicized. Apparently Baltimore, although not originally responsible for the fraud, defended the data largely for the reason that the truth would have tarnished several long-nurtured reputations, including his own.[9] The career of a young whistle-blowing scientist was crushed in the process. Another Nobel prize winning biochemist publicly admits that he "no longer puts his best ideas in his grant proposals,"[10] for fear that they will be stolen by the proposal "peer reviewers" (whose job it is to objectively decide if the idea should receive funds for development).

If such behavior is so widespread as to hamper a Nobel Laureate, consider the effect on struggling young Ph.D.s. Indeed, a loosely connected electronic network[11] of over a thousand Ph.D.s (discussing largely the horrific job market) discussed a feeling of having been cheated—used as inexpensive instructors for undergraduates, and to complete research projects and prepare lucrative proposals, only to be abandoned when their degrees qualify them for higher pay. Certainly no one should feel they have a "right" to a research job if society doesn't feel a need for the research. But science graduate schools seem almost in danger of becoming a sort of intellectual Vietnam. Surviving young Ph.D.s, having idealistically joined what they thought was a just and noble cause in search of truth, return bewildered to a thankless and confused society.

Less-than-exemplary ethical behavior is not new to science. Some historians argue that even the great Isaac Newton, 300 years ago, took credit for the invention of calculus from Leibniz by using his immense influence to prevent Leibniz from publishing in professional journals. Christian Huygens, upon discovering the nature of Saturn's rings 350 years ago, published the solution in code to prevent credit for his discovery from being stolen. But the evidence is that unethical behavior, or at least its effect, is growing. In *Nature* magazine, Sir Brian Pippard editorializes with kind understatement, "Such excess of confidence [among scientists] is a fairly recent development ... there are those ... who have gone further and assumed authority, in the name of science, to brand all belief as superstition. They have abandoned healthy scepticism in favour of bigotry."[12] The effects of this "excess of confidence" are far greater now because the remaining big issues in fundamental science are the foundations of its own materialist paradigm. The nature of Saturn's rings is intriguing (and incidentally dear to my own heart), but it does not affect great religions, basic political theory, the foundations of medicine or basic human understanding. The materialist paradigm does.

An open and unselfconscious example of "abandoned healthy scepticism in favour of bigotry" occurred in *Physics Today*, the magazine of the American Physical Society. Nobel Laureate and Princeton University professor Philip W. Anderson wrote a screed denouncing all those "who call themselves physicists" yet engage in experiments studying the possibility of ESP. Robert Jahn, a senior engineering professor, also at Princeton, wrote in defense of his experiments criticized by Anderson, "although [Anderson's] office is only a few hundred yards from my own, he has not visited our laboratory, discussed any of his concerns with me directly or apparently even read with care any of our technical literature."

1: Scientists—A Priesthood in Crisis

Anderson retorted, "I feel our differences would not be helped much by the pleasant collegial chat he suggests ... I am told that people who have looked in detail at Jahn's protocols have found some familiar problems—discarded data, in particular."

Anderson then again defends his position on simplistic philosophical grounds (grounds which, as I'll discuss later, do not withstand logic).[13]

The point here is not to defend Jahn's methods—I haven't studied them either. The point is the viciousness of his attacker. Jahn's earlier mainstream work (Jahn being tenured at the same exalted institution as Anderson) was presumably exemplary. As soon as he directed his gaze in the wrong direction, he apparently was considered fair game for the most destructive attack a scientist can receive: a charge of intentionally discarded data (that is, purposely fraudulent work), and this on the basis of third-party (or apparently fourth-party) rumor. Such a charge, in such a manner, would be inexcusable regarding any mainstream work. (It is quite commonplace verbally, and in anonymous reviews, but not in publicly signed writing.) Apparently, the mere direction of Jahn's inquiry makes him unworthy of civil discourse, much less, professional courtesy. Jahn is nearing the end of an otherwise respected career. He has tenure; he will survive. A younger scientist would not. The ideas we're discussing are indeed dangerous, but not to society—they are dangerous to the career of any scientist who would openly consider them.

The views of those looking into the scientific community from outside have not been rosier. British journalist Bryan Appleyard's book *Understanding the Present: Science and the Soul of Modern Man*,[14] indicts essentially the whole scientific enterprise as morally hollow and actively destructive to spiritual values. Pippard's review (in *Nature*—the same writer mentioned above) of Appleyard's book clearly goes to the heart of the issue in terms of our concerns in the rest of this book:

> "It is hard science that takes the knocks, especially physics as typified by the public figures who recount with breathtaking assurance the whole history of the cosmos from birth to death,

and promise the end of Real Science when a Theory of Everything is brought forth.

"If everything meant only the material world it would not be so bad, but it also includes the human mind, and sometimes even poor old God who appears to have had little choice in the sort of universe He would create. I wish one could say that Appleyard has simply been listening to the wrong pundits, yet this sort of triumphalism is unfortunately widespread. All too rarely do I find colleagues who will assent to the proposition (which I find irresistible) that the very ground-rules of science, its concern only for public knowledge, preclude its finding an explanation for my consciousness, the one phenomenon of which I am absolutely certain. Mostly they admit indeed that it will be a tough job, but like to believe that in due course the relationship of consciousness to brain activity will be made clear, and the ghost in the machine exorcised."[15]

Though Pippard is on the right track, we'll see later how the relationship of consciousness to human brain activity is only one example of a vast array of mysteries that permeate existence. The cause of the affront seen by Appleyard and others is scientists' failure to accept that the "everything" the triumphal physicists speak of is only the material world, and the material world only under certain restrictive circumstances. The assumption that matter described by the equations of mathematical physics is everything, always, without qualification, is the philosophical core of the materialist paradigm—and, as we'll see, it is not right.

A cautionary tale for American scientists can be found in the severe decline in British science in the mid-1980s, a decline from which it has not recovered. The editors of *Nature* magazine argue that the key to that decline surfaced in a newspaper commentary. British Member of Parliament Mr. George Walden was, for two years in the mid-1980s, minister in charge of government spending on science. At the time he was "articulate and argumentative, demanding" of heads of research. But scientists thought he was only cleverly mustering arguments with which to better obtain funding for them. Actually, writing in the *Daily Telegraph*, Walden later revealed that he held a "disgust" for some of the basic attitudes of scientists. Walden wrote of visiting CERN (the European high-energy physics consortium), and meeting there "soft-spoken zealots ... with a quasi-mystical belief in what they were doing," offering "the ultimate truth: the constituents of matter" in exchange for "enough government cash." The editors of *Nature* believe that Walden's previously hidden disgust is "part of the explanation why British science was so roughly dealt with [by the British government] in the 1980s."[16]

A similar situation may be occurring now in the United States. Even those government leaders whom scientists think are on their side are calling for a self-examination by scientists; and few scientists are doing that. Congressman George E. Brown, Jr., Chairman of the influential House Committee on Science, Space and Technology is spoken of as "one of science's best and most knowledgeable friends in Congress."[17]

Yet Brown writes, "... science and technology can promote concentration of power and wealth and even autocratic and dictatorial conditions of many kinds."[18] Brown refers to the famous warning of President Eisenhower, "... in holding scientific research and discovery in respect, as we should, we must also be alert to the equal and opposite danger that public policy itself become the captive of a scientific-technological elite." Brown calls for "genuine self-examination by the scientific community ... [and] ... of the role of science in human culture."

Elsewhere Brown writes that it is troubling and significant "that we have elevated science—to a position of predominance over other types of cognition and experience; that we have, unconsciously and ironically, imbued science with more value than other types of understanding which are overtly and explicitly value based. The Czech philosopher and playwright (and Former President) Vaclav Havel has called this the "crisis of objectivity."[19]

Brown's invocation of Vaclav Havel parallels, in the realm of government, the call for a shift to the hylozoic paradigm in science. The brilliant Havel, a key figure in Checkoslavakia's Velvet Revolution, who went from imprisoned critic of the Communist regime to democratically elected President, practically overnight, without violence, has been likened in stature to America's own Founding Fathers. Havel, in an astonishing moment during his address to the

United States Congress, said that a key principle in his own life, and a key to the continuation of human culture, was the realization that "consciousness precedes being." This key realization is analogous, in the political realm, to the shift to the hylozoic paradigm in science. Former Soviet Communism, against which Havel and others finally prevailed, could be called materialist/mechanist paradigm government. A cornerstone of authoritarian communism was materialist/mechanist paradigm science; for if the material universe was not entirely mechanistic then how could society, economics and government be unquestionably treated as such?

When Havel says that an important fundamental principle of human culture is that consciousness precedes being, he means it. If science, especially physics, is a quest for understanding how the world really works, then it must address what thinkers like Havel mean by "consciousness precedes being." If the prevailing mechanist paradigm science is the final understanding of Nature, of being, then consciousness does not precede being and Havel's guiding principle is wrong. It is a mistake for scientists to dismiss or ignore the insights of great humanitarian and spiritual thinkers, especially when those insights do not fit neatly into the scientific paradigm.

The complaints voiced by Appleyard, Pippard, Walden, Brown, Havel and others who have thought critically about the paradigms of science are not the voices of the merely ignorant. The problem is not that they haven't learned the techniques of complex analysis or field theory or quantum chromodynamics. The reasons for the present crisis of science may be on the scientists' own side of the fence—not recognizing the limitations of its own methods. It's time for the American scientific community to wake up and smell the coffee, or risk going the way of British science.

The old impetuses for increasing science research funding just don't work anymore; they were used for so long that they became implicit. We need explicit new impetuses and we don't have them. The Cold War is over; we have nuclear weapons in numbers beyond rational sensibility; Sputnik is ancient history. The race to the moon is over; we won. Now what? The language of technological spin-offs, space races and arms races has become as compelling as the gibbering of apes. Rather than searching externally for new enemies or new causes, maybe the answer lies in our own house: a renewed evaluation of our search for how the world really works and an examination of our own paradigm.

This crisis of science occurs at the end of a century of phenomenal successes for science—successes at describing and understanding the world, as well as technological successes. But crisis following success may be a natural sequence. Fundamental science, based largely on physics, has come to the end of its own paradigm. The crisis occurs now because that paradigm, though it was quite useful, is incomplete. To continue functioning in the old paradigm is to not remain true to the original purpose: the search for the truth about how things actually work. Defense of the old paradigm is defense of an incomplete truth in the face of evidence for larger truths. The larger truth, the new paradigm, is intuitively sensed but it is not yet explicitly clear.

Crises of Being

The founders of the scientific revolution struck a deal with the European Church: science was allowed to deal with the material world and not to trespass in the realms of spirit, and the Church was allowed its hegemony in the realm of spirit. In this way began the materialist/mechanist paradigm of science that continues to this day. But were the architects of that paradigm themselves true believers? What were their motivations? Most of them in fact were alchemists, astrologers and even magicians.[20] Did they mend their ways after creating the scientific paradigm—abandoning magic to become modern materialist scientists? Hardly. Johann Kepler,[21] for instance, continued to pursue his mystical "music of the spheres" after he had worked-out his laws governing the motions of planets—laws which we still use today. Isaac Newton spent most of the *second* half of his career in the pursuit of alchemy, having laid the groundwork for modern physics in the first half.[22] Jerome Cardan,[23] an important figure in the development of modern mathematics, continued to emphasize the importance of "prescient dreams, ESP and intuitive flashes of direct knowledge" throughout his life.

What was their motive, then, for creating this mechanist paradigm? Historian Morris Berman argues that René Descartes—the most powerful architect of the scientific paradigm—had spontaneous experiences of spiritual ascent, visions and "out-of-body" experiences. In these states, Descartes wrote in 1637, "I ... examined closely what I was, and saw that I could imagine that I had no body, and that there was no world nor any place that I occupied."[24] Berman argues that Descartes was so frightened by the strangeness, incomprehensibility and reality of nonmaterial aspects of being that Descartes was driven to define a tangible, understandable, rational world. Descartes thus created the materialist paradigm which sometimes bears his name ("Cartesian") as a pragmatic guide to functioning in an experientially mysterious world. Descartes' now cliched "I think therefore I am" was originally a statement that consciousness precedes being, that the spiritual world infuses the material world.

Berman argues convincingly that the creation of mechanist/materialist paradigm science then followed the same model as the creation of major religions. The paradigm of mechanist science, Berman says, "is a direct legacy of this two-step process, i.e., using an occult or somatic insight [Descartes' frightening mystical experience] to dislodge an old system, and then reacting with fear to the very tool that made this possible, dropping it [the tool] like a hot potato, and erecting a new (rigid) system in place of the old one, a system whose very existence depends on the mystical insight now being rejected."[25]

But materialist paradigm science, in addition to being ideologically similar to a religion, I will argue, did play a vital and specific role in the evolution of consciousness.[26] For prior to Descartes, Cardan, Kepler, Galileo, Newton and the other architects of this paradigm, the tools with which to deeply investigate matter and its workings, and hence its meaning, did not exist. Most importantly, materialist paradigm science allowed a completion. It has actually come to the end of itself. It does not need to be superseded through violence (either ideological or physical)—"dislodged" by a new insight—as in Berman's repeating cycles of religions. Old paradigm science created the tools with which to know that itself is incomplete, preparing the way for a vastly expanded paradigm of being. Those tools and their use are what this book is about.

At the time of its creation, the mechanistic paradigm was quite adequate for the science of the day. Then, the way even the most simple things work had yet to be analyzed in a formal experimental/rational framework. The most fundamental questions: *What are the most basic constituents of matter? What is life? How big is the universe? What is thought?* were so far removed from the tools of the fledgling new paradigm science that the Church, or anyone else, could have them, as far as a scientist could practically care. There was so much else, a wealth of everyday phenomena, to investigate. Even during much of the twentieth century, many of the fundamental questions accessible to mechanistic paradigm science remained to be investigated.

In Parts II and III of this book, we'll discuss how the adequacy of the mechanistic paradigm is now coming clearly to an end. The fundamental questions of that paradigm have been answered.

As the old paradigm has started to fail, the fruits it produced are taking on an ominous new dimension. They are taking on a global, planetary dimension. Consider the coincidence: accept for the moment that we actually have come, in a basic sense, to the end of our goal of understanding the functioning of matter; at precisely this moment, in historical terms, we are threatened by the possibilities of several global-scale catastrophes made possible by our use of the once-successful mechanist paradigm.

The possibly imminent catastrophes are well known. The burning of fossil fuels has increased the carbon dioxide content in the atmosphere significantly, and scientists predict that carbon dioxide and other "greenhouse gases" could trigger catastrophic global warming. The releases of ozone-destroying chlorofluorocarbons (CFCs) and other industrial ozone-destroying gases are significantly depleting the ozone layer of the upper atmosphere. This could cause disruption of the global food chain by affecting ocean microorganisms. Direct pollution of the oceans is becoming global in scope, again possibly impacting catastrophically on the food chain. The burning and cutting of forests is global in scope, impacting on the delicate atmospheric balance and the global ecological balance.

Science can tell us that our industrial actions *could* cause global catastrophe. In some specific cases, science can predict the exact outcome of our chosen actions. Possibly, for instance, we will be able to model the ozone layer and the rest of the atmosphere well enough to predict just how much ozone will be lost due to the CFCs we've released. However, science can only show that our actions are large enough to affect the global balance in some way, what the range of possible effects is; science cannot tell us which of the possibilities will actually happen. Such indeterminism is a property of the matter itself, not a failing of the methods of materialist paradigm science. Science can tell us that we are playing Russian roulette with our environment but it can't tell us where the bullet is. For reasons that we'll get into later, science shows that the bullet is not even in a well-defined spot until the trigger is pulled. The materialist paradigm can help describe what is happening, but it lacks a deeper framework for the meaning of these new crises and how to deal with them.

The experience of global crises, as we reach the limits of the mechanist paradigm, may be more than just coincidence. In Nature, when things are completed, they don't simply end; they change, often radically. When a fetus in the womb is fully formed, all of a sudden, crises occur in its environment—horrific physical contractions, near-suffocation and catastrophic changes in its fluid environment. The timing of our global crises with the culmination of the materialist paradigm is suggestive of more than simply an intellectual paradigm shift. It is suggestive of a major transformation to a new form of being.

Whatever the changes turn out to be, the hylozoic paradigm presented in this book may help us accommodate, at least intellectually, the new.

2. Transcendent Experience

Christian Huygens[27] wrote, "The world is my country, science my religion." Huygens also said that the then new scientific and astronomical world view was rejected only by those who were "a bit slow-witted" or those mistakenly holding onto belief structures created by "merely human authority"—meaning the Church.[28] Considering that Galileo died under house arrest for advocating precisely such a world view, when Huygens was thirteen years old, these were rather bold attitudes. What would Huygens say now, more than three hundred years later?

The Role of Transcendent Experience

Huygens would surely approve of NASA's exploration of the planets with the Voyager and other space probes. Huygens felt that other planets would likely harbor life, and that it would be "a waste" if Mars, especially, did not. He might be disappointed that the planets do not seem to harbor biological life as we know it, but I think he would be thrilled by the tremendous beauty and complexity that Voyager and the other space probes discovered on the planets and their satellites.

But would Huygens, the radical thinker, rejecter of "human authority," and investigator for the truth about how the world works, still be repeating what he said three centuries ago? I don't think so. Recently, even the Vatican rehabilitated, if begrudgingly, the reputation of Galileo. The bold truths and revolutionary ideas of Huygens' time are now the mundane beliefs of today.

I think Huygens would expose the "bit slow-witted," and the errors of "merely human authority" of today. And I think he would be chagrined to find them in the ranks of authoritarian proponents of the very science he pioneered. Huygens and many others boldly and refreshingly overthrew the absurd "Churchian" human authority. They did so by creating and using the observational/rational (and materialist and mechanist) scientific paradigm. Simply observe the world, with newly created instruments, and apply the principles of logic and rationality, formalized with mathematics, they said, and the truth is then apparent. If that truth is at odds with "human authority," then it is obvious which is right. If the human authority doesn't accept her error, then she is either slow-witted, or impaired by narcissism and megalomania.

All of that reasoning still applies. But a whole new set of authorities has arisen to defend the structure of the materialist/mechanist paradigm in the face of evidence for its incompleteness and inadequacy. In the light of present-day scientific knowledge, I think Huygens would be the first to point this out.

In the time of Huygens and Galileo, it was indeed bold, even foolish, to challenge the "human authorities." The Church-State authorities of Europe, especially Spain and the Italy which so persecuted Galileo, were at the height of their power. They were traveling to, trading with, profiting from, and claiming dominion over much of the planet. They were becoming immensely rich. They commanded huge armies. Their claim to authority depended on the rightness of their worldview. How could they be wrong? Today, the "scientific-technological elite" warned of by President Eisenhower largely fit the same description.

An examination of the roots of this new authority points to new origins today.

Just what was it that affected Huygens's teacher, René Descartes so much over three centuries ago that caused him to create a paradigm of being that still guides the dominant world culture? It was, surely, transcendent experience. Descartes' own words describing what drove his work, taking them at face value and not "interpreting" them, describe transcendent experience as the impetus. If true transcendent experience occurs, Descartes' was one of them.[29]

We'll consider examples of transcendent experience. But first, what does transcendent experience have to do with the shift to the hylozoic paradigm?

Transcendent experience is experience of something that transcends, or goes beyond, the ordinarily experienced environment of physical, corporeal, material objects and actions. Clearly one could argue endlessly about the distinction between objective perception and hallucination or delusion, but that avoids the issue. Taking the definition of transcendent experience at face value, the relation to our topic is clear. If the materialist/mechanist paradigm is correct, transcendent experience is not possible. If the hylozoic paradigm is correct, transcendent experience *may* be possible. Note that the hylozoic paradigm doesn't endorse all reports of such experience as unquestionably true; it simply opens the possibility that true transcendent experience may occur.

Abraham Maslow called transcendent experience "peak experiences" and brought their study into mainstream psychology.[30] Maslow said that all "core-religious," transcendental, mystical, and "unitive-consciousness" experiences were part of the same thing, "to the extent that all mystical or peak experiences are the same in their essence and have always been the same, and all religions are the same in their essence and always have been the same." Joseph Campbell arrived at this same conclusion of commonalty. His inductive studies of world mythologies led him to the realization that "all mythologies [religions] are true in this sense. They all point to something beneath, beyond the material world."[31]

If one is certain that the materialist paradigm is correct in the final analysis, then one must argue that Maslow and Campbell, and others we'll discuss below, were simply mistaken, if not fraudulent. In later chapters, we'll show how physical science, as presently understood, should be necessarily neutral on this point. One has a choice between the mechanist paradigm and the hylozoic paradigm. The choice however must be made on grounds other than what we know about physical science.

Maslow distinguishes between the essence of religion—transcendent experience—and organized religion. He says, "orthodox [organized] religion ... can lead to dichotomizing life into the transcendent and the secular-profane ... [it can] compartmentalize and separate them temporally, spatially, conceptually, and experientially. This is in clear contradiction to the actualities of the peak experiences."

As we saw in Chapter 1, this separation of life into the transcendent and the secular-profane is exactly what happened when Descartes, et al., originated the mechanist paradigm. In the same way that orthodox religion tries to usurp authority over transcendent experience, as described by Maslow, materialist paradigm science has taken authority over understanding the material world. The problem is that now, materialist paradigm science has gone beyond simply dichotomizing the world into matter and the transcendent; it claims that the transcendent cannot exist. As we will see later, there is simply no scientific ground for this claim. It is assertion, opinion only.

This opinion is widespread in our culture and is egged on by lazy adherence to the materialist paradigm. The importance of transcendent experience, to our investigation in this book, is therefore twofold. First, the hylozoic paradigm will allow a deeper definition of human health. Maslow says, "when we are well and healthy and adequately fulfilling the concept 'human being,' then experiences of transcendence should in principle be commonplace." This goes beyond the concept of health as absence of gross physical disease, and can validate the recent movements toward integrative concepts of health, life, and death. Second, reports of transcendent experience can tell us something about which paradigm (hylozoic or materialistic) we want to choose. The testimony of numerous high-functioning, intelligent (in some cases genius), integrated people, as to the reality of their own transcendent experience, points to an inadequacy of the materialist paradigm.

Also, a more practical consideration is involved. This point should be of interest to scientists whose research funds depend on the public trough, because transcendent experience includes the "other ways of knowing" spoken of (see Chapter 1) by government leaders such as Congressman George Brown Jr., Member of Parliament George Walden, President Eisenhower and Vaclav Havel.

Examples of Transcendent Experience

At the risk of clouding the issue by taking an example from an Eastern culture, I'll mention the transcendent experience of Gopi Krishna because a reader of his autobiographical account will see that he had a keen and scientific mind and his perspective, before his experiences, was essentially Western and skeptical. Also, his autobiographical account includes a professional commentary by well-known psychotherapist James Hillman. Gopi Krishna was essentially an ordinary man, an educator in the Indian province of Kashmir, with a stable family life. He considered himself mildly religious, but scientifically minded. He practiced a modest amount of yogic meditation, basically for health improvement, and he lived a simple lifestyle. One day, during meditation, he was in for a surprise:

> "Suddenly, with a roar like that of a waterfall, I felt a stream of liquid light entering my brain through the spinal cord. Entirely unprepared for such a development, I was completely taken by surprise ... The illumination grew brighter and brighter, the roaring louder, I experienced a rocking sensation and then felt myself slipping out of my body, entirely enveloped in a halo of light. It is impossible to describe the experience accurately. [My] consciousness ... grew wider and wider. I was now all consciousness, without any outline, without any idea of corporeal appendage, without any feeling or sensation coming from the senses, immersed in a sea of light simultaneously conscious and aware of every point, spread out, as it were, in all directions without any barrier or material obstruction. I ... no longer knew myself to be a small point of awareness confined in a body, but instead was a vast circle of consciousness in which the body was but a point bathed in light and in a state of exaltation and happiness impossible to describe."[32]

The similarity to René Descartes' description of his own experience is striking in that they both found themselves suddenly functioning independent of their corporeal bodies, and that their experience profoundly changed their views of life.

G. Krishna's experiences were by no means all "light ... exaltation and happiness," in fact he also experienced the polar opposite—fear of destruction, death, and insanity. "Ah, that's 'bipolar disorder,'[33] nothing common drugs won't fix," a psychiatry student might think. Indeed, Krishna himself was aware of the danger of confusing his experiences with psychosis. "I knew that but a thin line now separated me from lunacy, and yet I gave no indication of my condition to anyone." But Krishna also knew intuitively that the condition was something much more profound. "I [was] blaming myself bitterly again and again for having delved into the supernatural without first acquiring a fuller knowledge of the subject and providing against the dangers and risks of the path. ... [but] something inside prevented me from consulting a physician [or] psychiatrist."

This deeper interpretation of the events was later endorsed by psychiatrist (and subsequent president of the Jung Institute in Zurich) James Hillman. "It is to [Gopi Krishna's] credit that he avoided psychiatry, and even medicine, when later he was to go through the feverish experience of being burned alive from within. Again, however, from the viewpoint of modern psychiatry, such avoidance is typical of a man undergoing paranoid delusions. How close the borderlines [separating healthy transcendent experience and psychosis] are!"[34]

Gopi Krishna survived his ordeal not only intact, but transformed, through many years, into a vastly expanded and more productive self. He became a respected poet, author, and spiritual counselor whose presence uplifted those around him (including Hillman[35]).

The above account contains three key qualities of the sort of transcendent experience that is relevant to our discussion. The experience is, as far as the observer can tell, unmistakably beyond the ordinary experience of material reality. The experience is so unusual that it in some way threatens or destroys previous belief structures. And the experience, ultimately, expands and augments or heals in some way the personality of the experiencer.

Another example of transcendent experience is reported by American M.D., Richard Moss:

> "I was sipping coffee in a restaurant while rapidly scanning [a] book ... before [my] visit that evening. All at once, the words began to dance on the page. As I looked around, everything seemed alive with energy. The very air itself was on fire with radiant light and my body felt like an atomic reactor gone wild. I left the restaurant and [walked] up a country road toward the mountains. I felt nauseated, as though my body would explode. A shimmering brilliance pervaded everything, and I began to dissolve into the world around me. ... I sat down in some brush. A cow was grazing in the field. As I looked, I felt myself enter the plants. I coursed through the intricate tangle of stems, into the sap and cells. With a blink, my attention turned to the cow

2: Transcendent Experience

and at once I began to dissolve into it. 'I' and the world 'out there' were almost but not quite indistinguishable. ... My medical mind ... offered a chain of distressing diagnoses: seizure, stroke, psychosis, adrenaline-secreting tumor. ... I tried to breath deeply in order to settle myself. I found nothing I had learned gave me any authority over this experience."[36]

Though he intuitively knew, like Gopi Krishna, that he was not sick, Moss later submitted himself for extensive tests and nothing was found medically wrong. Moss also experienced that, over time, he was psychologically expanded, stretched, partially destroyed, and rebuilt by further transcendent experiences into a more effective and integrated self. If we trust the observer, Moss, then we must find evidence for considering the hylozoic paradigm. If a physical scientist wants to claim, on the basis of paradigm-preservation, that the observer is wrong and it actually was caused by a medical problem, then he must also claim greater authority in the medical realm than the observer himself, and his doctors.

Of course, if the description of the experience is accurate, then even if it was a medical condition, it must be a condition outside of the materialist paradigm.

American psychologist Paul Pearsall, who had run a successful clinic specializing in the psychology of the severely ill and dying, himself came down with cancer. During a long, and for many people fatal, treatment of radical chemotherapy and bone marrow transplants, he found himself in a near-death coma. He relates:

" 'He may never come out of this,' murmured the doctor to my wife. I was totally paralyzed, but I could feel every puncture and pull of the needles and tubes. I struggled to raise my eyelids, but my body was not responding. I tried to signal by twitching my wrists, which were bound to the bed to prevent me from trying to pull the breathing tube from my throat. 'Those little twitches are normal when you're dying,' said a nurse to my eighteen-year-old son. ...

"My body seemed strangely alien to me ... I felt that my family, my friends, my mother, my father, and all of my deceased relatives were with me. I felt more connected to everyone in my life than I had ever felt before, yet I was being declared disconnected by mechanics who read the gauges measuring my body machine as being beyond repair.

"I had never been able to see Betsy [a joyful and always-hopeful nurse], but I knew exactly what she looked like. I knew that she had dark hair curled around her head and that her teeth never showed even though her smile was broad and warm. I knew how tall and how heavy she was, and I knew her caring eyes were a light blue much like the light over my bed. I knew that the first finger on her right hand had a gold band and that she often cried when she laughed. I knew that, unlike many medical health workers, she wore her stethoscope over one shoulder instead of around her neck.... My body was unable to do the seeing for me, but I saw Betsy nonetheless. I 'saw' every nurse and doctor, even though I never opened my eyes before this wonderful moment. Freed by the tears of my family, my eyelids popped open. I recognized Betsy, my wife, my son, and every detail of the room ..."[37]

Again, either this trained observer's account (and the well-documented accounts of many other near-death experiencers) is completely wrong, or the materialist/mechanist paradigm needs revision. Pearsall also documented many similar experiences of other severely ill patients.[38]

An interesting description of transcendent experience is that of J. Krishnamurti, an influential philosopher and educator. Krishnamurti cannot be categorized as culturally or educationally Eastern or Western at the time of his experience. He underwent a painful series of transcendent experiences over many years leading to the maturity of his philosophy and teaching. He wrote about one of many experiences in a letter to a friend:

"Last 10 days, it has been really strenuous, my spine and neck have been going very strong [with pain and other sensation] and day before yesterday, the 27th [February, 1924], I had an extraordinary evening. Whatever it is, the force or whatever one calls the bally thing, came up my spine, up to the nape of my neck, then it separated into two, one going to the right & the other to the left of my head till they met between the two eyes, just above my nose. There was a kind of flame & I saw the Lord & Master. It was a tremendous night. Of course the whole thing was painful in the extreme. ..."[39]

In his philosophy, Krishnamurti taught of the hypocrisy and foolishness of most gurus and guru-worshipers, and he ridiculed the overemphasis on mystical and other "great" experience. Nevertheless, his philosophy was clearly transcendent in that he always emphasized that something profound, which is beneath thought, belief and knowledge, exists and is accessible. His circle of influence included, among others, Aldous Huxley (a close friend), George Bernard Shaw, Jawaharlal Nehru and Indira Gandhi (both Prime Ministers of India), and the Dalai Lama. He had an extensive association with well-known physicist David Bohm,[40] who later developed a system of "dialogue" aimed at realizing Krishnamurti's philosophy of the transcendent.

Interestingly, Krishnamurti refused to speak or write publicly about his own early experiences. He only allowed accounts, such as the one quoted above, by his close friends and associates who knew about "the process," to be published near the end of his life and after.

Transcendent Experience in Psychology and Psychiatry

In the 1950s, a Czechoslovakian student of Freudian psychiatry, Stanislav Grof, volunteered for a new type of experiment. The psychotropic drug LSD had just been invented and was being used by psychiatrists around the world as a research tool. A professor at Grof's institute was also doing research with stroboscopic lights, and decided to combine the two methods. Grof took a dose of the experimental drug and, after it had taken effect, was wired to electronic recording devices and placed under a strobe light. When the powerful strobe flashed, Grof was "catapulted out of [his] body." Grof then, similarly to Descartes, Gopi Krishna, Richard Moss, and Paul Pearsall, describes functioning independently of his body and experiencing consciousness much larger than his body.[41] Grof was so shaken by the reality of his experience that he was convinced the standard model of psychiatry was incomplete, and that transcendent experience was a key to understanding some forms of "psychosis."

Indeed, Grof (along with many others) has since come to believe that some "psychotic episodes" are actually spontaneous experiences, not drug induced, of the same nonordinary reality that was triggered in him.[42] He has had success treating otherwise hopeless cases by employing this model in psychotherapy.[43] Grof and others now guide large numbers of healthy people through similar experiences, using simple breathing exercises,[44] without drugs or light stimulus. They believe, as Maslow described, that awareness of the transcendent is a key element to health.

A number of psychiatrists and psychologists now believe that many people experience spontaneous episodes of nonordinary reality. If the experiencer is unprepared and without guidance, the experience can cause a "spiritual emergency" and even cause the individual to be falsely labeled psychotic.[45] When the process is handled within the context of transcendent experience as a part of normal life, it often becomes a passage to greater health and productivity. To people naturally sensitive to such experience, Grof's taking of a powerful psychotropic drug and exposing himself to a strobe light would seem humorously naïve and dangerous.

As stated above, Maslow brought transcendent experience into mainstream psychotherapy. Many others have worked professionally with the model, including Roberto Assaggioli, R.D. Laing, Otto Rank, Carl Jung and Arnold Mindell.

Italian psychiatrist and founder of the psychotherapeutic system called "psychosynthesis," Roberto Assagioli, wrote, "The incidence of disturbances having a spiritual origin is rapidly increasing nowadays, in step with the growing number of people who, consciously or unconsciously, are groping their way towards a fuller life. Furthermore, the greater development and complexity of modern man and his increasingly critical mind have rendered spiritual development a richer, more rewarding, but also a more difficult and complicated process."[46]

Scottish psychiatrist and author R.D. Laing is especially critical of our cultural blindness to transcendent experience. "We must remember that we are living in an age in which the ground is shifting and the foundations are shaking ... I wish to relate the transcendental experiences that *sometimes* break through in psychosis to those experiences of the divine that are the Living Fount of all religion ... Are these experiences simply the effulgence of a pathological process, or of a particular alienation? I do not think they are ... Our time has been distinguished, more than anything else, by a mastery, a control, of the external world, and by an almost total forgetfulness of the internal world ... society, without knowing it, is *starving* for the inner ... The outer divorced from any illumination from the inner is in a state of darkness. We are in an age of darkness ... Small wonder that the list of artists in, say, the last 150 years, who have become shipwrecked on these reefs is so long—Holderlin, John Clare, Rimbaud, Van Gogh, Nietzsche, Antonin Artaud, Strindberg, Munch, Bartok, Schumann, Buchner, Ezra Pound."[47]

Sigmund Freud founded modern Western psychoanalysis. His fundamental model of the psyche went through many evolutions and revisions during his career. One model he considered was that some psychological states were the result of trauma from the birth process. Freud did not follow up on this idea, but one of his closest students, Otto Rank, did. Rank published a book on this model, and the book turned out to be quite popular. Freud was initially stunned and apparently depressed that his student was taking over the international stage. Nevertheless he soon supported Rank's work. Other psychiatrists complained that the idea was too strange, and too different from Freud's biographical model based only on early childhood and subsequent life experiences. Freud eventually banned Rank from the psychotherapeutic professional society.[48]

Even later, "scientific" evidence that Rank's model must be wrong came in the discovery that the part of the brain associated with cognition is not "myelinated" until the baby is several months old. Myelination is the maturation of nerve cells in which they develop a protective sheath (myelin) that allows the cells to carry electrical signals in the normal way. The unmyelinated newborn's brain cannot cognize and store memory in the same way as the adult brain. Therefore, the reasoning goes, any birth trauma cannot affect later memories. The "therefore" is the problem. If consciousness sometimes occurs independently of, or is larger than the physical body—as Krishna, Moss, Pearsall, Krishnamurti, Jung, Grof, and many other trained and reliable observers describe—then it could possibly encompass the unmyelinated infant brain in some way. Some of the great saints and mystics also explicitly describe "memories" from premyelination time.[49]

Stanislav Grof, early in his career, effectively rediscovered Rank's model when he found that association with their own birth events was highly effective therapy for some patients. When he raised the issue with one of his professors, the professor shot back, "Of course not, the cortex is not myelinated." Grof, accepting the scientific authority, gave up the model.[50] Later, the mature Grof, faced with what he felt was overwhelming evidence of the effectiveness of using the model, returned to it.

Another close student, and early friend, of Freud's was Carl Jung. Jung underwent many transcendent experiences, some similar to those described above, and he became convinced of the reality of a "collective unconscious." According to Jung, in transcendent or nonordinary states, such as in dreams, one sometimes encounters, and becomes conscious of, parts of the collective unconscious. The collective unconscious contains generic cultural information not accessible to the ordinary consciousness, and even information never encountered previously in the biographical/biological life. Jung was so convinced, by his own direct experience, of the reality of the collective unconscious that he championed its use in psychotherapy, even though, as he reported, it "cost me my friendship with Freud."

Psychologist and Jungian analyst Arnold Mindell (who also has a graduate degree in physics) has attracted favorable attention with his "process-oriented psychology." Mindell calls much of psychotherapy a "garbage dump" because it is fixated on psychological "states" rather than psychological "processes." The overemphasis on states, Mindell feels, is fueled by a need to shore up one's own belief structure, rather than a desire to truly observe process objectively—whatever the process may be.[51] This defense of belief structures causes us (therapist, patient, whoever) to disengage from objective awareness of actual process, as in Freud's rejection of Jung and Rank and all transcendent experience. Mindell's success with this approach is more evidence for considering the hylozoic paradigm. If the mechanistic paradigm is correct, then Mindell's distinction between state and process is essentially meaningless—they are both simple deterministic material evolution. In the hylozoic paradigm, though, process may contain much more than the material state of any given moment (this will be shown in much detail in later chapters).

A final note on psychological models is inspired by Ken Wilber who writes, "I was starting to understand, both intellectually and personally, that consciousness could be divided into two great realms: the personal and the transpersonal ... Freud and his hysterics over religion in *The Future of an Illusion* is an example of a personal theory running riot over a transpersonal dimension. On the other side, although transpersonalists theoretically are supposed to transcend but include personal theory, I often found the opposite: They were so furious with Freud's treatment of the higher realms that they rejected *everything* Freud had to say, even about the personal sphere, which was nothing but a failure to acknowledge a lower and partial truth in precisely the realm in which it *is* true."[52]

I introduce the above examples of transcendent experience to make the case that such observations are robust enough to inform the paradigms of physical science, not to devalue the great body of work on personal psychology. If the materialist paradigm is the final word on physical science then transpersonal psychology and transcendental experience is impossible. The evidence of transcendent experience is evidence for the hylozoic paradigm. But it is not evidence that the great body of materialist/mechanist paradigm science is wrong or devalued, it is only partial.

Effect of Rejecting Transcendent Experience

Increasing numbers of people believe they have had transcendent experiences. Six out of ten Americans born after 1943 report having "experienced an extrasensory presence or power," compared with four out of ten of older generations.[53] Many scientists I know would take this as evidence of the increasing stupidity of the American public, especially the young. This attitude will not endear scientists to that public. Certainly, if the best *objective* and *properly understood* scientific model of the world did rule out the possibility of transcendent experience, then that's life—the truth—and scientists should stick to it and support it. But, as will be shown later, physics just doesn't require that we rule out transcendent experience.

Above, and in Chapter 1, I've tried to show that transcendent experience occurs in a cross-section of people that includes the clearly not stupid. I've focussed on the accounts of psychiatrists, psychologists, and medical doctors because they are trained experts qualified to judge the reality of such experience. A physicist is no more inherently qualified to judge the internal observations of a psychiatrist than is, say, a postman—and probably less so, because physicists on average may have less free time to think about it. A later chapter will consider the related topics of "parapsychology" and "mysticism"—these slopes are more slippery than those of basic transcendent experience. For now, I make the case that simple transcendent experience is quite common, and that there is strong evidence that it is quite real. For professional scientists to deny this may have severe consequences.

Historian Paul Boyer wrote, "Public intellectuals' rejection of (even disdain for) spiritual analysis has opened the door for freelance expositors who find meaning in the symbolic language of apocalyptic Scriptures."[54] Boyer was referring to the tragic events in Waco, Texas, where the followers of a charismatic and deluded prophet were led to violence, resulting in close to 100 deaths and great expenditure of public funds and attention. Boyer was indicating that the rejection of and disdain for analysis of the possibility that Spirit may exist actually empowers the sort of leader who would mislead the sort of follower who has no means of judging the validity of, or quality of, claims of spiritual authority. If the majority of Americans now believe in transcendent experience, while their intellectual leaders continue to reject and disdain the same, then we will be in an unstable cultural situation. And if that rejection is unfounded, we will surely be in a needlessly unstable cultural situation.

The transcendent experiences we have described are inconsistent with the materialist paradigm. Physics students learn to analyze the logical extremes of a proposition in order to ascertain the range of the proposition's validity. If scientists wish to support the ultimate authority of the materialist/mechanist paradigm, they should be aware of the implications. One implication is that, in addition to the artists mentioned above by R. D. Laing, the great saints of history—Buddha, Christ, Patanjali, Lao Tze, Mohammed, Moses, and others—should all be dismissed as psychotic, or at least ignorant and irrational, and not worthy of attention. The "out" taken by many scientists—that these great beings all spoke metaphorically, so that their teachings can be interpreted as simple polemics on basic ethics—does not hold up to scrutiny. On reading what they actually said, and not "interpretations," it is quite clear that they all taught of the reality of nonmaterial realms. As indicated above, the great mythologist and teacher, Joseph Campbell, concluded that this was the *key* point of the great saints' teachings and all the great world religions.

3. The Views of the Founders

In Chapter 2, I argued that the key point of the great world mythologies, and the conclusion of increasing numbers of contemporary psychologists, psychiatrists and pioneering thinkers in many fields, is that realms beyond those accessible to the senses, beyond all aspects of material reality, are real and of vital relevance. So, what of physicists whose job it is to study and understand all aspects of the material reality? What do they say about the relevance of the nonmaterial realms? There is an odd dichotomy here.

One of the key developments in this area was the quantum revolution in physics (indeed the quantum revolution in all of Western thought), which took place mostly in the 1920s. The creators of that revolution largely agreed that the quantum revolution in physics created an opening for the possible peaceful coexistence (though *not* homogenization) of physics and metaphysics—an opening that did not exist before. We'll look at portions of what these founders said on this topic. Several quotes are taken from Ken Wilber's compilation in the book *Quantum Questions*. Wilber argues that they all would have qualified as "mystics." Actually I'll introduce the more specific idea that they all would have agreed that the laws of physics indicate that matter is open to the influence of spirit. They would have had wide-ranging ideas about the effect if any of spirit, and what spirit might be. They would not have argued about the openness. They actually went beyond mysticism. "Mysticism"—associated with "mystery" or unknowable—carries a connotation of incommunicability, of disengagement from the world. As we'll see, the founding architects of contemporary physics advocated the co-pursuit of, and dual use of, mysticism and science. They were not merely mystics; I call them "esoteric hylozoists."

The dichotomy is that, in spite of the fact that developments since the 1920s in physics and other sciences, in addition with quantum mechanics, should reinforce and deepen the hylozoic attitude—the hylozoic view remains undeveloped. In later chapters, we'll discuss this loss and the further developments that should reinforce the hylozoic paradigm. But first, let's listen to the founders of quantum mechanics.

The Founders Became Hylozoists

Sir Arthur Eddington (1882-1944) was "the most distinguished astrophysicist of his time."[55] He was indeed the "founder of modern theoretical astrophysics."[56] He created the discipline of the structure, the constitution, and the evolution of stars. He did significant work on the theory of matter, and corresponded extensively on this topic with Einstein and the other founders of the contemporary quantum theory of matter.

Eddington reported clearly his belief in the possibility of the transcendent affecting matter; "Religion [Eddington means specifically mystical religious experience, and not religious dogma] first became possible for a reasonable scientific man about the year 1927. ... 1927 has seen the final overthrow of strict causality by Heisenberg, Bohr, Born, and others ... The materialist who is convinced that all phenomena arises from electrons and quanta and the like controlled by mathematical formulae must presumably hold the belief that his wife is a rather elaborate differential equation, but he is probably tactful enough not to obtrude this opinion in domestic life."

Eddington was referring to a major physics conference held in Brussels in 1927 at which it became apparent that matter at the atomic level really does behave according to the new theories of quantum mechanics. Eddington's point is that, as far as physics can tell, one's wife *is* a rather elaborate differential equation—but a differential equation that is open to outside, nonmaterial, influence—a differential equation with immensely varying possible ranges of solutions (eventualities) imminent in each moment. The mistake is in believing that one's spouse is the differential equation only, because quantum mechanics shows that *something else*, described at the atomic level by probabilistic terms, also occurs. What that something else is, is what all the fuss is about, and will be discussed in later chapters.

Eddington summarized, "If this kind of scientific dissection [by the materialist who believes that all phenomena arises from electrons and quanta only] is felt to be inadequate and irrelevant in ordinary personal relationships, it is surely out of place in the most personal relationship of all - that of the human soul to the divine spirit." Here, Eddington is not engaging in abstract poetic word games about the divine. He is describing the way he thinks the macroscopic world really *works*.

None of the fundamental physical equations or laws applicable to everyday phenomena have changed between the times of Eddington and now. And as we'll see, new understandings such as the insights from chaos theory, and other studies of complexity, actually bring the openness of quantum mechanics much closer to everyday occurrences, making the imminent nature of events even more apparent. Methods of calculation have vastly improved. The methods of quantum mechanics have been successfully applied to a dazzling array of phenomena, including simple biological molecules and other simple biological systems. But this only bolsters Eddington's point that the laws of physics are open, and therefore complicated systems such as human disease processes, much less psychology, much less religious experience, may or may not entail partially nonmaterial processes. Physics is entirely consistent with either possibility. As discussed in the introduction, physics after the 1927 Solvay Brussels conference (and even more so recently), became consistent with hylostochastism and hylozoism, but not consistent with materialistic determinism, or hylostatism. Eddington was a hylozoist.

It is said that in 1925, the Ph.D. thesis of French graduate student (and later Prince) Louis de Broglie was based on two handwritten pages.[57] The ideas in it won him a Nobel Prize four years later. (Graduate students should stop drooling—this kind of thing just doesn't happen any more.) De Broglie, working alone and guided by his intuitions about symmetry, showed that the wave-particle duality—then known to apply to light—can be extended to matter. De Broglie established that, given the quantization of mass energy, matter can be represented as a wave in space and time.

De Broglie, much later commenting on the meaning of these new sciences, deferred to French philosopher Henri Bergson's quote, "Let us add that this increased body [meaning the human organism increased by its tremendous scientific and technological power] awaits a supplement of the soul and that the mechanism demands a mysticism." De Broglie then strenuously supported this plea.[58] Bergson was noted for, among other things, asserting that an élan vital, or original life force, essentially governs all organic processes. Bergson and De Broglie were hylozoists.

German physicist Max Planck, at the turn of the century, dealt with some troubles in understanding the theory of black body radiation by suggesting that objects emit heat in discrete units rather than in a continuous flow. The heat energy is emitted in discrete, indivisible units mathematically equal to the frequency of the radiation times a constant that Planck called h. Planck's h is now called Planck's constant, and is known to be one of the small number of fundamental physical constants in nature. A few years later, Einstein, one of the few physicists then aware of Planck's quantum theory,[59] applied the same concepts of "independent quanta of energy" to electromagnetic radiation (light). Planck and Einstein thus initiated the move toward the quantum age. But, because the major professional journals and professional societies were heavily influenced by an "oligarchy of eminence"[60] with vested interests in nineteenth century physics, quantum theory remained unfashionable, if not dismissed out of hand, until many years later.

Decades later, after quantum theory had won the day, Max Planck spoke of the role of the transcendent:

> "The fact is that there is a point, one single point in the immeasurable works of mind and matter, where science and therefore every causal method of research is inapplicable, not only on practical grounds but also on logical grounds, and will always remain inapplicable. This point is the individual ego. It is a small point in the universal realm of being, but in itself, it is a whole world, embracing our emotional life, our will, and our thought.
>
> "... the individual can never consider his own future purely and exclusively from the causal standpoint ... The scientist as such must recognize the value of religion as such, no matter what may be its forms, so long as it does not make the mistake

of opposing its own dogmas to the fundamental law upon which scientific research is based, namely, the sequence of cause and effect in all external phenomena."[61]

Clearly, the "external phenomena" to which Planck is referring are those external phenomena which are measurable in controlled experiments, not for instance the minds of other men, which are of course also external phenomena. Not either, we will argue, those aspects of Nature which cannot be measured in controlled experiments, or completely modeled even in principle, and there are many such aspects of Nature, as will be described later.

Vienna physics theorist Wolfgang Pauli's brilliance, and deep physical intuition, and abrasiveness, became legendary even when he was still a young man. In his mid-twenties, he might tell Niels Bohr (Bohr himself a powerful leader of physicists), "Shut up, you are being an idiot."[62] Pauli pioneered work on the quantum numbers, quantum "spin," and discovered a key fundamental exclusion principle for particles that is still named after him. He predicted the existence of the neutrino twenty years before it was discovered. He won the Nobel Prize for this work. Nevertheless, the bizarreness and difficulty of the quantum revolution can be sensed from Pauli's 1925 remark, "Physics is decidedly confused at this moment; in any event, it is much too difficult for me and I wish I ... had never heard of it."[63]

Pauli much later collaborated with Carl Jung (who advocated the acceptance of the role of the transcendent in psychology) on a book about "Synchronicity."[64] Decades after the early quantum discoveries, Pauli wrote of the need to confront the paradoxical coexistence of the transcendent and the mundane:

"I believe, ... , that to anyone to whom a narrow rationalism has lost its persuasiveness, and to whom the charm of a mystical attitude, experiencing the outer world in its oppressive multiplicity as illusory, is also not powerful enough, nothing else remains but to expose oneself in one way or another to these intensified oppositions and their conflicts.... Warned by the miscarriage of all premature endeavors after unity in the history of human thought, I shall not venture to make predictions about the future.

But, contrary to the strict division of the activity of the human spirit into separate departments—a division prevailing since the nineteenth century—I consider the ambition of overcoming opposites, including also a synthesis embracing both rational understanding and the mystical experience of unity, to be the mythos, spoken or unspoken, of our present age."[65]

Pauli urged the investigation, and unification if possible, of both rational science and mystical experience—he was a hylozoist.

An interesting bit of folklore, favorite among physicists now, is that the mere presence of the brilliant theorist Pauli (who didn't do experiments) near a physics experiment would cause the experiment to go awry, and experimentalists wanted him nowhere near. Once an experimenter was completing a particularly difficult experiment that inexplicably broke. The event was later "explained," when it was found that at that precise moment Pauli's train had stopped at the station nearby. It seems that physicists sometimes feel that in their own folklore they can be mystical but no one else should.

In 1925, Werner Heisenberg, only 24 years old and on vacation with a lady friend in the hills of Helgoland, invented matrix quantum mechanics. One of the later results of Heisenberg's invention was the fundamental "Uncertainty Principle" that bears Heisenberg's name. He was awarded the Nobel Prize in 1932.

One summer night in 1952, after a meeting in Copenhagen, Niels Bohr, Wolfgang Pauli, and Werner Heisenberg discussed the meaning of quantum mechanics. Later, watching ships in the harbor, Pauli asked Heisenberg, "Were you quite satisfied with Niels' remarks about the positivists? I gained the impression that you are even more critical of them than Niels himself, or rather that your criterion of truth differs radically from theirs."

Heisenberg: "I should consider it utterly absurd—and Niels, for one, would agree—were I to close my mind to the problems and ideas of earlier philosophers simply because they cannot be expressed in a more precise language. ... I believe that, in the final analysis, all the old religions [Heisenberg means mystical religious insight, "the spiritual content of many cultures and different periods, even in places where the very idea of God is absent"] try to express the same contents, the same relations, and all of these hinge around questions about values. ... we ought to make every effort to grasp their meaning, since *it quite obviously refers to a crucial aspect of reality*; or perhaps we ought to try putting it into modern language, if it can no longer be contained in the old."

Pauli: "But where must we seek for the truth, in obscurity or in clarity? Niels has quoted Schiller's 'Truth dwells in the deeps.' Are there such deeps and is there any truth? And may these deeps perhaps hold the meaning of life and death?"

Heisenberg lapsed into "silent soliloquy" until Pauli asked quite unexpectedly, "Do you believe in a personal God? I know, of course, how difficult it is to attach a clear meaning to this question, but you can probably appreciate its general purport."

Heisenberg: "May I rephrase the question? Can you, or anyone else, reach the central order of things or events, whose existence seems beyond doubt, as directly as you can reach the soul of another human being? I am using the term 'soul' quite deliberately so as not to be misunderstood. If you put your question like that, I would say yes."

Pauli: "Why did you use the word 'soul' and not simply speak of another person?"

Heisenberg: "Precisely because the word 'soul' refers to the central order, to the inner core of a being whose outer manifestations may be highly diverse and pass our understanding. If the magnetic force [Heisenberg is saying 'magnetic force' metaphorically; he means some as yet not understood non-material organizing agent.] that has guided this particular compass—and what else was its source but the central order?—should ever become extinguished, terrible things may happen to mankind, far more terrible even than concentration camps and atom bombs. ... As far as science is concerned, however, Niels is certainly right to underwrite the demands of pragmatists and positivists for meticulous attention to detail and for semantic clarity. It is only in respect to its taboos that we can object to positivism, for if we may no longer speak or even think about the wider connections, we are without a compass and hence in danger of losing our way."[66]

In their laying to rest of the positivists, Heisenberg, Bohr, and Pauli were, as Wilber puts it, "lamenting the attempt of [modern] philosophy to ape physics." Heisenberg's frighteningly important "central order" is clearly a nonmaterial "inner core" that guides the "outer manifestations"—an aspect of spirit that affects matter. Heisenberg makes it very clear that the ancient accounts of mystics are not merely linguistic play. They "quite obviously refer to a crucial aspect of reality."

At the same time as Heisenberg et al. were developing matrix quantum mechanics, Erwin Schrodinger (1887 - 1961) independently developed "quantum wave mechanics." Schrodinger's wave mechanics is mathematically equivalent to the matrix mechanics but simpler and easier to use, and today much more commonly used. He was awarded the Nobel Prize in physics in 1933. Schrodinger has been called the "most mystical" of the founders of quantum mechanics. Though his equations are immensely widely used, his views on the meaning behind the mathematics are very little known or appreciated. He wrote, for instance:

> "Immediate experiences in themselves, however various and disparate they be, are logically incapable of contradicting each other. So let us see whether we cannot draw the correct, non-contradictory conclusion from the following two premises:
> (i) My body functions as a pure mechanism according to the Laws of Nature.
> (ii) Yet I know, by incontrovertible direct experience, that I am directing its motions, of which I foresee the effects, that may be fateful and all-important, in which case I feel and take full responsibility for them.
>
> "The only possible inference from these two facts is, I think, that I—I in the widest meaning of the word, that is to say, every conscious mind that has ever said or felt 'I'—am the person, if any, who controls the 'motion of the atoms' according to the Laws of Nature.
>
> "… it is daring to give to this conclusion the simple wording that it requires. In Christian terminology, to say: 'Hence I am God Almighty' sounds both blasphemous and lunatic. But …

consider whether the above inference is not the closest a biologist can get to proving God and immortality at one stroke.

In itself, the insight is not new. The earliest records, to my knowledge, date back some 2500 years or more. From the early great Upanishads the recognition ATMAN = BRAHMAN (the personal self equals the omnipresent, all-comprehending eternal self) was in Indian thought considered, far from being blasphemous, to represent the quintessence of deepest insight into the happenings of the world. The striving of all the scholars of Vedanta was, ... really to assimilate in their minds this grandest of all thought. Again, the mystics of many centuries, independently, yet in perfect harmony with each other ... have described, each of them, the unique experience of his or her life in terms that can be condensed in the phrase: DEUS FACATUS SUM (I have become God)."[67]

Given Schrodinger's profound grounding in the knowledge of the functioning of matter, when he talks about the mystical traditions like Vedanta (a detailed and precise system of mystical awakening), he is not merely making pretty words. He's talking about the way matter and spirit actually function in concert. So much for the "recently drawn parallels" between Eastern mysticism and physics. These guys were there all along. But somehow that is little appreciated. It seems that as we crawl our way out of this Kali Yuga (Dark Age—some of the major Vedantic lineages say it started about 4,000 BC and could be ending about now[68]) we have trouble recalling what the sages of 40 years ago said, even if they were only calling our attention to those of 3,000 years before them.

Niels Bohr (1885–1962) used the new quantum theory to explain for the first time the light emission spectra of hydrogen atoms. This first major application of the quantum theory to solve a fundamental mystery was a major part of the watershed move to the acceptance of quantum theory. Bohr received the Nobel Prize in 1922, but even more important than his individual contributions, Bohr was a teacher, leader, and organizer of other physicists and architect of the quantum revolution. Bohr led an institute in Copenhagen that became the center of the quantum revolution and attracted at one time or another essentially all of the major players. Bohr was concerned with how to use the new quantum theory—how to do physics with it—if indeed it is an accurate reflection of the way matter works, how to employ quantum mechanics to understand and predict matter.

The early 1920s saw intense debate (and as noted by Pauli above, confusion) about the interpretation of quantum theory. Bohr and his Copenhagen institute were developing the "Copenhagen interpretation," with major dissenters including Einstein and Schrodinger. The arguments were intense. Once, Bohr invited Schrodinger to Copenhagen and "immediately started to harangue him" about the inadequacy of Schrodinger's interpretation, and continued badgering him until Schrodinger became "physically ill."[69] Schrodinger left shaken but unconvinced. At the Solvay conference in 1927, though, the Copenhagen interpretation essentially "won."

We'll discuss later some more details of what the Copenhagen interpretation is, but for now the essence of it was that the fundamental indeterminacy to events, the indeterminacy that the quantum theory had discovered, was necessarily filled (for purposes of calculation) by random processes. The Copenhagen interpretation was immensely practical because it facilitated calculations to make predictions that further tested the quantum theory, and it discouraged fruitless concern (fruitless as far as doing calculations) with the metaphysical implications of the new theory—implications that are immense. The temporary, practical adoption of the Copenhagen interpretation seems to have developed into a dogmatic belief—a mistaken dogma that has twisted Bohr's Copenhagen interpretation (that experimental science cannot even in theory determine the deeper influences underlying quantum indeterminacy); twisted into a belief that somehow it was proven that the deeper influences cannot exist, that metaphysics cannot exist.

Bohr himself voiced his unhappiness with this "positivist" misinterpretation of the metaphysical implications for his physics theories. He related the following to Heisenberg and Pauli, at that 1952 meeting:

> "Some time ago there was a meeting of philosophers, most of them positivists, here in Copenhagen, during which mem-

bers of the Vienna Circle played a prominent part. I was asked to address them on the interpretation of quantum theory. After my lecture, no one raised any objections or asked any embarrassing questions, but I must say this very fact proved a terrible disappointment to me. For those who are not shocked when they first come across quantum theory cannot possibly have understood it. Probably I spoke so badly that no one knew what I was talking about.[70]

"... For my part, I can readily agree with the positivists about the things they want, but not about the things they reject. All the positivists are trying to do [the things they want] is to provide the procedures of modern science with a philosophical basis, or, if you like, a justification. They point out that the notions of the earlier philosophies lack the precision of scientific concepts, and they think that many of the questions posed and discussed by conventional philosophers have no meaning at all, that they are pseudo problems and, as such, best ignored [the things they reject]. Positivist insistence on conceptual clarity is, of course, something I fully endorse, but their prohibition of any discussion of the wider issues, simply because we lack clear-cut enough concepts in this realm, does not seem very useful to me. This same ban would prevent our understanding of quantum theory.

"... You mentioned Philip Frank's book on causality. Philip Frank was one of the philosophers to attend the congress in Copenhagen, and he gave a lecture in which he used the term 'metaphysics' simply as a swearword or, at best, as a euphemism for unscientific thought. After he had finished, I had to explain my own position, and this I did roughly as follows: I began by pointing out that I could see no reason why the prefix 'meta' should be reserved for logic and mathematics—Frank had spoken of metalogic and metamathematics—and why it was anathema in physics. The prefix, after all, merely suggests that we are asking further questions, i.e. questions bearing on the fundamental concepts of a particular discipline, and why ever should we not be able to ask such questions in physics?"[71]

Because of his emphasis on developing the practical use of the new quantum theory—an immense job in itself—Bohr wrote little about his own concepts of metaphysics. The above discussion, for instance, was related in an essay by Heisenberg. But, as he makes clear, Bohr certainly did not believe that metaphysics could not exist, or even that it was a fruitless endeavor. Though we do not know much about Bohr's metaphysics, we do know that he incorporated the yin-yang symbol of mystical Chinese Taoism into his family crest. Perhaps, as the ancient Taoist proverb goes ("He who doesn't know says a thousand words, while the sage who knows, says nothing."[72]), Bohr chose to *act* on his metaphysics, rather than speak them.

Einstein's "Mistake"

Einstein has become famous for (among, of course, many other things) supposedly having said, "God does not play dice with the Universe." That quote is also infamous because that sentiment was supposedly Einstein's mistake—his disbelief in quantum theory. For a long time, I believed this was a "mistake" also. Whenever someone would indulge in Einsteinian idolatry, I'd happily retort, "but he was wrong about the dice thing you know"—meaning he ended up behind the times, fallibly human after all.

What Einstein actually said was, concerning the statistical (Copenhagen) interpretation of the quantum wave equation, "An inner voice tells me that this is not the true Jacob. The theory accomplishes a lot, but it does not bring us closer to the secrets of the Old One. In any case, I am convinced that He does not play dice."[73] Einstein did believe that a model of the universe which represented, "things themselves and not merely the probability of their occurrence,"[74] could be found. Einstein apparently put out argument after argument trying to show that the Copenhagen interpretation would be superseded by deeper "hidden variables," and each argument was shot down by the persistent and equally brilliant Bohr.

One of Einstein's more famous thought experiments, in this vein of shooting down the Copenhagen interpretation, he published with two other physicists (Podolsky and Rosen), and it is known as the EPR experiment. We'll look at the EPR experiment later, but the bottom line was that, if the Copenhagen interpretation of quantum mechanics applied, then the results of the experiment would seem absurdly paradoxical. EPR were implying that, because of its inherent paradox, there must therefore be something wrong with the quantum theory. Bohr couldn't shoot that one down, but said essentially, "Well then, that's how the experiment will go."

Recently, the EPR experiment has actually been conducted. It behaves precisely as quantum theory predicts. The universe seems absurdly paradoxical.

Bohr and Einstein, through years of discussion on this issue, became very close. But their fundamental perspective was so different that it eventually drove them apart. Einstein wrote, in 1928, about the Copenhagen interpretation, "The Heisenberg-Bohr tranquilizing philosophy—or religion?—is so delicately contrived that, for the time being, it provides a gentle pillow for the true believer from which he cannot very easily be aroused. So let him lie there."[75]

Einstein may indeed have been wrong in believing that the deeper realities could be put into a precise mathematical physical theory. But his conviction that there *are* deeper realities that do affect material events, we will be arguing, was correct. And his above comment was prophetic, for a sort of "tranquilizing philosophy" has indeed perpetuated a dogmatic religion of materialism. So in the hylozoic paradigm, we can view both Bohr and Einstein as essentially right. The quantum theory may be utterly applicable in those cases where it can make statistical predictions. But it may not "bring us closer to the secrets of the Old One." And some of the secrets of the Old One may in fact be knowable, as Einstein thought they were, but not through experimental physical science—only through direct mystical experience or intuition—through the hylozoic paradigm.

So, the founders of quantum mechanics said: "the mechanism demands a mysticism." "The scientist as such must recognize the value of religion as such." "A synthesis embracing both rational understanding and the mystical experience of unity, [is] the mythos ... of our present age." "The spiritual content [mystical religious insights] of many cultures and different periods ... try to express the same contents, the same relations.... We ought to make every effort to grasp their meaning, since it quite obviously refers to a crucial aspect of reality."

The meaning of these quotes is unmistakable. The founders of quantum mechanics were esoteric hylozoists. The physical laws they discovered showed that matter is open to the influence of spirit. The hylostatic paradigm was incontrovertibly overthrown. They had a choice between hylostochastism or hylozoism. They chose, on the basis of their own experience, hylozoism. The Copenhagen interpretation for actually doing quantum mechanical calculations won the day. Even Bohr—from whose Copenhagen interpretation the now prevailing, largely implicit, "tranquilizing philosophy" of hylostochastism takes precedence—seems to have been a hylozoist.

4. The Present Concensus

Acalm, knowledgeable and soothing voice describes: "The way physics sees it, particles and forces are the authors of every event in our world from the exotic to the everyday."

Cut to a baseball game, fans cheering, a batter contacting a pitch, then overlay of photon exchange schematic during bat hitting ball. The show proceeds to describe the importance of the proposed 11 billion dollar superconducting supercollider.[76]

As that television show implied, there is a powerful scientific opinion that we've figured everything out, except for some minor details that can be acquired for large amounts of money. Just sit back and watch the tube and the purveyors of knowledge will reassure you that there's nothing strange, nothing profound or mysterious going on, nothing to worry about—just keep the tax dollars coming.

"There Are No Phenomena ... That There Is Deep Mystery About"

As a model of this opinion, we'll use the opinion of the late Richard Feynman. Feynman was a universally acclaimed physicist and physics teacher. He won the Nobel Prize in physics. He first became well known as the youngest (then in his early twenties) of the scientific group leaders at Los Alamos during the development of the atomic bomb. He is the subject of several recent books. He was not one to hide his opinions, and so he has explicitly stated what we can call the consensus scientific opinion:

> "... all ordinary phenomena can be explained by the actions and the motions of particles. For example, life itself is supposedly understandable in principle from the movements of atoms, and those atoms are made out of neutrons, protons and electrons. I must immediately say that when we state that we understand it in principle, we only mean that we think that, if we could figure

everything out, we would find that there is *nothing new* in physics which *needs to be discovered in order to understand the phenomena of life* ... In fact, I can say that in the range of phenomena today, so far as I know *there are no phenomena that we are sure cannot be explained this way, or even that there is deep mystery about* ....

"There are ... phenomena, such as extra-sensory perception, which cannot be explained by our knowledge of physics.... If it [extra-sensory perception] could be demonstrated, of course, that would prove that physics is incomplete, and it is therefore extremely interesting to physicists whether it is right or wrong. Many experiments exist which show that it does not work. The same goes for astrological influences."

I admire Feynman greatly, and as a student was immensely inspired by his teachings on physics, and I think a whole generation of students owe a great debt to Feynman. But on this one point, which is actually not a point of physics at all, we're going to have to take him head-on, and hold his comments up as representative of a glorious but outgoing paradigm, and argue that he was quite wrong.[77]

Concerning extra-sensory perception, there are many well documented anecdotes apparently supporting single episodes of, for instance, telepathy,[78] sometimes involving severe accidents or life-threatening situations of loved ones. Some examples will be dealt with in Part IV of this book, but Feynman is referring specifically to repeatable experiments, not anecdotal incidents. The best research in the area of carefully controlled and repeatable experiments, such as those by Charles Tart, have generally given inconclusive results.[79]

Actually the failure or success of such experiments is inconsequential to our question. Even if purposive extra-sensory perception were impossible, noumenal processes like the transcendent experiences described in Chapter 2 could play a major role in the functioning of our world. The world is, after all, a single event—never repeatable from moment to moment. True transcendent process may have large effect and be nonrepeatable at the same time.

Also Feynman, in his comment above, is assuming that the details of subnuclear physics, and cosmological scale physics, about which there are still clearly stated scientific mysteries, cannot affect everyday phenomena. For the arguments in this book, I will share that assumption.[80] The key to Feynman's argument is that "phenomena ... which cannot be explained by our knowledge of physics ... if ... demonstrated ... would prove that physics is incomplete."

The problem with this statement is that he does not specify incomplete what? If it is meant incomplete as a description of the laws which govern the functioning of all aspects of the universe (which may include nonmaterial processes), then the argument is demonstrably false. This is because the laws of physics, which govern the functioning of the material universe, are open. That is, if the statement is meant in the much more restrictive sense of understanding how only the matter behaves, in an average sense but not in any specific case, then it may well be right, but it's not much of a claim. There may be much more than matter. And there are some very important specific cases—like you and me.

The mechanistic belief structure is typical among many working scientists today. It's a largely unconscious belief structure that only comes out explicitly when challenged, but it silently colors attitudes and actions in many ways. This belief structure is seldom dealt with, probably because the actual work of physics does not require consideration of such issues, unless it is chosen to specifically address them, and such investigation is not encouraged, as shown by the example of the discouraged graduate student in Chapter 1.

Nevertheless, others have stated the same point of view. Stephen Hawking is another brilliant cosmological theorist and skillful popularizer of contemporary cosmology. Hawking says, "Mysticism is a cop-out. If you find theoretical physics and mathematics too hard, you turn to mysticism."[81]

Hawking also says, "I believe the Universe is governed by rational laws, and that we can understand those laws."[82] It is disconcerting to find oneself disputing such truly brilliant intellects as Hawking and Feynman, but their statements are quite clear. As the other great thinkers described in Chapter 2 indicate, the key here may be that the "other ways of knowing" have nothing to do with intellect. In fact, where can Hawking's belief "that the Universe is governed by rational laws, and that we can understand those laws" come from, given that he's clearly not there yet, if it doesn't come from some nonrational ideation?

That standard cosmological view was reiterated by a NASA scientist on the Larry King Show.[83] Asked specifically if he believed in God (meaning any sort of transcendent influence), the scientist gave the standard response that we've discovered all the laws of the universe except for some details relevant only in the first second of the Big Bang, but even if we figure those details out, we'll never know how or why the Big Bang was created. Meaning that the transcendent may have played a role before the Big Bang fifteen billion years ago, and fifteen billion light years away—quite a safe distance!—but not since then, certainly not here, now. Oddly, this is essentially the Newtonian wind-up-clock model of the universe which is clearly outdated, but this still seems to be the extent of thinking about the transcendent by a powerful contingent of scientists. As we'll see, this is an opinion, based on some sort of nonrational deduction, for there is nothing in the physical equations (the physical "laws") that rules out transcendent influence everywhere, now.

Leon Lederman, Nobel Laureate elementary particle experimentalist, explains to the layman, in his book *The God Particle*, the need for the Superconducting Super Collider as the next step to discover the "God particle"—a building-block subnuclear particle called the Higgs boson. When pressed by a television host to discuss the meaning of his book title, Lederman somewhat iritatedly remarked that it was a "whimsical title."[84] The feeling was as if it should be so obvious that there is no transcendent and that any scientist's mention of God should obviously be in some sort of jest.

Nobel Laureate elementary particle theorist Steven Weinberg, in his book *Dreams of a Final Theory* seems less certain. But he does argue that a completed theory of subnuclear particles (which he argues is very nearly at hand) would end "the ancient search for those principles that cannot be explained in terms of deeper principles." Elsewhere, Weinberg has said, "The more the universe seems comprehensible, the more it seems pointless," and that "it would be wonderful to find in the laws of nature a plan by a concerned creator in which humans played some special role. I find sadness in doubting that we will [find it]."[85] The hylozoic paradigm can possibly relieve the sadness by pointing out that while there may be no

4: The Present Concensus

special role in the *laws* of nature, and no authoritarian concerned creator, there may be special meaning in the actions in the moment of humans and other complex events.

Science fiction writer Isaac Asimov, writing for the Committee for Scientific Investigation of Claims Of the Paranormal publication *Skeptical Inquirer*, reiterates the same perspective. CSICOP is an independent organization of well known scientists, writers, and stage magicians that debunks "claims of the paranormal" and claims to represent a scientific perspective.[86] Asimov says:

> "If intuition is as important to the world as reason, and if the Eastern sages are as knowledgeable about the Universe as physicists are, then why not take matters in reverse? Why not use the wisdom of the East as a key to some of the unanswered questions in physics? For instance: what is the basic component making up subatomic particles that physicists call a quark?
>
> "What nonsense all this supposed intuitional truth is, and how comic is the sight of the genuflections made to it by rational minds who lost their nerve.
>
> "No, it isn't really comic; it's tragic. There has been at least one other such occasion in history, when Greek secular and rational thought bowed to the mystical aspects of Christianity, and what followed was a Dark Age. We can't afford another."[87]

Asimov's comment that rational minds that accept intuition have "lost their nerve" is similar to Hawking's indication that intuition (mysticism) is an exercise for those who aren't bright enough to do mathematical physics. This perspective seems to have degenerated from that of the great physicists described in Chapter 3. As for Azimov's first point, as discussed in Chapter 3, several very significant physicists did indeed find inspiration from Eastern mysticism. For example, Werner Heisenberg was a guest in India of Rabrindranath Tagore—a very significant mystical poet—and found inspiration for his physics in talks with Tagore.[88] Niels Bohr may have had similar contacts in China.[89] Oppenheimer regularly studied the Baghavad Gita and other mystical treatises.

Part of the reason for this degeneration of attitude from the founder's time to now might be indicated by Asimov's odd claim that the Dark Ages were caused "when Greek secular and rational thought bowed to the mystical aspects of Christianity."

Historians such as Morris Berman (see Chapter 2) and other contemporary thinkers are realizing the great historical importance of the difference between dogmatic religions and the mystical realizations from which they came—two antithetical forces. An appreciation of this difference indicates that Asimov has it upside down here. It was dogmatic organized religious Christianity (and other religions)—almost by definition the opposite of mystical Christianity (and the mystical origins of other religions)—that tended to plunge cultures into darkness.

Specifically, for example, in 325 A.D., the Emperor Constantine called the first ecumenical council at Nicea, and there declared in the name of organized and controllable religion that Jesus was the *only* son of God, that is, Jesus was declared the only possible recipient of mystical truths and the Emperor by this fiat was thus the only possible divinely-sanctioned authority.

Even at that time, long before printing presses, there was plenty of documentation to the contrary—writings about Jesus' studies with other great teachers, for example (fragments of which may now be resurfacing for instance in the Dead Sea Scrolls, the Nag Hammadi Library, and the Tibetan Pali manuscripts).

Just 64 years after the ecumenical council's declaration, their fear of the documented threats to their dogma seems to be a reason for the burning of the great Libraries at Alexandria—a major harbinger of the Dark Age.

Asimov's confusion of the two—dogmatic authoritarian religion, and mystical insight—indicates that we as a culture perhaps have (or had in the recent past) so little contact with the latter that it is confused with the former. Hence, when scientists believe to have disproved, or ruled out the possibility of intuition and mystical insight, perhaps they really mean they have disproved the dogmatic claims of certain organized religions (be they Eastern religions or Western religions)—which is something quite different.

Feynman's standpoint highlights the success of physics at explaining "everyday phenomena" and he does not explicitly rule out mystical religious experience, but his remarks would not be encouraging. The present general scientific world view does make the further assumption that the success of physics in explaining the material world precludes true transcendent experience. This final exclusion is not supportable by the facts.

Feynman detested philosophy, and wrote little on the subject, so it is not surprising that he did not follow all the avenues of his musings on the possibility of metaphysics.[90] His exclusivity may have been what nurtured his great talents as physicist and teacher which were a gift to society. But as the comments of others above indicate, the exclusive belief in rational positivism has a grip on much of science. Most of the great architects of modern physics, however, stated clearly their understanding that the laws of physics are open, as shown in Chapter 3. Nothing relevant to this point has changed regarding the fundamental laws or their interpretation since the time of the founders of modern physics quoted above. So what has happened to cause the entrenchment of this strong materialist opinion? At least three major factors can be identified. First, is the confusion between dogmatic religion and mystical insight, described above.

Second, mainstream science, I believe, has reacted to being embarrassed by numerous charlatans, frauds, and the merely deluded. Also, some recent physicists who have tried to express this openness of physics have then embraced some specific ancient, medieval, or modern mystical dogma—itself necessarily flawed—thereby diluting their influence. This problem of fraud, delusion, and inconsistency of result in such studies is dealt with in detail in Chapter 14.

Conversely, many in the New Age-type movements have reacted completely against all science, rationalism, and logic, or worse, have claimed that physics proves whatever dogma they are touting.

If true transcendent experience does occur, it is more fundamental than material experience and material causality, which are the fields of study of physics, and thus physics cannot prove any theories about the transcendent. Our point in this book is that physics also cannot disprove a large class of models of the transcendent, and that the transcendent may have significant impact on science. The material world studied by physics is an entirely valid and self consistent system, but it is open.

A third reason may be a lack of appreciation for the real impetus behind much of "fundamental" science funding. In recent years (early 1990s), at large annual meetings of planetary scientists[91]—those who study the planets, especially with space probes such as the NASA Voyager spacecraft—many younger scientists' eyes were opened. In spite of major successes like the fly-bys of the planets Uranus and Neptune, there was a growing malaise in the field. This was due partly to worse-than-usual difficulty in getting funds for research, but something deeper was going on. In large open searching meetings, it became clear that what was going on was the end of the Cold War. Older researchers, who'd been involved since the origins of the space program, made it clear that the unmanned exploration and basic research were just minor appendages on the manned and military space programs and that these were Cold War weapons.

A book by David DeVorkin chronicles how the military created the US space sciences after World War II.[92] DeVorkin documents how the whole institutional framework for space sciences is an outgrowth of the military's original development of the V-2 rockets, their successors and uses for them. The V-2 was developed using slave labor by the Nazis in World War II and used to deliver bombs to Britain. After the war, boxcarloads of V-2 parts were brought to the United States, and to the Soviet Union, by the Allied victors. These became the seeds of the US and Soviet Space programs (and weapons races)—somewhat unsavory origins for the many altruistically-minded planetary scientists.

Certainly many researchers had always operated with an attitude of, "Sure, our research money may only come as an appendage of politically motivated projects, but the basic science *is* important in its own right, so we'll do the best we can with the money that comes our way." But now that the root impetus—the Cold War—has suddenly disappeared and the research is forced to stand on its own merits, we are confronted with the question: Is this particular sort of basic research really that important? In the whole field of fundamental scientific questions of how the world really works, how do we justify, or should we justify our particular focus?

The other large consumer of funds for "fundamental scientific research" in the physical sciences—elementary particle and nuclear physics—of course has similar origins and root justifications. Daniel J. Kevles, in his book *The Physicists*[93] chronicles how support for

4: The Present Concensus

the hugely expensive accelerators used for high energy physics experiments was a direct outgrowth of the Manhattan (atomic bomb) Project, and continued support went hand-in-hand with the continuing Cold War and nuclear weapons race, all the way up to the Superconducting Super Collider. Without the frenzy of the Cold War, and the implicit justification that elementary particle research would somehow help us maintain military hegemony, as backdrop, the expense of the SSC begins to appear absurd. It is doubly absurd in light of the fact that the scientists themselves had no illusions that the SSC results would ever have any military or even any other technological applications.[94]

A weapon employing the physics at SSC energies—should such a thing somehow be possible—would make the hydrogen bomb look like a firecracker, but could never be built for a number of practical reasons, and in any case could not be used for anything less than interplanetary warfare. Many high-energy physicists, I think, like many space scientists, held the attitude, "Sure our research money may only come as an appendage of the Cold War, but the basic science *is* important in its own right, so we'll do the best we can with the money that comes our way." Now that the whole Cold War basis has changed, the justification for the research really needs to be articulated on its own merits.

Throughout history, many great scientists have functioned in a military context, for instance, Leonardo DaVinci. The problem is not the military context itself. In the decades since World War II, generations of scientists have developed the illusion that they were really just trying to find out how the world works while institutional and cultural inertia, fueled by the consistency of the Cold War and the new post war phenomenon of massive government funding of basic research, have skewed their perspective.

The problem with the SSC is not just the enormous cost of the SSC itself, but can be stated as a comparison. Is a 20 billion dollar SSC[95] really appropriate when we are spending essentially zero on trying to understand transcendent experience, and the transcendent in nature? There are about a thousand physics Ph.D.s granted per year in the US (many of whom now cannot find jobs). The vast majority of the SSC funds would not have gone to scientists but to construction and administration costs. For five percent interest on 20 billion dollars, we could give each new physics Ph.D. graduate a one million dollar research grant, in perpetuity. If that were done, surely some of the money would be wasted, but so much creative freedom would be granted that probably much more scientific advancement, and cultural advancement, would occur than the SSC could plausibly create.

Paradigmatic Inertia

Max Planck said, "A new scientific truth does not triumph by convincing its opponents and making them see the light, but rather because its opponents eventually die, and a new generation grows up that is familiar with it." The death of the hylostatic paradigm (Newtonian mechanism) was, however, so obvious that even opponents of the new at least acknowledged the deterministic mechanism's demise. The ensuing struggle should have been between the hylozoists—even if they didn't think of themselves as hylozoists—and the hylostochastists. The hylostochastists initially got the upper hand for practical reasons. Then World War II, and subsequent decades of Cold War mentality diverted the community from assimilation of the new paradigm. So now there is primarily old paradigm consciousness, with an incomplete new paradigm that you're not supposed to think much about. In the next part, we'll see that, along with the end of the Cold War, the newest scientific developments themselves are finally forcing us toward new paradigm consciousness.

Well-known physicist John Bell (for whom is named Bell's theorem relating distant quantum events, described in Part II), wrote, "The founding fathers of quantum mechanics were very proud that they dealt only with phenomena: they refused to look behind the phenomena, regarding that as the price one had to pay for coming to terms with nature. And it is a fact of history that the people who took that agnostic attitude towards the real world on the microphysical level were very successful. At the time, it was a good thing to do. But I don't believe it will be so indefinitely."[96]

In the following chapters, we shall see just what that agnosticism was. Note that Bell correctly states that the founders took an *agnostic* attitude toward the microphysical reality, in order to get on with their calculations. That temporary agnosticism for the sake of

4: The Present Concensus

expediency has degenerated, for many, into a certainty that there is nothing to consider other than the calculations.

Ode to Giordano Bruno

As Isaac Azimov's comment indicates, it seems that much of the anti-mysticism of scientists is actually a sort of echo of Galileo's assaults on dogmatic religion, using the then new tool of rational scientific investigation. Considering that the Vatican only recently rehabilitated Galileo's name, the continuing echoes of that event may not be entirely without redeeming value. The inertia of paradigmatic belief structures is tremendous, and the reactions to outside evidence in favor of paradigmatic change are severe.

In the year 1600, Italian philosopher Giordano Bruno, a contemporary of Galileo, was the last man burned to death at the stake by the Inquisition[97] (women, however, were burned until the 1800s). Bruno was burned for the suggestion that spirit lives in everything—make no bones about it, a form of the hylozoic paradigm. Compared to Galileo's punishment—Galileo spent several years in house arrest, had his academic career truncated, and lost his friendship with the Pope[98]—Bruno's punishment was severe. More than rational science, the worst threat to authoritarian dogmatic religion is true mystical insight, and the Inquisition knew how to deal with it. The fear of stake-burning was probably an effective deterrent for many intellectuals.

As we are only now putting the Galilean controversy behind us, it is fitting that the Bruno controversy is reemerging. Shades of Bruno can be seen now in many who suggest that spirit may have influence in nature, in matter. Fritjof Capra has written that, since he published *The Tao of Physics*, he never received funding to do physics despite his efforts in that regard. Formerly esteemed astrophysicist Fred Hoyle has taken tremendous ridicule and criticism, almost to the point of ostracism, for his suggestion that teleological influences exist in nature.[99] Buckminster Fuller, not a scientist to start with but an encroacher on the scientific turf, received much ridicule for his emphasis on meaning behind the observable world. Cambridge biologist Rupert Sheldrake is a favorite whipping boy for suggesting that biological organisms are connected by nonmaterial influences.

This comparison of Galileo and Bruno is not meant in the least to slight the importance of rational science. Rational science has created great and marvelous wonders. So, is it time now, 350 years after Galileo to proclaim—just as Emperor Constantine proclaimed 350 years after Jesus that the organized Church was the one and only recipient and purveyor of truth—to proclaim that rational science is the one and only acceptable mode of thought? Perhaps we should start burning the poems of Kabir and Tagore and Merton, the Vedas, the Baghavad Gita, and the Bibles, Korans, and Cabalas. But the written word is everywhere now, and can't be as easily disposed of as were the libraries at Alexandria, so the only recourse is to control the thoughts themselves, and with instant global communication, the best method of thought control is strenuous and excessive ridicule of any unacceptable inquiries.

PART II:

THE FACT OF MATTER

5. Matter in Motion

The task of this chapter is to describe the basic concepts of physics as it came to be at the beginning of this century. These concepts are known as "Classical physics" and they are not generally thought of now as being exhilarating topics of conversation. To appreciate what comes later, though, a review of them is really necessary. For those not numerically inclined, at least we will not use any mathematics. Some might say that this is impossible, for mathematics is the language of physics, and the essential language of all science. But that argument is only another form of the mystic's stance that essential reality cannot be communicated at all, or the stance of some Japanese poets that one has to speak Japanese to understand the essence of Haiku.

This very brief review of classical physics will be in the context of applying the concepts to understanding one single everyday sort of event. In the process of trying to understand this event, we'll find that a logical way to proceed is to review the fundamental state of physical science as it came to be in the first two decades of this century. At the turn of this century, physics consisted of Classical Mechanics (Newtonian Mechanics), Electromagnetism, and Relativity, and Relativity was brand new. Since these are completely deterministic theories, for this discussion, we'll call this pre-quantum scientific world view the "hylostatic paradigm." That paradigm has enjoyed many other labels—Newtonian, Cartesian (after Descartes), Newtonian-Cartesian, Mechanistic, Deterministic, Positivistic, Rationalistic, Materialistic, and Classical—all useful labels, but containing deep-rooted connotations. We use a new label, hylostatic, to help us think about it again in a new way, just in case we missed something the first times around.

As we review the development of physics, in the context of trying to understand an every day sort of event, some historical tidbits will be related to help develop a cultural perspective.[100] Some of this chapter is going to go a little fast. Others who've written about the sorts of things we're going to get into later have skipped this foundation stuff altogether, to get to the new stuff. Reviewing some threads of the development of the paradigm that we're moving out of should help us appreciate the shift to the new.

As an example of the need for gaining familiarity with established concepts first, there is a class of objects called Celt stones[101] that behave in a very bizarre way. They are smooth oddly shaped objects meant to be spun like tops. When you spin them one direction on a smooth, nearly frictionless, table they keep on spinning like a top. When you spin them the other direction, they quickly slow down, vibrate a little, and then *reverse* direction and spin the other way! To anyone who knows any science, this is bizarre behavior. It seems to violate a universal principle called conservation of angular momentum—a principle which should never be violated.

To a physicist who's never heard of Celt stones, an encounter with one can be quite unnerving. If you tell such a physicist about Celt stones, he's likely to say something like, "No. No stone could move that way. You must have something wrong." (This is a wonderful thing to do, especially to a physicist of the pompous variety.) Yet they do move that way. To understand how they do so without violating conservation of angular momentum is just quite a bit subtle and complicated. I love Celt stones. Thinking I might inspire a life of science, I gave my four-year-old niece a Celt stone. She was unimpressed. To her, it was just a top that didn't work very well. She was just starting to get a feel for momentum, much less angular momentum, less still any kind of concept of or belief in a universal principle of angular momentum. We do need to learn the way *most* things are first, before we will truly appreciate the exceptions.

Dynamics

So, keeping in mind that we will be outlining only the barest threads of the essential concepts of physics, and following a few illustratory side tracks, let's start. To get into the Newtonian mood, and to see how it really applies to everyday life, we'll go into one example in much detail. In the process, we'll cover physics from the 17th century to the turn of the 20th century.

5: Matter in Motion

Visit a tropical beach on a calm early evening, on the night of a full Moon. If you are foolish enough, or scientifically-minded enough, to do so without a companion, you'll have plenty of time to notice that a number of things will be happening.

The Sun is setting. The full Moon is rising directly opposite the setting Sun. The tide is flowing in. It will be one of the highest high tides of the month. There is a cool breeze blowing onto shore. Whoa, how do we know that these last five things will be happening? That the tide is rising instead of ebbing? That it will be one of the highest high tides of the month? That the breeze is blowing onto shore? One way to know this is to talk to a reliable observer who lives on the beach. He will tell you that at sunset on full moon nights on tropical beaches, the second highest tide of the month flows in, and the breeze usually blows onshore.

The power of Classical Mechanics is that we could also predict these things, even with no previous experience about them, only from our knowledge of Classical Mechanics. Even a computer, if given a simple model of the Earth, Moon, and Sun, and the relevant properties of each, and the laws of Classical Mechanics, could do the predicting. The computer would predict that, if the computer were setting on a tropical beach at sunset on a full moon night, the peak tide of the second higher tide cycle of the month would be flowing in, and an onto shore breeze would be blowing through its cables. The exact details of how the computer could predict this will be left "as an exercise for the serious student." But some idea of how, is as follows.

Tides

Before stating the key principles of Classical Mechanics that let us make predictions, a description of how the principles are used should get us ready for them. The Moon orbits the Earth, and the differences in the Moon's gravitational pull, on opposite sides of the Earth, cause the Earth's shape to deform slightly. The rocky part of the Earth deforms only a tiny bit because it is very rigid. The surfaces of continents, being rock, deform on the order of a few inches as the Moon moves over head. You too deform. You stretch out an imperceptible amount (at least I don't perceive it, I don't know about you), but nevertheless an amount several hundreds of atomic layers thick.[102] The watery part of the Earth's surface, being watery instead of rigid, deforms much more than the rock part—as much as a few feet—due to the Moon's differential gravitational pull as the Moon moves overhead. The water thus appears to rise, relative to the land, and the tide rolls in.

When the Moon is not overhead, but precisely underfoot (on the other side of the Earth), a similar but slightly less strong effect occurs. The pull of the Moon ("downward" now in our reference frame) is less strong where we are standing than it is at the center of the Earth, so the water and continents puff up slightly compared to where they would be without the Moon's pull - the water puffs up much more so than the continents. And so another high tide occurs at this time.

If the Earth didn't spin, there would be only two high tides per month, as the Moon makes a complete orbit around the Earth, and they would occur precisely when the Moon was overhead and when it was underfoot. But the Earth spins quite rapidly (every 24 hours) underneath the Moon. So there are two high tides per day—about, but not exactly, every 12 hours. And they don't occur exactly when the Moon is overhead, or underfoot, but a little before these times. This shift in times is because the tidal bulge on the rapidly spinning Earth takes some time to relax after the pulling Moon whizzes past.

So, we've just used Classical Mechanics to predict that, on our tropical beach at sunset on the full Moon night, the tide will indeed be flowing in. This is because the Moon is just rising and is a few hours yet from being overhead—about when Classical Mechanics tells us that the tide will be high.

Now how do we know that this high tide will be one of the highest tides of the month? The Earth and Moon orbit the Sun. The Sun is many times more massive than the Moon, and is many times farther away. So, the Sun causes tides on the Earth, just like the Moon does, except smaller tides. Both the Sun and Moon cause high tides on the sides of the Earth that are nearest and farthest to them. When the solar high tides and the lunar high tides happen at the same time, they add up to a higher tide than the average high tide. They will happen at the same time, any good physicist or computer will tell you, twice per month—when the Moon is directly between the Earth and the Sun (new Moon), and when the Moon is directly opposite the Sun (full Moon). The new Moon high tide is the highest of the month because when the Sun and the Moon are both aligned on the same side of the Earth the biggest total differences in their net gravitational fields are felt. The full Moon high tide is slightly less high than the new Moon high tide, but not much less. So, if we know it's going to be a full Moon, we know that it is going to be one of the highest tides of the month.

We've really only used one principle of mechanics so far—the Law of Universal Gravitation. We've used this, together with the basic methods of mechanics embodied in Newton's Laws of motion (which we'll get to in a moment) which are almost second nature to scientists.

Newton's Apple

The legend goes that Isaac Newton,[103] sitting in a garden one afternoon with the Moon overhead, noticed an apple fall and he suddenly intuited the Law of Universal Gravitation—that the Earth and Moon would pull on each other in exactly the same way as the Earth and apple pulled on each other (and that everything in the Universe would pull on everything else in direct proportion to their masses and inversely proportional to their distances squared)—and that this would explain a whole lot of things. It would explain exactly how the tides work, and why the planets followed Kepler's Laws so precisely, and why heavy and light objects fall at the same rate, and one heck of a lot of other things. As physical insights go, this one was a doosey.[104]

So, one single Law of Universal Gravitation, together with the basic methods of mechanics lets us predict exactly what sort of tide we'll have, and when, on our tropical beach.

Some Asides about Tides

We'll be getting back to understanding the breeze on the beach in a moment. But first, an interesting aside about tides is that everything in the Universe raises tides on everything else in the Universe. Now, the gravitational tide that I cause on you is quite small—about one ten billionth of the size of an atomic nucleus[105] assuming you are about a thousand miles away from me, or as big as about a hundred atomic nuclei if you are right next to me. These tides are clearly inconsequential. But one has to be careful to check when assuming that something is inconsequential. For instance, the planet Mars raises tides on Earth (along with the Sun and the Moon), that are not entirely inconsequential. Earth's atmosphere, being even more fluid than the oceans, experiences tides that affect the weather and climate. The tides that Mars causes on Earth's atmosphere (though much smaller than those caused by the Moon and the Sun) are quite large enough to affect weather systems on Earth.[106] The effect is in subtle and delicate ways that we can't predict exactly, but it is not inconsequential. So, when an old-fashioned physicist tries to tell you something like "the planets of the Solar System are so far away, and their forces are so small, that they couldn't possibly affect anything relevant here on Earth"—usually in the context of bashing something like newspaper astrology columns (these being one of the dead horses that some physicists love to beat)—don't believe him. He's clearly either a religious fanatic or he doesn't follow his own science.

If he means to actually say something like, "we know that the gravitational pull of the other planets does affect things like *weather* here on Earth. But as far as we know, there can be no material mechanism by which the relative positions of the planets could cause specific *emotions* in humans. Therefore our resentment of the fact that some astrologers make more money than most physicists is justified." Then he would be much more scientifically accurate.

Another interesting thing to note has to do with a general appreciation for the sizes of things. Ocean tides on Earth are, as we noted, a few feet high. Another class of objects that are a few feet high is us. Most humans are about 5 or 6 feet high. We are also made mostly out of water. Both of these coincidences are why tides are important to us. If humans were as big as mountains, we would barely notice ocean tides. If humans were as small as fleas, we also wouldn't think of them as tides—we'd simply be inundated by an appearing and disappearing ocean periodically if we happened to live in a tidal zone.

Humans and other mammals are essentially mobile water blobs—just about the same height as the tidal bulge that spins around the planet—rambling around on the continents feeling self-important. In many models of the origin of life, the tidal zones are essential. The lunar tidal zones are likely regions (possibly essential) where water and chemicals and solar energy first associated to form the most primitive living organisms.

For a number of reasons that we'll get into later, a few feet may well be an optimum size for complexity, especially here on Earth. A few feet is right in between the large sizes dominated by gravitational forces and the small sizes dominated by electrostatic and chemical forces, for instance. As the lunar tidal bulge keeps spinning around the planet, we tidal bulge-sized organisms are starting to wonder if there's something going on about complexity, something having to do with material complexity as a doorway for the nonmaterial and the material acting together.

Newton's Laws, Maxwell's Demons, and Boltzmann's Demise

That takes care of the tides on our tropical beach, but how do we know that the breeze will be blowing onto shore? This is a little more involved than the tides. Whereas for the tides one can sort of intuit how to make the predictions, now it will help to specifically introduce the basic laws of mechanics. These are called Newton's Laws of Motion. When Newton communed with that apple, the Law of Universal Gravitation didn't just appear out of the blue. He had been working very hard to understand, for a long time, how and why things move the way they do. (And when Basho was perturbed by that frog, he'd been working very hard to get to the essence of poetry.) Newton was developing Newton's Laws of Motion.

Newton's Laws of Motion are three:

1. A body at rest (or in motion) tends to stay at rest (or in motion).
2. The sum of forces on a body is equal to the mass of the body multiplied by its acceleration.
3. For every force acting on a body, the body exerts an equal and oppositely directed force on the forcer.

These are the only laws of Classical Mechanics. The Law of Universal Gravitation and a small number of other properties of matter (like the forces between electric charges) specify the exact sort of forces that go into Newton's Laws of Motion. The extraordinary thing about Newtonian mechanics, indeed about all of physics, is that a very small number of laws is universally applicable, and that they can predict correctly an enormous range of phenomena. Of course, a sophisticated mathematics is also needed to employ the laws to actually make predictions. By proceeding without mathematics, we're just displaying a flavor of things.

So, it's not obvious yet how Classical Mechanics will tell us which way the wind will blow on our beach, is it? The following development of this question will skip volumes, and is a different perspective from the way it's often done. The scientist may find it unusual, but perhaps interesting. Those completely unfamiliar with scientific methods will probably not follow it all. But hopefully some of the flavor of the Newtonian or mechanistic paradigm will come across. Some of the ideas introduced will seem unrelated at first. But stick with them. They come together.

In 1856, James Clerk Maxwell's doctoral dissertation won the Cambridge University "Adams Prize" contest for his study of the rings of Saturn.[107] Maxwell showed, using the methods of classical mechanics, that Saturn's rings are composed of particles (rocks or ice balls of some sort) because liquid or gaseous rings would not be stable. It was a good paper, and won the prize, but Maxwell knew that it didn't answer a lot of questions about Saturn's rings, and he returned to the issue throughout his career.[108] He wanted to know just how the ring particles behaved, and he felt that, by studying Saturn's rings, we could find out whether Newtonian mechanics really did work the same "in the Saturnian realms" as it does here on Earth. The dynamics of Saturn's rings, it turns out, are immensely complicated. They still dog some physicists. Maxwell never solved some of the questions he posed to himself about the rings but happily for science, his frustration led him to help develop a major new field of physics—the relation between statistical Newtonian mechanics and thermodynamics, known as the "kinetic theory of gases."[109]

The kinetic theory of gases shows that whole sciences—the theory of gases, and thermodynamics (the study of how and why heat flows), and fluid dynamics (the study of how and why fluids move), which had their own laws and results—are *derivable* from the simple concepts of Newtonian mechanics. Of course, some pretty fancy mathematics and some pretty subtle physical insights are involved in really showing this. But Maxwell and others opened up the field that showed that these (theory of gases, thermodynamics, fluid dynamics) are nothing more than Newtonian mechanics. Some of the intricacies of these relations are still being worked on today but, for our purposes, the relation can be considered as completed.

Another character worth noting on our journey from Newton's laws to our breezy tropical beach is Ludwig Boltzmann.[110] One thing that Boltzmann did was to develop a single mathematical equation, based on Newton's laws of motion, that embodied all these other sciences. He did this by thinking as follows:

1. Well, these sciences like fluid dynamics, and gas dynamics, and thermodynamics, are just about how fluids and gases and heat behave. Simple enough.
2. Fluids and gases and heat are, at the microscopic level, just a bunch of particles colliding and jostling each other. The particles may be molecules, or clusters of molecules, or ice balls like in Saturn's rings, or atoms, or even electrons and protons like in a plasma (though no one then knew about electrons and protons and plasmas).
3. If I make one single mathematical equation that applies Newton's laws of motion to all the particles, individually and together, then the same results should come out of that one equation as I get from fluid dynamics or gas dynamics or thermodynamics.

The resulting "Boltzmann's equation" does just that. The tricky part of Boltzmann's equation is that the "interparticle terms" of the equation—the part that takes into account the particles colliding and pushing and pulling on each other—complicates the equation a lot. In fact, the equation can almost never be solved exactly. That is probably one reason why Boltzmann's ideas were not as well recognized as they should have been.

Boltzmann was a very sensitive man. He was tormented by the lack of acceptance of his important theories. He ended up taking his own life prematurely. Boltzmann's equation is still little known, though some of his related work is now widely recognized as of key importance.

One of the things that Maxwell did was to show that the particles in an approximate sort of "ideal gas" would have a certain simply-described distribution of velocities. This "Gaussian distribution" or "Maxwellian distribution" can be used to make good approximations to Boltzmann's tricky equation. (A simple form of the same distribution is the so-called "Bell curve," widely used to rank students' test scores and other random distributions.) One gas that is often well approximated by this sort of "ideal gas" is air— Earth's atmosphere. We're getting a little closer to our beach breezes now.

In the 1880s, Yale University decided (against many of its Humanities-dominated faculty) to get in on the new European thing called "theoretical physics," just in case it turned out to be important. So Yale allowed J. Willard Gibbs, who had studied in Europe, to teach, without pay. Gibbs did very important work at Yale on thermodynamics, essentially supplying a rigorous mathematical base to the ideas of Boltzmann and Maxwell. Gibbs helped to formalize the concept of "entropy" (measure of disorder) and showed that the principle of increase of entropy of a closed system is also a direct result of Newtonian mechanics.

Gibbs's formalizations laid the groundwork for Ilya Prigogine's work on "dissipative structures" and "nonhierarchical approaches to reality."[111] We'll show later that Prigogine's nonhierarchical reality and his way of looking at dissipative structures is another way to appreciate the hylozoic paradigm. We can make this connection by working back through Gibbs, Boltzmann, and Maxwell (and the quantum and chaos discoveries we're coming to). After ten years of service and producing some of the most important theoretical physics ever by an American, Gibbs finally got a $2,000 salary from Yale—to keep him from moving to John's Hopkins which had offered $3,000.[112]

So Boltzmann, Maxwell, and Gibbs grounded the knowledge of fluid motion and gaseous motion in the "first principles" of Newtonian mechanics. Now we can predict which way the breeze will probably blow on the beach—using Newton's laws only. First, there's the little step of modeling the air molecules as tiny inelastic

5: Matter in Motion

balls (inelastic meaning perfectly bouncy). Then approximate their velocities with Maxwell's distribution of velocities. Plug that into Boltzmann's equation and out pop all the equations of fluid dynamics. Then simply apply the equations of fluid dynamics to the atmosphere around the beach.

On a calm tropical day, the Sun heats up the land and ocean. The land surface heats up more than the water surface because it does not conduct heat as well as the water does. The ocean conducts the heat from the sun down into its cooler parts. So, by sunset, the land surface is relatively hot and the ocean surface is relatively cool. As the sun sets, the land warms the air above it and the ocean cools the air above it. All this is predicted by those fluid dynamics equations (which come from Newton's laws). The warm air above the land rises, causing low pressure just above the land. The cool air above the ocean sinks, causing higher pressure above the water. The cool air above the water therefore flows to the lower pressure region above the land. And a cool breeze blows onto shore. We can even predict that it will be a cool breeze and not a hot breeze.

An instructive detour on our route arises here. Like any good paradigmaticist, Maxwell tried to shoot down supposed physical laws whenever he could. A look at one case of this illustrates how Maxwell thought, and also develops the sort of thinking that we'll be using for our route to the hylozoic paradigm. To shoot down the second law of thermodynamics, Maxwell once employed a demon.

The second law of thermodynamics is also called the "law of increase of entropy." Entropy is a measure of disorder, and a whole mathematical formalism exists around the law. But a simple example will suffice for our purposes, and will avoid the mathematics. A quintessential example of the second law (law of increase of entropy) is a box with two compartments connected by a hole with a valve on it. If we start with a hot gas on one side of the box and a cold gas on the other and then open the valve, the two temperatures will equilibrate. The entropy will increase. One hot container and one cold container is more organized (less disordered, and so lower entropy) than the resulting equilibrated containers. The second law says this will always happen and one side will not suddenly heat up as the other cools off.

But Maxwell invented a counter-example to the law, and a single good counter-example to a physical law denies its status as a law. He said suppose there is a little demon sitting on the valve watching the molecules that come toward the valve. The demon wants the left container to get hot and the right to get cold. So, when a fast molecule comes from the right, he opens the valve, and when a slow one comes from the right he closes the valve. Likewise, when a fast molecule comes from the left, he closes the valve, and when a slow one comes he opens it. Soon the left container heats up, and the right cools off. And the entropy of the system *decreases*—one good counter-example and so end of the second law, almost.

Actually, the counter example is close but doesn't win the cigar. The demon acts in such a way that the system of the gas is actually not isolated. The demon needs to "look at" the molecules and measure their speeds and directions. To look at them, the demon needs to bounce photons off each molecule that comes by and do calculations in his head as to their speeds. So, it turns out that the entropy of the whole system—gas, and photons, and demon—does indeed increase. The demon and his light source become highly disordered as the gas becomes more ordered. So the second law wins. But it is a sort of a Pyrrhic victory because to us sitting outside watching the gas, it would sure look like the entropy decreased. If we remember Boltzmann's equation though, and the derivation of the second law from it, then nothing strange seems to happen even with the demon there.

Another thought experiment that seemed to indicate that the second law is actually a fundamental law in itself, and not derivable from Newton's laws, also doesn't survive careful analysis. This thought experiment simply reverses the time for all the gas molecules. But this doesn't cause problems either, for reasons we'll show in the next chapter. So, there's nothing spooky or fundamental in the concepts of increase of entropy or thermodynamics or fluid dynamics. These are only derivative of Newton's laws of mechanics (together with perhaps a tiny bit of quantum indeterminacy that we're getting to).

5: Matter in Motion

Simple Electricity and Magnetism Begets Light and Relativity

So, in the last section we showed how to predict, for our beach experiment, which way the tide would flow, what sort of tide it would be, which way the breeze would blow and what temperature the breeze would be—all from Newton's laws of classical mechanics only. Right? Almost! But there was one tiny little thing we had to start with. We had to say, "first there's the little step of modeling the air molecules as tiny inelastic balls ..." And as we get into what is really behind that "little" starting point, an enormous new field will open up, and we'll get very close to the hylozoic paradigm.

Air molecules do indeed act enough like tiny inelastic balls so that the above method gives the right predictions, but why do they? Around the beginning of this century, experiments were starting to show that atoms are composed of positive electric charged things (protons) at their centers, surrounded by negative electric charged things (electrons). And air molecules are made of a few atoms each. And so, we run into a problem. Newton's laws alone don't tell us how these "electric charges" behave, and so cannot tell us why those air molecules behave like tiny inelastic balls. We need some more physics before we can rest at ease that we understand the breeze on our beach.

We need to understand how those electric charges behave. And for that, we need to understand electromagnetism. Fortunately we've already introduced one of the characters who first really figured out electromagnetism for us. Maxwell, besides wrestling with demons and worrying about Saturn's rings, is best known for "Maxwell's equations of electrodynamics." With those equations, Maxwell unified and completed the classical study of electricity and magnetism. (Except, again, for a nasty little detail that will open up a whole new field of understanding.) Maxwell's equations have an elegance and beauty such that it is not uncommon to see people wearing them on T-shirts. But we're not going to write them down. We'll just explain a little of how they came about, and what they mean.

One of America's favorite Americans, Benjamin Franklin, was instrumental in showing back in the late 1700s that two types of electric charge exist—positive and negative. Positive charges repel each other according to a law that is exactly the same as the Law of Universal Gravitation, except in place of the masses in gravitation are the charges of electricity (and a different constant of proportionality out front). Negative charges, of course, also repel each other. And positive and negative charges attract each other with the same strength. These forces between charges constitute the first of Maxwell's equations.

The second of Maxwell's equations was developed in the early 1800s by French physicist Marie Ampere. It shows how electric currents create magnetic fields, and that electric currents are just moving electric charges. It also settled the problem of magnetic origins. Magnetic stones are bipolar. They create oppositely directed magnetic forces on opposite sides of themselves. No matter how small the pieces you break them into, they remain bipolar. No one could find or isolate separate magnetic charges (like the electric charges). Ampere's law suggested that there may not be any magnetic monopoles at all. Still today, as far as we know, there are no magnetic monopoles. (And that's what Maxwell's fourth equation says—there are no magnetic monopoles—it is the flip side of the first equation about electric charges.)

The third of Maxwell's equations was developed by American physicist Joseph Henry, who noted a flavor of scientific culture in America in the 1840s: "Our newspapers are filled with puffs of quackery and every man who can ... exhibit a few experiments to a class of young ladies is called a man of science."[113]

The British scientist Faraday also discovered this third equation independently (this sort of independent discovery happens a lot), and it now bears his name. Faraday's law shows how changing magnetic fields create electric fields. It also begs the creation of electric motors. Dig up some magnets, and push them around some wire loops, and know something about Faraday's law, and pay attention to what happens, and eventually you're going to invent electric motors.

Those are the four Maxwell's equations, except for a key piece—the symmetrical version of Faraday's law, which says that changing electric fields also create magnetic fields. It could easily have been noticed by Faraday or Henry, but no experiments then indicated the need for it. So it fell to Maxwell to add this piece onto Ampere's law and complete classical electrodynamics in 1865.

5: Matter in Motion

All sorts of new physical phenomena were implied by Maxwell's addition, and the completed equations of electrodynamics. Since then, these phenomena have been verified by experiment. Remember that the equations themselves were all motivated by relatively simple experiments in electrostatics—with magnets and conductors and electrostatic generators (like rubbing a balloon on your head and sticking it on the ceiling). Add a little profound mathematical insight ala Maxwell, and shazam—light! Literally. Maxwell's equations predicted light of all sorts, as electromagnetic radiation. Remember that changing electric fields create magnetic fields and changing magnetic fields create electric fields. And a little mathematics shows that an electromagnetic wave continues to propagate on by itself. And it was quickly realized that electromagnetic waves are what light is.

Now we might have enough to go back and finish our prediction of the breeze on the beach. But we should make sure we understand light because, light being electromagnetic waves, if we don't predict light correctly then there might be something wrong with our equations of electromagnetism—and we need them to be correct. So, we need to talk about light too.

Mathematically, after 1865, light turned out to be very neat little electromagnetic waves. At that time everyone knew that waves were wiggles on something else. Ocean waves are wiggles on the water. Sound waves are wiggles in the air. Seismic waves are wiggles on the Earth. So, it was assumed that light waves are wiggles on the ether. Like all those other waves, the speed of light waves would then be relative to the medium in which it moved—the ether.

Scientists like Michelson and Morley devised experiments to measure the difference in the speed of light when moving with respect to the ether. They tried this at different times of day because the spinning Earth would be moving with respect to the ether. They tried it at different times of year because the Earth's motion around the sun is even faster than its spinning motion. They tried it while aloft in balloons in case the ether was dragged along with the surface of the Earth (probably also because balloons are fun). All the experiments gave negative results, even though they were sensitive enough to measure a difference. People started to doubt the ether.

Lorentz then rescued the ether in 1892 with the bizarre proposal that all objects contract in length by certain amounts when they move with respect to the ether. The experimental apparatuses of Michelson and Morley would then also shrink and appear to record the same speed. But experiments by Fitzeau (1851 and 1853) and Morley (1886) on the speed of light in rapidly moving fluids, also showed that the ether would have to be dragged along with the fluids in ad hoc ways, even if Lorentz's contractions happened too. So people again doubted either the ether or Maxwell's equations themselves. In any case, they were confused or should have been.

Then, in 1905, Einstein did his thing. He proposed that physics is independent of the motion of the observer. He also postulated the constancy of the speed of light. This solved the problems with understanding the experimental results. There is no universal electromagnetic ether. There is no *special* universal reference frame at all, for anything. So, the theory is called special relativity. Light waves do wiggle. But they don't wiggle *on* anything. They just wiggle.

1905 also is when the bottom started dropping out of the Newtonian-Cartesian understanding of the world. Einstein's relativity implied that Lorentz's bizarre contractions do actually occur, but not with respect to a universal ether. The contractions occur with respect to *any* inertial reference frame. So objects have different lengths in different reference frames.

If one thought that Lorentz's contractions were bizarre, Einstein's relative contractions were mind-blowing. Einstein's relativity meant also that Newton's laws of motion would have to be modified for fast motions, in a similar manner to Lorentz's contractions. Since Einstein's proposals in 1900, all manner of experiments have been done to test the predicted consequences of special relativity. They have all verified the theory.

We'll get back to understanding the breeze on the beach. In the interim, we've come to the end of something very important and should note the implications. We've come to the end of the deterministic models of matter.

Maxwell's equations, together with Newton's laws of motion, and the Lorentz transformations at high speeds, and Einstein's principles of relativity, finally completes electrodynamics and

5: Matter in Motion

material dynamics both classical and relativistic. These are all deterministic theories. In these theories, particles move precisely as the relevant equations describe. Some pretty bizarre things happen at high relative speeds, with objects shrinking, and masses increasing, and time running at different rates. But the theories are exact and precise according to the equations.

Classical and relativistic electrodynamics and mechanics are deterministic models of matter. In deterministic models, there are direct, exact, and precise cause-and-effect relations explicit in the mathematical equations. We call deterministic models of matter collectively, the "hylostatic paradigm." To appreciate the hylostatic paradigm, consider one single event. An event is something happening—anything. Many things may have contributed to the cause of that event. In the hylostatic paradigm, the causes are in the past. The outcome of the event, in turn, will become a cause and will affect many things in the future.

If you like to visualize, visualize the hylostatic paradigm as follows. Think of a large circle moving forward and getting smaller. The circle continues to move, becomes a point, and then becomes an increasing sized circle again. We've described a conical hourglass shape. The forward motion direction represents the passage of time. The initial circles represent the causal chain of events leading up to the single event of the present, which is the single point dividing past and future. The future circles represent all the future events affected by that single present event represented by the point. The size of the circles represents the spatial distance, away from the present single event, out to which causes could influence the present (because of the speed of light). Also consider that all events have similar cause-effect cones associated with them, connected with many other events.

Now picture, or imagine, one more-encompassing dimension—imagine the cause-effect structures in four dimensions with all of time included. In this frame of imagination, all the interrelated cause-effect chains are fixed and specified. Nothing changes. The material universe with all its events is a big, static and unchanging, four-dimensional object. Hence it is hylostatic. This will be one way of visualizing how different the hylozoic universe is from the hylostatic.

Sneaking Up On the Nature of Atoms

So now that we've really completed classical electrodynamics and classical mechanics, we can fill in that last little bit of understanding the breeze on the beach: Why do the air molecules act like tiny inelastic balls? Well, sort of.

Since the experiments were starting to show that atoms consist of positively-charged nuclei surrounded by negatively-charged electrons, we can try to make an approximate model of an atom and see if it behaves like an inelastic ball. Model the electron clouds as sort of negatively-charged globs attached around the positively charged nuclei. When two of these glob-model atoms bump into each other, we can now use the force equations of electrodynamics (Maxwell's equations) together with Newton's laws of motion to predict how they will move. Because negative charges repel each other, the electron globs will move slightly away from each other as the atoms approach. The positive nuclei will no longer be completely shielded by their electron clouds, and they will also repel each other. So, Newton's laws of motion tell us that the resulting net forces will push the two bumping atoms apart—just like two inelastic balls.

Have we finally now understood the breeze? The simple model atoms do act like tiny inelastic balls. But there is another nasty little detail that just doesn't fit into the picture. We know that air particles are actually molecules composed of two or more atoms each. Our glob-model atoms bounce apart whenever they come close, so they would never stick together to form molecules in the first place. There seems to be no simple model that uses the physics we now know (electrodynamics and mechanics) that will explain both the molecules and the inelastic bouncing.

So, if we really want to understand our breeze, we're going to have to understand atoms. And that is going to lead us to some revolutionary findings. We're also starting to see a pattern in which that last little detail that just won't fit actually becomes a doorway to a whole new field of completely different sorts of phenomena.

6. The Stochastic Universe

A story about an eccentric physicist who lost his house keys goes as follows. The physicist is searching vigorously around on the ground. A friend of his walks by, stops and asks, "What are you doing?" The physicist says, "Looking for my keys." So the friend joins the search, crawling around on the ground. Another acquaintance walks up, inquires about the search, is told by the friend about the lost keys and joins in the searching. A colleague of the physicist also arrives and is told by the others about the keys, and he too joins the search. After a while the second physicist who knows that his colleague's antics often have a meaning not initially apparent asks, "Where did you lose your keys?" The physicist says, "Over there." The colleague asks, "Why are we searching here?" The physicist says, "Because there is light over here!"[114]

Scientists look where the light is; and the light of science at any given time in the evolution of science can only shine on a limited range of phenomena. Physics and the science based on it is searching around in the light as it only can and should. But it has generally forgotten to ask whether the key thing—the truth about how the world really works—is likely to be in the areas where there happens to be light.

Science progresses by looking for anomalies: experimental results and phenomena that *don't* fit into the models of science. If experimental results or observed phenomena that don't fit into the present models are found, then new models are required that hopefully will be even more fundamental and simple than the old models. The key to experimental science is to know how to look, what to look for, and to look very vigorously. The key to relating science to the larger field of all human experience is to be aware that some important things may not be in the light at all, and to recognize that just because such things are not in the light of science does not mean that they cannot exist. The outgoing paradigm does not recognize the importance of this fact.

In this part of the book, we are looking around in the light of science and the history of science. In the next parts we attempt some initial ventures into the dark of spirituality and the history of spirituality. The keys that we are looking for we suspect were actually lost in the dark. But, to be able to venture into the dark at all, we do need to know the way that the part of the world that *is* in the light works.

In this chapter, we will look at how the discovery of the quantum mechanical nature of things answered many of those final questions left hanging after the completion of classical physics. By the end of the previous chapter, we almost came to understand the breeze on our beach. Conceptually, along with reviewing the state of physics at the turn of this century, we reviewed key concepts of classical physics. In order to tie up some loose ends in the theories, we had to accept that some pretty wild ideas of Einstein and Lorentz are actually quite true, as well as being wild. (And those ideas lead to a whole new range of phenomena that significantly alter our way of understanding the world; but that's beside the point for now because relativity is a deterministic theory just as classical mechanics is.)

We've just about understood our breeze, and by analogy just about everything else in our environment. That is a lot of analogy, but suppose for now that it would hold true; with a little more work we might expect that we'll explain those last details of the deterministic, hylostatic, models of our universe and that will be the end of it.

A Theory Of Everything?

Then we would have a Theory Of Everything. Our TOE would consist of mathematical equations, based on a few physical laws, that would accurately represent the evolution of everything at all times. Being a deterministic hylostatic TOE, it would show that the ability to predict all future events would only be limited by our ability to compute (to solve the mathematical equations of the TOE) and limited by our ability to measure the initial conditions for those computations. In practice, even if we had such a TOE, our ability to do the computations and to make the measurements would be limited. But a verified hylostatic TOE would tell us a lot about ourselves and the universe simply by its existence, even though we couldn't actually predict everything.

A hylostatic TOE would tell us that a lot of things must be impossible. Such a TOE says that all events are caused in rigid sequence by past events. It says that all events are caused by other events immediately before, in the immediate spatial vicinity. We could call this "contact causation." So a hylostatic TOE would show, for instance, that telepathic rapport with another human (any sort of nonphysical sensation of a distant other) is impossible.

Many people theorize that electromagnetic fields might explain telepathy. Very low intensity electromagnetic fields generated by the brain and body do occur and may affect others in one's immediate vicinity. In fact, low intensity electromagnetic fields seem to be the hypothetical mechanism of choice for scientists who consider the possible mechanism for telepathy. For instance, on a radio show, the featured guests were a "parapsychologist," a local mathematics professor playing the role of skeptic, and a local physics professor playing the role of sympathetic agnostic. The physics professor was asked, "How do you think telepathy might work if it did exist?"

He replied, "The brain does produce electromagnetic fields ... which could influence other brains."

If I were the parapsychologist, I would not be happy with such "help." These sorts of electromagnetic effects are within the hylostatic paradigm, and would be entirely deterministic processes. They could not possibly explain the many reports of telepathic rapport over long distances because the electric fields that the body and brain generate (at least, all those fields understandable in terms of the hylostatic paradigm of classical physics) are far too low intensity to be responsible for such effects.

So, if a hylostatic TOE could be found, it would mean that such reports of telepathic rapport are simply wrong. Similarly, it would mean that reports of mystical religious experience are necessarily either ignorant misinterpretations of fantasy, or lies. The present scientific paradigm, which informs the world view of the Western cultural elite, sure seems to be that such a hylostatic TOE, if not actually known, is close enough to reality to make the preceding conclusions true. We are investigating the facts to see if they support that worldview, and that leads us back to our development of the understanding of breezes.

Classical physics allows us to understand a lot of things—the tides, the motions of planets, a lot of thermodynamics and fluid dynamics (which covers a *lot* of phenomena), of course, ballistics and the related arts and horrors of war, the nature of light (at least, much of the nature of light), and all sorts of technologies (including combustion engines, electric motors, heat engines and the principles of heavier than air flight).

Given our great understanding prowess, and the physical power it confers, we might reasonably assume that soon we'll understand just about everything, if we just tackle those last little details. To make sure, we should at least briefly survey things and note those things that *cannot* be explained even in principle by classical physical science.

To many readers, the above sort of reasoning may already seem absurd because there are multitudes of phenomena that we have no idea how to explain with classical physics or any other physics. But there is a key way to think about these things scientifically. Rather than jumping directly to something like "consciousness" that is clearly too complicated to explain, the scientist looks for stuff in the middle ground of complexity. We look for things that are fairly simple and *should* be predictable by physical models, but do not behave as one would predict from the physics.

These types of mysteries indicate that there is something very fundamental in the physics that is not understood. This is what Maxwell was looking for when he studied Saturn's fairly simple rings to see if physics was the same "in the Saturnian realms" as it is here on Earth. If there are such "middle ground" phenomena that cannot be explained, then scientists have no basis for arguing that the higher order phenomena are just more complex versions of the basic concepts—because the basic concepts don't even explain the simple stuff.

Failures of Classical Physics

At the turn of the century, one very simple example that did not behave as the classical physics of the time would predict was the radiation from a small hole in a hot furnace. Another phenomenon that was completely mysterious was the spectrum of light that gases emit when an electric spark is sent through them. Both of these are very easily producible phenomena that you can find in most homes; almost any very hot object will glow like a hot furnace; fluorescent lights are examples of gas discharge tubes (though they are usually covered in white and otherwise designed to produce a broad spectrum of light, whereas a simple gas discharge tube only fluoresces certain very specific colors or wavelengths of light).

It is important to note that we are progressing through the basic concepts of physics with detailed hindsight. By thinking in terms of atoms and molecules, applying classical physics to them in order to try and understand the workings of a breeze, a very clear conceptual picture of the development of physics can be drawn. In fact, however, at the turn of this century, the fact of atoms' and molecules' existence was not even well established; a lot of leading chemists of the time did not believe in atoms at all.[115] They thought that the various chemicals, compounds, metals and gases were just different kinds of stuff, not divisible to a basic atomic constituent. Incontrovertible experimental proof of the existence of molecules and atoms only came in 1907 through study of "Brownian motion"—the incessant jiggling of microscopic bits of matter (grains of pollen) in a fluid due to pelting by individual molecules.[116]

So, pretending that we are turn-of-the-century scientists surveying our turf, we note that there are actually many "little details" that just don't fit. Let's look more closely at our two examples to get a feel for how quantum mechanics made them fit.

The Ultraviolet Catastrophe

How did the radiation coming out of the hole in a furnace revolutionize our understanding of matter? One of the first things noticed about this radiation is that it has a simple characteristic "spectrum" that depends only on the temperature of the furnace. Spectrum is a fancy term for the color; the color spectrum is the amount of energy radiated per unit time per unit wavelength of light. (Actually we'll use the general term "spectrum" for the technical term "spectral emittance" which is the energy per unit time per unit wavelength per unit surface area, around a given wavelength, at the surface of an object.) The spectrum of radiation that comes out of a furnace has a characteristic form that is centered around shorter or longer wavelengths, depending on the temperature of the furnace. Basically the spectrum tails off toward zero at both short wavelength and long wavelength ends, and has a hump in the middle around whatever wavelength of light is equivalent to the overall temperature of the object. This simple furnace spectrum, common to all furnaces, depends only on temperature; it is the sort of thing that physics theorists love to explain; they know it *should* be explainable from the first principles of physics.

The furnace spectrum became even more important when it was shown that it was the same as the spectrum of *any* "black-body." A black-body is any object that has no intrinsic color and thus emits light only in the form of heat. The furnace spectrum, or "black-body radiation spectrum," is a very important and fundamental concept; it applies, at least in an approximate sense, to any object that "glows" from heat. Warm objects don't glow at all (warm being about human body temperature). Hot objects glow red like an electric stove, and the insides of most furnaces. Hotter objects glow white like the sun. Really hot objects glow blue like some stars. But each one has the same characteristic blackbody spectrum, differing only in temperature—the spectrum peaks around the light color (wavelength) determined by the temperature. Actually the sun and stars have very complicated spectra due to the radiative processes in their atmospheres, but to very rough first approximation, they can be thought of as black-body radiators.

Just before the turn of the century, people were beginning to measure and characterize this black-body spectrum; theorists were busy trying to explain the observations in terms of classical physics; really good theorists were busy trying to *predict* from classical physics what the future observations should look like. That is what Lord Rayleigh was doing. In 1900, Rayleigh approached the problem in a very elegant and powerful way, as follows.[117] Classical physics says that a furnace is a cavity that can vibrate only at fixed frequencies, just as a string can vibrate only at fixed frequencies depending on the length of the string; hence the notes of a violin. Similarly, the radiation in the cavity is the vibration of electromagnetic waves; and the total radiation in the cavity must be some superposition of all the possible standing waves, all the possible vibration modes, inside the cavity.

A famous principle of classical statistical mechanics, the sort of stuff that Boltzmann and Maxwell were doing (see the previous chapter), says that each of the possible standing wave modes should contain the same amount of energy. This is called the law of equipartition of energy and is the basis of the law of increase of entropy. The law of equipartition of energy is due to the concept that energy rambles around and fills all spaces available to it in equal measures—like a happy dog trying to monopolize all its toys at once: the dog's attention is the energy, and the toys are the vibration modes. These two simple considerations led Rayleigh to predict a simple expression for the spectrum of a blackbody, based only on the principles of classical physics.

Rayleigh's prediction did indeed match the observations for the long wavelength end (red or cool part) of the spectrum. But on the short wavelength end of the spectrum the prediction did not match the observations. Rayleigh's expression for the energy per unit wavelength keeps getting bigger at smaller wavelengths. In fact, it would require the total energy in the blackbody to be infinite because there is an infinite number of possible tiny wavelength modes and equipartition of energy means they all have equal energy. Obviously, infinite energy violates classical physics, and thermodynamics and other considerations require that the blackbody is in equilibrium, so something was wrong with classical theory. It could not explain blackbody radiation. Since the shortest wavelength light known at the time was called "ultraviolet," this seeming tendency toward infinite energy was called the "ultraviolet catastrophe." Rayleigh's ultraviolet catastrophe means that something very basic about classical physics is wrong.

Meanwhile, in 1899 and 1900, Max Planck invented a mathematical expression that fit the observations of the blackbody spectra at both ends. (This kind of formula that matches an observation without being based on a physical mechanism is called an *empirical* formula.) In order to explain *why* his formula worked, instead of just that it *did* work, Planck had to learn some more physics. Planck had to go back and review Boltzmann's work from 1877 in which

Boltzmann recognized that the entropy of a state is a measure of the probability of the occurrence of that state.

The probability can be found by counting the number of different states available within the whole system, and assuming that each state is equally probable. In this case of blackbody radiation, the number of states is the number of ways of assigning various energies to each of the individual vibration modes in the black-body cavity. In order for counting the states to be possible, the energy of a given vibration mode cannot be a continuous variable (like the amplitude of standing waves on a string that can be big or small or anything in between), as it is in classical physics. For counting to be possible, the energy must exist only in integer multiples of a basic unit. This basic unit of energy could be incorporated into Planck's empirical formula (for mathematical reasons) only if that basic unit of energy is equal to a constant (now called Planck's constant) multiplied by the frequency of the electromagnetic vibrations. This distribution of energy into integer multiples of a basic unit is called the "quantization of energy." The smallest possible amount of energy is Planck's constant multiplied by the frequency of vibration of the mode that the energy is in.

(The above slightly complicated sentence is as simple as I can make it. It would be more fun if we could say that "the smallest possible amount of energy is N," where N is some number, but we can't because N depends on the frequency. The smallest possible unit of energy, E, is $E = h\nu$ where ν is the frequency and $h = 6.6 \times 10^{-34}$ Joule-seconds is Planck's constant. Note that Planck's constant has units of angular momentum and so there *is* a fundamental smallest amount of angular momentum—something to think about next time you are spinning around on an ice rink.)

With that great creative act of Planck in 1900, the quantum revolution started. Planck showed that the smooth and continuous blackbody radiation spectrum can be understood only if the internal energy states of the black-body are quantized in discrete fundamental units. It is still a common misconception that quantum effects are only relevant for submicroscopic processes like atomic transitions, and not relevant to macroscopic things like blackbodies.

The ultraviolet catastrophe is a beautiful reminder that, to even remotely resemble the world that we see around us, the world *needs* to rest on quantum mechanical grounds. If energy were not fundamentally quantized, objects could never reach temperature equilibrium with their surroundings. The high frequency states would continue to suck up some of the energy that is normally radiated away, until the object exploded or melted. Those things that had not exploded yet would not feel warm to the touch. The material world would seem cold, brutal and inexorably destructive.

Planck's own reaction to his discovery of the quantization of energy is interesting. First, he noted that it was merely empirical: "... I based my opinion of the usefulness of the formula ... especially on the simple structure."

Later, after establishing its foundations in terms of the quantization of energy, he said, "I do not place any value on the proof of necessity and the easy practical applicability, but only on the clarity and unequivocal nature of the directions given for the solution of the problem."[118] In other words when Planck understood what his model meant, he intuitively knew it pointed to something very fundamental.

Einstein, being one with a definite nose for the fundamental, was practically the only important physicist who recognized the importance of Planck's discovery early on. In 1905, Einstein noted that the entropy of the electromagnetic radiation in Planck's formula for a blackbody was the same as the entropy of an ideal gas (as in Maxwell's ideal gas, and Boltzmann's statistical mechanics, see Chapter 5). Einstein concluded that electromagnetic radiation behaved as though it consisted of discrete particles; he called them, "independent energy quanta."[119]

So Einstein went a big step further than Planck and said that electromagnetic radiation, which is light, behaved in general like a stream of particles; Planck had only showed that the internal energy states of an object are quantized. Einstein's light quanta explained a number of mysteries like the photoelectric effect in which cathodes (like your TV screen) exposed to ultraviolet rays emit electrons in a way that the wave theory of light fails to predict. Nevertheless Einstein's quantum light theory was by no means quickly accepted, even by Planck. As late as 1914, when Planck was arguing for the admission of Einstein to membership in the Royal Prussian Academy of Sciences, for Einstein's work on relativity theory, Planck urged that Einstein be excused for his wild idea to extend the quantum hypothesis to include light.[120] Planck's mild form of Frankensteinian lament at the wide ranging implications of ones own discovery was later to visit Einstein himself.

Those Troublesome Atoms

In the process of investigating those "little loose ends" of classical physics, we discovered that one of the loose ends was actually an ultraviolet catastrophe. The discovery that nature averts the catastrophe by quantizing energy puts us on a slippery slope, but if we want to understand the breeze on our beach, we have to slide down the slope. We still have no idea why some atoms bounce and some stick. It turns out that the other loose end that didn't fit into classical physics—the spectral emissions of gases—will be intimately related to the nature of atoms and so perhaps to the nature of breezes.

Since Newton, it was known that when you pass a beam of light through a glass prism, the colors of the beam separate; the intensity of each of the colors is the spectral emissivity of the source of the light. That is one way to measure the spectrum of the light from a furnace for instance. When you burn a chemical like the sulfur on a match or a pinch of salt, it emits a spectrum of light colors that is unique to that chemical. For simple compounds and elements, the spectrum of colors emitted is the same when you excite it in any way, such as by burning or sending an electric discharge through it as in a fluorescent light tube. And spectra generally consist of a series of very well-defined separate colors. The spectra of individual atoms are not at all continuous, as is the blackbody spectrum.

Why these different colors should be emitted was a mystery to classical physicists in the first decade of this century. They did know that it must be due to the way atoms work. At the time, conservative chemists notwithstanding, the atomic nature of matter was starting to be established. Experiments by Ernest Rutherford, who measured the scattering of atomic nuclei, were showing that atoms are composed of a dense central nucleus of protons surrounded by a diffuse outer part of electrons. Somehow these atoms could absorb energy and then emit the energy in the form of light, like a flame or an electric discharge; and the emission of a given atom is always one or more of the specific discrete colors of its unique spectrum.

6: The Stochastic Universe

Physicists tried to explain the spectrum of the simplest atom, hydrogen, in terms of its structure that consists of only one electron and one proton. Even such a simple atom as hydrogen emits a complex spectrum of many discrete colors. Rutherford, the experimentalist, suggested that a good first guess at the structure of the hydrogen atom should be that the electron orbits around the proton like a planet orbits around a star, except the attractive force in an atom is electrical instead of gravitational.

Niels Bohr showed in 1913 that the Rutherford model couldn't be right. According to the classical electrodynamics of Maxwell (described in Chapter 5), and Newton's laws of motion, the electron would be moving very fast in its orbit around the proton. That movement would create a rapidly changing electric field and, by Maxwell's equations, the changing electric field creates an electromagnetic wave that would radiate away the energy of the electron; the classical Rutherford atom would collapse in a tiny fraction of a second. And the radiated energy would have a continuous spectrum instead of the observed discrete spectrum. The theory failed to explain the observation; the Rutherford model was wrong.

But Bohr was on the trail of the right model. Because the discrete spectrum clearly implied discrete energies Bohr, realized he had to go back and study those crazy ideas of Planck and Einstein about the quantization of energy. When Bohr combined Planck's energy quantization with a Rutherford-like atom, he showed that the difference in energy of the spectral colors was exactly as could be predicted; the quantization of energy is actually a general principle and not only a peculiarity of black-body thermodynamics.

In Bohr's model of the atom, point-like electrons orbit the nucleus and can only absorb and emit Planckian quanta of energy as the electron jumps from orbit to orbit. This model explained a lot, but the spectra of more complicated atoms could not fit the Bohr model. Trying to fix these details, Heisenberg realized that the problem with the Bohr model was in the classical underpinnings: the idea that point-like electron particles actually move around the nucleus.

Heisenberg decided to forget about models of what was going on in the atom; by only focusing on "observables" like the spectra, and by discarding the conceptual underpinnings altogether, he was able to develop an elegant mathematics of quantum mechanics that incorporated the details that didn't fit Bohr's less mathematical model. Einstein's reaction to the younger Heisenberg's method, said to Heisenberg during a walk together, is interesting:

> "Einstein agreed that [Einstein] might once have worked that way [using a theory of observables only] but said, 'It's nonsense all the same.' Einstein ... explained that it was pointless to attempt to build theories on observables, for, after all, it was the theory itself which told physicists what could and could not be observed in nature."[121]

That dispute between Einstein and Heisenberg was the first rumbling of a general disagreement that continues today: what does quantum mechanics really mean?

Soon after that verbal rift, in 1924, the young Sorbonne graduate student Louis de Broglie submitted his thesis about the quantum hypotheses of Planck and Einstein. American physicist Arthur Holly Compton had shown in experiments on the photoelectric effect that Einstein's light particles have discrete momenta given by Planck's constant divided by the wavelength of the light. The young De Broglie said basically a particle is a particle, so maybe *all* particles that have momenta (electrons and protons and baseballs) also have wavelengths given by Compton's formula; photons have momentum depending on wavelength so maybe electrons have wavelength depending on momentum.

Because this was an original idea, de Broglie's professors were at a loss as to what to think about his thesis, so they sent it to Einstein.[122] Einstein approved. He even instructed influential physicist Max Born: "Read it. Even though it might look crazy it is absolutely solid."[123]

De Broglie was granted his Ph.D. A few years later, de Broglie's crazy matter waves were actually measured at Bell Labs in America and the still young Prince de Broglie was awarded a Nobel Prize.

In the meantime, Erwin Schrodinger in Zurich was considering leaving physics for philosophy. But de Broglie's idea caught his interest. Schrodinger invented a wave mechanics that describes mathematically how de Broglie's matter waves move.

By 1926, Schrodinger was able to show that, according to his quantum wave mechanics, the electron in the hydrogen atom could be treated as a "standing wave" that produced exactly the observed atomic radiation spectra. Einstein and Planck liked Schrodinger's method better than Heisenberg's method because it reintroduced a physical model that was continuous in time and space. The solutions to Schrodinger's equations were "smeared out" distributions in space. Schrodinger wanted to think of the distributions as actual smeared out electron blobs that would move continuously, although rapidly, from one state to another.

But quantum weirdness prevailed; Max Born argued for technical mathematical reasons, and because he knew that electrons at least sometimes act like concentrated point-like particles, that the distributions from Schrodinger's equation's solutions represent the *probability* of finding the electron in a given place. Born's statistical probability argument meant the particle would jump discontinuously from one stable quantum state to another. Niels Bohr enthusiastically took up Born's statistical interpretation and tried to convince Schrodinger of this new interpretation for Schrodinger's own equation. Schrodinger was not happy about this and even lamented at one point, "If one has to stick to this damned quantum jumping, then I regret having ever been involved in this thing."[124]

Wave-Particle Paradox?

A note here on the wave particle paradox will help us appreciate why these guys were having a very hard time agreeing on what was really going on. The wave-particle duality and "double-slit experiment" have been treated in many popular accounts. This review will be quick and I think will make a couple of points not usually included. The main point will be that the usually referred-to "paradox" is only a semantic problem, but the experiment does reveal something strange and profound about the nature of matter.

Electrons and all "particles" behave sometimes like a wave and sometimes like a particle. So what? Just because we want to think in terms of only the word "wave" or only the word "particle," is there really a paradox? Maybe electrons are just funny little things that behave in a strange but self-consistent way.

One of the simplest illustrations of the wave-particle duality is the double slit experiment. In the double-slit experiment, light is shone from a source through two slits and detected on a screen. The pattern on the screen shows bright and dark regions. The light waves from one slit interfere with waves from the other slit to add up to bright or dark bands, just like two sets of water waves passing through each other sometimes make a bigger wave and sometimes a smaller wave; they make an interference pattern.

The "paradox" arises when you make the intensity of the source so small that only one photon at a time passes through the slits. When this is done for many individual photons in sequence, the same bright and dark pattern emerges on the screen. The photons are detected as points that arrive individually, at the brighter areas only. If one thinks of a point-like photon, it must have gone through one slit or the other but not both; but since it obeys the interference pattern, it must have gone through both slits and acted like a wave.

This is not necessarily a paradox; maybe photons are neither particles nor waves. Relativity showed that time slows down as things approach the speed of light; photons travel at the speed of light and so do not "age." In the reference frame of the photon as it moves from source to detector, no time passes; it doesn't really move at all; it jumps from here to there. Everything in between here and there, both slits, can affect how it does so. This is interesting but it is not a true paradox.

Then again, we can do the same experiment with de Broglie's crazy electron waves. The electrons behave exactly as the photons do except the dimensions of the slits have to be different because the electron and photon wavelengths are different. Each electron "passes through" or "knows about" or "senses" both slits and interferes with itself, and lands only in the bright areas of the interference pattern on the screen. Electrons travel slower than the speed of light and so they do "age," and they do move from here to there. So electrons must be essentially waves that are only detected in a particle-like way. In this case, there *is* a paradox but it is only a semantic one. Our ordinary words fail to describe the particle. There is not a physical paradox though. The mathematics of quantum physics accurately describes the probability distribution of how the electrons will behave. If we push the experiments a little further though, something not a paradox but physically very strange indeed does happen.

Add a third slit far down on the screen. This will make a small but measurable change to the interference pattern. Now consider the third slit is so far down that during the time it takes the electron to move from source to detector, not even light could pass from the third slit to the first two. Consider also that the slit is covered by a door that is closed all the time, except when each electron is moving across from source to detector. Would the difference in the pattern still be there?

Quantum mechanics says, "Yes." And experiments performed recently verify that yes, the electron would "know" that the third slit was there and the door was opened. Now that *is* bizarre. This is not a wave-particle semantic paradox; it is even stranger. The electron—even if a wave—is not like any wave we've experienced before: it somehow "knows" about distant things. And there's nothing special about electrons; all particles act in a way that is dependent on distant things, and they act in a nondeterministic (probabilistic) way.

No wonder the physicists of the late 1920s were using metaphors like "the bottom dropped out" of their worldview. The bottom still hasn't been replaced.

"Uncertainty" or Complementarity?

Heisenberg was not convinced by Schrodinger's wave mechanics method, probably in part because it was eclipsing his "observables" mechanics in popularity. Trying to settle the issue of statistical versus continuous interpretations, he posed the following question. The electron in Schrodinger's distributions has an exactly defined momentum; could the exact position of the electron, even in principle, also be measured?

To answer, Heisenberg invented a little thought experiment. He considered a moving electron. If we measure its exact position at two exact times, then we'll know both its momentum and its position. To measure its position we have to bounce at least one photon off the electron and focus the photon, the observing light, with a microscope. The wavelength of light used limits the precision with which we can measure the position.

Also, as Planck, Einstein and Compton showed, smaller wavelength photons have larger momenta; so when we bounce the photon off the electron, the momentum of the electron becomes a little uncertain. The result of this "microscope experiment" is that the product of the uncertainty in the position and the uncertainty in the momentum cannot be smaller than Planck's constant; the electron's position and momentum cannot both be measured.

Heisenberg's mentor, Niels Bohr, hated Heisenberg's microscope experiment. Bohr agreed with the result; the position and moment could not both be measured; but he disliked the method because it implied that the electron actually *had* precise position and momentum. Bohr pressed this point so strongly that Heisenberg was "driven to tears."[125]

Bohr thought in terms of a more general and more profound "principle of complementarity" that was inspired by ancient Chinese philosophy. Bohr argued that position and momentum are complementary variables. Some experiments can measure position; other experiments can measure momentum. These complementary experiments allow us to build a general concept that encompasses both position and momentum. Bohr argued that electrons are not "things" with definite properties at all; electrons have certain "tendencies to exist." He even argued that generally, in Nature, there are no "things in themselves."[126]

Bohr and Heisenberg showed that, according to quantum mechanics, a general principle of indeterminacy exists for all pairs of complementary variables like position and momentum, or energy and time. Based on complementarity and indeterminacy, Bohr, Heisenberg and their Copenhagen group of physicists argued for the statistical and probabilistic interpretation of quantum mechanics that is now called the "Copenhagen Interpretation."

It is ironical, and a statement on the still unresolved meaning of quantum mechanics, that textbooks now refer to Heisenberg's argument as "Bohr's microscope," probably because Bohr published a paper on complementarity that used the example even though he didn't like it;[127] and the general principle of indeterminacy is referred to as Heisenberg indeterminacy, or the Heisenberg Uncertainty Principle.

6: The Stochastic Universe

The Uncertainty Principle would best have been called the No-Things-In-Themselves Principle (or the Bohr-Heisenberg No-Things-In-Themselves Principle because they both deserve credit for it). This appellation might have headed off a lot of wrong thinking. As Briggs and Peat note:

> "Nowadays some physicists still argue that Heisenberg's uncertainty principle is only a statement about the limitations of observation (maybe the particle has both position and momentum but we just can't measure it)."

Einstein Loses in Brussels

In October 1927, at the Solvay conference of physicists in Brussels, leading physicists met to discuss the meaning of quantum mechanics. Bohr led the proponents of the Copenhagen interpretation that says that the quantum equation solutions represent statistical probabilities of the outcome of an experiment or an event. Bohr's Copenhagen interpretation said that a deeper, classically causal, physical reality cannot exist. The Copenhagen interpretation says the buck stops here; physics stops with statistical probabilities.

Einstein led the opposition to the Copenhagen interpretation with the argument that a deeper theory that represented "things themselves and not merely the probability of their occurrence" should be searched for.[128] Einstein focused on finding counterexamples that contradict the uncertainty principle. Bohr consistently and clearly showed that Einstein's counterexamples were not really counter; quantum mechanics could calculate the correct probabilities of various outcomes.

Einstein lost. He became convinced of the usefulness of quantum mechanics for making calculations but he remained certain that a deeper reality existed. The Copenhagen interpretation won, and still reigns today. The accuracy of quantum mathematics has since been verified in many experiments and has not been contradicted. The Copenhagen interpretation allows physicists to make calculations and predictions. The problem is that the Copenhagen interpretation avoids the issue of what the quantum nature of reality really means; is the universe fundamentally partly random, or is the randomness only in our ability to make predictions?

The Hylostochastic Paradigm

Today, a sort of ossified pigmy version of Bohr's intended interpretation reigns. This ossified pigmy version is what I call the hylostochastic paradigm. The distinction between Bohr's subtle complementarity concepts and the contracted dogma of today is unimportant for making calculations but it is immensely important for metaphysical implications. Remember Bohr's Copenhagen interpretation was based on Bohr's no-things-in-themselves complementarity principle; it says there is no classical causal (deterministic) reality that determines the quantum statistics. The hylostochastic paradigm of today takes a big step backward by saying that *nothing* deeper can influence a quantum event: all quantum events are random, with probabilities determined by the solutions to the quantum equations.

Influential physicist Murray Gell-Mann says: "Niels Bohr brainwashed a whole generation of physicists into thinking that the whole job was done fifty years ago."[129] Actually, I would say that a whole generation of physicists brainwashed *themselves* into thinking that, because Bohr showed that infinitely precise mathematical predictions are impossible, the universe must be inherently random; and so any metaphysics must be in error. Bohr himself defended the importance of metaphysics (see Chapter 3). De Broglie, fittingly the only prince in our tale, even felt, "the mechanism *demands* a mysticism."

The mathematics of quantum mechanics can predict the probabilities of the various possible outcomes of a quantum experiment with crystal clarity. In a way, this mathematical clarity has increased the general muddle about the importance of the metaphysical implications. An example of the continuing muddle is the reaction to the theories of David Bohm, who carried on Einstein's tradition of disputing the hylostochastic paradigm. Briggs and Peat, 1984, point out that, "Unfortunately for his career, Bohm's message in this argument was profoundly misunderstood ... a well-known history of quantum theory ... portrayed him as a determinist. Though ... Bohm is probably as far from being a determinist as any physicist in the world today."[130]

A 1985 book by physicist Nick Herbert, *Quantum Reality*, is relatively lucid in its descriptions of quantum phenomena but is still muddy about the metaphysical implications, and one of its subtitles is "An Excursion Into Metaphysics and the Meaning of Reality." Herbert classifies Bohm's models as a return to determinism.[131]

Dissenters to the hylostochastic paradigm, which Herbert correctly calls the "orthodox ontology," have included such luminaries as Albert Einstein, Louis de Broglie, Erwin Schrodinger, David Bohm and John Stewart Bell. It is not really complete to say, as Herbert does, that "most physicists accept the orthodox ontology." Actually most physicists don't think about it at all. They do tend to react to information contradictory to the hylostochastic paradigm as if they had thought about it and concluded that the orthodox ontology was correct. How this reaction occurs is an interesting question but would require a digression about emotional reactions and mob mentality.

I think we can still say, as Richard Feynman did in 1964, "I think I can safely say that nobody understands quantum mechanics."[132] So in the rest of this book, we are certainly not going to try to understand quantum mechanics. We *are* going to try to understand how quantum mechanics does not imply or require the hylostochastic paradigm or the hylostatic paradigm.

Back to the Breeze

So, in the process of trying to understand the breeze on our beach, we ran into some "little details" that couldn't be explained by classical physics. In the process of investigating those details, we discovered that they were actually "cracks in the cosmic egg"[133] of the classical paradigm. To explain the "little details," we had to develop an entirely new paradigm of quantum theory in order to make mathematical calculations to predict events. An adequate mathematical theory was settled on, in which it is possible to calculate the probability of various outcomes of an experiment; a single quantum experiment cannot be predicted. In fact, a no-things-in-themselves principle indicates that classical causality does not occur at all. What this really *means*, we have no idea yet, but we can do statistical calculations; and the calculations match the observations and settle those "little details."

The little detail of the ultraviolet catastrophe of classical physics was averted by quantization of energy. The collapse of atoms Bohr showed would occur in any sort of classical atomic model was alleviated by the wavelike nature of the electron; and the little detail of the emission spectra of atoms was correctly predicted by quantum theory.

Can we finally understand our breeze? Well, one of the problems was to understand why some atoms bounce off each other like inelastic balls; this we can solve now. The quantum theory yields a consistent model of the atom, and a semi-classical model of electrostatic repulsion, like we tried in Chapter 5, explains why some atoms bounce off each other. A purist can also use Schrodinger's quantum wave mechanics to calculate the bounce result, or use the newer sophisticated Feynman method of particle exchange calculations to also get the bounce result.

The other problem was to understand why some atoms stick together to form molecules and some don't; this is called chemistry. The solution to this requires a new detail of quantum physics, but nothing that will alter the general quantum paradigm. This "little detail" will not destroy our conceptual universe like the other little details did, and it will not be important for the rest of the book. But we do need to be satisfied that it is understood in order to understand our breeze, and it is a good example of the sorts of details that exist in the quantum realms. So you may skip the next three paragraphs if you trust me that quantum mechanics explains in principle how chemistry works.

Remember that in the quantum model of the hydrogen atom, the electron exists in "states" and jumps between states when energy is added or radiated. Such quantum states are a peculiarity of quantum mechanics; they are represented by solutions to Schrodinger's equation. Quantum states have no classical analogue. A principle of quantum mechanics is that two identical particles (like two electrons) can exist in the same state only if their wave functions (solutions to Schrodinger's equation) are identical. Particles have charge, mass and spin. Spin is just that: a certain amount of spin angular momentum.

The following is due to essentially mathematical reasons that I will only outline.[134] There are two basic sorts of particles: spin-a-half (measured by a half of Planck's constant of course), and spin-one. For very elegant but sort of involved mathematical reasons, when you interchange two spin-a-half particles in the same quantum state, their mathematical wave functions change sign; they are not interchangeable and so they cannot share the same state. This is called Pauli's exclusion principle. Spin-one particles are not so restricted.

The principal constituents of matter (electrons, protons, and neutrons) are spin-a-half. Photons (and some other less common particles) are spin-one. For electrons in atoms, every sort of electron orbital solution has two paired states: one for spin-up and the other for spin-down (again for mathematical reasons). So the heavier elements—helium, lithium, everything heavier than hydrogen—have electrons existing in progressively expanding shells. Two atoms of those elements with an odd number of electrons each have a half-filled shell and so they tend to stick together and share one electron. This is the basis of chemistry; the study of how and why some atoms tend to stick together and others don't. If there were no Pauli's exclusion principle there would be no chemistry. It is interesting that Pauli's exclusion principle occurs for mathematical reasons (there is no simple physical model for it) and yet it makes predictions that have been verified in great detail. A number of such mathematical quantum mechanical discoveries have been found to actually occur. This quantum mechanics stuff really works, whether we understand it or not.

Proof of Nonlocality

Another quantum mathematical discovery that was recently verified seems almost as if Nature said, "Just try me" to a sort of, "I dare you to …" threat. Remember how Einstein was trying to find counterexamples to Bohr's Copenhagen interpretation? Einstein and two colleagues (Podolsky and Rosen) created a thought experiment to test quantum mechanics. The thought experiment was setup such that the results predicted by quantum mechanics were so bizarre that, EPR felt, they just would not occur and so something must be wrong with the quantum theory. In the 1980s, physicist John Bell developed a mathematical theorem that turned the EPR thought experiment into an ironclad test of whether "classical-type" causality could hold.[135] Bell's theorem meant that if the EPR thought experiment was actually performed, and if the results were as predicted by quantum mechanics, then it would constitute a proof of quantum mechanical no-things-in-themselves and of nonlocal connectivity. So, also in the 1980's, French physicist Alain Aspect and colleagues actually did the EPR experiment.[136]

A number of popular accounts of this experiment and the proof of Bell's theorem are available (e.g., Penrose and references therein). I will only review the main points and what they mean for our exploration in this book. Consider a source that spits out two particles with quantum mechanical spin, moving in opposite directions. (Aspect, et al., actually use massless photons but particles with mass work, too.) The two particles are in a correlated quantum state as they fly away from each other. Two detectors are placed to catch the particles and detect the direction of their spin. Actually, the detectors can detect whether the spin is closer to up or closer to down (or whatever the orientation of the detector) but not the exact angle of the spin.

EPR showed that quantum mechanics predicts the results of the measurements at one detector will depend on the orientation of the *other* detector, indicating distant connectivity. Because quantum mechanics is a statistical theory, it took Bell's statistical proof to show the results would actually prove the no-things-in-themselves principle. The average correlation between the results of the two detectors depends on whether classical causality or quantum causality applies.

Classical causality would be present if some "undetectable hidden variables" predetermined the true spin of each particle from before it left the source. Classical causality could also hold if there were some random aspect to the particles that caused a randomness in the detections.

No-things-in-themselves causality means that the probabilities of different spins detected for one particle at one detector actually *depend on* the orientation of the other detector; distant events instantaneously affect local events because the act of measuring one particle actually alters the quantum mechanical state of the distant particle if the two particles are in a correlated quantum state.

Aspect et al. did the experiment and it showed quantum-type causality. The probabilities at one detector depend on the orientation of the other detector and the detected state of the other spin. This result is almost universally accepted now. The full details would take too much space to cover here; the unconvinced reader is referred, for instance, to Penrose.

Many physicists have analyzed Bell's proof and Aspect's experiments; none have been able to escape that it means the two particles must be connected in some way across space, even at a large distance. Some sort of faster-than-light influence must connect them; this is called "nonlocality." Even to many quantum physicists, this is difficult to accept. It seems at first to violate the rule that nothing can travel faster than the speed of light, for one thing. Some physicists tried to get around nonlocality by suggesting that the apparatus in the experiments was somehow sensed beforehand by the particles.

To counter that claim, Aspect et al. set up their apparatus so that the orientations of the detectors can be rotated while the particles are in flight! The results were as predicted by quantum mechanics; again establishing nonlocality.[137]

This was just too much for some physicists; very competent mathematical physicists tried to hold onto their worldview by clinging to possible flaws in the experiment. They said the detectors only detect a percentage of the particles; being mechanical devices they naturally miss some particles; if all the missed particles behave differently from the detected ones (in itself a bizarre thought) then the nonlocal could still be wrong. So Aspect et al. went about employing the latest in detector technology and now I believe the efficiencies are such that even this last weasel is disproved.

These experiments are incontrovertible; they establish beyond any doubt the nonlocality of Nature and the accuracy of quantum mechanics.

Beyond the Breeze

Now that we know for sure that quantum mechanics really applies to atoms, we finally understand our breeze! In the process, we've had to realize that we don't understand one heck of a lot of other things, like what nonlocality really means, but we got the breeze nailed down. To recap, the air molecules are no longer mysterious. According to quantum mechanics, the different sorts of atoms in the air will stick together to form certain molecules, and those molecules will bounce off each other like tiny inelastic balls. We can then apply classical Newtonian mechanics to the inelastic balls via Boltzmann's equation to get the equations of fluid dynamics.

There *is* another little detail here. According to quantum mechanics, the position and momentum of each molecule is slightly non-existent. The molecules don't exactly behave like classical particles; there's a little wiggle to applying the Boltzmann equation. But that's okay because it means we have to put a little random statistical term into Boltzmann's equation, which is how Maxwell got the average velocity distributions that led to the fluid equations anyway (as described in Chapter 5). And the sort of breeze we are talking about is a near-equilibrium system for which those little fluctuations will not matter. So in the fluid equations, we find the warmer air rising over the land and the cooler air over the water, and we can predict that the breeze will blow onshore.

Along the way, we discovered that the quantum nature of reality started to take root in the 1920s and it unequivocally negates the hylostatic paradigm of classical physics. We saw that the meaning of the quantum nature of reality is so strange and so unfamiliar that it is still in dispute by those few scientists who seriously think about it.

What was settled long ago was a way of making calculations in order to make predictions. These predictions can only be probabilistic in nature because of the no-things-in-themselves and the nonlocal natures of reality. Extensive experimentation, some of it very recent, has shown that the quantum theory predictions are correct. This proves that the nonlocal and no-things-in-themselves natures of matter are true and fundamental properties.

The orthodox ontology (paradigm) has concluded that, because the best possible mathematical predictions for matter are probabilistic, the underlying mechanism is purely random. This is the hylostochastic paradigm—that the part of the universe that is not deterministic is random. This hylostochastic view is not required; the physics, mathematics and observations can also support what we will be calling the hylozoic view. The mathematics of quantum mechanics is the same in the hylozoic and hylostochastic views; the metaphysical implications the hylozoic and hylostochastic views; the metaphysical implications are completely different.

The founders of quantum theory, by and large, were not hylostochasticists. They merely accepted the probabilistic model in order to do calculations. Even Bohr, the greatest advocate of the probabilistic model, defended metaphysics and implied that something beyond the hylostochastic paradigm does have important influence in Nature. In the following parts of this book, we'll describe how the hylostochastic paradigm is finally dying, and why this is a good thing. But first, in the next chapter, we'll look at another "little detail" that is actually part of classical physics. This next little detail will help us appreciate the importance and relevance of the new paradigm.

In terms of our trying to understand the full Moon evening on the beach, this little detail arises as follows. After completing an understanding of the atom, using quantum mechanics we were finally able to understand why, on a calm evening, *on average*, the breeze blows onshore. The breeze doesn't *always* blow onshore though. Sometimes it blows every which way; it gusts; it flutters; there is a hurricane, or a tornado. Can we understand these "anomalies," even in principle, in terms of the hylostochastic paradigm? That is a big question. A small part of the answer is called chaos theory, which we'll introduce in the next chapter.

7. The Butterfly Effect

In the previous two chapters we covered a lot of ground. We indicated the power of Newton's laws of motion for predicting classical phenomena like tides. The application of Boltzmann's statistical mechanics to Newton's laws of motion gave them very general applicability to fluid flows like the breeze on the beach. To make sure though, that the statistical mechanics really does apply, we had to learn about the "little detail" of the nature of atoms. That brought us to understanding electricity and magnetism through Maxwell's equations.

Maxwell's equations completed electromagnetism and showed that we also could understand light as electromagnetic waves. Then some loose ends about how Maxwell's equations really work led directly to Einstein's relativity of measures of space and time. With classical electromagnetism finally under control, we were ready to really apply it to atoms, and we found that, according to Newtonian mechanics, we couldn't!

The problem of why we couldn't apply classical physics to atoms was solved by quantum theory. Quantum theory required that a no-things-in-themselves uncertainty principle, and a nonlocal connectivity principle, applied to the foundations of matter. These principles struck a mortal wound to the hylostatic paradigm of classical physics. We found that quantum theory, with its bizarre new understanding of matter, is absolutely necessary. Quantum theory is not just a microscopic detail about atoms. The very nature of everything around us depends on the quantum (no-things-in-themselves, and nonlocal) nature of reality.

Without this quantum nature, objects would not reach heat equilibrium, and there could be no chemistry, and thus no biology, and thus no readers. When quantum mechanics left them conceptually without a paradigm, physicists adopted the Copenhagen interpretation that the quantum theory solutions are accurately treated as the probabilities of events. This allowed physicists to return to their jobs of calculation and prediction, but the true issue of the conceptual paradigm was avoided.

The Paradigmatic Crisis

Over time, this avoidance of the real issue in favor of doing mathematics without asking questions, has led to a paradigm in itself—the hylostochastic paradigm. The hylostochastic paradigm holds that the part of the universe that is not deterministic (as in the hylostatic paradigm of classical mechanics) is random. The hylostochastic paradigm *is* an adequate paradigm for doing mathematical calculations. It may be inadequate for describing how the world really works. And describing how the world really works, after all, is historically part of physics. This leads to a historical crisis, because physics *also* has always been based on repeatable experiments.

The crisis is that, now, repeatable experiments *are* accurately described by the hylostochastic mathematical paradigm. But that paradigm may not encompass how the real world works. The real world includes nonrepeatable events and, in fact, the real world is generally composed of nonrepeatable events.

For physics, now, a choice is necessary—define physics as the study only of repeatable laboratory experiments, in which case physics becomes a limited branch of mathematics (which would greatly irk many proud physicists), *or* define physics as the study of how nature really works. If the later choice is taken, then it must be acknowledged that the reigning hylostochastic paradigm is inadequate—or at least that it has not been seriously investigated whether it is adequate or not. In the rest of this book, I will be arguing that it *is* inadequate.

This is the historical crisis of science that we are in now. If the first choice (of limiting science only to the study of mathematically predictable events) is taken, then physics essentially ends and becomes a sort of mathematics that is applicable only to a very limited portion of nature.

If the second choice is taken, then many of the old methods based on mathematical prediction will be inadequate and the whole basis of physics begins to look very little like the familiar realms of hylostatic classical physics and its clinging offspring hylostochastism.

Scientists who seem to want to have their paradigm and eat it too foster the general lack of understanding that the crisis exists. Such scientists insist that any concept that goes beyond hylostochastism must be tested in repeatable experiments. But they ignore that their own quantum theory shows that there is a fundamental difference between repeatable experiments and single events. When one talks about what really happens in nonrepeatable events like human consciousness, the reply is often, "well, that's not physics." And yet reports of anomalous events (like religious experience, telepathic intuition, etc.) are often dismissed as impossible because they "violate physics." These confused reactions would be unimportant academic squabbles, except that they seem to have significant and negative affect on the way our culture thinks and acts.

Back to Matter for Now

The choice of paradigms described above—actually the choice of the hylostochastic paradigm or, for the time being, no paradigm—is not just a philosophical choice divorced from understanding the way matter works. Nature, of course, has chosen already. Nature works one way or another regardless of what name we adopt for it. Our task is to determine what Nature does. Nature is either completely hylostochastic or it is not. If Nature is hylostochastic, then the actual events that we observe in meteorology, biology, geology, and physiology, will occur one way. If Nature is not hylostochastic, then the events will be different. So while the paradigm that we are talking about includes the metaphysical, its effects are material. How these effects might possibly come about will be the subject of the next chapters.

A further appreciation of why matter is susceptible to such metaphysical influences is the focus of this chapter. In the last two chapters, we completed our sketchy review of the fundamental laws and methods of physics that describe the way matter works. Now we will go back and look at another little detail called "chaos." Unlike the other little details that led to quantum mechanics and relativity and destroyed the old paradigm, chaos will not destroy any paradigms. Chaos will add an important perspective for understanding the new paradigm as an expansion out of the old paradigm.

The style of this chapter will be different from the previous chapter. Quantum mechanics is a very well established physical theory (at least its mathematical applicability, if not its meaning), and so reviewing its historical development and the points relevant to our discussion was straightforward. Chaos theory is technically older (not in name, but in foundation) than quantum mechanics but has only more recently become fashionable. It will be clear that this book is not intended to be a further hyping of chaos theory, but for now we'll hype it a little for fun. The revolutionary concepts of quantum theory are the roots of the emerging new paradigm, and chaos theory is the trunk and branches (we'll get to the leaves and fruits in the next chapters). I will not attempt a historical development of chaos theory. Instead we will jump right in with an example of the implications of chaos theory. Then we will fill in some of the groundwork of the physics of chaos. Also, of course, a couple of asides on meaning and metaphysics will be ventured as well.

The key important feature of what is technically called chaos in physical systems is "sensitive dependence on initial conditions." Sensitive dependence on initial conditions means that a very small change in the system (a change in the "initial conditions") creates an extremely large change in the state of the system at later times. This may sound like technical jargon, so let's look at a real situation. An eminent mathematical physicist who helped apply the theory of chaos to turbulent fluids gives a perfect example of what sensitive dependence on initial conditions means in Nature.

The Sensitive Universe

David Ruelle investigates a thought experiment in which a "little devil" creates a tiny tiny initial change that will affect the outcome of the Earth's global weather system. Ruelle's initial change is poetic in its smallness. Scientists especially will recognize how absurdly small this change is: Ruelle's little devil removes one single electron from the edge of the known universe!

Remember that air molecules bouncing off each other behave according to Newton's laws of motion. Boltzmann's equation applies Newton's laws of motion to the air molecules and then the bulk motion of the air can be calculated by the equations of fluid dynamics that come out of Boltzmann's equations. Also remember that a key feature of classical physics is that all matter exerts gravitational forces on all other matter according to Newton's law of universal gravitation. Ruelle's thought experiment starts with the tiny deflection that the gravitational impulse, from removing one electron from the edge of the universe, exerts on air molecules here on Earth.

In Chapter 5, we described how the equations of fluid dynamics depended on treating the velocity distribution of air molecules in a certain average statistical way, and that such a treatment would apply to any near-equilibrium fluid—like the air on a calm day. One of the things that chaos theory applies to is fluids that are *not* near equilibrium—like the air on a blustery day. Exactly how chaos theory is applied will be touched on later. For now, remember that chaos is motion fully according to classical mechanics and Newton's laws of motion; it is just more complicated motion than the near-equilibrium cases.

Ruelle's thought experiment illustrates the importance of chaotic not-near-equilibrium motion. The thought experiment is to calculate how soon after the initial deflection a significant change will be observed in a turbulent fluid like the weather—due to the gravitational force of that electron 15 billion light years away (the "edge of the known universe" is probably somewhere between 10 and 20 billion light years away):

> "Let us idealize the air molecules as [in]elastic[138] balls and, concentrating on one of them, ask after how many collisions it will miss another molecule that it would have hit if the gravitational effect of the remote electron had been acting. ... it would take just about 50 collisions!! After *a tiny fraction of a second* [air molecule collisions happen very, very rapidly], the collisions of the air molecules will thus become quite different, but the difference is not visible to you. Not yet.
>
> "Suppose that the air that we consider is in turbulent motion (all you need is a little bit of wind); then the sensitive dependence on initial condition present in turbulence will act on microscopic fluctuations of the sort created by the little devil (so-called thermal fluctuations) and magnify them. The net result is that *after about a minute*, suspending the gravitational effect of an electron at the

confines of our universe has produced a macroscopic effect: the fine structure of turbulence (on a millimeter scale) is no longer quite the same. You still don't notice anything, however. Not yet.

"But a change in the small-scale structure of turbulence will, in due time, produce a change in the large-scale structure. There are mechanisms for that, and one can estimate the time that they take using the Kolmogorov theory [of turbulence]. ... Suppose that we are in a turbulent part of the atmosphere (a storm would be ideal). We can then expect that *in a few hours or a day* the imperceptible manipulation of the little devil has resulted in a change of the atmospheric turbulence on a scale of kilometers. This is now quite visible: the clouds have a different shape and the gusts of wind follow a different pattern. But perhaps you will say that this does not really alter the carefully planned course of your life. Not yet.

"From the point of view of the general circulation of the atmosphere, what the little devil has achieved is still a rather insignificant change of initial condition. But we know that *after a couple of weeks* the change will have taken on global proportions. Suppose then that you have arranged a weekend picnic ... Just as you have spread your tablecloth on the grass, a really vicious hailstorm begins ..."[139]

Ruelle's time calculations are approximate, but they are not guesses. They are based on specific calculations using the standard models of fluctuations and turbulence (and physicists can check them using the references in Ruelle). Starting with as small an initial perturbation as is imaginable, after a minute's time millimeter scale flow is altered, after a few hours kilometer scale flow is altered, and after only a couple of weeks the whole weather pattern on Earth is noticeably different. How does that sort of extraordinary sensitive dependence on initial conditions come about, and if it is only part of Newtonian mechanics, how come it was not really noticed until recently?

A Need to Know

A prime example of the relevance and practical uses of understanding of sensitive dependence on initial conditions, and chaos

7: The Butterfly Effect

theory, is the motivation of the scientist who is largely responsible for bringing chaos to general attention. World War II interrupted Edward Lorenz's graduate studies in mathematics. Assigned to predict the weather for the Army Air Corps, this student-aged mathematician suddenly found himself applying mathematics to the vaguely defined science of weather prediction, with his results responsible for the lives of pilots fighting a world war. That responsibility is enough to make one want to know what's *really* going on, and forget about the usual squabbles of academic egos. Lorenz stayed with meteorology after the war, and in 1960 he pioneered the use of computers for weather prediction. The use of computers for weather prediction sparked the now general appreciation of the importance of sensitive dependence on initial conditions.

As one motivation for our high-speed journey through the basics of physical science, we are still wondering about the breeze on our moonlit sunset beach. We understood the calm steady-state average sort of breeze very completely in terms of classical physics and the hylostatic paradigm. We did have to accept a small random element to the motions on atomic scales because of quantum mechanics. But this was only an unimportant detail as far as the near-equilibrium bulk motion of the breeze on a calm steady-state average sort of day. But can we understand and predict, in the same hylostatic way, all the changes, variations, and surprises that actually happen in real weather? That's the question that Lorenz addressed.

Nonlinear Weather Is Unpredictable

The specific case that Lorenz studied was actually close to that of our beach breeze after sunset. Lorenz considered the seemingly simple case of the motion of air that is above a warm ground—so that the higher up air is cooler than the air near the ground. (This is even simpler than our beach example because it is like the air above the warm ground only, without the added affects of the cooler ocean.) The case that Lorenz studied is known as the simplest form of "atmospheric convection." The ground is warm due to the sun's heating, and so the lower layers of atmospheric air become warmer and lighter than the layers of air above them. The light, warm air near the ground tends to rise, and the dense cool air above tends to sink.

Now, how can we apply the mathematical methods of physics to predict exactly how these sinking and rising air motions will actually occur? For the time being, we will ignore completely the quantum uncertainty associated with atoms and assume it is unimportant (which it is for this part of the problem). Then the atoms and molecules can be thought of as tiny inelastic balls subject to Newton's laws of motion. We remember that Boltzmann's equation applies Newton's laws of motion to all the molecules individually and together as time proceeds. So all we have to do is solve Boltzmann's equation for a convecting atmosphere. But it is immediately clear that Boltzmann's equation is far too complex to be solved in this case. So we go to the next lower level of complexity—the equations of fluid dynamics that come out of Boltzmann's equation. The equations of fluid dynamics arise out of the Boltzmann equation if you treat large groups of molecules as acting in an average sense (and mathematicians have shown that in this case of atmospheric convective motions, this level of approximation is plenty accurate enough).

Now the equations of fluid dynamics are still pretty complex, but they at least look like we might have a chance of solving them in some cases. The main problem with solving the equations of fluid dynamics is that they are "nonlinear." The definition of nonlinear is a mathematical one, and since we are not using mathematics, we cannot define it precisely. But an example of nonlinearity should suffice. In nonlinear equations, a small change in one variable may create a very large change in another variable. If you set your computer near the edge of your desk and slowly nudge it toward the edge, you are making small changes in the horizontal position variable. That is linear. At one point, a tiny nudge will cause a large and interesting change in the vertical position and the disposition of your computer. That is nonlinear. The dynamical state of the computer's position is a nonlinear system when it is near the edge of the desk. But when it is in the middle of the desk, it is a linear system.

The problem with nonlinear equations is that they are difficult, and often impossible, to solve with paper and pencil-type mathematics. (Computers can solve them in many cases, at least in principle, but we'll get to that later.) The fact that most of the equations

7: The Butterfly Effect

describing real physical systems are nonlinear has always been rather irksome. Until very recently, when scientists encountered nonlinear equations, being can-do type people, they would not lament but would proceed by "linearizing" them. There are sophisticated and complex methods for "linearizing" equations. In some cases, linearization yields adequate results. But since it was the only technique available, it was overused to the extent that the real systems were often ignored in favor of "linearized" versions that are not at all like the real systems. Those few physicists and mathematicians who really thought about it knew the problems of doing such linearization all along, but since they could offer no better calculation method, they were paid little attention.

Lorenz's specific case is a convective fluid heated from below (the air motion above warm land). Linearized solutions to the fluid dynamics equations would show that on average there would be up and down convective motions of the air, and that, on average, there would be "convection cells" of certain sizes depending on the temperature of the land and the temperature of the air above. Such calculations are quite applicable in an average sense. But Lorenz wanted to know about a single specific case, and not the average. Specific cases can be very important. If I am on an airplane about to takeoff, I don't really want to hear that "on average there is an 80 percent chance that in this sort of weather the plane will not encounter a severe microburst wind that will cause it to crash at takeoff." I want to hear that "in this specific case, we will not encounter a microburst."

So Lorenz did a very clever thing. There seemed to be only two choices: One, linearize and solve for the average behavior as was the standard practice, or two, move onto another problem because a lot of very clever mathematicians had shown that this sort of nonlinear equation just can't be solved exactly. Instead, Lorenz did a third thing. He greatly simplified the nonlinear equations so that they were still nonlinear but so that they preserved the basic physics that he wanted to study.

The resulting nonlinear equations are *still* too complicated to solve with pencil and paper-type mathematics. Lorenz's good idea would have remained one of many good but not very important ideas, except that he applied a new technology.

Lorenz's simplified nonlinear equations are quite simple to solve with a computer. So Lorenz used the new, and then rather unpopular tool of the computer to simulate solutions to his simplified nonlinear convection equations. Such computer-generated solutions are called "simulations" because the output from the computer is a sequence of numbers that represent the evolution of the equation solutions in time, and so simulate the evolution of the real system in time.

What Lorenz actually simulated was the evolution of hybrid variables, from his simplified fluid dynamics equations, that related only indirectly to real physical things like air speed or air pressure. To get a feel for what the results mean, though, we can imagine that the results represent the actual motion of a little parcel of air molecules. Lorenz's simulations showed that the air parcel would circulate up and down and around like in a convection cell, just as expected from the linearized averaged solutions. But they did so in a peculiar way.

Each time around, the air parcel would go near a sort of turning point (think of it as a boundary between two convection cells). Sometimes around it would end up in the right-hand convection cell, and sometimes it would end up in the left-hand. And it would always end up coming near this turning point again. And when it came out of the region around the turning point, it would end up on a slower or faster circulation track depending on whichever convection cell it ended up in. And which cell it ends up in, and which part of the cell, depends only on very slight differences in how the air parcel approaches the turning point. And the whole convection cell also changes shape depending on what this parcel of air does when it goes past the turning point.

This means that a tiny difference in where Lorenz started the air parcel (in his simulation) would soon become a large difference in the system—it could be in one convection cell or the other, and it could be on the fast type circulation or the slow type, and the whole flow pattern would also depend on this. After Lorenz made sure that he hadn't made some sort of mistake, he began to realize three things. First, the physical system he was simulating was exhibiting mathematically sensitive dependence on initial conditions. Second, that real air flow, real weather, actually behaves in such a sensitive way. Third, if what Lorenz's simulations showed could be verified, it meant that long-term weather prediction is impossible. On average, certain basic principles of large-scale atmospheric flow are applicable, but any given single weather system is quite messy and unpredictable.

The Butterfly Effect

In this book we are trying to dig deeply into a few specific examples in order to grasp the basic concepts that inform the new paradigm. Ruelle's example of global turbulence, and Lorenz's local convection, both exhibit sensitive dependence on initial conditions. The recently developing science of chaos has shown that sensitive dependence on initial conditions is a precisely defined quality of nonlinear dynamical systems.

The popular and well-written books *Chaos*, by James Gleick, and *Turbulent Mirror*, by Briggs and Peat, discussed the wide-ranging applications of chaos theory. Because chaos theory contains so many intriguing applications, colorful and beautiful computer simulations, and fresh concepts, it is a seductive topic. But the mathematics of chaos theory is only a small part of the larger picture that we are trying to look at. So, we'll resist the seductions and try to extract the core elements of chaos theory that are relevant to our larger picture.

Sensitive dependence on initial conditions has been called the "butterfly effect." In a sensitive dynamical system, like Ruelle's turbulent global climate, a small local cause like the flapping of a butterfly's wings can yield a very large effect like altering the course of a hurricane, a few days later, on another part of the globe. Sensitive dependence on initial conditions is, mathematically, the exponential growth of small uncertainties, or small fluctuations like the flapping of a butterfly's wings.

The chessboard allegory illustrates the difference between exponential growth and linear growth. A king once felt indebted to a court fool and offered to give a present of the fool's choice. The fool asked only for some rice—to be measured out on a chessboard, as follows. Put one grain on the first square of the chessboard. Put two grains on the second square, four on the third square, eight on the fourth, and so on to fill up the board. The king vowed to grant the fool's modest wish. Less than half way through the 64 squares on the board, the king knew he had a problem. He called in the court astronomers who calculated that the fool had asked for the equivalent of many times the total economic output of the planet. Exponential growth is growth at a constant rate (in the chess board allegory, a rate of doubling with each square), as opposed to growth by a constant amount in linear growth. If the chessboard is filled by linear growth, it contains 2,080 grains of rice. If it is filled by exponential growth, it contains 2 to the 64th power (which is about 10^{19}, or one followed by 19 zeros) grains of rice.[140]

Linear dynamical systems exhibit linear growth of "errors" (small differences, or initial uncertainties). Many nonlinear dynamical systems exhibit exponential growth of errors. Exponential growth of errors in a system is one of the mathematical definitions of chaos. Chaotic dynamical systems exhibit exponential growth of uncertainty. Chaos theory contains many technical details on how to measure exponential growth in uncertainty, and why there really is a clear-cut difference between linear growth and exponential growth. This clear difference makes chaotic systems a clearly definable and different class of systems (different from the linear systems usually studied in physics). For our purposes, we can take the mathematical technicalities for granted, and see what chaos means.

Strange Attractors

Two aspects of chaos theory worth noting are "strange attractors" and turbulence. Ruelle points out that sensitive dependence on initial conditions of nonlinear dynamical systems has been known at least since French mathematician Jacques Hadamard published a paper on it in 1898. The recent popular interest in chaos (sparked by Lorenz showing that it applies directly to weather) has been amplified by the beautiful computer generated images of strange attractors. Strange attractors are the swirling, colorful, intricately complicated, and familiar-looking objects such as the famous Mandelbrot set. The term "strange attractor" was first used in a paper by Ruelle and Florence Takens, in 1971.

Ruelle and Takens were trying to understand the dynamics of turbulence in fluids (like the weather, air flow past an air plane, etc.). Turbulence is fluid flow that is all jumbled and swirly. Turbulence is one major class of fluid flow. The other major class of fluid flow is "laminar" flow. Laminar flow is smooth, layered, and

7: The Butterfly Effect

predictable (and described, of course, by linear equations). Basically from the time that anyone studied fluid flow, they knew that there are great differences in laminar and turbulent flow. Laminar flow can be studied and modeled with linear equations. Turbulent flow was always mostly mysterious (and, of course, nonlinear). Slow and gentle flows are laminar. More rapid flows are turbulent. Turbulence is everywhere—a rapid stream, most of the weather, some of the airflow around airplanes, gas jets flowing out of young stellar objects, probably some of the flow in the Earth's lower mantel, the blood flow in a heart—and so is important.

Before Ruelle and Takens' paper, there was a standard idea about turbulence. (This is common in science. There are large fields of phenomena about which the most accurate statement would be, "We really have no idea how it works!" But nonetheless there is usually some sort of "standard idea" or "standard model" that is generally accepted.) The standard idea was that turbulence was a combination of a large number (or infinite number) of linear flow modes—the same old idea that the way to solve nonlinear problems is to "linearize" them. Ruelle and Takens showed, for mathematical reasons, that turbulent flow is probably better described by what they called "strange attractors."

To get a little of a handle on what a strange attractor is, let's try first to describe an "attractor." The key is to visualize any dynamical system as being described by a single point moving through a multidimensional space—as many dimensions as are needed for that particular system. (Don't panic at the prospect, it's quite simple.) A swinging pendulum can be described well with one dimension—the angle to the vertical.

The dynamical system of the pendulum is described by a point moving back and forth on a one dimensional line giving the angle. Now add some sort of dissipation or damping and, of course, the pendulum will slow down and stop. It is then described as being at a single point representing zero angle. That point is an attractor in the space representing the dynamical system of the pendulum. If dissipation is added, the pendulum is always attracted to that point. More complicated systems need two, three, or more dimensional spaces to represent them. And the attractors may also consist of lines, areas, or spaces, instead of points. But the concepts are similar to the pendulum attractor.

A strange attractor is an attractor that has special properties. Ruelle describes it: "The strangeness comes from the following features, which are not mathematically equivalent but usually occur together in practice. First, strange attractors look strange: they are not smooth curves or surfaces but have "non-integral dimension"—or, as Benoit Mandelbrot puts it, they are fractal objects. Next, and more importantly, the motion on a strange attractor has sensitive dependence on initial condition. Finally, while strange attractors have only finite dimension, the time-frequency analysis reveals a continuum of frequencies."[141] For our purposes, we only need to go into the "fractal" character of Ruelle's criteria. (We've already noted sensitive dependence on initial conditions.)

Fractal Nature

To get an idea of what a fractal object is, consider an example. Think of a piece of a straight line, say one inch long. Remove the middle half of the line, a half-inch portion. From the two remaining pieces, remove their middle halves (each one eighth inch pieces). From the remaining four pieces remove their middle halves *ad infinitum*. The remaining object is a fractal object. It is called a "Cantor dust" after mathematician George Cantor who described this sort of set in the 19th century. The Cantor dust has dimension between one (like a line) and zero (like a point)—actually 0.6309. The famous Mandelbrot set is another fractal object that has dimension between one and two (a plane has dimension two).

One of the keys to the chaos revolution in science is that Lorenz, Ruelle and others have shown that sensitive dependence on initial conditions occurs in dynamical systems that have strange attractors. The most important thing for our purposes is the sensitive dependence on initial conditions—which causes exponential increase in uncertainties. A little more discussion of fractal objects and strange attractors, though, will help us appreciate the ubiquity of chaotic sensitive dependence on initial conditions.

Lorenz showed that his simplified atmospheric convection model also has a strange attractor (one of the most famous, now called the Lorenz attractor—in fact some argue that all strange

7: The Butterfly Effect

attractors be named after Lorenz). Ruelle and Takens showed that turbulent flow in general probably has strange attractors. Now, many nonlinear dynamical systems are being found to have strange attractors. Just how general a principle strange attractors are is still being worked out.

Fractal objects were brought to popular attention by the perseverance of Lithuanian-born mathematician Benoit Mandelbrot. Working purposely outside of overspecialized academic disciplines (and so often in obscurity), Mandelbrot drew connections between the mathematical objects (fractals) and an astonishing array of phenomena in the physical and social sciences.

Exemplified in his book, *The Fractal Geometry of Nature*, Mandelbrot used a number of methods to show the ubiquity of fractals in Nature. He started by examining the strangeness and beauty of fractals mathematically. Sometimes, he found the fractal nature in statistics from things like commodity prices (like the price of cotton, or stock index futures). Sometimes he showed that simplified equations from physics, or economics, yielded fractal solutions—like Lorenz did. Sometimes he created colorful fractal images from pure mathematics, and then showed that they *look like* common things in Nature—mountain ranges, clouds, coastlines, turbulent rivers, patterns of leaves.

Detractors from Mandelbrot's approach complain that showing that a mathematical function looks like a mountain range (or leaf pattern) doesn't mean that there is any meaningful scientific connection with the physics of mountain forming (or leaf growing). This is true, but the work of Lorenz and Ruelle and others—that relates fractal strange attractors to nonlinear physical systems and the sensitive dependence on initial conditions of chaos—adds a lot of weight to Mandelbrot's view that fractals are one of the most important geometries of Nature. Conversely, the ubiquity of fractal-like structures and processes in nature suggests a ubiquity of chaotic sensitive dependence on initial conditions. The ongoing work of chaos theory is to flesh-out the meaningful connections in more detail.

Deterministic Chaos

Chaos theory, developed mostly in the past twenty years, quantifies the sensitive dependence on initial conditions common to nonlinear dynamical systems. It is becoming apparent that much, or even most, of the interesting and important dynamical systems in Nature have some sort of sensitive dependence on initial condition. This sensitivity is an exponential growth of uncertainty. I like to think of a sort of blooming of uncertainty packets everywhere—like a time-lapse film of a field of flowers blooming.

The label "chaos" has added to the popularity of this science. It is important to reiterate that "chaos" is a partially misleading label because chaos connotes randomness. Mathematical chaos theory (and the associated physics) contains no randomness. Chaos is more completely called "deterministic chaos." The sensitive dependence on initial conditions in deterministic chaos amplifies the initial errors or uncertainties. But if there is no initial uncertainty in a chaotic dynamical system, it will behave just as deterministically, and repeatable, and therefore predictable as any linear Newtonian system. Whether it is physically possible to have no initial mathematical uncertainty is another question that we'll get to later. Chaos theory itself, though, is a part of deterministic Newtonian mechanics—classical physics.

The recent blossoming of chaos science and fractal geometry, facilitated by the development of microcomputers, can be looked at two ways. First, it brings under the understanding umbrella of deterministic classical physics a huge range of nonlinear phenomena that had been beyond reach. The signature of chaotic dynamics is seen in phenomena ranging from the frequency and timing of ice ages, the orbits of planets, the reversal of the earth's magnetic field, the patterns of climate and weather, the frequency of mass extinctions in the geologic record, the structural form of plants and animals, heartbeats, and human brain waves. These phenomena can now be studied in a context of deterministic models.

The second point, and the thing that is frustrating for the scientist, is that chaotic phenomena are deterministic in an unpredictable way. Chaotic systems behave according to intricately modeled strange attractors that clearly show relation to real-world phenomena. But the butterfly effects of sensitive dependence on initial condition—those blooms of unknowingness—mean that any single

7: The Butterfly Effect

chaotic event cannot be predicted. Unlike quantum mechanical unpredictability (which is unpredictability because of initial nonexistence), chaotic unpredictability is deterministic and classical (and existing) unpredictability. What the two together mean is where we are headed in the next chapters.

A Mathematician on Mathematicians

Before we move on into the meanings of the new paradigm, we can make use of Ruelle's comments about the psychology of science to further understand the inertia of the old paradigm. Ruelle cites a theory from his colleague about the mental development of mathematicians:

> "Mathematical talent often develops at an early age. ... To this [notion], Russian mathematician Andrei N. Kolmogorov added a curious suggestion. He claimed that the normal psychological development of a person is halted at precisely the time when mathematical talent sets in. In this manner, Kolmogorov attributed to himself a mental age of twelve.
>
> "He gave only an age of eight to his compatriot Ivan M. Vinogradov, who was for a long time a powerful and very much feared member of the Soviet Academy of Sciences. The eight years of Academician Vinogradov corresponded, according to Kolmogorov, to the age when little boys tear off the wings of butterflies and attach old cans to the tails of cats. Probably it would not be too hard to find counterexamples to Kolmogorov's theory, but it does seem to be right remarkably often. ..."[142]

Ruelle's description may explain the cause of an experience that many young scientists have. Often, during student years, any accomplished scientist is assumed to also be a generally exalted human as well—probably because of desires similar to the desire for great sportsmen to be great people. Then one day, often at a professional conference or in a more informal setting, it becomes quite clear that one of one's intellectual heroes is motivated largely by a sort of psychological "tearing off the wings of butterflies." As Ruelle and Kolmogorov imply, the sort of motivations consistent with stunted mental development are not inconsistent with, and can even be an aid to, professional development and accomplishment.

While Kolmogorov's model is specifically for mathematicians, it undoubtedly has some bearing on mathematical physicists too. The paradigm shift we are talking about has often been couched in mathematical terms—because of the highly mathematical natures of quantum theory, and chaos theory. In fact, discussions relevant to our topic have often degenerated into purely mathematical debates that lose track of the meaning altogether. This is why this book is not developing any new mathematical models—it is only putting into context, and relationship, very well-established (if in some cases newer) physics and mathematics.

Ruelle's observations on the sociology of physics are not more encouraging: "Fashions currently play an essential role in the sociology—and in the funding—of physics and other sciences (mathematics being relatively spared [probably because there is relatively little funding in mathematics]). A specialized subject (such as chaos, string theory, or high-temperature superconductors) comes into fashion for a few years, and then is dumped. In the meantime, the field has been invaded by swarms of people who are attracted by success, rather than by the ideas involved. And this changes the intellectual atmosphere for the worse. ... [Ruelle then describes how research library copies of his own papers have been defaced with razor blades.] This kind of vandalism remains exceptional. It is characteristic, however, of a new situation in which the main problem is no longer to convince other scientists that your controversial ideas represent physical reality, but to get ahead of the competition using whatever means are available."[143] Given such an environment, it is not surprising that a new and unfashionable paradigm (especially a paradigm that cannot be touted as a new sort of certainty) is slow to be accepted—if not even vilified and loathed.

"Complexity Theory"

A well-written example of the sociology of science at work is the book *Complexity*, by science journalist M. Mitchell Waldrop, about the creation of a research organization called the Santa Fe Institute. At first encounter, *Complexity* seems to be about an exciting effort by brilliant scientists to come together and investigate fresh, new, nondogmatic, and open approaches to understanding the way things work. Exciting statements seem to characterize the intent of the institute; "... a guerrilla war against reductionism;" "the fundamental laws and the fundamental particles are [*not*] the only things worth studying." A rebellion against the "enforced tunnel vision" of overspecialized academia. Liquidity [in phase transition in liquids] is an "emergent" property. "Life is an emergent property." Even advocacy of a "holistic" perspective!

In light of Ruelle's observations, a second look at the motivations described in *Complexity* reveals a parallel perspective. Initially discussed by a group of senior scientists at the Los Alamos Nuclear Weapons Laboratory, the institute was (in the perspective of one of its, non-Los Alamos, founders) "shaping up as a cushy retirement home for aging Nobel Laureates from Caltech—complete with megabuck endowments and lots of scientific glitz and glamour."[144]

The founding director (and originator of the idea) of the institute was George Cowan, former head of research at Los Alamos. Precisely as Los Alamos was sensing a future of major funding cuts due to the post Cold War weapons reductions, Cowan, "privately thought of the [Santa Fe Institute] as an 'institute on the art of survival.' "

Another founder felt that "it can be as much fun to start an institution as to write a good scientific paper." Another felt that "we needed anything that could organize and reinforce the intellectual capability in the state [of New Mexico]."

The formation of the institute took the form of a search for a "$100-million angel." The focus of the institute quickly shifted to economics when it seemed an angel might appear in the form of John Reed. Reed had just taken over as CEO of Citicorp. And Citicorp, having just lost billions of dollars on defaulted foreign loans, was realizing that its sophisticated world economics models didn't work. Citicorp didn't cough up the $100 million, but the several hundred thousand dollars needed to jump-start the institute (chump change for a corporation that loses billions) was given in the hopes of generating "new ideas" for Citicorp's economists, and because John Reed enjoyed the Santa Fe meetings.

The economics at Santa Fe *is* fascinating and different. And the story of its development highlights the problem of paradigmatic inertia. Spearheaded by William Brian Arthur, the new economics is based on the concept of "increasing returns." Increasing returns says, basically, that large portions of economies are unstable in ways such that a small initial influence can create increasing future effects (increasing returns) out of proportion with the initial influence. Increasing returns economics predicts that inefficient or arbitrary technologies will "lock-in" in economies. A prime example of lock-in is the QWERTY typewriter keyboard (now universally standard) that was created to *slow down* typists on the early typewriters because fast typing would jam the mechanisms.[145]

Arthur nearly left economics early on because of the resistance to, and ridicule of, his emphasis on increasing returns economics. He thought that he was only revealing the obvious about what we observe happening in economies, and yet his ideas were ridiculed. His eyes were opened as to the source of that ridicule by a brilliant Eastern European economist. She pointed out to Arthur that the reigning "neoclassical" economics in the West, which is based on the assumption that economies are in, or very near, states of equilibrium and so economies cannot have the sorts of instabilities in Arthur's models, is actually the prime reinforcer of the myth that unregulated pursuit of individual (corporate and personal) accumulation necessarily leads to the most efficient economy.

If completely free economies, based solely on the motivation of unlimited accumulation by whatever means possible, really lead to instabilities, increasing returns, and lock-in of inefficiencies, then the economic justification for many Western political and psychological beliefs disappears! And so the "neoclassical" economic paradigm, which touted itself as really just trying to understand the way economies work, was actually based on deeply held psychological and emotional biases.

The Santa Fe Institute seems definitely stimulated by the whiff of new paradigms, but as Waldrop described it, it seems driven by old paradigm motives and methods (or at least the verdict is still out on this). Briggs and Peat note that:

> "The new holistic vocabulary may conceal a traditional reductionistic impulse, the impulse of an assembler and manipulator of parts. The co-opting of language indicates that the reductionist urge in science is powerful, so powerful, in fact, that it is almost

7: The Butterfly Effect

impossible to think of science without that drive to get to the absolute bottom of things, to find that absolute part, to learn the absolute basis of forms. ... The desire to have a reductionist answer is often accompanied by the need to have a mystery to work on. The difference between reductionism and holism is largely a matter of emphasis and attitude. But, in the end, that difference is everything."[146]

If I am motivated by a need for a "a $100-million angel," my attention is necessarily limited. Such a funding source, in our culture, is generally motivated to find new ways to predict and then manipulate and control—economies, weapons, biological entities. There is no value judgment meant in that statement—simply an observation. The motivation to profit from the manipulation and control of economies and industries has a long and exalted history in contemporary culture. It is just important to be clear about what we are doing, if we say we are doing science. It's great if we want to develop new prediction and control methods, but it may be something entirely different from trying to find out how Nature really works, without any emotional bias. Nature may involve aspects that are far subtler than, and even contradictory to, prediction, manipulation, and control.

All of those with significant input into the direction of the Santa Fe Institute, according to Waldrop's account, were chosen specifically to have major influence in (and therefore stakes in) status quo old paradigm physical sciences (and the highly mathematical branches of economics and "theoretical biology"). There is no one with a psychological, spiritual, or religious background. There is no mention of spirit, soul, transcendent influence, or nonmaterial reality of any sort. There is a sense that serious consideration of the nonmaterial aspects of reality is as taboo as ever at this supposedly new paradigm institute. If their intent is not merely to spiff-up and reinforce old paradigm motivations with some of the more exciting new paradigm language (and perhaps mathematical methods), then the reports of the seemingly sympathetic Waldrop do not serve them.

Waldrop ends his account with an appropriate quote. One of the Santa Fe Institute's permanent researchers admits, a few years into the effort, "All these terms like emergence, life, adaptation, complexity—these are the things we're still trying to figure out." Well, in this book, we're trying to state quite clearly what will really make these concepts new paradigm concepts—hylozoic paradigm concepts. It will be the inclusion of nonmaterial influences (spirit, soul, prana, etc.) and material aspects, both.

Paradigms Completed, and Lacking

With the end of this part, we come to the end of the foundations of physics and its understanding of how matter works.

So far, we've noted three main reasons why the new paradigms have not been developed:

1. The skills of the mathematical physicist are not the same skills needed to explore completely new paradigms. This is caricatured in Ruelle's model of arrested mental ages of mathematicians and physicists.
2. The historical definition of physics includes prediction and controlled repeatable experiments which, if strictly adhered to, precludes even asking the questions necessary to the new paradigms.
3. The social motivation of science funding agencies has reinforced the old emphasis on prediction and control. (Other reasons like general pigheadedness and corrupt motives are also present, but are less specific to the discussion at hand.)

Physics has come to the end of old paradigm descriptions of the functioning of matter. But it is incomplete and open-ended. First, the old paradigms ran up against the walls of quantum mechanical nothings-in-themselves uncertainty, and nonlocal connectivity. Then, the inadequacies of steady-state, and near equilibrium, and average descriptions are greatly magnified by the sensitive dependence on initial conditions of chaos.

There is something about our culture that pushes scientists to abandon the real search for truth about how things work, in favor of the peddling of certainty. But is the purveyance of false certainty really the way we want science to be oriented?

One way to search for gifted children is to ask questions such as, "Who discovered America?" The developmentally challenged child may say, "I don't know." The bright child will say, "Columbus!" The gifted child may say, "I don't know." If you badger the gifted child to explain her answer, she may say (probably less grammatically) something like, "Well, of course the popular idea that Columbus discovered America was discounted long ago. There is strong evidence that the Vikings were in the region that is now Canada hundreds of years before Columbus. And, of course, before that there were many "indigenous" civilizations in the America's. And there is even some evidence of contacts between the ancient high cultures of Central America and the ancient Indo-European high cultures. ...."[147]

Before educators realized that there were such things as gifted children, many of them were labeled as retarded. Is the labeling of "kook" (given to any scientist who doesn't advocate the materialist party line), a similar practice? Science—at least that portion of science that colors and infuses the attitudes of culture and society as a whole—should be gifted, and not just aggressively bright. It is time to again start saying, "I don't know."

PART III:

THE EFFECT OF SPIRIT

*"There are more things in Heaven and Earth, Horatio,
than you have dreamt of in your philosophies."*[148]

8. The Creative Universe

If you made it through the previous three chapters, you might have already made the connection that this chapter is going to make. Readers who got stuck on some of the technicalities can resume here and still find out where we're going, without the detailed background of Part II.

While the new paradigm is pulling the comfortable rug of certainty out from under us, all we can do is try to recognize the new, whatever it is. As Hamlet felt, we probably haven't even dreamt about the possibilities yet. The chapters of this part can be seen as a discussion of why it is reasonable to expect that it will be very new indeed.

The example we explored was that of really trying to appreciate, in contemporary scientific terms, how the events we observe at sunset on a full moon night on a beach, come about. The scientific principles we revealed are assumed to apply everywhere. The principles apply to all material functioning—even to me sitting here typing, and to you sitting there reading. In Chapters 5 and 6, we found that classical hylostatic physics did very well at explaining and predicting regular, large-scale phenomena like the tides and the average local air flows on calm days. The large-scale, macroscopic, universe we described is composed of the small parts of Nature (especially atoms) that behave according to quantum theory.

Chapter 7 showed that actual specific events—like the details of weather on a given day, instead of the average weather—are quite unpredictable because of the sensitive dependence on initial conditions of chaos theory. Chaotic systems, though unpredictable in practice, are deterministic in principle. Quantum systems are nondeterministic in principle because, in some actual sense, they don't exist before they happen. Classical deterministic (hylostatic) causality has been proven inapplicable to quantum events.

Layers of Reality

Keeping to our method of extracting the essential points of a paradigm, the present scientific understanding can be modeled as having three levels or layers. The first layer of reality is described by classical physics—classical mechanics, electromagnetism, and relativity. This layer is governed strictly by classical deterministic causality. It is hylostatic.

The second level of reality is that of quantum physics, the realm of quantum events that Bell, Bohr, Heisenberg, and Aspect showed cannot be governed by classical determinism. How *are* the quantum events of this second level eventuated? This question brings us to the third level of reality. The third level is the realm from which quantum events come. The classical events of the first level of reality come, in turn, from the quantum events of the second level, which come from the third level. The orthodox ontology of the outgoing paradigm—the present standard idea—is that the third level of reality is purely random. This idea—that Nature is random on the deepest, third, layer—is the hylostochastic paradigm. The hylostochastic paradigm says that the various possibilities predicted by quantum mathematics eventuate at random. Hylostochastism is material determinism modified with a little randomness.

The three-layered model is a conceptual aid for thinking about the standard ideas of physics, and contains no new ideas or theories. What is new is our focus on layer three. The orthodox idea that layer three is entirely random and meaningless is not based on any evidence, experiments, or mathematical proofs. Hylostochastism has flourished for the social reasons mentioned in the previous chapters, and for two reasons related to the physics. The first reason is that quantum mechanics is taught as applying only in the realm of the very small and very brief. All large and enduring phenomena—everything we experience—is taught as the deterministic outcome of the statistical average of billions of quantum mechanical events. Repeatable experiments with large systems, composed of very many quantum events, behave according to the laws of the other physical theories (classical mechanics, electricity and magnetism, and relativity). The smallness of the quantum realm is measured by a physical quantity known as Planck's constant. Planck's constant is so small that the idea that quantum mechanical openness must be completely divorced from our experience was often convincing. That is, people argued that the effect of the third layer on the first layer is so small that it is unimportant, and so we might as well call it random. This is now changed by chaos theory. The exponential growth of unknowingness in chaotic Nature brings the third layer much closer to the first layer.

The second reason is that the Aspect-EPR experiments, and Bell's proof, show that single quantum events cannot be predicted even in principle, and that very many quantum events will follow the probability distributions of quantum theory. If it is not deterministic, and if it does follow probabilistic distributions, must it be random? Randomness is one logical possibility, but it is not required by the two conditions of nondeterminism and probability distributions.

Spirit and Matter

Another possibility, instead of randomness, is that a deeper influence in layer three of reality—neither random nor deterministic—is present. Such a deeper influence is what, in this book, we are defining *spirit* to be. I can already hear the more dogmatic mystics complaining, "No, you cannot *define* spirit ..." Well, for our purposes, I must take issue with such enforced ignorance. The same writers who are so sure of the indefinibility of terms sometimes engage in long pontifications advocating some sort of definite belief or dogma and then claim that such belief is supported by the indefinibility of terms! The taboo on defining key terms perpetuates the existing (materialistic) paradigm, for if the basics aren't defined, then the details that rest on the basics can be thought of as merely "poetic" or metaphorical, or wrong, allusions to one's core pre-existing beliefs.

Note that our definition of spirit is not a description of characteristics, or limitations. This definition is certainly not a "measure" of spirit. It is a description of what spirit is not. Spirit is that aspect of reality that is not contained in, or described by, or arising out of the mathematical equations of physics. Matter is that aspect of reality that *is* contained in, described by, and arising out of, the mathematical equations of physics. Matter is the measurable. Spirit is the immeasurable.

The no-things-in-themselves principle of quantum theory leaves the equations open to "something else." The hylostochastic paradigm makes the assumption that the something else is purely random. The hylostochastic paradigm is the assumption that spirit doesn't exist.

The Hylozoic Paradigm—Planckian Butterflies

The hylozoic paradigm is the allowance that spirit does exist and that spirit does interact with matter by means of the third layer of reality—the "beyond quantum" layer. The development of chaos theory brings layer one—the classical reality of ordinary experience—much closer to layer three—the realm of spirit. The exponential increase of unknowingness in chaotic matter brings quantum mechanical openness into play in macroscopic events much more effectively than the linear increase in unknowingness of linear models.

We now introduce the term "Planckian butterfly effect" to describe this closeness of spirit and matter. Planck's constant (also called Planck's quantum of action) is a measure of the tiny windows of nonexistence in each of the myriad quantum events that make up our world. These collective windows of nonexistence propagate exponentially, by deterministic chaos, into immense possibilities inherent in the future. Postulate something, call it Planckian butterflies, that chooses in layer three—the quantum eventuating layer—to eventuate one of those possibilities.

Layer three is necessarily nonmaterial because quantum mechanics does not allow any deeper "hidden variables" which would apply to a more elusive, but still material, component. Quantum mechanical experiments predict a distribution of possible outcomes. Repeatable experiments, repeated many times, exhibit results according to the predicted distributions. Any single event cannot be predicted. The single events are where the Planckian butterflies can do their work. In single events spirit affects matter. Repeated trials of isolated repeatable experiments always produce the predicted distribution of outcomes.

Are the Planckian butterflies therefore unimportant because they always obey quantum mechanics? No, they are important because the interesting aspects of the universe, such as creative thought and conscious choice, are definitely not repeatable experiments. They are single events. In other words, each moment in any real, complex, and unique world process is the outcome of trillions of quantum events, and contains tremendously varying possibilities. While each atom, or particle, over time will exhibit the predictable quantum distributions, in the actuality of complex events, the Planckian butterflies are of great importance.

Prana, Lifetrons, and Subtle Realms

The concept that I labeled "Planckian butterflies" is not new. What *is* new is the clarity that science, especially physics, has given us. Science shows unequivocally that matter (which we define as that substance which behaves according to the mathematical equations of physics) is open to the influence of something else. Following the language of physics itself, the term Planckian butterflies joins the concepts of the butterfly effect of chaos and Planck's quantum of action.

The spiritual scientists of the past have described exactly the same concept. Here is where one of the image difficulties of this discussion can occur. If we are not careful, the development can look like we are trying to "prove mysticism with physics." We are most definitely not doing that. If anything, the information flows the other way. But that flow also has to be treated carefully. If we pick out ancient mystical language that sounds like, or uses similar metaphors to, the metaphors of physics, we risk trivializing the whole discussion. It all becomes a play on language ("all is one"—end of discussion). If we are going to use the language of pre-contemporary-scientific philosophers (call them yogis, or spiritual scientists, or spiritual masters, or saints, or yes even mystics), it serves us to only use that which is very clear and specific.

The best example of clear and specific description of the Planckian butterfly concept that I have run across is from Paramahansa Yogananda. Yogananda (1893-1952) was the first major Indian spiritual teacher to live and teach in the West.

Starting with hugely popular appearances at an International Conference of Religious Liberals in Boston, in 1920, Yogananda lectured and taught in America, and India, until his death. He initiated many, including the world-renowned American botanist

Luther Burbank, the great physicist Jagadis Chandra Bose, and Indian liberator Mahatma Gandhi, into the practice of a certain type of mental and physical yoga. US President Calvin Coolidge officially received him at the White House. Luther Burbank published an endorsement which said, "The swami's idea of right education is plain commonsense, free from all mysticism and non-practicality; otherwise it would not have my approval."[149]

The Indian Ambassador to the United States, Mr. Binay Ranjan Sen, said, in 1952, "If we had a man like Yogananda in the United Nations today, probably the world would be a better place than it is. To my knowledge, no one has worked more, has given more of himself, to bind the peoples of India and America together."[150] No serious investigator questions Yogananda's expertise in Vedanta, world religions, and physical and mental yoga, and the sorts of scandals that have dogged many recent gurus never tarnished him.

Concerning our concept of Planckian butterflies, Yogananda wrote in 1946, "The different sensory stimuli to which man reacts—tactual, visual, gustatory, auditory, and olfactory—are produced by vibratory variations in electrons and protons. The vibrations in turn are regulated by *prana*, 'lifetrons,' subtle life forces or finer-than-atomic energies intelligently charged."[151]

The Sanskrit word "prana" is the name of a very basic Vedantic concept. Prana is usually translated vaguely as "life force" or "vital principle." Those usual translations are meaningless for any rigorous understanding in the terms of contemporary physical science. Yogananda's brilliant translation as "lifetrons," which are finer-than-atomic, and intelligently charged, makes it quite clear that he is talking about what we called Planckian butterflies.

Yogananda continues, "Sri Yukteswar [a revered 19th and 20th century Indian holy man, and Yogananda's teacher] used the word prana; I have translated it as "lifetrons." The Hindu scriptures refer not only to the anu, "atom," and to the paramanu, "beyond the atom," finer electronic energies, but also to prana, "creative lifetronic force." Atoms and electrons are blind forces; prana is inherently intelligent."[152]

"Atoms and electrons are blind forces; lifetrons are inherently intelligent." That is exactly the key to the hylozoic paradigm. The fascinating thing is that the precise quality that Yogananda (and his teachers and their teachers) ascribed to lifetrons—that of being inherently intelligent, and different in quality from the blind forces of electrons—is actually required by what we now know about quantum mechanics. (The fact of lifetrons's existence is *not* required by the physics, that lifetrons must have qualities different from matter if they do exist *is* required.)

Matter is that substance which behaves according to the mathematical equations of physics. The functioning of matter is open to the influence of another agent, but it cannot be an agent that is deterministic or strictly local. Physics is entirely consistent with an agent that has some sort of purpose in the moment, or intelligence. This deciding among various imminent possibilities is the active function of lifetrons, or prana, or Planckian butterflies.

Yogananda continues, on the specific relevance of lifetrons, translating his teacher. "Physical death is attended by the disappearance of breath and the disintegration of fleshly cells. Astral death consists of the dispersement of lifetrons, those manifest units of energy that constitute the life of astral beings. At physical death, a being loses his consciousness of flesh and becomes aware of his subtle body in the astral world. Experiencing astral death in due time, a being thus passes from the consciousness of astral birth and death to that of physical birth and death. These recurrent cycles of astral and physical encasement are the ineluctable destiny of all unenlightened beings. Scriptural definitions of heaven and hell sometimes stir man's deeper-than-subconscious memories of his long series of experiences in the blithesome astral and disappointing terrestrial worlds."[153]

Yogananda says that lifetrons act on deeper-than-subconscious levels. Thus he implies that conscious and subconscious thinking is a material process, and that thought can be influenced by something deeper—something composed of lifetrons. Also, lifetrons are general subatomic influences that choose among the quantum possibilities imminent in electrons and protons. There is nothing special about the atoms in a human. Lifetrons may inform the functioning of all matter—not only human life and biological matter.

Apparently, the late Yogananda's mission of bringing together East and West included, in part, a specific emphasis on bringing together science and spirituality. Yogananda's teacher describes the origins of that purpose as a "chance" encounter with the near-mythical reclusive Christ-like spiritual master known as Mahamouni Babaji. Sri Yukteswar encountered Babaji at a *mela* (Indian festival meeting of diverse spiritual seekers and teachers) and had the following exchange:

" 'Sir, I [Yukteswar commented to Babaji] have been thinking of the leading scientific men of the West, greater by far in intelligence than most people congregated here [at the mela], living in distant Europe and America, professing different creeds, and ignorant of the real values of such melas as the present one. They are the men who could benefit greatly by meetings with India's masters. But, although high in intellectual attainments, many Westerners are wedded to rank materialism. Others, famous in science and philosophy, do not recognize the essential unity in religion. Their creeds serve as insurmountable barriers that threaten to separate them from us forever.' "

[To this, Babaji indicated his approval and said ...] " 'East and West must establish a golden middle path of activity and spirituality combined. India has much to learn from the West in material development; in return, India can teach the universal methods by which the West will be able to base its religious beliefs on the unshakable foundations of yogic science. You [Sri Yukteswar] have a part to play in the coming harmonious exchange between Orient and Occident. Some years hence, I shall send you a disciple whom you can train for yoga dissemination in the West. ..."

That disciple was the highly influential Yogananda. We have been a little slow. But a few Western scientists are finally starting to catch the passes sent by the great spiritual teachers like Babaji, Yukteswar, Yogananda, and many others [from other traditions as well as from Vedanta].

Different Religions and the Hylozoic Paradigm

The key to the hylozoic paradigm is the possibility that Planckian butterflies, or Yogananda's pranic lifetrons, exist. It should be emphasized that the hylozoic paradigm is not dependent on, or related to "the advocacy of Hinduism." Some critics, usually "fundamentalists" of some sort, of the emerging nonmaterialistic paradigms use the charge that the new paradigm advocates a rival religion in order to claim that it is thus evil, if not wrong. The fact that the major advocates of what we are calling the hylozoic paradigm do tend to the ecumenical, if not even to the completely nonsectarian, seems to have two sources.

First, the spiritual traditions that are most rigorously clear about the point, like Yogananda is clear about lifetrons, are also the least sectarian. The Vedantic tradition, of which Yogananda is a part, emphasizes the importance of recognizing "the essential unity in religion."

The Sufis, who also have a technically detailed philosophy of the relation between matter and prana, recognize 125,000 prophets—including of course Mohammed, as well as Jesus, Abraham, Moses, (and probably Buddha, Krishna, the Vedantists, etc.). Esoteric Buddhism is also explicit on the subject of spirit and matter being distinctly different aspects of the unitary universe, and also is highly inclusive of other religions. Kabbalism, and even some Shamanism as in that of the American Ogalala Sioux holy man Nicholas Black Elk, also fit the pattern.

The same, even, applies to Gnostic Christianity[154] such as described by Perre Teilhard de Chardin. Teilhard de Chardin (1881–1955) was a distinguished paleontologist, as well as a Jesuit Father. Teilhard de Chardin went to great pains to rigorously reconcile the standard findings of contemporary science with the transcendent aspects of Christianity. He is largely viewed (by those who have sufficient scientific and spiritual backgrounds to study his work) to have succeeded.[155]

Teilhard de Chardin postulates two distinct components of the basic energetic fount of the universe; "tangential energy" which "represents 'energy' as such, as generally understood by science," and "radial energy" which "draws [material elements] towards ever greater complexity and centricity."[156] He then carefully solves "the only difficulty [which] is to explain the interplay of tangential arrangements in terms of the laws of thermo-dynamics." Essentially, he does so by noting that the radial energy creates an "intervention of arrangement" among the various possible future eventualities—all of which are allowed by thermodynamics and conservation of energy and the other "laws" of physics. This is, of course, the same way our Planckian butterflies get around the same "difficulty," which is actually no difficulty at all.

Teilhard de Chardin's radial energy, and our Planckian butterflies, and Yogananda's lifetrons, and the Vedantist's prana are all the same thing. If one believes, or asserts, that none of them exist then one has the hylostochastic paradigm. If they do exist, then the hylozoic paradigm is possible. Standard physics as it is now understood is entirely consistent with either case.

The second reason why truly new paradigm thinkers tend to the nonsectarian is that the hylozoic paradigm requires thinking for oneself. The staunchest advocates of deterministic materialism (and also hylostochastism), if they have any sort of religious interest, tend to associate with the dogmatic and authoritarian wings of the major faiths (excluding the special case of "existentialism").

Dogmatic authoritarianism can manifest in a single charismatic demagogue, or in a major world organization. Dogmatic authoritarians persecute scientific visionaries like Galileo, and mystical visionaries like Teilhard de Chardin, alike. Obviously, dogmatic authoritarians resist change, and a new paradigm requires change. Also, as soon as an aspect of the new outlook gains a foothold, new dogmatic authoritarians try to co-opt it. The hylozoic paradigm cannot serve a dogmatic authoritarian because it requires seeing for oneself (whether the deeper, nonmaterial, influences exist) instead of following an authority.

The hylozoic paradigm refers specifically to an aspect of scientific understanding of the working of matter. This paradigm for science may be a small part of a larger world cultural movement away from authoritarianism, in the religious, economic, and political realms. The case that authoritarianism (that is, its demise) is the key difference between the emerging new cultures and the slowly dissipating old cultures is made in an eloquent book called *The Guru Papers: Masks of Authoritarian Power*.[157]

The authors of *The Guru Papers* use "guru" as a "metaphor for anyone who manipulates others under the guise of 'knowing what's best' for them, whether leaders, mothers, or lovers," and I would add many "scientists." They argue, also, that the outgoing authoritarianism is not simply categorized as a victim-oppressor relation-ship. The damaging aspects of authoritarianism are authorities we invest in others out of ignorance, emotional weakness, and laziness. The hylozoic paradigm, like all of the new nonauthoritarian cultures, requires self-involvement.[158]

So, in this book, if I tend to use Vedantic models—as examples of preexisting spiritual systems that can inform contemporary science—I do so specifically because Vedanta seems to me the most inclusive and respectful of other religions, and Vedanta can be seen as a metaphor for the source of *any* significant spiritual discipline.

Another example of this coincidence—of inclusivity of religious perspective, together with clarity on the issue of matter-spirit, or matter-prana, or matter-Planckian butterfly, relationship—can be found in an extraordinary contemporary source. Indian holy man Sathya Sai Baba's main epistemological point is the essential unity of all religions. (There will be further discussion of the extraordinary figure Sai Baba in a later chapter.[159]) Concerning the skepticism of old paradigm science, Sai Baba says:

> "It is the scientists who are so unsure of themselves that they indulge in escapist theories. For example, they say that the moon is lifeless. Simultaneously, they maintain that all matter consists of moving atoms. Now isn't the moon also a conglomerate of the same moving atoms? Then how can it be lifeless? There is no matter that does not consist of atoms, electrons, neutrons and protons, which are all constantly moving. This energy [of specific sort of movement], too, is God. So also there is no human being in whom there is no divinity. To say that there is no God in man is like saying that there is no atom in the moon or any large lump of matter. The omnipresence of God has been described in our ancient texts as: "ano baniyam mahatoo maniyam" (God is a small particle in the smallest of particles and a large mass in the largest of masses). In this context, how can one say that God is not in man?"

Is it radical to say that "if I am alive, the moon is alive"? Given the contemporary understanding that biology is organic chemistry, and that there is no fundamental physical difference between organic and inorganic chemistry, that cannot be a radical statement. So what is the fuss about? From the perspective of the hylozoic paradigm, it is the old paradigm scientist who seems absurd—for he seems to believe first that he is alive but nothing else is alive, and second to believe that prana, or lifetrons, or Planckian butterflies don't exist.

Sufis call the childishly egotistical core of our personality "the Pharaoh." The Pharaoh is certain that he is omniscient, and omnipotent, and that he is the center of the universe. He will go to great lengths of self-deception to reinforce that belief. For, how could it not be so? The Pharaoh is genuinely surprised to learn that he is one of many Pharaohs, and that there is not even anything universally central about Pharaohs at all. Since there is no logical scientific reason to disallow the possibility of spirit, there must be a cultural Pharaoh that reinforces the materialistic old paradigm. The Czech-American philosopher Erazim Kohak also sees such a cultural Pharaoh. Kohak says, "that the notion of a fundamental discontinuity between humans and their natural world should have come to appear evident is itself a curious phenomenon."[160] And Kohak means by this that the whole is infused by spirit and so is alive, not, as the materialists would have it, that the whole is dead.

The Dreaded Dualism

Some new paradigm advocates say, "You shouldn't talk about" spirit and matter because articulating them separately is 'dualistic.' "Dualistic" has become one of those code words like "reductionistic." If anything is labeled "dualistic," it then becomes obviously wrong or taboo, because everyone knows that "holism" or "monism" is the answer to everything. "Dual" has become a bad four-letter-word apparently for two different reasons.

One reason is because of the authoritarian dogma of theistic dualism that has been abused by the Western "Christian" church. Theistic dualism is the assertion that God and human are separate and disconnected. Theistic dualism is used to strengthen the dogmatic authority of organized religions because, if God and human are separate, then the church organization can claim to transmit the truths of God to man—man who is held unable to reach the truths himself.

One of the tragedies of history is that "Christianity" is associated with theistic duality, whereas Jesus himself taught the exact opposite; "the kingdom of heaven is within you." Theistic dualism has absolutely nothing to do with the dualities of spirit and matter. The difference between the obvious truth that everything is *connected*, and the deep mystical insight that everything is *one*, is confused by those who use the doctrine of unity to support some sort of dogma of their own. "All is one, so don't talk about matter and spirit, or mind and body, or this or that,—listen to me instead!" Isn't this obviously absurd? Probably in some fundamental way, far beyond the myriad realities we experience, all *is* one. Personally, I haven't become[161] this pinnacle of Godhead yet, and so it is still useful to talk about what I experience[162]—a great variety of things.

In his book attractively titled *Consciousness Explained*,[163] Daniel C. Dennett articulates the second reason for the taboo on discussing dualities:

> "The idea of mind as distinct ... from the brain, composed not of ordinary matter but of some other, special kind of stuff, is *dualism*, and it is deservedly in disrepute today .... The prevailing wisdom, variously expressed and argued for, is *materialism*: there is only one sort of stuff, namely *matter*—the physical stuff of physics, chemistry, and physiology—and the mind is somehow nothing but a physical phenomenon."

Dennett's definition of matter is the same as ours, and he verifies that materialism is the "prevailing wisdom." Dennett's interpretation of "mind" though, is problematic. He seems to define mind as active thinking processes (conscious or unconscious). In essence, he defines mind as that part of mentation[164] that the hylozoic paradigm says *is* material process anyway. The implication of the sort of materialistic anti-dualism of Dennett is that, since the active thinking function is a material process, there cannot exist spirit of any sort. In other words, if spirit does not exist in one's little egoic self-identity, then spirit cannot exist at all! The Pharaoh *must* be the center of the universe.

Proofs Of Materialism Are Still Wrong

Dennett, a "cognitive studies" researcher, says that the "standard objection to dualism" comes from "standard physics." Dennett says, "How ... do they [our Planckian butterflies, or prana, or spirit] make a difference to what happens in the brain cells they must affect, if the mind [spirit] is to have any influence over the body [matter]? A fundamental principle of physics is that any change in the trajectory of any physical entity is an acceleration requiring the expenditure of energy, and where is this energy to come from? It is this principle of the conservation of energy that accounts for the impossibility of ... dualism."

By this point in our book, it should be clear that, while the principle of conservation of energy is quite applicable, Dennett's proof of materialism is quite wrong. Physics shows in detail that, based on the present initial conditions, future events (like, say, the precise global weather two weeks from now) may assume an extremely large range of possibilities. How one specific case of those possibilities eventuates is unknown to physics. It is known that, however it eventuates—by Planckian butterflies or by prana or by randomness—conservation of energy is not violated because all the future possibilities have the same total energy.

Since Dennett calls his proof of materialism the "prevailing wisdom," one wonders how Eddington, and de Broglie, and Bohr, and Einstein, and Bohm didn't know about it. (See Chapter 3, for evidence that all of their conclusions were the opposite of Dennett's.) Dennett says, "ingenious technical exemptions [to the putative proof of materialism] based on sophisticated readings of the relevant physics have been explored ... without attracting many conversions." Does he mean all of quantum mechanics? Apparently he does because he also says, "[this] standard objection to dualism was ... familiar ... in the 17th century."

The fact that the rest of Dennett's book, on cognitive studies itself, is fairly lucid, while he is so stunningly wrong on this point, indicates that there really is a paradigmatic underpinning that needs to be finally smashed. While Dennett's ignorance of basic physics is excusable, his basing his whole approach to his own field of cognitive studies on a wrong physical assumption is not productive.

To be fair, some physicists still do claim to make the same proof of materialism as Dennett does. Retired physics professor Milton A Rothman, associated with the debunking organization called CSICOP, writes, "All descriptions of ESP [specifically telepathic rapport] imply violations of conservation of energy in one way or another, as well as violations of all the principles of information theory and even of the principle of causality. Strict application of physical principles requires us to say that ESP is impossible."[165]

Well, very standard physics says that Rothman is just plain wrong on all three counts. We've dealt in detail with the "conservation of energy" claim. It is depressing that Rothman follows one wrong blanket claim with two others, implying that they have the weight of scientific authority. His "principle of causality" is violated by the theory of quantum mechanics, and even, in fact, by the experiments![166]

Of course, the Pharaoh just doesn't care about reality—if he believes in a materialistic "principle of causality" that is somehow proved by physics, then there must be a "principle of causality."

Finally, the "principles of information theory" is another of the vague and in fact wrong arguments that are occasionally offered as "proofs" of materialism. Rothman gives no reference[167] or explanation, but we can assume he is referring to the idea that all processing of information requires the dissipation of energy (another form of the "conservation of energy" proof). This idea goes as follows. In order to manifest any sort of intelligence, rather than pure randomness, the Planckian butterflies would have to process information. And "the principles of information theory" show that information processing requires the dissipation of energy. And so the Planckian butterflies cannot exist or, if they do exist, they must be conventional matter.

The problem with this argument is that "the principles of information theory" do not, in fact, show that. More recent analyses have shown that those supposed principles were not truly quantified, and were based on "physical plausibility arguments," which made initial assumptions equivalent to assuming in the first place that the information processing was to be done materially. Recent truly quantitative information theory has proven the opposite—so-called "reversible computation" or computation without dissipating energy *is* possible in theory.[168]

Cognitive scientists such as Dennett color their approach to the study of the mind by outdated assumptions from 19th-century physics. The putative proofs of materialism have been shown, repeatedly, explicitly, and unequivocally, to be wrong. The influence should really go the other way. An unbiased observation and study of mind functioning (which may involve much larger processes than simple cognition and active thinking) can inform the choice between materialism and hylozoism—a choice that is left open by physics (in fact, proven to be open by physics).

Dennett believes that physics proves his materialistic assumptions about brain functioning. It is interesting that an equally distinguished biologist finds succor from physics for precisely the opposite position from Dennett. Dr. George Wald, emeritus professor of biology at Harvard and co-recipient of the 1967 Nobel Prize for physiology says in a 1985 lecture:

> "I, and practically all biologists and most other people, had supposed that consciousness or mind was a late product in the evolution of animals. The idea came to me that instead of that, the constant pervasive presence of mind guided matter in that direction. I realized that I was in the best of company; that ideas of this essential kind were millennia old in the Eastern philosophies. And numbers of people among the monumental group of physicists [of the first half of the twentieth century] had come to exactly that kind of thought. I found Eddington at one point saying the stuff of the world is mind stuff and giving it the primary place over matter. Von Weizsacker, a rather philosophical physicist, spoke of what he called the identity principle, that mind and matter are the twin aspects of all reality."[169]

These eminent biological scientists need a little self-empowerment. The fact is that most physicists think very little about these issues—in fact many avoid them on purpose because of their swamp-like nature—and there is zero content on these matters in most physics Ph.D. (and masters and bachelors) courses.

That some of the most eminent physicists, like Eddington, as Wald notes, felt compelled to make known their conclusions on these matters in an ironic way also adds apparent authority to superficial pronouncements like those of Rothman. If physics proves *anything* about the nature of the mind, it proves that the mind, like all matter, is open to transcendent influence (which may or may not exist). That is all a physics education qualifies a physicist, in the sense of specific professional training, to say on this point.

Personally, I think a physics education would benefit from some content in this regard, but at present there is none. (In fact, I think that the discipline of physics is in the process of withering because of lack of such content.)

This book argues that old paradigm scientists keep themselves blind in one eye by rejecting spirit. A certain type of the so-called new-agers would blind us equally in the other eye. This type misuses the subtle concept of nonduality to justify sloppy and unclear language and thought. Such enforced vagueness is as much a tool of authoritarianism as is dogmatic materialism. Having the vague dogma fight the one-sided dogma can be a lot of fun, but it is not progress.

Planckian Butterflies In Action

As an example of Planckian butterflies at work, let's return to the example of chaotic turbulence making the global weather uncertain (see Chapter 7). In that example, the cascade of uncertainty started with the absurdly small cause of the change in the gravitational pull from removing an electron from the edge of the universe. Quantum effects were not considered. After the initial small perturbation, it took only 50 collisions of air molecules until the molecular motions became much different. That takes only a fraction of a second. Then the chaotic turbulent motion of the air caused the small collisional difference to propagate to millimeter-sized fluctuations in about a minute—and so on, until the whole global weather is different after a couple of weeks.

Now consider quantum effects as an initial perturbation, instead of the electron at the edge of the universe. Quantum indeterminacy means that the precise momentum and position of each air molecule is slightly nonexistent—an emergent event. This means that after only about *one* collision, the inherent quantum uncertainty will start the same cascade of uncertainty leading to emergent weather[170]—we don't even have to wait for the 50 collisions. The millimeter-scale changes will again take about a minute, and the global-scale changes a couple weeks. This means that the gravitational influence of electrons at the edge of the universe *is* unimportant. But it is unimportant not because it is so small, as old paradigm science would have it. It is unimportant because the inherent quantum uncertainty (quantum emergence) is much larger! Our third-reality-layer Planckian butterflies then, if they exist, are very important to real-world physical phenomena.

Ruelle also notes another example. Instead of air molecules, consider billiard balls. Consider perfectly bouncy billiard balls moving and colliding on a perfectly frictionless billiard table. The billiard balls exhibit sensitive dependence on initial conditions, like other chaotic dynamical systems, like the air molecules in the previous example. Now consider the small change in the balls' motions caused by the gravitational pull of a human billiard player standing three feet from the table. It can be calculated that after only about nine collisions, the billiard balls will be moving completely differently than they would if the human was not there (or if she were standing on the other side of the table, or moving around the table—the gravitational influence of sticking one's tongue out would take only a few more than nine collisions to manifest in the motions).[171]

Billiard balls are often taken as examples of eminently classical systems—no weirdo quantum effects on those billiard balls! Well, let's see. The same quantum uncertainty that applies to air molecules does apply to things as large as billiard balls—it is just a much smaller effect. The exponential increase of trajectory uncertainty of the colliding balls amplifies even the quantum uncertainty. After about 15 collisions, the billiard ball trajectories are a completely undetermined property due only to the quantum effects.[172] If we estimate about a half second between collisions, the quantum indeterminacy of billiards manifests in only a few seconds. (The Planckian butterflies can play billiards, too.)

All around us, many natural phenomena exhibit chaotic sensitive dependence on initial conditions. These can be visualized as blooms of unknowingness, or blooms of creation out of transcendence. Collectively, all those individual blooms become large transcendent systems—like humans, global climate systems, storms, and stock markets.

In the hylostochastic paradigm, the universe in inherently random, and the apparent order and meaning of events and things, like humans, are mysteries, or are mis-observations. In the hylozoic paradigm, the universe is inherently creative. The proverbial monkey banging randomly on a typewriter would eventually, after an impossibly long period of time, produce a few lines of Shakespeare. But real monkeys don't bang randomly on typewriters, and we want to know how the real Shakespeare worked.

As air molecules and billiard balls, after a short period of time, are emergent phenomena, so too was Shakespeare's brain. A human brain, especially a well-exercised one like Shakespeare's, is an unimaginably complex dynamical system. Mind functioning is a highly emergent process. As such, the Planckian butterflies associated with Shakespeare's brain had a vastly diverse range of possibilities out of which to create Shakespeare's plays. In order to do so, the individual atomic Planckian butterflies of Shakespeare's brain molecules would needed to have, at least sometimes, some sort of organization or association, or trade union, that would make them function together to produce the plays.[173]

This sort of hierarchy of transcendent realms is also a common feature of those ancient philosophical systems, like Vedanta, that are explicit about transcendent (spirit) and matter. How such super-Planckian-butterflies, or nested realms of pranic lifetrons, are in fact organized is the stuff of metaphysics. Teilhard de Chardin, for instance, postulates a global "noosphere" that affects the minds of all humans. The purpose of this book is not to advocate the specific details of the metaphysical realms—it is to present a framework in which the interaction of the metaphysical and the physical can be appreciated. The first step is to accept that the metaphysical, or spiritual, realms may exist at all.

We are not trying to prove by the mathematics of probability that teleological influences must be present. Others have attempted such proofs. The details of such calculations are necessarily uncertain and foster arguing about mathematics instead of reality. The point of the hylozoic paradigm is the converse—science and its calculations show that matter is open to the *possible* influence of Planckian butterflies. Whether such influence occurs or not cannot be calculated. It can only be sensed directly, intuitively.

In the following chapters of this Part, we will consider the importance of the effects of spirit (or prana, or Planckian butterflies, or lifetrons, or radial energy), should they exist, in Nature.

We will consider what the hylozoic paradigm means for:

1. What is commonly thought of as "natural phenomena"—intermediate-scale events affecting and effected by humans;
2. Larger-scale phenomena, such as planets;
3. Human-scale phenomena, specifically humans.

Then, Part IV indulges in some speculations about the sorts of outlook and actions that the hylozoic paradigm in action might lead to.

9. Life in the Valleys

Physicist Freeman Dyson[174] uses the metaphor that physics is very successful at understanding the "mountain tops"—like repeatable quantum experiments, the orbits of planets, the propagation of light, the spectrum of the hydrogen atom, idealized gears in idealized machines—and poor at understanding the "valleys," nonrepeating phenomena involving many length scales and time scales and varied processes—like weather, thunderstorms, earthquakes, life and consciousness.

It is in the "valleys" where the Planckian butterflies (spirit acting on the scale of Planck's constant in such a way as to choose among a range of possible macroscopic events) can do great things. "Mountain tops" are simple, clearly defined and predictable. "Valleys" are complicated, messy and difficult to define precisely. A "mountain top" is the orbit of a single isolated planet about an idealized star. A "valley" is the long-term orbital evolution of many planets all pulling and pushing on each other. A "mountain top" is the convective flow of an ideal fluid heated precisely from below and cooled from above. A "valley" is the actual movement of the earth's crustal plates—earthquakes, volcanoes and all—driven by the flow of the underlying hot molten mantle.

The emerging hylozoic paradigm reveals that the idealized "mountain tops" and the "valleys" differ in an important way. The "valleys" are not simply complicated idealized "mountain tops." The complications, messiness and uncertainties of the "valleys" open them to the entirely different effects of spirit. These effects are not present in the idealized "mountain tops" described by the mathematical equations of physics. The equations of mathematical physics stop at the "open window" of indeterminacy of quantum mechanics. The mechanistic hylostochastic paradigm asserts that there is nothing outside of the window, and that nothing passes through the window. The hylozoic paradigm says the window is open; let's check it out before we assert the other side is empty.

As real-world natural phenomena are more "valley-like" than "mountain top-like," the process of moving from the old mechanistic paradigm of science to the new hylozoic paradigm promises to be complicated, uncertain and messy. This chapter and those following will explore specific examples of natural phenomena in light of the hylozoic paradigm. But first, I'll describe part of a messy valley-type process in my life, involving intellectual, emotional and physical changes all at the same time. This process helped further my own investigation of the new hylozoic paradigm.

An Earthquake Triggers an Inner Quake

The following events happened basically as I describe them. Later medical examination revealed no physical or psychological disorders except for some elements of common anxiety attack. Anxiety attack, or panic attack, affects a large percentage of people at some time during their lives. It is characterized by various temporary, sometimes severe, somatic (bodily) symptoms that have no apparent cause. It is considered a reaction to stress and is especially common among people undergoing major, long-term change stresses like moving to a foreign culture.

There is growing recognition though, that very similar symptoms also occur in relation to some spiritual experiences and mystical experiences—the sort of thing described in Chapter 2. In this view, it is important to distinguish among a range of experiences from pure physiological reaction to experience of deep spiritual insight.

A most famous example is the experience of Saint Paul on the road to Damascus. His great mystical experience was accompanied by somatic symptoms similar to common panic attack. The mechanistic paradigm interpretation is to attribute the whole event to physiological stress reaction, probably caused by Paul's stressful job of persecuting early Christians, and to dismiss the great saint's own spiritual interpretations as ignorant fantasy.

Similar experiences are a part of all the major world religions, and the native spiritual traditions, and are probably more common among ordinary people than is appreciated. My interpretation that my own experience also contained real spiritual meaning—that physical science itself can benefit from spiritual insight if viewed from a hylozoic perspective—can also be questioned. Only the

9: Life in the Valleys

weight of numerous such insights, shared with discrimination, will change the consensus view. And so I share my own:

> One evening during dinner at a dear friend's house east of Tokyo, the earth started to shake. This quake seemed more violent than the several quakes I'd felt since moving to Tokyo. Soon the shaking stopped and we laughed at our own fearful expressions and tried to continue dinner. But it was taking me longer than usual to "come back to myself." I felt as if I'd shifted partway out of my body—a highly disconcerting feeling. Nothing seems the same. It is difficult to focus on any thought, feeling, or sensation. Everything continually shifts and flows. There was sensation of heat in my head and back with no apparent cause. As the experience continued, my inability to bring myself back to usual created a powerful fear. I had to use the toilet three times in a half-hour. There was a clear sense that the earthquake and my body's reaction to it had started a process that I was powerless to stop.
>
> I checked for the hyperventilation characteristic of anxiety attacks but was breathing normally. Nothing from my experience with several types of meditation and breathing practices was able to relieve the feelings of dislocation, heat and energetic movement in various parts of my body. Even a highly effective relaxation posture from yoga could not help. Finally I started to allow whatever was occurring in me to happen.
>
> While in the relaxation posture my body shook involuntarily for several minutes. My thoughts were mostly extreme fear and bewilderment. The sensations were so extreme that I considered this may be what the process of death feels like. There was also a sense that the process was a necessary result of a very deep part of myself coming to fruition. This sense allowed the strange events in my own body to be just bearable to my mind.
>
> This inner quake was one of a series of inner events characterized by feelings of psychological undoing and physical body restructuring, and at the same time a coming-in of an expanded appreciation for the aliveness of nature. I'd come to accept this process as a bubbling over of, or encounter with, the deep unconscious or collective unconscious described by Carl Jung.

This aspect of the collective unconscious seemed to be associated with living natural processes normally considered inanimate.

Afterwards, my body felt as exhausted as if I'd run a marathon or been beaten up. I was emotionally shaken as if after a terrible accident but I was mentally relieved. I felt that I'd been allowed, indeed survived, a rare glimpse of a deep part of my/our psyche that is not matter, but spirit as defined in this book. I also felt a deep identification between this aspect of spirit in us, and the actual earthquake that triggered the process.

The friend I was with happened to be a registered nurse, and a highly trained physical therapist. She confirmed I was not hyperventilating or exhibiting other obvious signs of panic attack during the process. She also sensed something beyond the ordinary occurring. She felt heat and sensation not only on my body but also in the space nearby. Though her calm presence comforted me, she later confided that she'd actually been very frightened because what was occurring seemed beyond any standard medical or physical model.

The experience clearly had some similarities to common anxiety or panic attack. My own interpretation that it was also something more—something that brings the experiencer in contact with his spiritual self—cannot be objectively proven. In that interpretation, it fits a model of a relatively common sort of spiritual experience. The hylostochastic paradigm dismisses the possibility of any experience ever containing any spiritual meaning. The hylozoic paradigm says, "Maybe it did, maybe it didn't." Only study of the spiritual traditions, physical science and physiology, and careful observation of one's own experience can determine whether there was meaningful spiritual content or whether it was simply a physico-mechanical reaction.

As I continue to integrate that and other experiences into my own belief structure, I become more certain that the primary lesson from those experiences is that material processes in nature are affected by spirit. In terms of the model of matter described in Chapter 8, these experiences lead me to believe that the third level of material process—the level where spirit can have effect—is not purely random. The Planckian butterflies are intelligent in some sense vastly different from our own intelligence, but equally real.

This is a subjective interpretation of experience that cannot be proved or disproved logically. It can be objectively and logically shown why such an interpretation is plausible and why it should be considered—as I am doing in this book.

The event described above was part of my own physical and psychological process mentioned earlier in this book. I view it as an example of the sort of transcendent experience containing spiritual meaning common, in degrees and in many different ways, to all of us. A detailed psycho-physiological examination of this sort of experience is not the point of, or within the scope of, this book. I include my experience mostly for readers who know they've experienced this sort of thing and often feel isolated because of bias against accepting it as meaningful experience.

Also, our personal experiences of this sort can be viewed as a metaphor for the process of society as a whole shifting paradigms. As such, a clear lesson is that this major paradigm shift is not a simple, painless, trivial process.

Real joys are involved, but also real dangers. We may see intellectually the truth of the new paradigm, and intellectual understanding can be a first step. To underestimate the power or difficulty of the shift, though, will leave us unprepared. Our intellect has a tendency to think, "Yes, that's right, just think that way now!"

But to come to really know the new paradigm, to feel it in our bones, involves a death-rebirth process with all its pitfalls, pleasures, dangers and ecstasies. The social, cultural and psychological aspects of transformative journeys are dealt with in the mythological studies of Joseph Campbell[175] and the psychology of Jung, Grof and others.[176]

Our exploration now, however, is of the basis in physical science for the shift to the hylozoic paradigm. Whatever may be the correct interpretation of my own experiential journey, the scientific contents of the following discussions should stand or fall on their own merits.

Predicting the Next Great Tokyo Earthquake?

If the next Great Tokyo earthquake is due to be, say, five years from now, how precisely are its magnitude, time of day and location contained in the present state of the earth?

In a crowded little restaurant near Tokyo University, in 1992, we hunched over our plates. The only foreigners in a crowded and cozy place, our young waitress was nearly paralyzed at the sound of an American more fluent in the language (my companion) than most Japanese. Oblivious after years of such circumstances, Bob turned to me and went garrulously on, in English, about his earthquake theories.

Though worried about exposing my unusual opinions to my senior research colleague, I decided—probably stimulated by our slightly bizarre circumstances— to say what I really thought. "In general, I think scientists focus too much on what is known rather than what is not known. That's why I like your article."

To my relief, he agreed and asked me to comment further on his paper. All the while, as we chatted, deep in the earth beneath us, the next Big Tokai earthquake was brewing.

Geophysics professor Robert Geller is one of the first tenured Westerners at the prestigious University of Tokyo, and I was a postdoctoral researcher at the same institute as Bob. His paper was about the fact that we don't know how to predict earthquakes and in it, he criticized the Japanese government's approach to earthquake prediction research. The article was the rough draft of a controversial letter he published in *Nature*,[177] lambasting the $60 million per year earthquake prediction program of the Japanese government.

That discussion led me deeper into basic questions that I was wrestling with. Will unique natural phenomena like earthquakes, tornadoes and explosive volcanism ever be precisely predictable? Does the earth itself, the matter in which these things occur, even "know," in the sense that the future events are exactly determined by the present state of the matter? Is it possible that, in a subtle but real way, such things are alive?

I'd spent years obtaining credentials in a field dominated by scientific materialist opinions, and here a part of me was wanting to blurt out to a superior, "don't you see, ... matter is alive!" I managed to settle on the middle ground of, "I think scientists focus too much on what is known."

9: Life in the Valleys

The Great Tokai (Tokyo area[178]) earthquake is of interest to far more of us than only geophysics researchers. When the tremendous energy of this earthquake is released, it may cause major damage to the city; hundreds of thousands of deaths could be caused. Tokyo is a world financial and industrial center and, depending on the severity, timing and exact location of the quake or quakes, major disruption of the world economy could occur.[179]

Bob Geller's article argued that the Japanese earthquake prediction program was running on inertia from an outdated concept that earthquakes could be predicted from seismographic data precisely enough to evacuate or warn populations. He argued that the scientists benefiting from the program created a false belief among the Tokyo public that they would be warned a few hours before the next huge quake.

The Tokyo government has in place an entire public earthquake warning procedure. The procedure begins with six university professors on 24-hour beeper call. The professors are to be notified of anomalous seismic data and called together to decide if the public should be warned. Then, a system of radio, television and civil communications procedures is waiting to instruct the public on emergency procedures. Official posters in public places describe the warning system plans. The farcical aspect of the plan is that there is no way to decide what sort of anomalous data should require beeping the professors in the first place.

My conversations with Bob Geller occurred only a short time before my "inner quake" described above. This sort of coincidence often accompanies encounters with the collective unconscious.[180] As these experiences guided me to a newly intuitive understanding of the physical world, I became aware of the danger of arrogantly projecting an inflated image of our understanding of nature. Will more people than necessary die in a major earthquake because of a false complacency caused by scientists' holding a flawed world view? Could my own self-centered concern with how my statements will further my career indirectly endanger the lives of thousands, by contributing one more bit of complacency? Is the future time, magnitude and location of the quake predetermined exactly in the present physical state of the material earth? Are the people who will die and the lives disrupted therefore also determined? Or is there inherent indeterminacy in these things, as there is in the fundamental quantum events on which all matter depends? If there is material indeterminacy, will the event be determined purely by random and meaningless process or can there be deeper spiritual cause?

Bob's article sparked a public debate in the pages of *Nature* and a short flurry of international news coverage.[181] The issue was whether the expensive earthquake prediction program of the Japanese government is a waste of money because earthquakes are not predictable by the methods being pursued. The prediction program is based on an empirical approach. The hope of an empirical approach is that some event that occurs before earthquakes can be identified and watched for as a precursor to future quakes.

Most of the program focuses on sophisticated instrumentation such as seismographs, pressure sensors and strain sensors. A bizarre example of an earthquake detector funded by the program was a Chinese catfish in a Tokyo government office. The catfish was monitored for possibly strange behavior preceding quakes, at a cost of $60,000 per year. The motivation was probably the ancient Chinese fairy tale that the earth's crust rests on the back of a giant catfish, whose twitches cause earthquakes. In 1992, the catfish was fired for failure to predict several moderate quakes, but most of the $60 million program remained intact.

The problem with empirical methods is that most large quakes may be unique and have no consistent precursors. The scientific debate focuses on the interpretation of data, and the precision of observable quantities like seismograms. Scientists create physical models and compare these models to measurable physical quantities. If the models prove accurate enough, we can make predictions from them. The details of data interpretation and model accuracy are argued about and focused on while a major implicit assumption remains unexamined. The assumption is that macroscopic material processes—the destructive forces of earthquakes in this case—are completely predetermined material processes. The assumption is that matter is dead.

Bob Geller's argument was that the empirical method of trying to predict earthquakes is hopeless without a sound physical model on which to base the judgments. He proposed that much more of the budget should go into better understanding physical models, and that money is wasted if the approach is only empirical. The extreme case of monitoring a hapless catfish illustrates the point. Even if the fish acted strangely before a quake, we wouldn't know why it did so, and we couldn't trust that it would do so again before the next quake. A balance of physical models and empirical data is a more correct scientific approach. But an even more complete approach is to also consider information from beyond the boundaries of present science, while accepting everything science can tell us.

In the previous chapters, we showed how the assumption that matter is dead may be wrong. Improvement in our ability to monitor seismological activity and improvement in our understanding of the traditional scientific questions can only help our preparedness for earthquakes; this approach should continue to be pursued. But we should not foster a belief that all natural phenomena are entirely predetermined material processes until we've examined the belief carefully. To examine this belief is not to abandon the scientific method but to enhance our understanding of the entire picture. This question of the degree to which matter may be subtly alive is so far unexamined in the mainstream scientific literature. The few examples that do exist in the literature are largely ignored.

The arguments that follow can only be a rough first attempt to quantify the question in specific cases. The goal is to redirect some interest to this very important question of whether material phenomena can be subtly alive by means of the influence of spirit. Refinements, corrections and different approaches by other scientists would be great.

Many dissertations and rigorous studies have been done on earthquake models and seismological measurements. Many good dissertations by scientists more clever than I could also be done on the precise boundaries of determinism. (Remember that we are working with the specific definition of determinism as that aspect of the functioning of matter that is strictly predetermined by linear causality: material past causing only one possible material future not affected at all by the "no-things-in-themselves" indeterminism of quantum mechanics.)

The boundaries of determinism are also limits of predictability. For that reason alone, these studies are of more than philosophical interest. The answers to these questions have direct bearing on understanding the way matter works. The ideas presented here are not meant to be final answers, but we have to start somewhere.

Sensitive Earthquakes: A Link to Planckian Butterflies?

To what degree are the magnitude, location and time of future earthquakes predetermined by the present material state of the earth's crust and its environment? To some degree clearly they *are* predetermined. Stress builds up because of large-scale crustal plate movements. The stress must inevitably be relieved by earthquakes. But the deeper question of how much fundamental indeterminism exists in earthquakes remains to be examined.

Clearly, to some degree future earthquakes are *not* determined by the present state of the crust. Do we too rapidly accept that the indeterminacy is small and should not be considered? Our ability to measure the earth and to model it are far from the limits of determinability. But to reject the importance of the emergent spiritual effect because we cannot yet measure it, does violence to our understanding of our earth and ourselves.

My state of mind five minutes from now is largely determined by what I know and feel now, and what my senses will encounter in the meantime. But it is also largely *undetermined* because of the complexity of mind functioning. To what degree are the exact time, location and magnitude of a future earthquake similarly undetermined by its own complexity?

The microphysics and macrophysics that go into a given actual earthquake are extremely complex. On the largest scales, the basic concepts are simple. The motions of the earth's fluid mantle push on the crustal plates, causing stress to build up. The stress builds up until it is stronger than the friction on preexisting faults. The plates then move, causing an earthquake.

On finer scales, the process is much more complex. There are tiny and large movements, stresses and strains, pressures, flows, frictions, waves, heat flows, crystalline phase changes, chemical reactions, electromagnetic fluctuations and more. The preexisting faults are actually extremely complex systems of cracks existing on all size and length scales. Consider descending, with your mind, to the smallest precisions of size and time scales in an earthquake zone. The complexities of an earthquake at some level of detail will be as great as the complexity of the chemical, electromagnetic, and neural processes that determine our own thoughts.

Physicist Per Bak has studied how "large interactive systems perpetually organize themselves to a critical state in which a minor event starts a chain reaction that can lead to a catastrophe."[182] These systems behave entirely differently than the near-equilibrium models with which scientists tried, and failed, to explain things in the past. Bak and others propose a theory called "self-organized criticality" to model these systems. They demonstrate with experiments and models that many basic systems of geology, economics, biology and meteorology show signs of self-organized criticality. They show that earthquakes especially exhibit signs of self-organized criticality.

In self-organized criticality, "composite systems naturally evolve to a critical state in which a minor event starts a chain reaction that can affect any number of elements in the system." This means that a large earthquake, at an earthquake-prone fault, may be triggered by a tiny event. Just how tiny? As tiny as can be, because in self-organized criticality, the system is already critical—ready to go at the slightest touch. This doesn't mean that it is cocked like a hair-trigger gun and will necessarily fire at the next twitch. It is critical on all size scales; the tiny event may trigger a tiny quake or it may trigger a giant quake. Many tiny quakes occur between each large quake.

In a self-organized critical system, it could be possible to predict whether a given trigger will cause a small local quake, but a catastrophic quake cannot be precisely predicted. The catastrophic events depend on the history of the entire system and are too complex to predict. Self-organized criticality is still a deterministic theory, however, because each of the composite self-critical elements behaves according to the classical mechanistic laws of physics. So, though we can't predict catastrophes, the system itself "knows" what sort of triggers will create catastrophes.

Are the tiny triggers where the Planckian butterflies can come into play—where metaphysics, as well as physics, comes into play? In systems as large as earthquake zones, "tiny" is still not anywhere near as small as the quantum mechanical size. We might demur at this discrepancy. But we've determined to get some idea of just where spirit might meet matter in earthquakes, so let's continue.

What kind of earthquake triggers are we talking about? Little fluctuations (changes) in pressure, velocity, or density of tiny pieces of the crust at or near the earthquake fault. Now remember from Chapter 7 how physicist David Ruelle showed the extreme sensitivity of fluctuation in a turbulent fluid to events as small as the quantum jumps of an electron. Ruelle showed, with scientific rigor, that the millimeter-scale structure in a turbulent fluid is altered within a minute due to *the gravitational force of removing an electron from the edge of the universe!* He showed that turbulence on the scale of kilometers is similarly affected in a few hours.

In a self-organized critical earthquake zone, fluctuations on the order of a millimeter to a meter should be plenty large enough to cause the difference between a catastrophic quake and a minor quake. The rock in an earthquake zone is not a turbulent fluid, but fluctuating physical processes similar enough to turbulence occur. As in a turbulent fluid, small changes in these complex interacting perturbations (jiggles) rapidly grow into large changes. Also, much larger perturbations than removing an electron from the edge of the universe are caused by local quantum events.

For instance, much of the rock is in crystalline states and a sort of vibration or sound wave called a "phonon" travels through crystals. Tiny phonons are created and altered by tiny quantum fluctuations in the vibrational and rotational states of the rock molecules. Atoms and molecules are never still; they jiggle, vibrate and rotate; their rotational and vibrational states are quantized and they constantly jump among neighboring quantum states. The timing of these jumps is subject to the same quantum indeterminacy described in Chapter 6.

The precise movements and strengths of the phonons, bouncing off crystalline imperfections, can be expected to be as sensitive to "initial conditions" (that portion of the state of matter which is undetermined because of its quantum nature) as the molecules bouncing off each other in Ruelle's turbulent fluid. So the inherent quantum uncertainty or "unknowingness" in the vibrational states of the rock molecules becomes large uncertainty (millimeter-scale) in the vibrational structure of the rocks themselves in only a few minutes. These larger vibrational states may then provide the tiniest triggers for the cascade of self-organized critical earthquakes.

Crystalline vibrational modes are only one of the myriad small-scale events that may cause the triggers. In summary, extremely tiny quantum fluctuations alter the evolution of larger elements through chaotic sensitivity to initial conditions, until tiny but macroscopic fluctuations occur in a few minutes. Then these fluctuations trigger catastrophic events through self-organized criticality. Thus our best physical models of earthquakes indicate that the Great Tokai earthquake may be poised in self-organized criticality, ready to go in a few hours from now or a few years from now.

The whole spectrum of possibilities is contained within the uncertainty of the present state of the matter. The Planckian butterflies, by choosing the quantum fluctuations, could "decide" to cause the quake anytime, within that window of uncertainty, without violating the known laws of physics. So if there is something more, if there is a spiritual dimension that does sometimes choose among the possibilities inherent in matter, then the job of really understanding earthquakes is not complete until the spiritual aspect is considered.

Volcanoes

Minutes before the eruption, a camera crew shot the last footage of a young volcanologist: Harry Glicken. He and a famous volcanologist couple from France were taking samples and observing on the slopes of Mount Unzen in southern Honshu, Japan. Harry was excited. He was doing what he loved. He moved quickly and talked as he scooped fresh, unadulterated samples of volcanic ash—the hardest kind to sample—into sample bags. Such fresh samples provide important data for scientific models of volcanic eruptions. Aware of the danger, he glanced at the camera crew, indicating they really shouldn't be there, and they should run at the first sign of unusual volcanic activity.

Suddenly a rare type of explosive eruption, called pyroclastic flow, released thousands of tons of superheated rock, ash and gas. The eruption was by far the largest of the series that had been rocking Unzen. The hellish mixture roared thousands of feet down the mountain and into the air at speeds over 100 miles per hour. Harry and his colleagues would have known for at least several seconds what was going to happen. The explosive cloud was so large they probably didn't even try to run. The three volcanologists, several reporters and villagers—43 people in all—died in moments.

Ten years before his death, Harry's first research advisor came to relieve Harry on his watch at their observing post on Mount St. Helens. After a routine change of shift, Harry headed down the mountain. A few hours later, Mount St. Helens exploded. Harry's advisor was killed when an entire side of the mountain slid over him.

Harry became scientifically dedicated and personally obsessed with understanding volcanoes. He was nagged by the apparent randomness of why his advisor was killed and not he. A month before he went to Unzen, I rode with Harry on an express train from Tsukuba Science City to Tokyo. He talked about the difficulty of finding research funds and good research posts. His scientific dedication and focus were clear. Unaccustomed to my own new views on the limitations of experimental science and the inadequacy of the materialist world view, I didn't mention my strong interest in these questions to Harry, and our conversation stayed on a "lower" level of aliveness. A month later, when I heard his name on the evening news and saw the horrific videos of Unzen's eruption, I remembered our conversation and I regretted my hesitation.

Volcano predictors have been more successful than earthquake predictors. If magma is observed rising rapidly into the rock beneath a volcanic crater, volcanologists can give a good indication of whether a series of eruptions is likely in the near future. The sort of explosive volcanism that killed Harry, however, is much less predictable. At the top of Mount Unzen a volcanic bulge formed. Inside the bulge, magma and superheated gases were rising under pressure from below. The outside of the bulge cooled to a rigid rock shell riddled with cracks as the bulge expanded.

As the bulge grew, pieces of it would fall off. When this happened, part of the magma and gases were suddenly exposed to the cool air. A combination of explosive thermal and chemical processes then caused an explosion that blew superheated rock and gas (pyroclastic flow) down the mountain and into the air. The process of small, large and catastrophic pyroclastic flows breaking off the volcanic bulge is very likely governed by self-organized criticality.

9: Life in the Valleys

The same sort of highly sensitive triggers that cause earthquakes determine the exact timing and size of the pyroclastic flows. The subtle shifts in the cool outer shell of the volcanic bulge occur by processes very similar to earthquakes. The same sort of cascade—molecular quantum fluctuations altering larger but still tiny material fluctuations, finally triggering the start of a cascade of triggers leading to a pyroclastic explosion—would determine the difference between a catastrophic flow and a small flow. The whole cascade, from complete indeterminism to catastrophe, would be as short as a few minutes.

In this model, the explosion that killed Harry and his colleagues was only one of a large number of possible scenarios. In some scenarios, they would have been safe. The best current models agree that such a wide range of possibilities is the case. The old paradigm of mechanistic science assumes that randomness determines which of the possibilities happen. The hylozoic paradigm recognizes that there may be deeper cause. The Planckian butterflies may "decide" which possibility to make happen.

The Weather

Journalist James Gleick, in his report on the development of chaos theory,[183] considers the example of global weather prediction. The weather is modeled with supercomputers at the National Center for Atmospheric Research (NCAR) in Boulder, Colorado. A global grid of input parameters such as temperature, pressure, humidity and wind velocity are input into the computers. The finest-meshed grid for global weather computing now in use is about sixty miles between data points, and a few layers vertically in the atmosphere, all over the Earth. The mathematical equations known to govern the weather are then "run" by the computer, on the input data, to predict the future weather. The calculations are difficult and time-consuming. The massive supercomputers at NCAR are just faster than, but less accurate than, the actual evolution of the weather. For major climate trends, the model predictions are pretty good up to a couple of days ahead.

The sensitive dependence on initial conditions, however, causes the predictions to become useless for more than a few days ahead. A finer-scale grid and faster computers can improve the accuracy of the predictions somewhat, but the sensitivity of the chaotic weather and climate always will cause the predictions to err much more rapidly than if the weather were governed by simple nonchaotic processes.

Gleick uses the example of a very fine global weather mesh of data sensors one foot apart all over the globe and up into the atmosphere to illustrate the importance of chaos dynamics. To appreciate the way the model simulates the actual weather, imagine the large matrix of sensors. Now imagine taking data from the grid of sensors, and feeding the information into an imaginary "hyper-supercomputer." The computer inputs the data into equations known to exactly describe the way the weather evolves, and computes the future weather. In about a minute, small fluctuations between our sensors, which we could not have measured, spread to fluctuations more than a foot across, already causing minute errors in the predictions. In a few hours, these fluctuations spread to kilometer-scale errors just like in David Ruelle's turbulent fluid example. In a couple of days, local predictions of rain or sun will be in error. In a few days large climate systems will be unpredictable and in weeks the global climate is unpredictable.

The point of chaos theory is that there is nothing wrong with the equations in our computer. They mimic the evolution of the weather perfectly. The weather itself is just extremely sensitive to very small fluctuations. As our imaginary experiment with weather forecasting shows, weather's sensitivity forever dooms certain types of forecasting because we will never be able to measure accurately enough or compute fast enough.

The hylozoic paradigm, though, goes a giant step further, beyond the limitations of the practicality of computing the future. The hylozoic paradigm recognizes that very significant future events are more than uncomputable: the future is not completely contained in the present material state of the universe. In fact, it may be that the future is *created* by the influence of spirit, within the wide range of possibilities allowed by matter.

To appreciate this, we can repeat our imaginary weather forecasting experiment on a deeper level. This time, imagine sensors on the molecular and atomic scale. Imagine that somehow we can sense the exact condition of every atom in the atmosphere right now. We sense the excitation levels of the electrons, the vibrational states of molecules, quantum rotational states, velocities, everything.

We remember, from Chapter 6, that much of what we sense can only be quantum probabilities of possible ranges of states. Quantum mechanics tells us that this quantum uncertainty is more than an inability to sense more accurately. It is an actual nonexistence of an exact state of the atoms themselves. Our sensors sense everything that can be known, and everything that the material atoms *are*.

Then we feed this data into our "hyper-hyper-supercomputer." Never mind that a machine powerful enough could never be built, even in theory. We are not doing engineering. We want to know how the universe works. Now, a very subtle but important glitch occurs. To proceed with its calculations, the computer needs to decide which of those uncertain quantum states the atoms are actually in.

When a real atom bumps into another atom, that atom "observes" the first one and causes it suddenly to be in one or the other of its uncertain vibrational states. Our computer can't know which state and must pick at random. The random choices of the computer will be slightly different than the actual choices of the atoms themselves, causing a tiny error in the first prediction of the computer. Then, again as in Ruelle's turbulent fluid, these small errors rapidly propagate into kilometer-scale errors in our weather prediction after only a few days.[184]

These "errors" in our imaginary most-accurate-possible weather predictions are unavoidable. The predictions depict one of the many possible weather futures. There is a large spectrum of possible weather futures allowed by matter. Our prediction selects one of those possible futures. The weather itself selects another one of the possible futures.

Experimental/predictive science cannot tell us whether Planckian butterflies in the atmosphere choose among the possible weather futures, or if the choice is purely random. Will a new science, operating under the hylozoic paradigm, be able to tell us? We don't know. We do know the old science can't tell us. We should at least try the new.

The "Clockwork" Motions of the Planets

At a large meeting of astronomers in October, 1991, Massachusetts Institute of Technology physicist Jack Wisdom revealed an astonishing result of his calculations concerning the orbits of planets.[185] "A small comet hitting the planet Pluto now could cause an ice age on Earth a hundred million years from now." This result is astonishing because Pluto is a very small planet very far from Earth, and until recently Pluto was considered totally irrelevant to the motion of Earth or any events on Earth.

Wisdom's calculations showed that the orbits of the planets in our solar system are chaotic. Before you quit your job in anticipation of the Earth crashing into the Sun, be assured that the Earth will travel around the Sun this year almost identically to the way it did last year. Chaos theory and butterfly effects aren't going to allow us, or spirit, to sail the planet about the galaxy willy-nilly. We've seen that the Planckian butterflies may affect earthquakes, volcanoes and weather on human time scales; but how possibly could they affect the orbits of planets?

To appreciate the distances in the solar system, find a small marble-sized object to represent the Earth. Place a bowling ball at your feet to be the sun, and the marble thirty yards away for the proper distance scale. The planet Pluto would be the size of a pinhead ten football fields away.

Jack Wisdom has a special computer that does nothing but simulate the paths of all the planets around the sun as they pull ever so slightly on each other. Kepler's solution for the orbit of one planet around a star stood for over four hundred years. The solution for the orbits of two or more planets together cannot be found.

Since Newton, astronomers have been able to calculate that the orbits of Earth and the other planets would change only very slowly, and essentially not change at all over hundreds of thousands of years. Except on long time scales, the planetary orbits are very similar to the simple case of a single planet orbiting a single star, seemingly as dependable as clockwork. However, the longer-term evolution of the solar system was not known. Now, Jack Wisdom has shown that the orbits of the planets are subtly chaotic and hence highly sensitive to small perturbations.

Wisdom has so far only been able to track the solar system backward about one fifth of its age, a billion years. In that time, the basic orbital paths of Earth and the other major planets change only slightly, but the path of Pluto changes a lot. More importantly, the obliquities (tilt of the spin axes) of all the planets change a lot.

Studies of the Earth's climate history tell us that changes in the Earth's obliquity cause major ice age periods. (Short ice ages seem to happen any time, but major ice age periods depend on the obliquity.) The changes in obliquity, over hundreds of millions of years, are caused by the subtle gravitational pulls of all the planets on each other. Even the pull of tiny Pluto is important.

Wisdom's calculations can show how much the orbits change, but can't track the actual planet motions exactly because of other unmodeled and unmodelable effects. (Like our hypothetical weather forecast could show one of the possible weather futures but could not show the exact one.)

During times as long as hundreds of millions of years, all the planets are pelted by small comets and asteroids, like the famous one that apparently killed the dinosaurs on Earth sixty million years ago. The calculations do show that the effect of a small comet hitting Pluto would change Pluto's orbit enough to pull on all the other planets' orbits and so change the obliquity of Earth enough to cause a major ice age a hundred million years later.

These orbits, though, seem far removed from spirit or Planckian butterflies. But perhaps not. Consider: where do comets come from? They fall into the inner solar system from the outer reaches of the sun's gravitational influence, a hundred times again as far as Pluto. The comets were thrown out there at the very beginning of the solar system.

Comets are big ice balls that formed between Jupiter and Neptune at the same time as the planets and the sun formed, about five billion years ago. All of these—planets, sun, and comets—formed from the gravitational collapse of a featureless cloud of gas and tiny dust particles. The cloud first collapsed into a swirling disk, kind of like the rings of Saturn, around a central blob. The central blob became the sun and the planets and comets accreted in the disk. Most of the comets—trillions of them[186]—were slung out of the solar system by the gravitational slingshot effect of the planets.

A small fraction of the comets were slung to the edge of the solar system. They hang there, like a punted football at the top of its path, for billions of years. Some of them are perturbed ever so slightly by galactic gravitational pulls and fall back toward the planets. A few of those that fall back hit Pluto. If they hit Pluto just right, they cause an ice age on Earth a hundred million years later.

The comets formed from kilometer-scale fluctuations in the turbulent planet-forming disk of gas and dust. The present best evidence indicates that this happened during about a hundred thousand, or a million, years. David Ruelle's turbulent fluid analysis showed that quantum fluctuations can affect kilometer-scale turbulence after a few hours. A tiny change in where and when a comet forms, before it is slung to the edge of the solar system, will determine whether it will hit Pluto a few billion years later. Thus it may be that the Planckian butterflies decide on the sequence of major ice ages on Earth, during the birth of the solar system, by tweaking the formation of the myriad comets.

To appreciate further this sort of cosmic-scale no-things-in-themselves principle, do the following thought experiment. In your imagination, go back to that turbulent planet-forming disk of gas, dust and the featureless cloud from which it collapsed. The formation of the planets from this matter is basically understood by mechanistic science, in broad principle. Even such basic aspects as the future orbits of the planets, though, are not determined, not existing, in the state of the matter from which they form. It would be absurd to claim that the utterly more sensitive weather, earthquakes, volcanoes and other natural phenomena here on Earth now are determined in that initial turbulent disk.

I have given rough estimates of the rapidity with which spirit can affect material outcomes. More precise calculations may show that it happens more or less quickly. But the argument can only be about degree. That the emergence from nonexistence to actuality occurs on many time and size scales, and affects to some extent essentially all complex real world phenomena, is without doubt.

The same sort of emergence we traced for the formation of comets in our solar system can be traced for the collapse of galactic gas clouds to form solar systems, the clumping of giant gas clouds in the galaxy into smaller gas clouds, the formation of the galaxy itself, and other galaxies.

All these processes are contained within the known equations of physics. There is no deep mystery about them in that sense. The emergence into actuality of one from among the myriad possibilities, at each time, in each place, is where the mystery is tremendous. That emergent possibility is where spirit can create effect, and where spirit can create effect is what we call "alive." The weather, earthquakes and volcanoes may be alive in ways that profoundly affect us on human time scales. The Earth may be alive in ways that affect earthquakes, volcanoes and climate. The solar system may be alive in ways that affect the long-term evolution of the planets. The galaxy may be alive in ways that affect the evolution of the solar system.

"Just Because We Can't Predict Tornadoes Doesn't Mean the World Isn't Round."

That quote was made by celebrated astrophysicist David Schram,[187] discussing the great unsolved problems of science. Characteristic of the defense of a dying paradigm, that quote combines implicit ridicule, assertion of authority, and lack of clarity. The dynamics of tornadoes are poorly understood, but it is likely tornadoes are among the most sensitive weather phenomena, highly sensitive to the affects of Planckian butterflies or whatever you want to call spirit. Schram's quote implies that to even consider spirit is to regress to prescientific beliefs, when "the world wasn't round," and thus be subject to ridicule. The statement is asserted in the vaguest manner, with an air as if it were not worth considering.

Presumably a topic considered more worthy than the mysteries in our immediate presence is the theory of the Big Bang, which is associated with the origin of the universe. The Big Bang is an event as far removed in space and time, from us here now, as one can get. The cultural forces that celebrate the assertion that the only remaining mystery is the Big Bang, are likely the same cultural forces that make spirituality something to be endured from a preacher on Sunday, or something attained only once by an ancient near-mythical teacher, completely removed from ordinary life. These are the cultural aspects that will require a transformative crisis before they can accept the hylozoic paradigm.

It is becoming clearer that those scientists who refuse to consider the hylozoic paradigm will either go the way of papal pronouncements on science—maintaining irrelevant pockets of authority—or they will go the way of 19th century skeptics who refused to "believe that rocks could fall from the heavens." These skeptics were talking about meteorites. Conservative rationalist skeptics play a useful mediating role in change. Convincing skeptics is a challange. If we stoop to skeptic-bashing, we've failed; we may note that no less a great thinker than Thomas Jefferson was one vocal nonbeliever in meteorites.[188]

The analogy of meteorite awareness is apt because we came to accept the reality of meteorite falls through an increase of sensitivity. In the 18th and early 19th centuries most scientists, and generally educated people like Jefferson, did not believe that rocks fell from the sky.[189]

As the world became more populous and more connected by communications and travel, the populations became more aware of the scientific worldview. This knowledgeable populace became, among many other things, a sort of planetary meteorite detector. More and more meteors and meteorite falls were reported, and meteorite samples examined, until the evidence became overwhelming. Even the skeptics began to accept that rocks fall from the heavens. Now, specialized radar can detect hundreds of tiny meteors, smaller than visible size, per day, and thousands of meteorite samples have been collected in the Antarctic where they are easy to spot.[190]

Similar to the way in which we became sensitive to the fact of meteorite falls, increasing knowledge of, and sensitivity to, spiritual experience is stimulating acceptance of the hylozoic paradigm. As two centuries ago, reputable people and even scientists began to report seeing meteorites falling, today reputable people and even scientists are beginning to report their encounters with spirit. We can't know what sort of techniques and technologies of the future will emerge to bring us closer to knowing spirit. But it's time to start looking for ways because technically the materialist paradigm is bumping up against its own limits, and because the indiscriminate use of the fruits of materialist science are threatening our future.

Concerning the foundations of physics, another celebrated physicist said, with the characteristic humility of celebrated physicists, "the difference between physics and mathematics is like the difference between sex and masturbation."[191] Mathematics can be as profound and beautiful as any other art, but it is only concerned with abstract symbology. Physics applies mathematical understanding to the real world —to matter.

Physics has done very well at discovering just how matter works, but there are growing bodies of evidence indicating that the functioning of the real world requires more than matter alone. Scientists who ignore this confine themselves to nothing more than a sort of restricted mathematics, removed from much of the subtle functioning of the real world, and not very advanced mathematics at that. Scientists who accept the hylozoic paradigm will accept the challenge and embrace of the real world.

Just Turn Off the Terminals and See What Happens

How will the new hylozoic paradigm emerge? I don't know. I'll discuss possibilities later, but let me offer a story from my experience as a possible metaphor for the emerging sensitivity that will be required. In my second year at graduate school, I was transferred to an office with two older graduate students. As usual when we enter new environments there was adjustment stress. They were Ph.D. candidates; I was a lowly new student. I was still taking courses; they were already doing research and publishing papers. They were experts in the upper atmosphere; I planned to study the rings of Saturn. The major stressor however was our different relationships to the computer graphics terminals. I would turn them on only when necessary and make sure they were off when nobody was using them. They hated to wait the thirty seconds for the terminals to warm up, so they liked to keep them on all the time.

We had big old-fashioned, industrial-type graphics terminals that made a terrible racket. Many large electronic machines, especially older TVs, computer terminals and fluorescent lighting systems emit a very high-pitched hum. The frequency of this hum is just beyond the hearing range of most people. But a few percent, perhaps ten percent, of people hear it quite clearly and some people are quite bothered by it. I happen to be one such hearer. Before I realized this,

I often felt mysteriously unsettled in shopping malls, and around large TV's and computer terminals. When I realized that a racket that most people didn't even hear was the source of disturbance, I was relieved and better able to deal with the stresses. Those graphics terminals were like dog whistles. I was the dog, squirming in irritation at my desk, while my office mates heard nothing.

I tended to work late at night in my new office and turn off the idle computer terminals that were like noise machines to me. My senior office mates would arrive in the morning and be annoyed to have to wait for their terminals to warm up. This tension continued for a couple of weeks until one of them brought in a new shortwave radio he was playing with. Tuning in a distant signal, he got only noise.

Being experts in the physics of the upper atmosphere, they said, "must be a lot of turbulence in the K band today." A certain layer in the upper atmosphere is called the K band, and has properties such that shortwave electromagnetic signals normally bounce off the layer making distant reception possible. I, aware that those graphics terminals were electromagnetic noise machines as well as audible noise machines, suggested, "It might be these terminals."

"No, idle terminals couldn't create such strong interference," they assured me, and they continued to fiddle with the radio and theorize about atmospheric disturbances.

"Just turn off the terminals, and see what happens," I finally piped up.

When we clicked off the last terminal, the radio came in crystal clear. After that, they had more tolerance for my sensitivity to terminal noise.

The hylozoic paradigm will become accepted through new appreciations of sensitivity to spirit. That's what the hylozoic paradigm is: the acceptance that matter can be and is affected by spirit. How this sensitivity will be documented, observed, accepted and used is the problem waiting for solutions. Most likely, the indications will be closer to home than expected. Spirit will probably not be seen in the mathematics of Big Bang cosmology but in something like undeniably sensing the emotional/mental states of those around us in ways clearly beyond anything explained by physical models. Or spirit may be seen in sensing the connection of our own bodies and

9: Life in the Valleys

minds to nature, or a growing awareness of our own spiritual souls. A more complete appreciation for the openness of "valley-type" material processes to the effects of spirit allows us to accept, conceptually, these connections.

The tools of materialist paradigm science can help us intellectually understand, but the connections to spirit will probably be made in unanticipated ways. These ways will probably be much closer to home than expected, and often closer than is comfortable. Hylozoic paradigm examples of, "Just turn off the terminals and see what happens," are likely to be suggestions like, "Just stop thinking and try to sense your environment, your self, other people, the weather," or, "See what happens when your body and mind are completely still," or, "Find out what thought is, find out what fear is." The signals that come in, sometimes, might just be crystal clear.

Nature Spirits

Does the hylozoic paradigm advocate a "return to superstition"? Absolutely not. Superstition is the irrational fear of something unknown or mysterious. The hylozoic paradigm suggests that mechanistic paradigm believers reject, sometimes out of irrational fear, that mystery exists. The mechanistic paradigm is thus a superstition because, as we have been describing, mystery abounds. The hylozoic paradigm is more encompassing than the mechanistic paradigm. The hylozoic paradigm accepts everything materialist paradigm science gives us, accepts that science restricted by the materialist paradigm has limits and that there may be something beyond those limits.

Does the hylozoic paradigm believe that "nature spirits" exist? Yes, in the sense that nature spirits are whatever causes the third level of matter (described in Chapter 8) to affect the second level. The mechanistic (hylostochastic) paradigm is the belief that the nature spirits generate only random and meaningless process. The hylozoic paradigm doesn't specify whether they are only random or are sometimes purposive. The nature spirits may even be conscious Planckian butterflies, actively choosing from among the immensity of possible futures allowed by matter. The hylozoic paradigm doesn't constrain our investigation but urges us to find out what the nature spirits are.

10. Consciousness Not Explained

In the previous chapter we presented arguments that "natural phenomena" might be highly complex interactions of matter and spirit. The primary perspective of this book is that the truths of physics show that the question whether spirit and matter act in concert, or whether matter alone acts, is an important open question. I hope we have finally established that main point.

So, those readers still with us can be considered to share the common perspective that there is a profound open question in our, Western, view of our world—whether spirit and matter both act in nature, or whether matter acts alone. In this chapter, we extend the same question to include an especially odd hunk of matter—the human brain.

Some Facts about the Brain

The human brain weighs about three pounds. It consists of billions of nerve cells interconnected by hundreds of billions of synapses. The synapses in turn have variable shapes and connection networks that change over time. Malleable protein molecules mediate the electrical signals running around in the synapses. It is estimated that the brain depends on at least 10 trillion operations (of some sort) per second when thinking.[192] Brain function—memory, thinking, emoting, dreaming, creating, etc.—depends on some combination, as yet unknown, of electrical signals passing through the synaptic circuits, changes in the circuit structure, and chemical changes in the molecules themselves. It is very, very complex.

Brain waves are rough measures of the gross electrical behavior of the brain. Statistical studies of the brain wave electroencephalograms measured by electroencephalograph machines show that the familiar signatures of chaotic dynamical systems occur in brain waves. This chaotic signature indicates that brain function is at least in part chaotic. Some of brain function can be described by the mathematics of deterministic chaos. Also, the physical component of mentation (mind functioning) is not contained only in the brain. The whole nervous system, and its related sensory apparatus, is involved in thinking and mental processes. And these other parts of the nervous system also involve chaotic processes. For instance the heart, and the nerves controlling it, has a chaotic component to its rhythms (this recent discovery has advanced the understanding of heart attack mechanisms).[193] Probably even individual nerve cells have chaotic aspects to their rhythms.

The nervous system is not only extremely complex, it is also infused with chaotic sensitive dependence on initial conditions. As in the natural phenomena considered in the previous chapter, real-world brain functioning is a highly sensitive and complex and unique event. The gross matter of the brain has set itself up to have exponential increase of emergence, through sensitive dependence on initial conditions. The emergence of mind-brain functioning occurs in many ways, at many levels of functioning with varying complexity. The exponential growth of possibilities (thought of in reverse) brings us rapidly down to the level of Planckian butterflies, or prana, or lifetrons. We'll return to this point later in this chapter. For now, let's review the tenets of Dennett's models of consciousness, and why he considers "consciousness explained."

Cognitive Models—Open or Closed?

There are many brain researchers and many consciousness researchers. In actuality, their opinions on the basic question we are considering range from the staunch materialist to the complete transcendentalist. Since Dennett in his book claims that his completely materialist perspective represents the orthodox ontology, we take his arguments as the standard model. Dennett does not attempt the sort of ground-up, building-block model, of brain function that we started above.

A complete model in that vein—starting with a bunch of atomic elements, combined into biological molecules, functioning as cells, that behave in such a way as to determine all of human functioning—is far beyond present knowledge, if indeed it is possible at all. Dennett's axiom is that such a conceptual model *is* a complete representation of human beings. He believes that the constituent atoms, molecules, proteins, cells, synapses, emotions, and mentations, behave in deterministic mechanistic ways. He states his mechanistic beliefs quite clearly. His models do contain some random behavior, so we assume he is hylostochastic in his mechanism—that is, deterministic with a little randomness.

Starting with Dennett's axiom of materialistic mechanism, the rest of his book sets out to justify it. He does not, however, build his mind-brain from first principles of physics (if it were possible to do this, that would be the closest possible proof). Instead Dennett introduces a series of sophisticated philosophical arguments meant to model some of the components of mind functioning—sensation, cognition, comprehension, ratiocination. I found these descriptive models interesting, and convincing. For our purposes, there is no reason to review details of his models. For even if they are correct in essence, they only bolster the emerging hylozoic view of brain-mind functioning.

In the hylozoic view of brain-mind functioning, thought *is* a material process—just as Dennett describes. Call this deterministic, material entity that does the thinking, the "ego." Models, such as those described by Dennett, show how active thinking, usual cognition, even emoting, can be entirely material processes. The point of the hylozoic paradigm is that the material aspect is only part of the story, and that the brain-machine is not a closed system.

Let's go back to the basics about this issue. Postulate, for the moment, that there is both spirit and matter, as described already in this book. On a basic level, we know that the brain can be entirely devoid of spirit. For example, a recently dead brain can be thought of as devoid of spiritual component. But a dead brain presumably also has no ego. One step up from a dead brain, perhaps a living brain may have an ego but still be entirely devoid of any influence of any sort of spirit (or Planckian butterflies, or prana, or lifetrons). Even at this level we may have a problem because the matter (the atoms) necessarily functions in a way that nondeterministic properties are present (as described in detail in previous chapters). But assume that the nondeterministic aspects are entirely random (the hylostochastic paradigm). Then we can conceive of a living brain, with an ego, and entirely without influence from spirit—this is what is described by the Dennett models. The only difference between Dennett's mechanistic perspective and the hylozoic view is that the hylozoic paradigm indicates that such a living brain with ego is an open system. It is open to the possible influence of spirit.

Models such as Dennett's are essentially plausibility arguments. Plausibility arguments are useful but not always definitive tools in science. Astronomers for instance, when they are trying to understand how distant astronomical phenomena work, need to distinguish between theories that are merely plausible, and theories that are plausible and also likely. In practice this determination is much harder in astronomy than in the laboratory sciences, because you can't study astronomical events, neutron stars, say, in the laboratory. We can only watch them at a distance. For that reason, many highly complex astronomical phenomena have yielded only to a wide variety of plausible explanations, but not to a generally accepted model.

Those mysterious astronomical phenomena are far less complex than the human mind. And the human mind similarly cannot be studied in the laboratory. Of course, some of the most rudimentary sensory and cognitive functions can be studied by experiment. But extrapolating from them to the full-blown human mind in all cases, is like extrapolating from laboratory studies of simple molecules to a complete understanding of galaxy formation—it is not possible.

Dennett's models make the case that it is plausible that a living brain with ego present can be no different from a dead brain—that is, functioning entirely without spirit. Sure, that is plausible, but is there any evidence that it is also true in all cases? Is there any evidence that a nonmaterial component does not, sometimes, play some role?

There is absolutely no inconsistency of the mechanistic sensory and cognitive models with the hylozoic view. This sort of model in fact is essentially what the spiritual teachers have described. They say that our usual state of self-centered ego-affixed consciousness is mostly devoid of spirit. The goal of spiritual practice, they say, is to attune the nervous system to a state where it can be sensitive to the very subtle influences of spirit. And that state, all spiritual traditions say, is beyond thought. In Zen, they say it is beyond "no-mind." One of the basic Sufi practices is to silently chant (the Arabic equivalent of) "the subtle, the subtle, the subtle is God." The Zen practice is to repeat the word "mu" (void, not, nothing, absence) as if it were a question that can be answered from the void.

J. Krishnamurti worked toward the same ends by dialogues—repeatedly pointing the egoic mind toward its limits—hoping that a momentary opening to the subtle may be glimpsed. (Krishnamurti actually felt that the chanting sort of meditations usually lead to a sort of deluded stupor.) Our point is not to advocate a certain technique. As Krishnamurti so emphasized, techniques often are barriers. The point is that normal material mind functioning may actually be capable of opening to, at least momentary, coherence with the beyond material, the spiritual. And from those rare openings have come the origins of all the great spiritual traditions, and indeed all truly compassionate human functioning—so the hylozoic model goes.

Of course, Dennett does not even consider these expanded possibilities. He starts with the axiom that connection with the transcendent is impossible. The problem is not with Dennett's sophisticated models of cognition—they are very good models. The problem is that his fundamental axiom is wrong.

Computer Fear

While Dennett approaches the materialistic model of mind functioning from the philosophical direction, some computer researchers do so in an applied way. One camp of artificial intelligence researchers believes that human mental functioning is entirely mechanistic, and so machines can eventually be built that will behave and think in exactly the same manner as humans do. An instructive example is the idea of building a robot, with a computer brain, that will "feel" and act on fear.

Consider a simple ambulatory robot, built in an upstairs laboratory. Such robots that can wander around on their own, and identify and plug into electrical outlets when they are "hungry" have already been constructed. A next step toward instilling human-like (or at least animal-like) qualities in the robot is incorporating fear of destruction. The robot might wander into an open stairwell, perhaps thinking there is a tasty electrical outlet there, and fall down the steps to its demise. So, for the robot's computer brain, researchers envision creating sophisticated programs that can recognize when its television-camera eyes spy a stairwell. Then a very complex and sophisticated set of interactions between rudimentary sensors (pressure feelers, probes, and spatial measurers) might be devised to allow the robot to test whether in fact it is a stairwell or something that just looks sort of like a stairwell—such as a hallway.

There would always be some uncertainty in the determination, and so some internal decision in the robot's program must decide how much uncertainty to accept. That measure of acceptable uncertainty is also an inverse measure of the fear of that particular robot. Very fearful robots would never go near anything. They wouldn't even amble down a hallway, for fear it might be a stairwell. Fearless robots would be much more adventuresome, and a few would occasionally fall down a stairwell, thinking it just might be a strange sort of hallway.

Such a demonstration is an entirely mechanistic analog of what we experience as fear. The robot's external actions are very similar to a fearful person's. Even the robot's internal experience might seem similar to our own.

This example also leads to seeing how, in the hylozoic idea, the nonmechanistic aspect of mind functioning can also come into play. Fear is a response in favor of preservation. I don't want to fall down a stairwell because I might cease to exist. As our robot friend illustrated, it is plausible that fears related to simple bodily preservation are plausibly an entirely mechanistic process. But there is another sort of fear. There is existential fear.

Existential fear is fear of knowing that which exists. Existential fear is similar in concept to fear for bodily preservation. To understand existential fear, first consider what it is that is doing the fearing. It is the sense of "me" that comes from accumulated memories, concepts, beliefs, ideas, and self-images, that is doing the fearing. It is the same self-image that fears death. The fear of death, though, is hard to untangle from the fear for bodily preservation. Existential fear occurs not only in relation to death, but also in the moment, right now.

Assume that Dennett is right—that this fearing self-image, this little egoic self-identity (us), is the result of sophisticated mechanistic feedback loops, accumulated sensory memories, reactive image construction, and the like. All are entirely material processes.

Assume also that there is a realm of existence related to spirit (as defined in this book), and that the material mind can, under certain circumstances, possibly experience some sort of contact with this nonmaterial aspect. Would the material mind want to make such contact? No, for two reasons.

First, it is highly conditioned to resist fundamental change, out of self-preservation. ("Do not fall down stairwells.") The nonmaterial aspect of existence, if it exists, is by definition going to be very different from the material, and so contact with it might cause radical change to the material mind—changes of belief, self-image, even self-identity. So the material mind fears such contact.

Second, the special circumstance under which the contact can be made, the spiritual traditions tell us, is detachment from the material self-image in the first place. Such detachment is, from the material mind's perspective, a sort of momentary death. The ego does not want to do that—"do not fall down those stairs." Existential fear is fear of knowing the totality of existence. It is attachment to the partiality of the egoic self-image. In robot-computer terms it is fear of software change. If you have a meditative contact with the transcendent, your body is not going to explode. That would be a hardware change. Your mind, your self-image, might change, however. That's a software change.

So, the mechanisms of fear, especially existential fear, are examples of the hylozoic view of consciousness. Mind functioning may be largely modeled as a material, mechanistic, process. And yet it may also be, as is much of nature, associated in a very relevant way to the transcendent.

We can probably build robot-computers that exhibit, and perhaps even "feel," fear for self-preservation. Can we build robot computers that experience existential fear? I would say maybe. In principle we are made of the same matter as are machines. So there may be nothing special about our matter, relative to computer-Joe's (or Commander Data's) matter. But the question of whether the transcendent quality would relate to the artificial fearing machine, in the same way as it relates to us, is a metaphysical question beyond our scope here.

Dennett's Wrong Axiom

We've already described (in Chapter 8) why Dennett's proof of the materialist axiom is wrong. Dennett claims that physics proves that the transcendent cannot exist. In fact, for the reasons already detailed, physics proves the opposite. (Physics does not prove that the transcendent *does* exist, it simply proves that it *might*.) The majority of physicists who have thought seriously about the issue (which might be a minority of the total) agree, as was described in Chapter 3.

Among such physicists can be counted Neils Bohr, who is universally regarded as one of the great figures of modern physics. Bohr recognized the possibility of applying quantum indeterminacy to human brain functioning, and he carried out some rudimentary calculations to estimate its importance. Bohr did conclude that the realm of quantum indeterminacy is so small that it could not be the primary source of mind functioning in the physical brain.[194]

For a number of reasons, Bohr's negative conclusion on that point still leaves the basic question open. First, Bohr did the study in the first place because he recognized that physics shows the opposite of Dennett's basic axiom. Second, in the half century since Bohr's work, our knowledge of the physical brain has increased, and the brain is found to be even more complex than then thought. Third, the application of the new results of exponential increase of indeterminacy from chaos theory might alter Bohr's results. Fourth, Bohr was considering the basic self-identity egoic functioning of the brain, whereas yogis, mystics, and saints speak of the spiritual realm as being beyond thought. Extra-normal momentary coherence with the transcendent may be quite consistent with even Bohr's preliminary results.

In any case, the issue of transcendent influence in mind-brain function must, from a rational, physical scientific point of view, be taken as an open question. The arguments of this chapter are qualitative. A quantitative analysis might be informative, but is beyond the scope of this book. Any analysis we could do here would still leave the question open.

From another perspective, the hylozoic view again seems suggested. To appreciate this perspective, conceptually design a machine. This machine must satisfy a number of requirements. It must be highly survivable on earth, in changing environments, for a long time. As such, it must be self-reproducible, mobile, not too big, and not too small. The primary requirement is that this machine have the capacity to get as much matter as possible in a state that can be sensitive to the very subtle, and minute, influences of spirit—through Planckian butterflies and lifetrons.

Now consider what we know about the human nervous system. It is extremely complex. It functions simultaneously on many timescales—from extremely rapid molecular vibrations to a lifespan of about a hundred years. Its size is in an in-between realm of physics—small enough to be sensitive to molecular and perhaps even atomic changes (the eye, for instance, can detect single photons of light under optimal circumstances), and also shaped by intermediate-scale electrical, mechanical, and frictional forces, and also sensitive to the large-scale force of gravity. It seems likely that the best possible machine to satisfy the above requirements would be something like the extremely complex and subtle human body with the human nervous system and the human brain.

The first requirements (of survivability and self-reproduction) could be maximized by something far simpler than a human. The view of the neo-geneticists is that humans are only the outcome of DNA molecules trying to maximize their number of copies. They view the primary human purpose as to create as many DNA copies as possible. If that is the case, then the DNA assumed a very strange sort of host in which to maximize its copies. Alternatively, we can view the conditions of survivability as only being secondary to the primary condition of sensitivity to the transcendent, and so it is plausible that sensitivity to the transcendent is the sole purpose for matter assuming forms like humans.

In any case, Dennett's axiom that physics proves materialism is simply not accurate. That error does not make his models for the mechanisms of cognitive processes wrong. It does negate his opinion that such models support the mechanistic paradigm. The mechanistic models for aspects of mentation are a valid subsystem of a larger, inclusive, hylozoic model. The hylozoic model includes the material brain-mind mechanisms as a part of total mind processes—processes that may include, to some degree, sometimes, the transcendent.

Evidence for Larger Models

The spiritual traditions generally find that there are many components to the human mind-body. (Of course, by "spiritual traditions," I include the more sophisticated readings of Christianity such as by Teilhard de Chardin, as well as Vedanta and the other major traditions already mentioned.) Three basic components are the physical, emotional (often called astral), and mental bodies. Also higher-level components like the soul and the causal body are usually included, but we don't need to worry about those for now. The physical body is the basic protoplasm, including the brain. The emotional and mental bodies include material protoplasm aspects and nonmaterial spirit, or lifetron, aspects. These complicated systems are said to have many levels of functioning—from the essentially mechanistic as described by Dennett, to the largely spiritual. As the material brain consists of hierarchies of organization—from electrons, to atoms, to molecules, to proteins, to clusters, to membranes, to cells, and tissues, so also the spirit aspects of the mental and emotional systems have levels of organization—from basic lifetrons, to clusters of lifetrons, to organ-like clusters ("chakras"), etc. The two systems (material and spiritual) connect and interact by the opening of matter described by the hylozoic paradigm. Plausibly each (the matter systems and the spirit systems) could function in the absence of the other, but each would function quite differently than they do together.

The different spiritual traditions hold different variants on this model. The common element of all of them is that functioning of the human being, to some extent, includes some sort of nonmaterial component. Science should *not* be viewed as contrary to this core point of the spiritual traditions. (Luckily for science in my opinion.) The erroneous dismissal, by science, of the spiritual aspect perpetuates ignorance and irrational sectarianism.

In Part I, we discussed individuals, including many physicists who, through various observations, decided that the transcendent and the material both exist. Interestingly, there are few people who have seriously investigated (through meditation and other types of self-observation) and then vigorously concluded that only matter exists. Exceptions may include existentialists like Jean Paul Sartre. But even the materialism of the existentialists is questionable. The existentialists can be interpreted as finding spiritual realms, but spiritual realms that are no more hospitable and no more meaningful than the desperate and depressing war-torn material environment.

Some scientists have claimed, as Dennett does, that the material sciences prove that only matter exists—but such claims can no longer be taken seriously. (If I seem overly repetitive on this point, well, the act of stating it imparts a feeling of doing something that really should have been done long ago, and so feels good to finally do—try it.) The job of physical scientists is to delineate and describe the knowable and the measurable. The most apparent way to answer the question left open by the physical sciences is through observation of consciousness.

The obvious experts in observing consciousness include psychiatrists. A notable example of a psychiatrist who, through standard clinical methods, and against all his personal and professional prejudices, came to realize the existence and the importance of the spiritual aspect of human functioning is Brian L. Weiss. Trained at Yale University School of Medicine, and chairman of psychiatry at Mount Sinai Medical Center in Miami, Dr. Weiss has the appropriate professional positions and credentials. (We're beginning to see that credentials are only given weight when one parrots the orthodox ontology, but one might as well mention them.) For years he practiced and fully believed in the standard materialist view of psychiatry. One of his patients changed his perspective. Catherine was a physically fit, but emotionally paralyzed, 27-year-old. After 18 months of conventional therapy, focusing on the patient's biological history, she showed no relief from her fears and phobias. Dr. Weiss decided to use a standard technique of hypnotherapy, in which the hypnotized patient is asked to "go back in time to the source of the phobia." Catherine went back to 1863 B.C.

Weiss says:

> "This was ... the first time I had come across this, so I was really considering that she was experiencing some sort of fantasy or dreamlike material, or even imagination."[195]

But other aspects of his clinical training indicated otherwise, so he suspended judgment. He says, "There were several things that did not fit with the idea of fantasy, or dreamlike material or imagination. ... the recall was so vivid and detailed ... she is not a suggestible person in that sense, and is not prone to elaboration." And clinically, "Her symptoms started to improve and improved dramatically right after that session [though] she had been fairly resistant for a year and a half previously, to conventional psychotherapy. Dreamlike material and fantasy do not cure symptoms, so something did not fit there."

If there were nothing unusual about the date of Catherine's memories, then psychiatry would take Catherine's improvement as obvious evidence that the therapy method was working. Traumatic events in Catherine's past (dying in a battle, drowning in a flood) caused related phobias in her present. The only problem was that they were past lives and not this life. The orthodox materialist perspective of his profession caused Dr. Weiss to be confused and doubtful.

Then, after the fourth such session, Catherine started to relate and analyze information from Dr. Weiss's own distant past—specific factual information that he believed no one except himself, certainly not his patient, could know.

Also, as Catherine's symptoms relieved, and Dr. Weiss allowed her psyche to do what it pleased, a profoundly wise intelligence began to speak through Catherine. This intelligence spoke directly to Dr. Weiss in a manner incapable of Catherine in her ordinary state, and this aspect seemed unnecessary to Catherine's own healing—it was for Dr. Weiss.

The bonus-intelligence that came out had the purpose of teaching Dr. Weiss spiritually and convincing him of the relevance of the spiritual aspect for psychiatry. Dr. Weiss changed his perspective, and in turn, this relieved his own symptoms of overstress and anxiety. He reports the case of Catherine in his book *Many Lives, Many Masters*.

As seems always the case when scientists encounter observations related to a spiritual aspect of reality, Dr. Weiss was reluctant to report his important observations. He says, "I did not write [the book] for three or four years after the sessions with Catherine ended because I was afraid of my reputation. ... I thought my professional colleagues ... would not be receptive to this."

After he published his book, he found that, "Many *are* receptive, but they won't admit it, they don't talk about it. It's fraught with peril, it may endanger their reputations and their careers for them to admit it. ... I have received 75 or 80 positive letters from psychiatrists around the country. [Some] write me they've been doing regression therapy for 10 or 20 years, but in the privacy of their office, and 'please don't tell anyone, but ...' "

In a subsequent book, Weiss reports on about a hundred more cases that corroborate his model that events of former lives affect the psychology of this life. Of course, a number of progressive therapists now do regression therapy. But, as Weiss mentions, the few fully credentialed psychiatrists who do allow this sort of perspective do so privately. Only a handful of such psychiatrists have published research on past life regression, and nonordinary spiritual consciousness. The major mainstream research departments are still completely inert in this respect.

What qualifies as proof in psychiatry? The sort of controlled repeatable experiment that is so important in physics is impossible. Should psychiatric evidence be accepted if it supports gang opinion, and rejected if it doesn't? In the case of past life recall, one might think that the recall of details like a specific name and date of birth, or death, for instance, could be verified in records, and this would supply a sort of physicist's proof. There have been a number of such cases, but they can always be suspected. If there is any vagueness or inconclusiveness, the case can be dismissed. If the specifics are too clear, then it is dismissed as fraudulent or circumstantial.

A common objection to the model of consciousness that includes multiple incarnations is that most of us are not aware of previous incarnations. But this objection doesn't carry much weight as evidence that multiple incarnations don't exist—it just is not positive evidence that they do. Most of us remember few of our dreams and little of our other mental processes during sleep. Does that mean they don't occur?

I am not suggesting that the mechanisms for remembering dreams are the same as for accessing information from other incarnations—I would think the mechanisms would be completely different. The meanings of dreams and other existences may be similar though.

Most psychologists believe that the content of dreams has significance for understanding our waking personalities. The contents of former incarnations may have similar meanings. Fully integrating the meaning of a few major dreams can take years, and yet we have many dreams every night. Most of us make plenty enough of a mess of this incarnation to occupy us during our lifetime. There may usually be no immediate need to revisit our former messes from other lives.

Of course, another common objection to the multiple incarnation model is the belief that the most common orthodox interpretations of Christianity reject the possibility. This would seem like odd grounds for a scientist to base his beliefs on, but many seem to, unconsciously anyway. But, increasingly, rigorous studies of what Jesus taught, including new scholarly translations, and newly discovered accounts from the time[196] indicate the contrary. These studies indicate that Jesus did not reject the multiple incarnation model, and even sometimes obliquely referred to it, he just felt it should not be emphasized. That was probably for the same reason that theologians today find fault with the belief in karma. An undeveloped view of karma can lead to the opinion that suffering is predestined, and so lead to a lack of compassion and to cruelty.

This chapter is about how the hylozoic paradigm encompasses the mysteries of consciousness, and how studies of consciousness can be used to determine between the hylozoic paradigm and the materialist paradigm. I emphasize the recent studies from psychiatry because positive psychiatric evidence of reincarnation would support the hylozoic paradigm.

In the materialist paradigm, no information could pass from life to life because the mechanisms of biological conception and development have no material links between lives. If links exist, they must be nonmatierial, and so finding such links would establish a hylozoic model of matter. A small number of physicians are also doing rigorous studies of "near-death" experiences. These studies also indicate that some sort of consciousness continues after physical/material death (that is, between incarnations). If such studies finally become conclusive, then the existence of both spirit and matter, and their mutual interaction, will also finally be concluded.

10: Consciousness Not Explained

A Note on the Mechanism

Assume for the moment that psychiatry is starting to uncover evidence of "past lives." The key point for us is that events of one material object (a human body in the past life) somehow affect another material object (the body in this life). Whether the former is, in fact, a past individual life, or a completely different individual, or some sort of collective experience, is not important here. The mechanistic paradigm says that there can be no influence—the material entities are separate and unconnected, and so no influence can pass directly from one to the other. If we accept the psychiatric data, we have to supply some mechanism for the influence to be transferred.

The Vedic and Esoteric Buddhist philosophies contain detailed descriptions of exactly these sorts of mechanisms. But we can't really use those systems without first laying the groundwork in contemporary Western scientific terms, because of problems of translation. How do you translate "prana"? "Life force" could be incorporated into a completely hylostatic (mechanistic) paradigm view. "Lifetrons" requires a hylozoic paradigm view.

If the experience of a past human body can affect the thoughts of a present human body, how can that happen? We've described how the living brain is a highly complex system with extreme sensitivity to initial conditions. This creates a certain degree of unflowering of possibility in each moment, and some of that possibility is connected, at the existential level, to Planckian butterflies. Planckian butterflies are not bound by the same rules of physics as are material particles. I have no idea how Planckian butterflies work in detail.

We know from the Aspect quantum mechanics experiments (see Chapters 6 and 8) that there is some sort of connection across space and time, and Planckian butterflies function in that connected realm. Let's postulate that some set of Planckian butterflies can carry the essence or kernel of an experience across the spatial-temporal gap from one body to another.

How can this kernel of experience then affect the receiving body without violating the laws of physics? The receiving brain is moving through its immense range of possibilities in each passing moment. Think of these possibilities as a large packet of possible future thoughts. A musical bell might be an analogy. The bell starts out quiet, now. One minute from now the bell might be ringing or it might still be quiet. In order for the bell to ring, an external material source must whack it, thereby imparting some energy.

In the living brain, various possibilities all have the same energy, and all can come out of the same initial state. Call one future brain possibility "ringing" and the other possibility "not ringing." The Planckian butterflies impart the kernel of experience to the brain and the result is the ringing state. The occurrence of the ringing state or the not ringing state is each consistent with standard physics.

Probably the brain then interprets its "ringing" state in terms of past experience and worldview. Any "past life experience" then would be some combination of imagination, fantasy, and true experience. Some experiences are probably completely fantasy, and some closer to truth. It is the job of psychiatrists to help distinguish between the fantasy and the reality. It is the job of physical science to be clear about what the possibilities are.

The Decision

A major way to decide the question of spirit and matter, or matter only, is through self-observation. In this book, I am advocating that scientists report what they really observe, and say what they really think, and advocate the study of what they really think is important—not what they think the funding authorities and "the profession" want to hear. I consider myself as equally unqualified as anyone else to observe my own mental processes. In the spirit of what I am advocating, I should report why I find Dr. Weiss's observations credible.

These self-observations occurred while I was working in Tokyo, where predictable routine seems always to hide a substrate of the extraordinary. The city of Tokyo is inhabited by hordes of enormous black ravens. These huge birds inhabit the skies and share the city with the sewer rats, inhabiting the underground realms, while we humans vie for hegemony at ground level with the flying cockroaches.

Those four primary inhabitants, crowding tightly together amidst frequent earthquakes and typhoons, all behave usually in highly predictable and uniform ways—punctuated by moments of shear strangeness. The ravens, for instance, usually adhere to their role of being noisy, troublesome, and stupid. And yet, one day, early in the morning, one of the ravens was spotted in a deserted schoolyard. The raven, alone, was sliding down the children's slide. It would slide down the slide, then turn around and fly straight to the top, and slide down again. And the raven returned mornings, regularly, for more rides, only when no one was nearby.[197] Like all good Tokyo residents, the raven would perform his acts of incredible individuality only when he thought no one was watching.

One day I was watching one of these black ravens (not the Leonardo-of-ravens that discovered slides) and a series of out-of-the-ordinary moments began in my own life. To present the context of these events requires a little background. I had always been motivated by a drive to understand what might be called the classical "mind-body problem."

That influenced my decision to study physics. Philosophy and the spiritual traditions might be faster routes to the mind-body question. Physics means to understand all matter, including the matter of us, and so physics seemed a plausible secondary route. And I thought physics was more socially acceptable. By the time I looked out the window at that raven, I was trying to concentrate mostly on the specific subfield of planetary science I had ended-up in, and to put aside the mind-body stuff.

As often happened though, when my work was not progressing, my mind wandered back to its old obsession. Something about that old question seemed to be falling into place, almost subconsciously. I stood up from my chair, looked out the window, and saw that raven alight near the windowsill. There was a sudden rush of understanding, like the common "eureka" feeling. What the rush contained is essentially what I am trying to describe in this book. The feeling of the moment was visceral—physical, emotional, and intellectual. No really new physics theories or anything like that came, just as there are no new physics theories in this book.

What came into me was a conviction, and a perspective of context, that I am trying to convey. In the months that followed that moment, a number of experiences happened, some of which I have already mentioned. These deepened that momentary conviction and perspective. Something very similar to Dr. Weiss's observations happened.

A few weeks after the raven experience, I was in my small apartment reading when a minor earthquake occurred. After the earth shaking stopped, my body started trembling. Since moving to Japan, I realized I had an irrational fear of earthquakes, and I was experiencing that fear. This time, instead of resisting the fear by tensing up and reassuring myself mentally, there was an impulse to go into the experience. There was a sense that there "was something there" in my psyche that could be accessed. So I went into a relaxed, semi-self-hypnotic state.

A sort of waking dream then occurred. In the dream, I experienced viewing an earthquake scene. Two figures were present—a young woman and her daughter. This earthquake was very strong. The woman and child were in a large wooden structure that was collapsing. They were killed. In the "dream" they were experienced as my beloved wife and daughter (though my waking self is unmarried). The experience of being in the scene was very realistic. The sadness, anger, and pain were overpowering. A wrenching scream emerged, as if from my heart.

When I "awoke" from the waking dream, I was amazed. The experience was very short, but all the sensations, feelings, and thoughts were as if it had actually happened—more realistic than an ordinary dream. It seemed very clear that those occurrences were related to my fear of earthquakes.

Was this a "past life"? I don't know. If I suspend judgment, and just report the experience, it was a spontaneous identification with another life, probably in the past. Was it *my* life in some specific sense? Was it identification with another person's experience, because of my own fear of earthquakes? Was it only fantasy, or the same as an "ordinary" dream? The hylozoic paradigm does not preclude any of these explanations. The effects were not the same as a fantasy or normal dream. When relating, or just thinking about the experience, powerful grief and compassion (for the victims and for the dream observer's pain) would occur. Tears would come.

Another waking dream occurred about the same time. The visceral feelings that I felt when I saw the raven by my window, and the feeling after the earthquake, and before the above dream experience, were similar—a sort of bodily fear. On another disconcerting occasion, I felt the same thing. I went, very late at night, to the soccer field to run laps to alleviate the fear feeling and the stress.

Again, in the midst of strenuous running, there was a sense of "something there" in my psyche. Instead of resisting, I went into it, and experienced another time, another place, in another body. This experience was stranger. The dream-body was in the midst of a sort of panic attack and sensory overload. It wasn't a fully human body, but a sort of animal-man. The experience was again very real. It was a sort of pre-verbal experience. So this description isn't exactly it, but is my later interpretation. It was an experience of a sort of animal-man expansion of consciousness.

At some point in our evolution, we (humans) developed all the thinking and feeling abilities associated with our unique capacity for abstract language. The dream experience was as if that expansion of thinking-feeling capacity happened rapidly, in a spurt, and that particular animal-man was experiencing it personally. Imagine it for a moment. He had neither language nor concept to describe it to others, or even to understand it himself, but he was undergoing a horrific, and fantastic change. In the pre-linguistic state, the feeling effects of such changes are amplified because they cannot be intellectually conceptualized.

In the midst of the run, I came out of the "dream," exhausted but relieved of the fear. Was this a past life experience? If it was, it was millions of years ago, and not just thousands. Was it experience of a sort of Jungian collective archetype? Was it simple fantasy or imagination? Again, the hylozoic paradigm does not rule out any of these models. When trying to decide amongst the models, all we can do is learn as much of the relevant science as is possible, and then be honest about our experiences in the realms where science can't go.

A third waking dream occurred under similar circumstances. This time the experience was of observing bloody mayhem in an ancient battle in an Asian country, and a feeling of personal responsibility compounded the horror of the scene. I had given some sort of advice to the commander to engage in battle. It was rational, logical, advice based on the best information available. Something unforeseen happened and the mayhem ensued, wiping out hundreds of people, within my own view. The "dream" ended with myself being beheaded, in disgrace, in a sort of assisted suicide. The dream experience was unusually real, and after the experience, there was again great relief.

My interpretation of my own experience is not yet conclusive. My opinion is that the expanded consciousness models merit serious consideration and study. Each of the "dreams," or regressions, or fantasies, whatever you think they are, seemed to have their own meanings, and seemed to have a connected meaning.

As I review the first one, the man who lost his young family to the earthquake seemed to have a very religious worldview. It was a simplistic religious view with a personal deity. He believed that if he was "good" and followed the rules, then his god would protect him. In his life, he did try to be good. And then nature, controlled he thought by his god, did that horrible thing to his innocent family. He was psychically crushed. It was not a good life. The mystical-irrational god-as-controlling-authority worldview was obliterated.

The bad advice "dream" was the other side of the coin. The figure in that life viewed himself as the logical, rational, controlling authority. He was completely identified with that perspective. This objectivist/materialist worldview was also obliterated, not theoretically, but by direct experience of its failure.

The animal-man expansion dream figure seems to be a metaphor for the present. We as a world culture are undergoing transformation. All we really know is that things are changing faster than our ideational concepts can adjust to them. That can be a horrific experience. Many of us in the West are materially comfortable, but we are not separate from the rest of the world. When we experience this connected aspect of the whole, the experience might be like that animal-man felt when he first experienced full individuation—at the same time, incomprehensible partial obliteration and partial expansion.

The animal-man regression, or dreamlike experience, brought me back to the initial moment when I saw the raven. There is no mind/body problem—it is a duality that we create by our contracted perspective. Culturally, socially, religiously, and intellectually, there is still a problem, because we don't have the language and the traditions of the incoming nondual perspective.

10: Consciousness Not Explained

In *Consciousness Explained*, Crick highlighted problem. A highly capable, authoritative, positioned, funded investigator, he claimed that the mechanistic, explicitly aspiritual models of consciousness should be the standard discourse of science.

Culture of Disbelief, by Stephen L. Carter, supports Dennett's being right about the contents of the standard discourse (if wrong about its correctness). Carter describes how contemporary law, politics, and elite social discourse trivialize spiritual devotion. Carter says that it is taken for granted that the motive for introduction of spirituality into public discourse could only be the advocacy of a hidden, exclusive, conservative, authoritarian religious agenda. Carter, a religious liberal, points out that in fact such agendas *are* present. The lack of serious liberal spiritual perspective, he says, then trivializes spirituality.

The common assumptions of the recent past are the primitive delusions of the present. In polite Victorian society, racism and classism were assumed substrata of correct cultural discourse. In contemporary elite Western society, the disbelief in sophisticated spiritual reality is a required assumption of acceptable adult discourse. A spiritual aspect that is a relevant and important component of realistic political, economic, and scientific discourse is dismissed by false assumption. This assumption is often believed to be supported by "modern science." It is to the detriment of science that scientists fail to clarify this error.

To be fair, there are plenty of reasons for the failure, not the least of which is the extreme specialization of scientific disciplines. In the first part of this century, Millikan spoke of the problem of overspecialization blinding scientists.[198] That was when the number of scientific sub-disciplines was orders-of-magnitude smaller than it is now. Herman Hesse described the effects of overspecialization in his Nobel prize-winning novel *The Glass Bead Game*. In the novel, the scientific, intellectual, and religious elite are seriously engrossed in an elaborate "glass bead game." Beautiful, intricate, and intellectually challenging as the game is, it is divorced from reality, and is artificial. The resulting society at large is in decay. Hesse's characters find deliverance from malaise only through personal embrace of spiritual reality, and material reality, together.

Hesse, a German living in Switzerland, was writing at the time of Hitler's Reich. His "glass bead game" was a metaphor for the cultural conditions that fostered the rise of Hitler. A spiritually barren and ignorant cultural elite, combined with economic disorder, left the people ripe for any leader who would explicitly declare a spiritual revival. Enter Hitler—truly evil, irrational, and mystical. If the overly materialist cultural elite had not created the spiritual void in the first place, Hitler would have remained the clownish failure he started out as. The former Soviet Union, today, is in a similar situation.

The Western press talks only about Russia's economic problems, while the Russian people themselves speak of spiritual degradation (though, of course, they don't want to be hungry either). Aspiritual authoritarian communism was revealed as a fraud. It froze in place the primitive sectarian (and sometimes even racist) religious aspects of a century ago. A Hitler-like figure (Zhiranovsky) was until recently dismissed as a clown—until he received startling percentages of votes in an election. Still, the Western press speaks only in terms of economic causes.

These large social movements take us a little far afield from the issue of university researcher's theories about brain function, but not too far I think. Claiming to prove that there is no spiritual aspect to existence does affect larger society. The alternative is to claim that the research is irrelevant anyway—not really serious about its claims—and just a sort of academic glass bead game. Staying within the artificial game is the safest approach. As Weiss describes, there is a sort of mob mentality in which it is believed that the mob will turn on any dissenters to the materialist rally. In such a circumstance, a sophisticated and hollow set of plausibility arguments can pass as a complete explanation of consciousness. And even a great weight of evidence of the spiritual aspect can be dismissed without a second thought.

11. The Lives of Planets

"There is, brothers, an unborn, a not-become,
a not-made, a not-manifest.
If there were not this that is unborn, not-become,
not-made, not-manifest,
there could not be any escape from that which is born,
become, made, manifest.
But, brothers, since there is this unborn, not-become,
not-made, not-manifest,
an escape from what is born, become, made, manifest,
is therefore made known."[199]

— The Buddha, in a discourse in the Jeta Grove of Sravasti, circa 500 BC, clarifying the events of his own enlightenment.

What comes to mind when we try to think of our "planet" as a whole? Many think of a landscape of hills or plains containing trees, plants, grasses, and perhaps animals. We might think of our immediate surroundings. We might think of towns and cities, and our friends and relatives.

Geologists might think of the interior structure of the earth—the mantle, and cores, and rock formations, and plate tectonics of the continents. Biologists might think of the biosphere—the thin layer of biological activity, species, ecological communities, and individuals, that rest on the geology.

Historians and anthropologists might think of the evolving structures and interrelations of human cultures. Economists and business people might think of a dynamic global marketplace of peoples, goods, and organizations.

Astronomers might think of a dark little hunk of rock orbiting a brilliant star. Astrophysicists might think of a complex interplay of plasmas, solar winds, and atmospheric molecules. Meteorologists might think of the dynamic and semi-predictable global climate and weather.

Increasingly, we think of the beautiful photos of the whole Earth taken by the Apollo astronauts, and the unmanned space probes. Most of us tend naturally toward one or more of these perspectives when the words "planet Earth" jostle our minds.

The Gaia hypothesis (after the Greek Earth goddess "Gaia") was first proposed in the 1970's by atmospheric chemist James Lovelock and microbiologist Lynn Margulis.[200] The Gaia hypothesis supposes that the Earth environment is kept at a state favorable for life by the living organisms. According to Lovelock, the Gaia theory "sees the Earth as a system where the evolution of the [biological] organisms is tightly coupled to the evolution of their environment. Self-regulation of climate and chemical composition are emergent properties of the system."[201] The Gaia hypothesis is commonly thought of as the idea that the Earth is "alive." What can the hylozoic paradigm tell us about the idea that the Earth is alive? Is it a preposterous proposal?

Medical doctors use arthroscopes to peer inside human bodies. Imagine using an arthroscope on yourself, to look at an e-coli bacterium in your gut. Then imagine that you get the impression that the e-coli bacteriae are debating among themselves whether the beast on the other end of the arthroscope is alive. That is analogous to the debate about the Gaia hypothesis. How could the planet *not* be alive, if we are alive? We are a small component of the planet. If the planet is dead, then we, as a subsystem of it, must also be dead.

Those who balk at the idea that the planet is alive seem to think something as follows: "The planet is the accumulated geology, meteorology, and biochemistry of a bunch of interacting systems—all of which are understood in terms of the material laws of physics—and so the planet should not be called alive in the same sense that *I* am alive."

It is strange that those who argue most forcefully in this vein tend also to be those who would agree with Dennett that all mental and conscious processes in humans are also material processes determined only by the laws of physics. Talk about irrational dualism—that is a prime example. Yet some present it as the orthodox ontology of "rational science."

Why does the Gaia hypothesis cause a stir? Probably the unsaid part of the disagreement is that the Gaia hypothesis seems to imply not only life in the most general sense of some sort of self-regulation, but also an emotional or mental consciousness.

Apparently only humans mentate or think specifically and abstractly, as a self-defined activity. Only animals, including humans, apparently, emote or feel emotionally in a self-identified way. Inorganic matter, we believe, cannot think or emote. For the moment, let's accept these assumptions—that only humans mentate, think, and emote in a fully self-identified way. There are thus two aspects of the Gaia hypothesis. First, the weak aspect is that the systems of the earth exhibit regenerative and self-propagating qualities similar to that of any life form. Advances in Earth systems science have made the weak Gaia hypothesis hardly in question. Nearly all knowledgeable scientists would agree with that.[202]

The strong Gaia hypothesis then might be that the planet as a whole has some sort of thinking or emoting consciousness, like humans. This is what is irksome to many scientists—the anthropomorphic aspect. Myself, I think the anthropomorphic Gaia model is mistaken (as I think Lovelock and many Gaia proponents would agree). But in the hylozoic perspective, the Gaia question changes. In the hylozoic paradigm, the Gaia question becomes, "Since all matter is alive in the sense that spirit and matter interrelate, what is the specific nature of the planetary life?"

The planetary life probably does not think and feel in the same sense as humans do, but does that mean that it is not as evolved as a human is? The planetary life contains the human, and the animal, and the plant, and the equally active inorganic (or "mineral") kingdoms. In the sense that I think I am more evolved than are my white blood cells, maybe the Earth is more evolved than am I. Is such an idea relevant, in a scientific sense, to our understanding of how things work and how to live effectively, or is it just philosophical fun?

To approach that question, the first step is to develop an appreciation for the vastness of the emergence associated with the planet—the immensity of its aliveness. To do so, consider, as we started to in Chapter 9, how this planet of ours came to be. The "standard model of solar system formation" is how science answers that question. In the following review of the solar system formation model, I will stick to the well-accepted, scientific consensus (as much as there is a consensus).[203] Later in the chapter, I will get back to speculations about what the scientific models really mean.

Formation of Earth

Out in the galaxy are enormous clouds of gas and "dust." Clumps of this gas and dust collapse to form stars and planets. In order of increasing size, we have our planet, our solar system (centered on our sun), our galaxy, sometimes called "the Milky Way," which is composed of many solar systems, the gas and dust clouds, and other stuff, and the universe as a whole which is composed of many galaxies and clumps of galaxies and other stuff.

When we look out at night, the stars we see are mostly Milky Way stars nearby in our own galaxy. The dark regions of the Milky Way—that look as though someone splattered black paint in front of the background field of star light—are dark because large galactic clouds of gas and dust obscure the star light. Those gas and dust clouds are what collapse to form the stars and planets.

We will focus on what happens during and after one of those collapses, but first note where the clouds come from. The galactic gas clouds are a mixture of stuff that was originally there when the galaxy first formed, together with stuff from the explosion of old stars (novas and supernovas). This is important to note because the only (regular-type[204]) matter that was formed in the initial "Big Bang" origin of the universe was hydrogen and a little helium.

The initial hydrogen and helium then clumped into the galaxies. (Cosmologists don't really know how this clumping occurred—thereby calling the model into doubt, some say—but we won't worry about that detail for now.) So the first stars that formed in the young galaxies, and specifically in our galaxy, were only composed of hydrogen and helium—because that is all there was. Any planets that formed were also composed only of hydrogen and helium. And hydrogen and helium are essentially always gaseous (except in the center, high pressure, parts of planets).

So the first planets would have been giant Jupiter-like things with no solid surfaces, and no solid things anywhere possible, and so no biology as we know it. The first stars, though, especially the bigger ones, were busy fusing hydrogen and helium together into larger elements like carbon, nitrogen, oxygen, and all the other good stuff we normally associate with the idea of "matter." This fusing of the initial hydrogen and helium into more complex atomic nuclei can only occur on a large scale in stars, and occasionally in cosmic rays (and more recently in accelerators, and in bombs) but only on a large scale in stars. When many sorts of stars use up their burnable gases, they explode—releasing the new carbon and oxygen, and other stuff back into the dark gas and dust clouds. Parts of those clouds then collapse again into new stars and new planets, and the very small trace amounts of "metals"[205] tends to be concentrated on the planets that form. Exactly how this concentration of the hard stuff in the planets occurs, instead of equal distribution among planets and sun, is also not really understood, but this glitch in the theory won't deter us for now either.

Finally the "metals" are available on hard surfaces on appropriately sized planets (continents on planet earth for instance) that are warm but not too hot, and they can then form plants and animals and astronomers. This is why we get shivers down our spines when Carl Sagan says "we are made of star stuff" because it is true in a direct, concrete, sense.

In reviewing the above familiar story, I do not mean to add to the impression that it is all understood, and all deterministic, and mechanistic. That is the impression that is often imparted along with the repetition of the story.

The story becomes a concrete myth in itself, like the book of Genesis, except instead of "the Bible says so" being the ultimate evidence of accuracy, "the astronomer on TV said so" becomes the sanction, and there can be allowed no deeper significance, meaning, or influence, other than the simple recitation of sequence and the assertion that there might be nothing miraculous about it.

To the contrary, we are now going to focus on a small part of the sequence that is sometimes dispatched as a detail. We are going to focus on the collapse from gas-dust cloud to star with planets, and the evolution of planets themselves, and we will find enormous space for emergent possibility.

I recited the standard story of cosmology, above, to show that all of what we are talking about in this book occurs without basic contradiction to the standard physical knowledge. The hylozoic paradigm is contradictory only to the standard metaphysical assumptions of many scientists, not contradictory to physical knowledge.

The Collapse

The standard models of Big Bang cosmology and the models of the initial formation of galaxies, mentioned above, give us the existing galaxies, populated with huge clouds of gas and dust. There are still gaps in those models, but for our purposes, we can assume that those gaps will be filled with future observations. We want to know now how those gas and dust clouds get to be us, our solar system—the sun, planets, and all. The "dust" is actually tiny, tiny grains of ice and rock, about one ten thousandth of a millimeter across. The clouds are called "molecular clouds" because much of the gas is in molecular form. They are over 98 percent gas and less than two percent dust.

As the clouds orbit around in the disk of the galaxy, they develop clumps and knots. Occasionally one of these cloud lumps becomes so lumpy that the gravity of itself pulling on itself becomes stronger than the gas pressure of itself pushing out on itself. Then the lump starts to collapse under its own gravity. The lump collapses from the inside out, so that a central blob rapidly develops. "Rapidly" is about a hundred thousand years, or more, in this case, because the sizes of these clouds are so large. The inner blob begins to spin, just like an ice skater spins when he pulls his arms into his chest. As the rest of the lump collapses, it starts to form a disk because of the spinning motion, and the loss of energy due to friction, similar to the way the rings of Saturn formed.

What happens during the collapse depends on exactly what sort of molecular cloud lump initially collapsed. If the lump has too much angular momentum, then the outer part will actually "bounce" back out into the molecular cloud, instead of forming a stable disk. If the lump has essentially no angular momentum, it would all collapse into one giant spherical star with no disk at all. But this almost never happens because even the tiny amount of intrinsic angular momentum—due to the fact that the cloud was orbiting the center of the galaxy—is enough to cause rapid spinning when it collapses into a star.

The type of friction present in the collapsing process is the major determining factor whether a disk will form. (We're so worried about whether there will be a disk around the star because that is where we live—on a planet that formed in such a disk.) As well as the usual rubbing friction of the gas, there is also electromagnetically caused friction. The big molecular clouds have magnetic fields associated with them, just like most planets, and stars, and most large astronomical objects have magnetic fields (like the Earth's familiar dipolar field). The giant molecular cloud magnetic field passing through the cloud lump as it collapses slows down the spinning. If the magnetic field is just right and the cloud lump is just right, then the lump will collapse into a central blob and a stable disk. This occurs in probably less than a third of collapsing clumps (many collapse into double or triple star systems without disks).

At one point in the collapse, there is a central blob, about the mass of the sun, and a collapsing disk, some fraction of the mass of the sun. The central blob is close to spherical and is many times the size of the sun. It is still collapsing and just dimly starting to ignite into a star. The inner part of the disk, around where Earth and Mars will be, is very hot because of the gravitational energy of the collapse changing into heat energy. The outer part of the disk, around where Uranus and Neptune will be, is still very cold, though much warmer than the ambient space temperature of a few degrees above absolute zero.

Most of the elements heavier than helium in the solar nebula disk are in the form of "volatiles" like water vapor, or water ice, and perhaps some liquid water, and the different phases of carbon dioxide, methane, nitrogen, and other low freezing temperature compound gases. The rest is in rocky and metallic material (just like ordinary igneous rocks). Somewhere around the location where Jupiter will be, temperatures in the disk tend to be around the freezing point of water. There may have been a sort of cosmogonic snowing around the nascent planet Jupiter's location.[206]

Throughout the disk, the different heating and cooling processes also caused convective flow, like in a pan of soup on your stove. With all that heating and cooling and convecting and snowing, there was large scale turbulence in the disk.

Another detail is that sometime during the evolution of the planet-forming disk, the amount of ice and rock, relative to the amount of gas, greatly increased—that is, much of the gas was "dissipated"—how the gas dissipation occurs is not known.[207]

Also during this time, the icy and rocky stuff begins to clump together, at first probably in roughly one kilometer-sized lumps. These lumps (called "planetesimals") then start to stick together to form large dominant planetesimals. The biggest of these eventually form the cores of the giant planets (Jupiter, Saturn, Uranus, and Neptune), and the bulk of the lesser, "rocky" planets (Mercury, Venus, Earth, and Mars). The remaining gas accumulates to form the envelopes of the giant planets.

The remaining planetesimals (now called comets and asteroids) continue to zing around the solar system, occasionally colliding into the planets. For instance a large comet called Shoemaker-Levy 9, hit the planet Jupiter around July 21, 1994, and the impact explosions were visible even through backyard telescopes on Earth. Many of the comets are mostly water ice, and the impact of one or more of these icy comets, soon after formation of the bulk Earth, may be the source of our oceans.[208] And then life formed, and that's it—here we are.

The Turbulence

The above synopsis of the standard model of the formation of the planets was necessarily sketchy. Hundreds of academic papers have been published, about only parts of the process.[209] These academic studies can be seen as approaching a general model of planet formation. What we are getting at in this chapter is an understanding of what can be meant by a "complete" model.

Consider the stage of the solar system formation just after the initial collapse of the molecular cloud lump into a central protostar and a surrounding stable disk. The disk is beginning the process of forming the planets, and comets and asteroids. Scientists have created a very sophisticated family of models that describe how this process occurs.

Probably some subset of those models is quite applicable to real molecular cloud collapses. The point here is that whatever set of models is ultimately correct, they must be open models. The best models will be able to predict that such and such a molecular cloud lump is likely to collapse into such and such a sized star surrounded by planets of typical sizes such and such, at such and such typical distances from the stars. They will be probabilistic models. That type of predictive model would be a great advance over the present state of understanding, which still consists of a sophisticated set of plausibility arguments with little observational evidence and few quantitative predictions.

The point is that a specific probabilistic model would also be the limit of what is possible for physics to achieve. This is a limit not only because of the difficulty of measuring initial states and the practical limits on computer speed, but also a limit inherent in the matter itself. The hylozoic paradigm allows us to include both the predictable aspect and the emergent aspect in our understanding.

The Solar Nebula Thought Experiment

To understand this limit of predictability in the case of solar system formation, we can do the same sort of thought experiment as we did for weather predicting, in Chapter 9. In the weather thought experiment, we imagined that a mythical supercomputer could calculate as fast as we needed it to. We programmed the supercomputer to apply the laws of physics to any initial input conditions we might supply. Then we imagined that we could supply all possible measures of the initial state of the atmosphere, including all possibly existing knowledge of the parameters of the atoms and particles allowed by quantum theory.

So we supply to the mythical supercomputer all information about the state of the matter itself—we are not even limited by impracticalities of actual measurement. Then we allowed the computer to predict the weather. We found that, after a week or so, the computer could only predict a wide range of possible scenarios.

Now do the same thought experiment with the entire collapsing solar nebula. (The solar nebula is the cloud of gas and dust and plasma, and electromagnetic fields—all the matter—out of which the present solar system formed.) Of course this is going to be a little more complex to visualize than was the weather, but the principles are the same.

Some readers will jump right to the quick and point out that we don't really need to do this thought experiment, because the weather thought experiment is strictly a subset of the solar nebula thought experiment, and the weather thought experiment already showed what we will conclude. That is a subtle and elegant way to look at it. The weather here on Earth this week is composed entirely of only a very small part of the matter in that initial solar nebula.

Even including the interaction of the weather with the geological processes like volcanoes, and ocean currents, and the sun's rays, and the solar wind, it is all a small part of the initial solar nebula mass. If this small subset is emergent on a time scale of a week or so, as we showed that it is in Chapter 9, then the whole solar nebula contains some significantly emergent properties. So, even though that logical argument seems to make our point, a description of the larger solar nebula evolution might give some other insights.

Continuing with more detail in the solar nebula thought experiment is a little difficult because even less is known about the early solar system than is known about weather and climate mechanisms on Earth. We can get an idea of what was going on, though. We are starting with the stage of the early protostar surrounded by a disk of orbiting gas and dust that extends out to about where the planet Pluto is now. Even if we start with an initially smooth, "featureless," equally mixed disk, something interesting happens right away. No matter how smooth and featureless we imagine the disk, there *are* features on the atomic scale. The different velocities of the atoms themselves are individual features, and these velocities will have some amount of quantum no-things-in-themselves nonexistence. The initial state has some degree of emergence in it.

So, in our thought experiment, we let our smooth "featureless" solar nebula disk start evolving. Because of the heating due to gravitational infall, and internal friction, convection will start. Convection also occurs because of the differences of temperatures between the surfaces and middle of the disk, and the temperature changes with distance from the central star.

The temperature differences also cause chemical phase changes. In some places, water goes through a "snow to ice to gas" cycling. In the hottest places, rock melts and refreezes. In places of more rapid convection, turbulence automatically starts. The initial quantum uncertainties begin growing exponentially in the turbulent disk, just like Ruelle's turbulent weather. The emergent uncertainties in the exact flows of the turbulence again propagate to kilometer size in only a few days' time (although there is no "day" and "night" in the solar nebula).

At the same time as there is turbulence in the solar nebula disk, there are also regular and predictable processes that occur. If the disk gets flat enough, there is a large-scale gravitational instability that will cause the matter, especially the ice and rock, to clump into kilometer-sized planetesimals. Alternatively, with all the heating and cooling and colliding and sticking, the dust begins to clump into larger sized objects eventually becoming planetesimals. For some reason, possibly the snowing-type of environment, a large planet core accumulates first at about the location where Jupiter is now. The gravity of this core begins sucking onto itself the surrounding gas, and the first giant planet of our solar system forms. The other planetesimals, still spread in the region from where Mercury will be, to where Neptune will be, continue orbiting the sun slowly accumulating into the planets.

These more regular processes arise out of the initial and ongoing turbulence. Physics predicts basically how the regular processes will proceed. The turbulence propagates the initial emergent zone into a rapidly expanding space of emergent possibility within which the regular and predictable processes eventuate.

The turbulence is highly emergent. In the hylozoic paradigm, the emergence is affected by spirit. In the old paradigm, the emergence is strictly random. As far as physics can tell, there is no difference between the two cases. The equations of physics (which are now very nearly the full equations of matter itself) predict a wide range of possible initial states and subsequent evolutions. In that sense, the formation of Earth and the solar system has already been "explained." The only problem with the explanation is that a wide range of other outcomes, some of which would appear radically different from the others, are equally "explained."

For instance, instead of the four rocky inner planets (Mercury, Venus, Earth, and Mars), two larger planets about where Venus is now might be equally possible to have come out of the same solar nebula as created the Earth we know. That is a radical difference.

Even slight differences, though, would change the whole history of Earth. If the spin axis of Earth, for instance, ended up essentially straight up, instead of tilted, or if it were flat on its side, like that of the planet Uranus, the climate of Earth would be radically different. And since, over the age of the Earth, the climate is coupled with the actual evolution of the atmospheric composition, the composition of the atmosphere (relative amounts of oxygen, and carbon, for instance) would also be radically different, to say nothing of the day-to-day weather or the evolution of sensitive biology.

All of that emergent possibility is from only the initial state uncertainties, propagated by the turbulence in the solar nebula disk, assuming that completely stable and predictable planetary accumulation and evolution processes occur from then on. Actually, highly emergent phenomena continue to happen, at many size-scales, throughout the evolution of the planets, after their initial formation.

One of these emergent processes is caused by what is called "resonant orbit commensurabilities." Between the orbits of the planets Mars and Jupiter lies a belt of asteroids ranging in size from hundreds of kilometers in diameter, down to dust particles. The asteroid belt is the remnant of planetesimals, and material from the early solar nebula, that never accumulated into a planet.

Most astronomers think that the asteroids were not able to accumulate into a planet because of the resonant orbit commensurabilities, with the planet Jupiter, in the asteroid belt. What that fancy term means is really quite simple. In the asteroid belt, there is a certain orbit distance where asteroids orbit the sun exactly three times while Jupiter orbits the sun twice. So such asteroids get a gravitational "kick" outwards precisely at the same orbital longitude, every third time they come around. That is a "resonant forcing."

To appreciate resonant forcing, consider a pendulum clock. Open the clock. Every third time the pendulum comes up to one side to turn and fall again, give it a little push. If you apply the push just as it turns, after only a few pushes the pendulum will be swinging with much higher amplitude. If you keep applying the little pushes, just right, the amplitude will increase and increase until the clock breaks—all from those tiny pushes.

In the case of the asteroids, the gravitational pushes from Jupiter pump up their orbital eccentricities and inclinations until something happens. The something that happens is not that the asteroid breaks, but it gets such an elongated orbit that it collides with another planet, or comes close to a big planet like Jupiter and gets slung out to the edge of the solar system, to hang-out with the comets, or it gets slung completely out of the solar system to wander about the galaxy. So, with the 3:2 Jupiter orbital resonance in its midst, and also other resonances, the asteroid belt was unable to form into a planet.[210]

The relevance of the resonances for our point in this chapter is that scientists have shown that, near resonant locations, there are almost always chaotic zones. In the case of the pendulum, if you push it not exactly at resonance, but a fraction of a second longer than the period of the pendulum, each time, then the pendulum will swing in a mathematically chaotic way. The same with asteroids near the orbital resonances. And, as we discussed, chaotic motion has sensitive dependence on initial conditions. And the initial conditions are sensitive to the initial turbulence from which the asteroids formed, and the turbulence is sensitive to Planckian butterflies, or pranic lifetrons, or randomness (whatever belief structure you hold regarding the emergence).

Exactly how sensitive are those asteroid orbits? A rigorous mathematical analysis is beyond the scope of this book (and beyond my own ability) but is possible in theory. If we assert that materially identical solar nebula clouds can spawn significantly different specific asteroid orbits—all contained in the initial no-things-in-themselves nonexistence—I am certain we would be correct, and I doubt most astronomers would disagree. There are trillions of asteroids and comets (a trillion is 10^{12}).[211]

There are many times that many if one includes the smaller objects that are better called big rocks and iceballs, or meteoroids, rather than asteroids or comets. These objects continually pelt all the planets including Earth and, during the initial formation process, the pelting rate was much higher. So the exact orbits of the planets themselves are emergent processes. The planetary orbits are emergent because of the influence of the emergent asteroids and comets, and also because of their own chaotic dynamical component (mentioned in Chapter 9).

The Lives

So, the specific make-up of the solar system—whether the planets' orbits will be here or there—is "up to the solar nebula." It is up to the solar nebula in the same way as it is "up to you" whether you continue reading this book or throw it out the window—both possibilities are contained in the present state of the matter that is you. In the above description, we were referring to the gross orbital parameters, like distance from the sun, and eccentricity of the orbits of the planets. We could do a similar study of the finer details like the spin rate (length of day), spin axis tilt (seasonal solar insolation variability), trace element composition (like oxygen, silicon, etc.), and amount of initial water content, of the planets. All would be emergent in the solar nebula to some degree or another. Two materially identical solar nebulas could "decide" to become vastly different solar systems.

This new view of the orbits of the planets is especially telling because of the special significance of planetary orbits. If one is asked to name the most stable moving thing known in the universe, the orbits of planets is the likely candidate. Planetary orbits last billions of years. They last longer than their host stars. In most cases, the star will go nova (explode), or enter a giant stage and so consume its planets, before the planet's orbit itself decays or otherwise alters. Even galaxies evolve on the time-scale of planetary orbit stability.

The universe itself is estimated to be about 15 billion years "old"—shorter than many planetary orbits would last if their host stars lasted that long. Nevertheless, there are subtle chaotic effects that, coupled with outside influences on the orbital motion, create emergent changes within the lifetime of planetary orbits. And the initial formation parameters themselves, in the solar nebulas, are emergent.

Planetary orbits are emergent on time-scales comparable to the age of the solar system. Processes on the planets (like weather and animals) are emergent on much shorter time-scales. In Chapter 9, we discussed how the details of weather are emergent on time-scales of only a few days. Deep geological processes, like the mantle flows that drive the motions of continents and the magnetic field of the Earth are probably emergent on intermediate time-scales. The precise timing and details of a specific volcanic eruption may be emergent in a few days. Major earthquakes may be emergent in years or shorter. The huge convection cells of deep mantle flow that drive the continents and build mountains may be emergent on hundreds of millions of years.[212]

All of these processes are in turn affected by the planetary orbital changes, due to differences in gravitational pulls and differences in strength of the sun's rays, and all are emergent out of identical solar nebulas.

In this chapter, we have only discussed so-called "inanimate" planetary processes. These inanimate changes then affect and are affected by the biological processes. And much of biology is emergent on more rapid time-scales—seconds or less. Planet Earth is all of these—is it alive? Consider one subsystem like the composition of the atmosphere. Scientists are increasingly noting the importance of the complicated feedback mechanisms that control the atmospheric carbon dioxide and oxygen contents (as well as other atmospheric gases).[213] This feedback includes, for instance, the collection of carbon on ocean floors from dead sea animals and plants and algaes.

The subduction of the ocean floor continental plates back into the Earth's mantle cycles the carbon dioxide back into the atmosphere through volcanoes. Depending on the rate of volcanic activity, the carbon dioxide recycles back into the atmosphere in about 100 million years. The carbon dioxide content in the atmosphere in turn affects the heat and solar insolation, which affects the growth rates of sea plants and animals that accumulate on the ocean floor when they die. All contribute to a self-regulating feedback loop that controls the carbon dioxide content of the atmosphere.

Similar atmospheric chemistry feedback loops—some that don't include biology—also play a role in the control of atmospheric gases like ozone.[214] These feedback loops that maintain a comfortable planetary atmosphere range are analogous to the homeostatic feedback loops that keep a human body alive and warm. Because the hylozoic paradigm tells us that matter is alive anyway, the difference between a human life and the planetary life is only one of degree.

The other planets in our solar system do not have biological life as we know it, as far as we can tell. The other planets do have, though, complicated, active, and dynamic processes and evolutions. In terms of sheer energy processing, bulk activity, and dynamic changes, a lot more happens on Jupiter, for instance, than on Earth. Because empirical science cannot address the questions of the internal lives of planets, does that mean they don't exist? This is not a "merely philosophical" question, because if planets do have internal lives, those internal lives affect their material evolution, just as your internal life affects your material behavior.

After the Voyager II spacecraft flew past the planet Neptune, one of the principal investigators on the imaging camera team of scientists stood in front of a large public lecture hall in Pasadena, California. Over a thousand people in the audience were attentive as the scientist showed slides and moving images of the first close-up photographs of the planet Neptune. Many people find that viewing the spacecraft images, clear and up close, of other planets, is a moving experience. I am one of them.

Voyager discovered many surprises at Neptune. One surprise was the very active weather system on the planet. Since the atmosphere of Neptune is very cold, and since it receives very little heat from the sun (about one in 1600 less per unit area than Earth does), many scientists had predicted an inactive atmosphere, as was discovered on Uranus. The speaker, a planetary climatologist, openly marveled at this surprise.

One of the weather systems on Neptune became known as The Great Dark Spot. The Great Dark Spot is an enormous hurricane-like storm in the atmosphere of Neptune. It stretches perhaps a quarter of the way around the lower part of the planet, and appears dark in the photos. The Great Dark Spot was so named because it is very similar to the Great Red Spot, which is a storm on Jupiter.

The enormous Great Red Spot (many Earth-sized objects could fit inside it) has stormed away for at least the few hundred years that astronomers have been able to see it with telescopes. Has it been there ten thousand years, or even a million years? Might it blow itself out next week as terrestrial hurricanes are wont to do? We don't know. Similarly, the Great Dark Spot on Neptune was only observed for a few weeks as little Voyager hurtled past toward other adventures. Will the Great Dark Spot still be there the next time we send a spacecraft to Neptune—perhaps twenty years from now?

Those are the sorts of questions that the speaker and his team of investigators wanted to answer. They created detailed computer models of Jupiter's (or Neptune's) atmosphere. They ran the computer model to see if a Great Red Spot-like thing happens. They have had some success in creating rough simulations of such storms. Those studies will increase our understanding of planetary climates, including Earth's climate, in general, and are certainly valuable in that sense. But the speaker's comment on why he does it was telling. To that large public audience in Pasadena, he said, "Why do I do it [try to understand the observed atmospheric dynamics]? Because I want to know how it works. I don't want to give up, and say, 'God did it.'"

Some scientists seem to be motivated as if by a challenge to prove that God doesn't exist—to show that Spirit can have no effect in Nature. But that contest was lost in 1926, and lost repeatedly since, as quantum theory has been verified by experiment. It may still be that the universe is, at the emergent level—at the quantum level—random (hylostochastic). But whether it is random, or whether spirit, and Planckian butterflies, and pranic lifetrons, exist cannot be determined from experiments on, or observations of, the outer world. Certainly, we will never predict the weather on Jupiter more precisely than we can predict the weather here on Earth.

I think that what the speaker really meant was as follows. The transcendent (God) referred to by some "fundamentalist" strains of the major Western religions, is couched in irrationality and dogmatism. And many of those dogmas have been shown to be wrong by science. Indeed, the authorities and advocates of the Western religions, in the past, actively battled against science and rationality. Therefore, that image of God is rightly discredited by the experiential truths of science. So, in our exploration of the universe, we should continue to apply science, mathematics, rationality, observation, and experiment because they have yielded the highest truths that Western general culture has experienced.

What that speaker did for me was highlight a generation gap. He was born at a time when the cosmological religious dogmas still claimed a veneer of credibility. So cultural progression, for him, is to advocate rational science as a higher truth. The younger generation of scientists, and people in general, however, came of age in a time when the secular truths of science had already thoroughly supplanted dogmatic religious cosmologies (in the observable world, if not the mythological world). For this generation, the cultural progression is to pursue the rational perspective all the way through and beyond its limits.

That pursuit leads to the conclusion that there may be metaphysical truths of the inner worlds, just as there are physical truths of the outer world. It is also to see that there may be cosmological metaphysical truths, as well as the inner truths of one's own separated mind.

Finally, it is to see that all matter may have inner lives, just as the matter of one's self has an inner life, and to know that the inner life affects the outer manifestation, and vice versa. This is where true rationality, coupled with inner experience, followed all the way to the end, may lead. For instance, a prominent contemporary Vedantist argues just that: "Vedanta holds that reason is the most precious possession of humanity, that it should be kept bright and pure, and that nothing should be indulged in that weakens or destroys it."[215] Vedanta[216] also finds that planets have inner lives, as do humans, and forests, and continents.

To be sure, the inner lives of all these things are vastly different, in degree of self-awareness, coherence, scope, and organization, just as the outer manifestations of all those things are different.

If we are alive, the planets are alive. As an actual butterfly modifies the course of a large weather system, each of us is a metaphorical butterfly altering the course of the whole planetary system. The specific bio-geo-chemical evolutionary track that the planet has taken is the result of the interplay between spirit and matter, not the controlled clockwork of a supernatural physicist. This is now relevant in a direct, and concrete way, as we become conscious of our enormous affect on the global ecosystems and atmospheric balances. When we ask, politically, socially, and personally, "How do we affect the global environment?" the spiritual aspect of the functioning of nature, and of ourselves, becomes highly relevant.

The Seventh Makham of Andalusian Sufism

"There exists in nature that which is emergent. If there were not this that is emergent, there could be no escape from determinism.

But since there is an emergent aspect in nature, an escape from determinism is possible, and is made known." (If I might be pretentious enough as to try to update the Buddha's original language, from the quote at the beginning of this chapter.) The Buddha himself made it explicitly clear that this fact of emergence, among possibilities inherent in matter, is very relevant. The Buddha was emphasizing relevance for spiritual growth of the individual.

The fact of emergent possibility also affects the outer world. The spiritual aspect of nature is highly relevant to the specific behavior of matter, and so also is relevant to the study and practice of science.

I emphasize here the Buddha's words about emergence in nature hesitantly. I do not want to appear to be advocating the idea that "physics proves a certain mystical dogma." As I've emphasized, physics does not and cannot prove that. Instead, I think we can take the Buddha's 20-20 inner insight as indicating that the hylozoic interpretation of 20th century scientific advances is relevant and meaningful for both science and for spiritual paths.

How can we verify such relevance and meaning, if we can't test it with traditional laboratory experiments? We can verify it in a number of ways. First, on the traditionally scientific side, more detailed analyses of the sorts of complex physical phenomena mentioned in this book can be carried out with the intent of investigating the hylozoic idea. On the personal side—the inner verification—I can only describe the way my own conviction developed. In this regard, there was the initial feeling that the hylozoic insight was important, as I have already mentioned. There was also the "waking dreams" with somatic experience that I've mentioned.

Another of those experiences relevant to this chapter occurred as follows. I began to feel the energetic bodily sensations that indicated that another dreamlike occurrence might happen. Still unaccustomed to that sort of thing, I was unsettled, but I'd learned that simply taking a walk could alleviate the feeling, so I went for a walk to Ueno Park.[217]

The sun was setting as I walked through the trees, trying to find a quiet place. I came to the back fence of a baseball diamond. I normally find watching baseball slow, but the unusual energized state made anything more than exciting. A poor transient man was sitting nearby, and we looked through the fence at the amateur baseball game.

As I tried to allow the energized feeling in my body to calm itself, it seemed to expand beyond myself. This is hard to describe because it wasn't a vision of my surroundings, but a sensation of the surroundings. The whole environment seemed alive in a way that I don't normally notice. It was as if there was a momentary sensation of the surrounding animate and inanimate things—a sensation of what *they* were feeling. And the sensation was that the environment felt a lot more than we usually assume it does, and that there was "more there" than the mechanistic paradigms of science would allow. The whole environment had an internal life, not the same as, but just as real as, our own ordinary internal lives.

Later, feeling relieved to be back to my ordinary state, I walked to my apartment and sat down. I thought about creating a sort of mental exercise that might convey some of the concepts of the experience. The exercise was to envision the scientific models of the environment—from the atoms with their quantum vibrations and fluctuations, to the jiggling and shifting molecules, to moving biological cells and mineral crystals and chemical compounds, to organisms and rocks and humans and all, to city and continent-sized environments, to the planet as a whole, to the solar system and its formation, to the galaxy and its structure and movement—and then, with that visual picture in mind, to ask myself if there was anything else there, along side the matter. As I plotted this idea out in my mind, an inner voice said, "Don't just think about it, do it." With that, the somatic sensation returned, and there was again a sensation of feeling the environment. This time the imagery and sensations became larger than the immediate surroundings, and larger than the city, and then the planet, and solar system, to something like solar and galactic sizes.

The striking thing of that dream-experience was that on the solar/galactic scale the sensed "inner life" and relevant processes were even more intense, and active, than those on the human size scale.

Clearly the experience just related doesn't prove anything. One could dismiss it as healthy imagination. From my perspective, the accompanying somatic sensations indicated more than imagination.

But such inner experience should be verified by outer knowledge and observation.

As part of a whole picture, I take it as evidence in favor of a hylozoic interpretation. Once I allowed that possibility, the logical thing to do was to investigate the spiritual traditions to see if they contained any helpful information. A cursory study indicated that the spiritual traditions had been there all along, and I was just reinventing the spiritual wheel (or one of many such wheels). Even the relevance of integrating contemporary science with the rational-based spiritual traditions, like Vedanta, has been advocated by some of the most significant and respected spiritual teachers (as already described).[218]

This fact, of the perennial existence, even though not predominance, of the hylozoic view, came home to me again when I did a workshop with a Sufi teacher. The teacher showed us a series of seven practices that form the basis of a major strain of Sufism.[219]

The seventh practice (or "makham") was to envision one's self expanding to include the entire universe, as best described by science, and then to actively envision the spirit of God infusing the whole thing. I felt as if I had stumbled onto a small part of practices developed by 12th century Sufis. The teacher said that the seven makhams had been kept secret by Sufi initiates until this century, when it was decided to gradually release them, and other formerly secret practices, to general knowledge.

In my opinion, the making and keeping of spiritual and religious secrets (and scientific secrets for that matter) only creates mischief. It does seem, though, that a number of spiritual traditions are recently making generally available formerly secretly held knowledge and practices. This may represent a sort of democratization of spirituality, in which people generally have available all information necessary to make their own decisions, rather than relying on authorities who maintain power through secrets. If so, it is probably meaningful that this democratization of spirituality is occurring at the same time as the general knowledge of physical science is also running, of necessity, into the same territories as spirituality runs. Maybe we've matured enough that our higher Selves can finally trust our lower selves with full knowledge.[220]

For myself, the only obstacle to accepting the hylozoic interpretation was the consensus view of many contemporary scientists and "intellectuals." A more careful look at that consensus opinion indicated that it was based on emotional reactions and incompletely analyzed assumptions, apparently influenced by outdated religious dogmas. In fact, many of the most significant physicists came to an essentially hylozoic perspective (as described in Part I).

If great scientific minds, and great spiritual sages, and even one's own experience, all point in one direction—a direction opposed only by a great inertia of half-thought-out and jealously guarded folk opinions—how much more evidence does one need?

PART IV:

FREEDOM FROM THE KNOWN

To the God Who is in the Fire and Who is in the waters;
To the God Who has suffused Himself through all the world;
To the God Who is in summer plants and in the lord of the forest;
To that God be adoration, adoration.
— Sh'vet Upanishad, II.17[221]

12. From Superstition to Intuition

In Part II, we've shown the openness of matter as science understands it. In Part III, we argued that this openness may be filled by spirit, both in nature and in living systems. Upon realizing the presence of spirit, many argue for a return to the ways of pre-scientific and pre-technological societies that emphasized the role of spirit.

Such denial of the success and value of science is, in some ways, worse than the blind scientific materialism it reacts against. Pre-scientific societies honored and respected spirit in ways that can teach us much. However, the reactive impulse to remain ignorant of science and technology, because they can be associated with destructive influences, spawns superstition, irrational authoritarianism, and new belief structures, themselves flawed. Those mistakes cause others to deny, by association, all aspects of spirit and its influence in our world.

Science has now, in a basic sense, completed our search for the most fundamental laws governing matter. We find matter open. The only way at present to explore that openness is to develop our intuition, with all its pitfalls and apparent imperfections. Intuition is the use of our own extraordinarily complex human body-minds to sense, and eventuate, the integration of spirit and matter.

A theme of this part of the book is that the hylozoic paradigm will be part of a larger movement characterized by:

1. A re-vivifying of the great spiritual and religious traditions in a way that they will be fully compatible with scientific knowledge, and that they will be accepted as not incompatible with (though different from) each other, because they originate from the same source.
2. The emergence now, or becoming newly accessible now, of teachers and teachings that will help us make these realizations. These range from great teachers, akin to the great

spiritual heroes of history, to unusual world events like the peaceful overthrow of authoritarian communism, and unusual environmental events, and to many individuals making known the relevance of point one above.

Obviously my own viewpoint on this is based on inner experience and opinion, as well as a reading of outer events. I will give examples of both. The first three parts lay the groundwork for the possible relevance of this sort of world-view.

This part should be read as one person's ongoing struggle to view a variety of emerging topics (some extremely controversial) with an informed hylozoic perspective. The opinions of others on these topics will be quite different. Such conflicts at this stage are good if we're honest about our own prejudices. They will hasten the emergence of new syntheses.

The following material presents a certain slant on the immensely open hylozoic paradigm. One reviewer has said that this part undercuts the "scientific objectivity" of the previous parts. I don't agree. The scientific facts and arguments already presented in Parts I, II and III can be verified, or refuted if possible, by any investigator on the basis of available information. Likewise, the sources and references in this part can be studied and verified openly.

That I include subjective interpretation, intuitive experience, and very controversial subjects in this part should not undercut anything already presented. The fact is that even the most objective scientist does hold a body of opinion and outlook on these issues. It seems to me that to make known one's own perspective, and the awareness that one has a perspective, only adds to the objective usefulness of the information given. To pretend otherwise—to pretend to know an exclusive objective truth about these matters, or to pretend not to have any internal bearings at all— would be disingenuous.

In this chapter, we suggest that the shift to the hylozoic paradigm in science is a key aspect of a larger world cultural phenomenon— the meeting of East and West. This meeting requires a movement from superstition, through rationalistic positivism, to transcendent intuition. We also look at a barrier to this movement—the dark side of spirit—in order to put it aside.

East and West

The Dalai Lama, in his autobiography, describes his own keen interest in science and technology as well as his profound spiritual training, and he advocates both heartily. He also describes his early meetings with Mao Tse Tung. The immense cultural forces involved in the paradigm shift can be seen acting on a personal level, in the Dalai Lama's description of his final meeting with Mao. Mao implied that the Dalai Lama couldn't really believe in his own religious practices, and the Dalai Lama describes:

> "The only possible explanation was that he had misinterpreted my great interest in scientific matters and material progress. ... that my cast of mind is basically scientific. So it could only be that Mao had ignored the Buddha's instruction that anyone who practices the Dharma should personally test its validity. For this reason, I have always been open to the truths of modern science. Perhaps this was what tricked Mao into thinking that my religious practices were nothing more than a prop or convention ... he had misjudged me completely."[222]

The unusually harsh, for him, tone of the above comments indicates the depth of the Dalai Lama's break with Mao whom he'd almost begun to trust. Chinese Premiere Mao's failure to grasp that the Tibetan leader could be both scientifically literate and capable on the one hand, and profoundly spiritual on the other hand, without contradiction, catalyzed the horrible crises in Sino-Tibet relations that still continue today.[223]

The Dalai Lama had "tested the Dharma" and found it quite valid. Rather than making him anti-science or anti-technology, this gave the Dalai Lama a foundation on which to use scientific and technological knowledge in a wider and more complete context, and heightened his interest in science.

Since this is the subjective part of the book, we can take off our scientist hats and speculate that the rift between the Dalai Lama and Mao is symbolic of the rift between the old and the new paradigms in science. That the Dalai Lama and Mao are both "Eastern" points to a fundamental cultural development that parallels the shift to the hylozoic paradigm.

The fundamental difference between what we call the East and what we call the West can be stated as "the East went completely over into the immeasurable, and the West went completely over into the measurable."[224] This is also the fundamental problem with each.

The measurable is, of course, what science deals with. The correspondence is complete. Science deals with the measurable only, and all of the measurable can be represented at least theoretically in terms of science. The immeasurable is spirit, as we have been using the term. Any and all of the nonmaterial stuff that may jump into the openness in matter to precipitate events is immeasurable. The way matter works, as we saw in Parts II and III—the connectivity across space and time—means that spirit is necessarily immeasurable (at least as we now understand the word measurable).

An awareness of, and emphasis on, clear measures can be very powerful for certain sorts of purposes, such as running large organizations. When NASA chief administrator Goldin was appointed the task of repairing NASA administration, I interestedly read his early speeches on e-mail. One of his first acts was to require all the senior executives under him to present a description of how their own performances could be measured. Talk about a powerful management tool! But consider applying that standard to all your social, cultural, emotional, and inner, activities—that's what the Western materialist paradigm does. If all the great sages, seers, and religious teachers of history—who said that there is an important immeasurable, spiritual, hylozoic, aspect to the world—are correct, imagine the collective psychic damage that the materialist paradigm does.

The East, in recent history, had the opposite problem. The short flourishing of authoritarian communism in the East (Russia and China) can be seen as an overreaction to the problem of the East—its overemphasis on the immeasurable. As the Dalai Lama suddenly realized in his meeting with Mao, authoritarian communism is based at its core on "scientific" Marxism or perhaps Marxist scientism. Authoritarian communism requires, at its philosophical core, a mechanistic deterministic (hylostatic) universe, or at least a mostly mechanistic and partly random (hylostochastic) universe. It cannot rest on a living (hylozoic) universe. Authoritarian communism can be seen, at its best, as the attempted imposition of an exclusively measurable worldview onto a culture immersed in the immeasurable.

12: From Superstition to Intuition

Its happy failure can be seen not as a triumph of the immeasurable but as the need for synthesis of the two—a meeting of East and West.

The need for a synthesis was the conclusion the Dalai Lama had long since come to. He had tried to improve the technological development of his country while maintaining its spiritual growth.[225] Unfortunately, a rapid and extreme swing into scientism and authoritarian communism does impart more control, at least temporarily, over matter and thus a more rapid technological development. This can be seen in the material and military superiority that China uses to wield power over Tibet.

Forward thinkers in the West are voicing the same interpretation of the fall of authoritarian Communism as being related to the dissolution of mechanistic deterministic paradigm science. Preeminent social philosopher and Czech Republic president Vaclav Havel writes:

> "The fall of Communism can be regarded as a sign that modern thought—based on the premise that the world is objectively knowable, and that the knowledge so obtained can be absolutely generalized—has come to a final crisis. This era has created the first global, or planetary, technical civilization, but it has reached the limit of its potential, the point beyond which the abyss begins. The end of Communism is a serious warning to all mankind. It is a signal that the era of arrogant, absolutist reason is drawing to a close and that it is high time to draw conclusions from that fact.
>
> "Traditional science, with its usual coolness, can describe the different ways we might destroy ourselves, but it cannot offer us truly effective and practicable instructions on how to avert them. There is too much to know; the information is muddled or poorly organized; these processes can no longer be fully grasped and understood, let alone contained or halted.
>
> "We all know that civilization is in danger. The population explosion and the greenhouse effect, holes in the ozone ... the threat of nuclear terrorism ... the danger of famine, the depletion of the biosphere ... all these, combined with a thousand other factors, represent a general threat to mankind.

"We are looking for new scientific recipes, new ideologies, new control systems, new institutions, new instruments to eliminate the dreadful consequences of our previous recipes, ideologies, control systems, institutions and instruments. We treat the fatal consequences of technology as though there were a technical defect that could be remedied by technology alone. We are looking for an objective way out of the crisis of objectivism."[226]

In an attempt to rebut what he views as an attack on science by Havel, a physics professor of the older generation writes, "I do not believe that the traditional goal of science—to understand nature—is socially irresponsible. The contributions of science to this nation and to the world need no apology."[227]

On the contrary though, I do not believe that Havel is attacking science. Havel is attacking objectivism. He is attacking rationalistic positivism—the belief, like Mao's apparent belief, that "the world is objectively knowable, and that the knowledge so obtained can be absolutely generalized." As should be abundantly clear, science itself as we now understand it presents no evidence to support such a belief. In fact, the adherence to the belief structure of objectivism is itself unscientific. If we falsely equate, as does Kleppner, science with objectivism, with rationalistic positivism, we will indeed doom science as Kleppner and others now fear it is doomed.

The East's diversion into the immeasurable leads to superstition. However, the West's exclusive belief in the measurable—the belief that the immeasurable just doesn't exist—is also superstitious. Leaders like the Dalai Lama and Havel are moving toward a meeting of East and West, metaphorically, an acceptance of both the measurable and the immeasurable. They arrive at this meeting through intuitive insight in the sociopolitical and philosophical realms—realms larger than that of limited science. We've arrived at the same meeting, as described in the earlier parts of this book, through the smaller field of science itself.

The same movement toward the acceptance of both the measurable and the immeasurable, toward the meeting of East and West, can be seen in the world of religion, in the growing interest in esotericism. Esotericism is the synthesis of, or interest in any one of, the esoteric cores of the major religions. Esoteric Islam is called Sufism. Esoteric

Judaism is called Kabbalism. Esoteric Christianity can be equated with Gnosticism. Esoteric Hinduism is Vedantism. Esoteric Buddhism can be seen in Zen, Theravada, and Tibetan Buddhism.

Esotericism is marked by an inclusive attitude toward the other paths. In Sufism, for instance, it is held that there are "125,000 doors into the Garden," meaning that the other major religions and many subdivisions, and many other paths, all lead to the same spiritual source—and all are respected. Esoteric Christianity can be represented by Jesus' even more inclusive statement, "the Kingdom of Heaven [the Sufi's Garden] is within you." The same inclusive attitude is echoed in Vedantism,[228] Esoteric Buddhism, and Kabbalism.

These esoteric cores can be antithetical to their counterpart organized religions—which tend to the dogmatic, authoritarian, and exclusive—and have been consistently persecuted. The Inquisition's campaigns for instance have become legendary, and one of the Inquisition's prime targets was esoteric spirituality. As mentioned in Chapter 4, Giordano Bruno's advocacy of an inclusive and esoteric attitude toward the transcendent was even more threatening to the Inquisition than was Galileo's science. Sufism is outlawed now in some fundamentalist Islamic countries.

In the same way as dogmatic authoritarian religion is antithetical to mystical insight, the dogmatic, authoritarian, and exclusive elements of the science establishment vigorously resist the shift to the hylozoic paradigm. This occurs even in the face of tremendous evidence that a shift is warranted. Exclusive emphasis on, or belief in, either the measurable or the immeasurable is propped-up by dogmatic authoritarianism, be it an Eastern religious dogma or Western scientism or Communism. The hylozoic paradigm lets East meet West, and the measurable meet the immeasurable.

Barriers to Intuition

One barrier to the much needed movement to the hylozoic paradigm is simple resistance to change—the perpetuation of authority for authority's sake, and for the sake of power. Another barrier has to do with the necessarily experiential nature of the shift. We alluded to this barrier earlier (in Chapter 1) as the frightening aspect of Descartes' experience of "occult or somatic insight"—that is, intuition. This barrier manifests, historian Berman describes as, "then reacting with fear to the very tool [somatic insight, or intuition] that made this possible, dropping it like a hot potato, and erecting a new (rigid) system."

Numerous other reliable accounts indicate that initial openings to the intuitive realms are accompanied by frightening as well as illuminating experiences. This aspect is symbolized in the mythic accounts of the Buddha enduring numerous demons on his way to illumination, and Jesus resisting illusory temptations on his way to crucifixion (and resurrection). The same principle is alluded to as the makyo, or "illusory realities," described in Zen and other meditative practices.

Democracy of the Transcendent

Lest we dismiss this sort of confrontation with the transcendent as relevant only to near mythical or superhuman figures of the past such as Buddha and Jesus, we reiterate that a number of ordinary, educated, reliable contemporaries also describe quite clearly intuitive or transcendent experience (see Chapter 2, for instances of these).

Also, as to the ordinariness of the transcendent, Edgar Cayce, for instance, was known as the "sleeping prophet," because he received his intuitive insights in a sort of a sleep trance. Cayce was invariably described as a simple man who, in his ordinary state and with his limited educational background, could not even understand some of his intuitive medical and other insights.

Similarly, the accounts of scientists experiencing flashes of insight that they take decades to understand are always popular—such as Einstein having insight into relativity theory when getting onto a bus, or Newton seeing an apple fall and intuiting the theory of universal gravitation. Some idiot savants (severely developmentally retarded individuals) seem to display skills that may only be explainable by intuitive connection with a very limited specific field—their "savant" quality.[229]

We can look from the superhuman Buddhas through the eminently human sleeping prophets, scientists, and idiot savants, to even the subhuman, and still find intuitive-spiritual rapport. Some researchers report that individual unrelated animals, such as monkeys and mice, learn new tasks more easily after other members of their species have learned them. The sudden ability of many humans to run a four-minute-mile, after one had done so, could also be an example of this.

With humans, though, one could describe a mechanistic explanation in that after it was done once, others might *think* they can do it, and so could. With laboratory mice it is more difficult to suggest that they overheard the researchers talking and conditioned themselves ahead of time. But task learning experiments with animals have been notorious for inconsistent results and subtle queuing of the experimenters or other uncontrollable factors. The point here is not to sanction any given example as proof that this effect occurs. The point is that if it does occur, it is essentially a sort of intuition, and it does not violate a hylozoic understanding of science.

Moving further down the evolutionary scale to the completely nonbiological systems described in the previous chapters, their opening to the effects of the Planckian butterflies, are also exhibitions of a sort of intuition. So, human intuition may be only one aspect of material rapport with the transcendent, a rapport that occurs literally everywhere. One does not need to be grandiose, or an egoist, or a TV preacher, to consider intuitive rapport with the transcendent as a reality. The hylozoic paradigm shows that one does not have to be "unscientific" either.

What is sometimes called a "spiritual opening," we can model as a human simply noticing that this material rapport with the transcendent is occurring. And according to many accounts, this noticing is often accompanied by a frightening as well as an illuminating aspect. What is the source of this? In following chapters, we'll discuss possible practical uses of intuitive insight in light of the hylozoic paradigm in science. But now, it may be useful to consider the source of the frightening aspect.

The Dark Side

Consistent with the hylozoic paradigm, intuitive insight, transcendent experience, or spiritual opening, could be some sort of sensation, by our material senses and brain-minds, of some aspect of the nonmaterial realms. It may be simply an awareness of a process that is always occurring, ordinarily below conscious awareness. For instance, a subtle sensation of the general thought quality or emotional quality of others in one's vicinity or even one's whole cultural group or species may be a constant subconscious process (which Carl Jung called the "collective unconscious").

Why might this sort of sensation be frightening? Anyone who's looked deeply into their own thoughts and emotions, and considered that similar thoughts and emotions are probably common to others, would not have difficulty answering that.

Indeed, the spiritual traditions say that it is best to view this sort of sensation of one's group as insight into the self, or Self in a collective sense. Treating it as an individual looking out onto a hostile external environment, the spiritual disciplines say, leads to destructive good-evil dualisms that are ultimately mistaken. Keeping that in mind, it is useful to consider the way things might look initially to the ego surprised to have this sort of insight or opening.

Given that in such instance, one is just starting to intuit the nonmaterial aspects of one's environment, it makes sense that some of the initial insights will be with the baser emotional and thought forms of others as well as one's own subconscious. More subtle and refined aspects are more difficult to intuit than the gross and base aspects.

The contemporary accounts, such as of Gopi Krishna, Richard Moss, and many others (as mentioned in Chapter 2), as well as the classical accounts of spiritual teachers, agree with this model. Given the sort of suffering, confusion, and pain that must have existed in the time of Inquisitions, openly practiced torture, and public executions, it may not be surprising that one such as Descartes starting to feel the subtle realms would not be thrilled.

If this model of the transcendent has some bearing in reality, it implies an inner responsibility for each of us. Rather than only being of curious interest as one aspect of the "way the world works," it implies as well a very real collective responsibility. Our thoughts, intentions, and will toward others, even if not acted out, may cause effects in peoples and objects throughout this level of reality.

This is not the grandiose "magical" delusion of the infantile personality that cannot differentiate between self and other. It is a fully rational and critical observation of the way things may actually work. Another responsibility is that those capable of investigating critically this subtle aspect of reality, and how to work productively with it, should do so.

The hylozoic paradigm of science shows that this sort of thing may or may not occur. The only way to determine for oneself whether it does occur, as far as I know, is careful observation of one's own thought, somatic experience, and creative process.

J. Krishnamurti, in considering whether becoming aware of violence can dissipate it, asks:

> "So is there such a thing as absolute evil? I don't know if you have ever considered this: I have seen in India little statues made of clay in which needles, or thorns, have been put; I have seen it very often. The image is supposed to represent a person whom you want to hurt. In India there are very long thorns, you have seen them, from bushes, and they are stuck into these clay statues."
>
> A questioner replies: "I didn't know they did that in India."
>
> Krishnamurti: "I have seen it. Now *there* is a determined action to produce evil in another, to hurt another."
>
> Questioner: "An intent."
>
> Krishnamurti: "The intent, the ugly, deep, hatred. ... Organized disorder, which is the organized disorder of a society that rejects the good. Because the society is me. I am the society; if I don't change, society cannot change. And here is the deliberate intention to hurt another, whether it is organized as war or not."
>
> Questioner: "In fact, organized war is the group manifestation of the phenomenon you are speaking about in India, putting the thorns through the little statues."
>
> Krishnamurti: "This is well known, this is as old as the hills. So I am saying this desire to hurt, consciously or unconsciously, and yielding to it, and giving it sustenance, is what? Would you call it evil?"

There is a lot of vicious stuff to be sensed if one begins to sense our collective thought forms. My own observations lead me to accept that collective thought and emotional forms do sometimes impinge on our awareness. I too started to encounter the fearful aspects when accepting this viewpoint. Being in Asia at the time, this aspect may have been amplified for me because, the East being more immersed in the immeasurable, the sort of practices mentioned above by Krishnamurti seem to be more prevalent there.

There is meant no judgmental attitude toward the East here. The prevalence of such consciously subtle violence in the East is probably surpassed by the prevalence of unconsciously subtle violence in the West. And the advocacy of consciously directed subtle violence is alive and well in the West also. For instance, under the pseudonym "Hakim Bey," an American writer and college teacher advocated making a list of one's enemies and putting formal curses on them, again using dolls and pins, complete with the use of potions of blood from a black rooster, dried scorpion, graveyard dirt, corrupted versions of sacred Islamic prayers, and the invocation of names of deceased adepts.[230] And he's not kidding. The writer also draws in the gullible with vague references to "mathematical chaos theory" as support for "ontological anarchism."

Physician Larry Dossey has recently reviewed the studies of prayer, and other remote (necessarily hylozoic) effects in healing and medicine. Dossey concluded that the clinical evidence, and even controlled experiments, overwhelmingly support the conclusion that nonlocal hylozoic practices like prayer (both for healing, and for harm—which he calls "black prayer" that reports may have sometimes contributed to death), do sometimes have effect, though not in as consistently measurable a way as simple drugs or surgery.[231]

The point here is not only to chastise that sort of violent intent. As Krishnamurti and many others point out, at deeper levels it is all aspects of ourselves anyway. We are acknowledging the dark side of initial encounters with the subtle or intuitive realms, in order to surpass it. For example, there was a specific time when I actually became frightened that I might be open to harm from this sort of thing, even though I had always dismissed superstition, because I felt momentarily unusually close to the intuitive realms.

An odd "coincidence" then occurred that seems to illustrate the sort of help that materializes if one bears with experience, rather than rejecting it. When I realized that I was specifically becoming afraid of the violence in the subtle realms in my environment and in the history of the culture I was surrounded by, I discussed this with a friend. The very next morning, an unusual encounter occurred:

12: From Superstition to Intuition

I was on my way to a meeting at the Institute of Space and Astronomical Sciences, south of Tokyo. Changing trains, I was standing alone, waiting near the end of a mostly empty platform, looking like quite an ordinary and unremarkable foreigner in my Japanese salaryman-style haircut, black-rimmed glasses, and briefcase.

Then a man came onto the platform and walked all the way toward me. He had a shaved head and was wearing an unusual sort of monk's robes—different color and style from the common Zen monks' or Zen priests', clean but worn with use, not merely ceremonial. He sat down right next to me on the empty platform—another unusual thing to do in Japanese society.

Then he spoke directly at me, again unusual. "I am a monk."

I was too taken by the weirdness of the events to be witty about his opening with the more than obvious, and I merely nodded. He asked me where I was going. I answered reservedly and disinterestedly, figuring this guy was probably a kook of some sort. Then he said, "I'm a Shingon Esoteric monk." My ears perked up. I'd heard vaguely of Shingon, and I was familiar with esotericism (as described above), but I'd never heard of Shingon Esotericism much less Shingon Esoteric monks. So I was now interested.

We sat down together on the train and there was a feeling that he wanted to tell me something. He was slightly agitated or vibrant. Whatever sort of meditation he practiced it tended toward vivification rather than serenity or complacency. I asked him where he was going, and he said without irony or sarcasm "this way," pointing in the direction the train was moving.

He explained to me that Shingon Esoterics were both Buddhist and Shinto—Shinto being the traditional or state religion of Japan with the Emperor the highest Shinto priest. He said that Shingon Esoterics were, in modern history, the priests of the "ruling classes," the other Buddhist and Shinto sects being more generally open to anyone.[232] He said that Shingon Esoteric monks and priests had no temples or fixed addresses (unlike the orthodox Shinto shrines and Buddhist temples), and they do not evangelize or preach or seek students. Students seek them. They are semi-hidden.

Then the most extraordinary part of the conversation occurred. He said, "But Shingon is terrible."

"Huh?"

"Shingon is also terrible."

Still unsettled by the unusualness of the encounter, which I had been attempting to treat as casual chitchat, I said something like, "Why do you say that?"

He repeated, "Shingon is terrible." And then he explained. He said that Shingon Esoterics were heavily involved, for instance, during World War II. He said that a certain priest, who was also a University professor, used Esoteric religious techniques to try and kill US President Roosevelt, remotely. He said that it was believed that a sort of boomerang effect, from that practice, was the cause of the professor and his son soon thereafter dying terrible deaths. He even said he thought it was that sort of wrong use of spiritual practice that brought the atomic bomb onto Japan.[233]

He concluded with, "We don't do that [sort of abuse of Esoteric practice] anymore." He said that they now pray for *all* people, and all races. He said that if, for instance, he were to hate Americans, Karma works in such a way that he would probably be reborn as an American in his next life. So, that sort of hatred makes no sense practically, or morally.

By then, long past my stop, I thanked him and disembarked.

That chance encounter seemed very clearly to come as if the universe were replying to my fear of the subtle realms. The message was obviously a verification—yes, you were sensing an actual aspect of your cultural environment, your intuition is accurate. It was also a lesson—don't be afraid, the apparent evil is only superficial, on deeper levels the subtle realms lead toward peaceful evolution for *all* humans. If the subtle realms are used to inflict emotional violence, then even worse violence will come to the inflictor. Intuition *is* a vital part of human being, and the dark side is real but engaging with it is futile at best—and it is best ignored completely. Intuition is simply the paying of attention, in the deepest sense.

All I can report is that my own experience seems to verify the intuitive insights of J. Krishnamurti, and the clinical and experimental studies reviewed by Dr. Dossey—that hylozoic effects are important in physical and emotional healing. One of the difficulties in accepting this view, as Dossey notes, is that it implies a responsibility that most of us would rather not have. If our internal thoughts, emotions, prayers, and intentions affect other people, and if we would prefer to have positive effect on others, most of us have a lot of self-improvement to do.

One of the first things that any meditator notices is the tremendous, ugly, mess of rampant thoughts, desires, and emotions seething in his near subconscious. Putting reins on them, or using other methods to allow them to dissipate, is not easy. But if the evidence is that our internal states are connected with, affect and are affected by, external events, then it is our responsibility to accept the truth, if apparently unpleasant, and go forward from there.

A Responsibility to Investigate

Obviously, my interpretation that my encounter on the train platform contained meaning, conveyed via the subtle nonmaterial realms, is subjective. If one wants to argue that the subtle realms just don't exist, and so events like this cannot have meaning that is subjective opinion also. The probability of that event cannot be calculated. We cannot send out an experiment of billions of Thomases all thinking and feeling exactly the same thing and see how many of them happen to meet a Shingon Esoteric monk who happens to convey such a tale. It is a safe bet that the precise event will not be repeated in the history of the universe. Humans are so complex that any given human event just does not repeat, and is not repeatable in full detail.

The hylozoic paradigm says that human events, indeed all events, may contain meaning and connectivity via the subtle nonmaterial realms. The decision as to whether such meaning and connectivity does indeed exist must be made by means other than experimental science—by intuition, and methods to develop intuition.

The hylozoic paradigm shows that rejecting the immeasurable, whether out of fear of the dark aspects or ignorance of the openness of matter, is just as superstitious as is blind belief in magical spells.

Also, considering that throughout history most of those who have capably and honestly investigated have concluded that both the measurable and the immeasurable do exist and do have effect in events, a responsibility is implied. The responsibility is that at least some of those trained in, and capable with the measurable (e.g. scientists), should bring some honest investigation to the meeting of the measurable and the immeasurable. If this area is ignored by our cultural, scientific, and political elite, then this possibly important realm will be left to the Hakim Beys, other would be petty black magicians, and the less than competent.

13: Intelligence—Allowing Spirit into Matter

"We have grasped the mystery of the atom and rejected the Sermon on the Mount. The world has achieved brilliance without wisdom and power without conscience. Ours is a world of nuclear giants and ethical infants."
— General Omar Bradley, ca. 1950[234]

"Like all else at this time, science itself is in process of transformation, and, little as it is realized by many, their work with what they call matter, and their investigations of the atom are entering into a new field. In this field the older techniques and mechanisms will gradually be discarded and a new approach and a different fundamental concept as to the nature of matter will mark the new age."
— The Tibetan Lama, Djwhal Khul, 1934[235]

"The most beautiful and most profound emotion we can experience is the sensation of the mystical. It is the sower of all true art and science. He to whom this emotion is a stranger, who can no longer wonder and stand rapt in awe, is as good as dead. To know that what is impenetrable to us really exists."
— Albert Einstein

"What humanity owes to personalities like Buddha, Moses, and Jesus ranks for me higher than all the achievements of the inquiring and constructive mind."
— Albert Einstein

There is one thing about which great warriors, great spiritual teachers, and great scientists agree: the world is hylozoic. If we accept that spirit and matter exist in concert, act in concert, and interrelate; and we accept that science as it is has been defined, limited, and practiced, has excluded consideration of the entire aspect of spirit, and so science has limited its range of validity, and limited its ability to confront the most important issues emerging now, where do we go from here, and how do we go there?

Trying even to address that question feels a bit pretentious. All I can do is expose some of my own intermediate efforts to discriminate among various models, theories, and practices. The core concept is the shifting paradigm of science, and that the new paradigm must be some sort of hylozoic paradigm, and it must have closer association with all the spiritual traditions than did the old paradigm. The following ideas about where to go from that basic realization, ideas about what spiritual traditions might help, and how, are just that—ideas to be investigated further, discriminated among, perhaps discarded, or adopted.

Horses' Teeth

A story from the time of the beginning of the scientific revolution can help remind us about how science got to be where it is now. In a book dedicated to the cooperation between contemporary science and spiritual traditions, that has been called the first such book written by a major spiritual leader, Swami Ranganathananda relates a telling story from Western Europe during the latter half of the 15th century:[236]

> "A group of scholars of Oxford University was assembled in its library hall and engaged in solving what to the participants was a momentous problem in zoology, namely, how many teeth a horse has. They followed the method of the centuries old tradition for solving such problems, namely, reference to ancient authorities. The scholars vied with each other in taking ancient books out of the library and consulting their authors. The author most consulted was Aristotle (384 – 342 BC) whose authority, already binding, but still more reinforced by the patronage of the medieval church, was unquestioned and supreme.

When the scholars were warmly engaged in the debate, quoting authorities to uphold one's position or refute that of one's opponent, one young scholar quietly left the hall and, in a few minutes, came back, to the horror of all those present, leading a live horse; and stationing it in the center of the hall, he calmly addressed his fellow scholars: "Gentleman, you want to know how many teeth a horse has? Here is a live horse. Please open its mouth and count its teeth, and thus ascertain the truth for yourself."

The rest of the scholars were thoroughly shocked by the foolhardy audacity of the young scholar and condemned him for believing, and asking them to believe, that a horse could have more or less teeth than what Aristotle and other authorities had provided for it in their books!"

The spirit of that young 15th-century scholar embodies the spirit of modern science. As the brash physics hero Richard Feynman eloquently put it, "it doesn't matter who you are, or what your name is, if your theory doesn't agree with experiment, then it is wrong." So, scientists have been counting horses' teeth ever since.

Counting a horse's teeth is a bright thing to do when the question is how many teeth a horse has. Empirical observation is the proper ultimate authority when the question is one suited to empirical verification. During the course of the last five centuries of science, though, the empirical method has in turn overstepped its rightful boundaries and tried to usurp ultimate authority over all questions, of any sort.

When the question is, "What is the horse feeling?" old paradigm scientists would reply with the metaphorical equivalent of, "Well, we can approach that question by first counting the horse's teeth."

Actually, the approach would be more like mapping the horse's nervous system, weighing its brain, quantifying its molecular structure, and so on. But the question cannot be answered by observation (counting) or by repeatable laboratory experiment. When the inability of the empirical method is realized, the answer is often asserted to be negative: "Horses don't feel at all."

Our hypothetical scientist gets into a bit of a bind when he sees that the question, "What is a person thinking or experiencing?" is essentially the same as, "What is a horse feeling?" However, he seems to have no problem sticking to his paradigm and asserting, "People must not think or have relevant inner experience either—a human is all perfectly determined, or partially random, mechanical material processes."

Similarly he asserts that the emergent weather must not have meaning—it must be random. Equally rational people, however, have concluded the opposite—that emergent matter is alive and is in touch with the transcendent. As old paradigm scientists dismiss that other view, they gradually lose credibility, and so does science itself if it doesn't move into the new paradigm. It is because I love science that I stress this point. If science dismisses experience, it loses credibility, and I want it to be credible.

Questions such as, "Do we have souls, and if so, what is their function and relevance?" are met with patronizing dismissal, and a return to the laboratory, to count horses' teeth again. What would the unaffected young scholar advocate now, five centuries later? Empirical science has been astonishingly successful, and productive. It has even run into the end of itself. Questions of how matter works—how the matter of our everyday environment works—have come finally to nonempirical questions.

Now, a relevant question becomes, "Is matter hylozoic, or is it hylostochastic"? The room full of scholars is sitting around saying, "Well, the answer to that question is not contained in the mathematics of quantum theory, and it can't be answered by ordinary laboratory experiments, so it must be a meaningless question."

The brash young scholar would say, "If you want to know if matter has a relevant inner life, study your own inner life!—you all agree that you are matter."

A Kogi Message from the Past

We need information on how to function in the spiritual realms. Do metaphysical realities exist? Do metaphysical truths exist? How do they affect material reality? How do our actions, thoughts, meditations, prayers, curses, wants, whatever, participate? Not in terms of abstract theology, but in a direct, concrete, immediate sense. When one is confronted with a new field where expertise is needed, the thing to do is to look around and see who is purported to have expertise, and see what they have to say. In that regard we will first look at a startling voice from the past, and then at some lesser-known but established existing systems, and finally at an astonishing voice from the present.

In 1976, a lone Colombian tomb robber pressed into the nearly impenetrable tropical forest at the base of the remote Sierra mountains in northern Colombia. He was in search of a fabled lost city. He found it. An enormous complex of roads, paths, ceremonial sites, and abandoned villages, the Tairona city is described as architecturally even more advanced than were the Inca cities. Tomb robbers plundered what they could for years, and then led the archaeologists to it.

Gradually it became apparent that the development was not entirely abandoned. In the higher reaches of the Sierra, a native people called the Kogi still live. The Kogi had successfully hidden themselves from the outside world since early post-Columbian times. After their "discovery," a number of factors, such as extreme physical isolation, acted to allow the Kogi to continue to keep out any unwanted visitors, which includes essentially all outsiders.

The lost city itself is a stonework masterpiece of architectural harmony with the environment—a sort of Frank Lloyd Wright-style city of stone in the jungle. The lowest level of the mountains is guarded by impenetrable jungle and guerrilla warriors of both the drug dealing and the revolutionary types. Above them on the mountains are bands of Native peoples, who have successively less contact with the outside world.

The few explorers, anthropologists, and missionaries who had tried to penetrate the upper regions were met with a wall of passive resistance that worked to protect the Kogi. Also, a young Colombian government Indian affairs officer (Amparo Jimenez Luque), stationed at the base of the Sierra, recognized the importance of the Kogi and staunchly protected them.

Several years ago, the Kogi determined that they would have to break their silence, just once, in order to deliver a vital message to the outside world. "Coincidentally," a BBC (British Broadcasting Corporation) documentary filmmaker (Alan Ereira) happened to hear about the lost city and the Kogi.

When Ereira asked Amparo about the possibility of doing a film for the Kogi, her reply astonished him. Amparo said, "Many television companies have come—from Europe, from North America, from Japan—wanting to film the Kogi. ... She has turned them all down ... [But, since] this was the first time anyone had proposed a collaboration with the Kogi—not to make a film about them, but to make a film with them ... she will support it. She will ask the Kogi."

The Kogi agreed. In fact they had been training one of their own people for years, to act as interpreter for just such a purpose. No outsiders can speak Kogi. The Kogi recruited a half Kogi, half Arhuaco (Ramon), who knew Spanish. Kogi society is run by a hereditary and divinatorily determined elite called the "Mamas." The Kogi Mamas had taught Ramon their spiritual ways for 14 months, and sent him to Santa Marta (the nearby Colombian city that has been a Wild West-like center of the marijuana, cocaine, and tomb artifacts trades) to learn proper Spanish. At the right time, along came Ereira, resulting in a 1992 book (*The Elder Brothers: A Lost South American People and Their Message about the Fate of the Earth*), and a BBC documentary film (*From the Heart of the World*).

When Ereira was finally allowed into the High Sierra, he found there "the last functioning pre-Columbian civilization." The people are clean, well-dressed in white tunics, intelligent, soft-spoken, articulate, and courteous. The Kogi Mamas really do not want any more contact with us. They consciously risked their successful isolation, only to convey a message of vital importance, just once. Their BBC film, and Ereira's book are meant to convey that message. The parts of that message relevant to our point, in this book, are as follows:

> The Kogi call themselves the "Elder Brothers," and us the "Younger Brothers." The Younger Brothers, the Kogis say, came about thousands of years ago as an immature group unable to interact with the spiritual aspect of nature. We were "given knowledge of machines" and sent across the oceans. Now we are back, and more dangerous than ever, and on a new global scale.

> In Ereira's words, "The Kogi are not hunter-gatherers, or a wandering tribe. They are a nation [of thousands] whose fields

have been continuously cultivated and towns continuously occupied for more than a thousand years.

Fragments of related civilizations, Maya and Inca, live on in isolated communities in the Andes and Central America, but they are fragments, coexisting with our world and all, to a greater or lesser extent, reshaped by it. The Kogi alone survive as a proto-state, maintaining the authority of their own theocratic institutions, exerting the power of their ancient laws, living in a universe that they perceive in an utterly different way than we do. These Elder Brothers look on us as children, dangerous, irrational and essentially helpless. In Spanish, they call us 'civilizados', the civilized people. It is an expression of deep irony." The astonishing images in his film support this description.

The Kogi Mamas are highly trained priests and priestesses—healers, spiritual teachers, and most importantly, guardians of the world, they believe. The training of a Kogi Mama is extraordinary. In early childhood, or infancy, those who show promise to become Mamas are identified. The child is put in a special building, or prepared cave, and kept there in isolation from the world. He is fed carefully prepared special foods, and given only enough sensory stimulation to keep his senses functioning. He is constantly attended by a spiritual teacher, and often massaged to keep his body healthy. He is taught to learn from the inner world of spirit, the world that they call "aluna." He is taught of the natural world—of plants, animals, weather, everything—and taught to learn about them, from their spirit forms.

Importantly, the Mamas say that *they* do not teach the student, they guide him to learn directly from aluna. The student is kept this way if he continues to show promise and ability and predisposition to endure the isolation for nine years or more (apparently sometimes 18 years, or more). Then the Mama is taken out, and he sees the brilliant outer forms of the world that he has only known on the inner side. As Ereira puts it, "he must be astonished by this, for the rest of his life."

The successful Kogi Mama, and only a few truly achieve such a state, is a bridge between the inner world of spirit and outer worlds of matter. The description of their training is part of their message. They documented it for us so that we might take them seriously.

The message of the Mamas, as related in Eriera's film, is this:

"I'm here, we all [Kogi Mamas] are here, to give a warning. I'm speaking on behalf of us all. To send a message to the Younger Brothers. And I'm going to have to say it in a way that they can understand. Not just a message for the men who've come [Ereira], and whatever place, wherever it is that they come from. I want the whole world to listen to the warning that we speak to you. ...

"She taught. The Great Mother taught ... we listened to the Great Mother's teaching and we lived by it. We all still live by it. But now, they are taking out the Mother's heart. They are digging up the ground and cutting out her liver and her guts. The Mother is being cut to pieces and stripped of everything. From their first landing, they have been doing this. The Great Mother too has a mouth, eyes, and ears. They are cutting out her eyes and ears. If we lost an eye we would be sad. So the Great Mother too is sad, and she'll end, and the world ends.

"If you do not stop digging and digging ... Younger Brother, we know the water down below has started drying up. Don't think that we are responsible. It's you. We are doing our work properly. And neither you nor us know whether the world will end. Isn't it so?

"Now, sending this message, I ask, can they think? ... I want to give some advice, to tell the real truth to the Younger Brother. If they go on like this, and they don't change their ways at once, they will see what will happen. I don't know when the world will end. But their looting will destroy it. They've taken so much. They've taken the Guardians of the stars and the Moon. The world will go black. What would happen if all we Mamas died, and there was no one doing our work? Well, the rain wouldn't fall from the sky. And it would get hotter from the sky. And the trees wouldn't grow, and the crops wouldn't grow. Or am I wrong, and they would grow anyway?"

The Mamas form their message as a question. They emphasize thinking, very seriously, about these questions, and they hope that we may see "the way things really are." They aren't urging us to accept their belief systems. They are asking us to see for ourselves how the world really works. They ask us, as we live, to think, very carefully, about what we are doing, and what we are going to do, and about the internal lives of the plants, animals, and global systems that we encounter. This sort of attention has a twofold effect. First, it brings useful practical awareness of the outer world. Second, it conveys courtesy to the inner lives, the spirit selves, the Guardians of the world.

> One of the younger, and most articulate Mamas, says:
> *"Humans need water. They have to have water to live. The Earth is the same ... and now it is weak and diseased. The animals die. The trees dry up. People become ill. Many new illnesses will occur, and there will be no treatment for them.*
> *The reason is that Younger Brother is violating fundamental principles continually and totally drilling and mining, extracting minerals, petrol, and striping away the world. This is destroying all order and damaging the world.*
> *Tell the Younger Brother open your eyes—hear the Mama's story. Learn how things really are!"*

The Kogi, of course, have no modern technology. The only outside influence they have allowed into their society is iron agricultural tools. No outsiders speak Kogi. What the Kogi Mamas know of the world as a whole they verify through aluna. They are confident of its accuracy and they hope that we will verify that accuracy for ourselves.

Are the Kogi Mamas talking about global atmospheric change, global warming, ozone depletion, AIDS, cancer, epidemic mental disorder and famine? It sure sounds like it. They are telling us that these things, and the way to deal with them, are fundamentally spiritual as well as material. And they are telling us that knowing this is finally urgent. They are not urging us to accept their dogmas or obey their orders or to apologize. They don't want any more physical-plane contact with us at all. They are saying simply, "Learn how things really are" – that is the essence of physics.

A measurable effect has alarmed the Kogi of the urgency of the situation. The Sierra mountains that the Kogi live in encompass representatives of practically all ecosystems on Earth—from sea level tropical forest, through progressively cooler regions, to permanently snowcapped peaks. They have lived in harmony and attunement with that microcosmic ecosystem for over a thousand years. Now, the paramo, the high tundra-like region, is drying up and dying. All the lower realms depend, successively, on the life of the paramo. The Kogi know that the paramo is not dying due to local environmental causes—they have observed it for over a thousand years. They believe it is an effect of the sickness of the whole planet. This is why the Kogi Mamas can no longer maintain harmony by themselves. They need our help.

A senior Mama says:

> "We must explain these things. We shouldn't threaten or insult. But it is good that we speak. We must show them how we work and how we offer our tribute to the Great Mother, so that they will know that we are working for the Younger Brother too. The Mama's work not only for the Kogi, but for all the people in the world. The Mama is not angry, not even with the Younger Brother, although he did harm. The Mama must look after the Younger Brother, and the Elder Brother, and plants and animals—all that is natural."

The Great Mother that the Kogi Mamas speak of is the mind inside nature. While the name given, "Great Mother," is metaphorical, the reality it alludes to is not metaphorical—it is the nonmaterial, spiritual, component of planet Earth. They allow the Great Mother to speak to them through divination, and through meditation.

The Kogi creation myth shares much in common with the other great world creation myths. A key point in the Kogi myth though, is they emphasize that "in the beginning there was ... memory, and possibility," and memory and possibility both exist, still, in the world. If we interpret memory as matter—that is material influence from the past—then this is also what quantum mechanics tells us.

13: Intelligence—Allowing Spirit into Matter

Matter has inherent emergent possibility (see Part II). Then, according to the Kogi Mamas, the Great Mother, acting through aluna, creates the phenomenal world from that inherent possibility. This is precisely the hylozoic perspective. There continues to be possibility in the world now. This is why the Mamas say they don't know exactly when the things they warn of will happen. They do know that the possibilities are moving in that direction.

This is, if you like, the scientific basis for divination. Divination is the observation of a "chance" event in order to decide on a course of action. Given that the event is truly emergent, the precise pattern of bubbles and waves in a pool of water for instance, the diviner sees it as an opportunity for spirit to speak to the diviner's embodiment in matter. If one is contemplating a decision that is truly immeasurable, then, at worst, divination can be no poorer a method of decision than thinking, as long as the diviner is honest. At best, divination can be the advice of the Great Mother Herself. One articulate modern advocate of a role for divination, and a widely regarded leader as well, is the Dalai Lama.[237] The standard "scientific" argument against divination has rested on the assumption that there is no immeasurable spiritual component to events. But it is apparent now that there is an immeasurable component to nature.

The other argument against divination is that divination can be abused by the dishonest, and the corrupt; but that applies to all decision-makers.

The Kogi Mamas are quite serious about their divinations. They have their nine years or more of internal training, and then, for a divination, they may fast and meditate for nine days or more. One of their requests is that we stop flying noisy airplanes over their land, so that they may meditate properly.

The Kogi are unimpressed by flying machines. In 1987, two *Miami Herald* reporters accompanied a small group of tourists on a helicopter visit to the Lost City archaeological site. The group happened to get stuck overnight by innavigable weather, and two Kogi "happened" to visit them. One was a Kogi Mama later featured in Ereira's film—Mama "Valencio" (the Kogi use Hispanic pseudonyms).

According to the reporters, "When Mayr [the group's guide] told Valencio that we were Americans, [Valencio] asked what our people do best. After thinking a minute, we told him Americans are best at doing things that have never been done before. As an example, we mentioned that Americans had flown to the moon in a space ship. Valencio gave us an amused look. 'Why would anyone bother going to the moon with a machine when you can go there so easily with your mind?' he asked. We didn't have any answer to that."[238]

The reporters seemed to have dismissed his remarks as quaint and irrational. That was only a year before the Kogi started negotiating with Ereira, and the BBC. If the reporters had been more open in their attitude, they might have stumbled into a much bigger story.

Myself, I am definitely a Younger Brother. I was deeply moved when I watched the first space shuttle landing—on TV no less. I enjoy riding on airplanes, and I love the shinkansen (Japanese bullet train). I would forego a lot to be able to ride in a machine to the Moon. I am not prepared to reject all technology or even to claim that much of it is not real progress. If we are going to incorporate the spiritual dimensions into our culture, we are going to have to do so starting from where we're at now, with all our technological gear. Perhaps even a co-evolution of the machines themselves will help us in some unforeseen way.

But I know enough to recognize that the Elder Brothers may have a point. If the world is a profound and vibrant living being and Great Mother, and if she is quite sick, and if we wake-up to that fact too slowly, the awful tragedy may be that we finally come to know Her only when it is too late.

The Ageless Wisdom

What the Kogi Mamas say about their identity as "Elder Brothers" working for the world on the inner spiritual planes is surprisingly consistent with a strain of both Western and Eastern spiritual and religious traditions. Aldous Huxley, and more recently Ken Wilber and others, called this the "perennial philosophy." It is similarly called the "ageless wisdom" by esotericists. I prefer the latter term because "philosophy" seems to have fallen into ill repute, although "perennial" is a better descriptive than "ageless."

The ageless wisdom holds that humans are all on a developmental spiritual journey leading eventually to God-realization, which is the same as Self-realization. That is, we are held to be divine spirits inhabiting material bodies for the specific purpose of spiritualizing matter—creating harmony between the two—and so evolving both spirit and matter. All the great world religions and spiritual traditions are said to be founded by individuals who were one or more steps ahead of the average on that way. This is why they appear to their followers to be Divine—because they are a bit more Self-realized to some degree.

A problem of organized religions comes when the followers start asserting that their path and their belief structure is the only correct one. They are confused because their founder invariably said that there is only one God—one ultimate Divine Source—while the founder also seemed himself to be divine. So, an incorrect (though seemingly logical) deduction is that their founder and their way and their belief structure must be the *only* truly Divine way.

Compounding the problem is that major scriptures, such as the Bhagavad-Gita and the Bible, are written in parables, allegories and metaphors, and can be understood on several successive levels of realization. The followers who believe in the exclusive authority of their own religion and its founder tend also to accept only one exclusive reading of scripture.

Assertion of exclusive Divinity is what is called Fundamentalism. All the religions now have their Fundamentalist strains. They all also have esoteric strains. Esotericism is a fundamental principle of the ageless wisdom and is the opposite of Fundamentalism—esotericism is inclusive and Monistic and sees the ultimate unity of the great spiritual and religious traditions. Esotericism holds *both* rational analysis and experience (which may be mystical and nonrational) as authorities.

Fundamentalism holds fixed scriptural dogma, and sometimes the decrees of appointed officeholders, as ultimate authorities. Science can be recognized as a subset of esotericism and Fundamentalists can be even more vicious in their attacks on esotericists than in their attacks on other Fundamentalists. With the rise of the scientific and secular belief structures, we are starting to see scientific Fundamentalism as well. Fundamentalism is on the rise in the world but may be only a sideeffect of a general spiritual upheaval which is signaling the movement toward a new world emergence of the ageless wisdom. This is what many proponents of the ageless wisdom believe and seem to be experiencing.

The ageless wisdom, being ageless and perennial, has been around for a long time—at least as long as the major religions, which go as far back as we have detailed knowledge of human culture. A number of recent cultural and social phenomena could possibly be seen as part of the reemergence of the ageless wisdom; the founding and strengthening of the United Nations; the disintegration of the authoritarian Soviet Empire; the dissolution of South African apartheid; the ongoing democratic revolutions and evolutions.

Some of these have exhibited dramatic reversals such as Vaclav Havel moving from prison to president of Czechoslovakia, and Nelson Mandela being elected president of South Africa. It also seems to be starting to appear in the mainstream discourse. US president George Bush and final Soviet president, Mikhael Gorbachev spoke of the New World Order.

The roots of the US itself may have had early influence from the same ageless wisdom principles. The US dollar bill features the words NOVUS ORDO SECLORUM, Latin for "New World Order."

Many people criticize the phrase New World Order as too vague, or not having real meaning. Well, maybe the New World Order is the reemergence of the ageless wisdom—this time on a worldwide and democratic scale, not only among an elite priesthood. Recent spiritual movements are also part of it; serious interfaith dialogues like the 1893 and 1993 World Parliaments of Religions; many smaller interfaith groups like Theosophy, and the popularity of Joseph Campbell's interfaith interpretations of mythology; and, yes, the general "New Age movement" which ranges from exploitative emotional solipsism to profound spirituality.

More or less accessible systems of theoretical structures for the ageless wisdom can be found in Theosophy, Esoteric Buddhism, Taoism, Vedantism, Kabbalism, Sufism, and Gnostic Christianity (except not as Al Gore uses "Gnosticism" to mean theistic dualism, but as in "gnosis"—emphasizing direct inner knowing). Various proponents of each of the above succumb to the Fundamentalist allure and claim that theirs is the true way, above all the others.

Also, as with all religions, adherents to each of the above include nonserious and degenerate groups and individuals that can easily discredit the serious inquirers. A little more will be said on this problem in the next chapter. For now, though, I'll try to summarize what these systems seem to mean in regard to the subject of this chapter, and consider them as a working hypothesis for a way to think about integrating spiritual and material concepts as an update on the ageless wisdom.

Recently, the founders of transpersonal psychology, such as Ken Wilber, have tried to integrate the various ageless wisdom systems with Western (Freudian and Jungian) psychology. As mentioned in Chapter 11, the Esoteric systems hold that the spiritual aspect of humans can be thought of as consisting of a series of bodies or levels. The levels are associated with the physical, emotional, mental, spiritual, and higher aspects. Spiritual evolution consists of integrating each of these aspects into full consciousness and embodiment in the material body. The progression of sequential integration is roughly in the order listed, though in some ways everything all progresses at once.

Most of the Esoteric systems say that it takes very many human incarnations for a soul to even start true integration of these aspects. But when it starts, it can proceed rapidly, completing in only a few incarnations. When the spiritual aspect (or, according to some systems, a higher aspect such as "causal") is fully integrated, embodied, and controlled, the soul is said to be God-Realized or Self-Realized. And when this happens, the soul no longer needs to incarnate as a human body. As Buddhism says, the soul is liberated from the samsaric circle of life and death, though the soul has further evolutionary tasks on other nonmaterial planes. This is why there are billions of humans and only a relatively small number of embodied God-Realized people.

Esotericists say that, in a difficult to understand way, humanity as a group also is on a similar path of spiritual-material integration. Perhaps this is akin to each cell in a human body participating in the Self-Realization of the human organism. The worldwide movement toward spiritual and human value-oriented thought is, Esotericists say, due to the movement of the whole human group toward a first integration of spiritual and material aspects. And the human group can be thought of as one of the major components of the planetary body. (Other major components may be the plant, animal, and mineral Kingdoms.)

The contemporary explosion of scientific understanding of material functioning could possibly be part of the preparation for this movement to a new level of humanity. While that would be a momentous advance, it may not be assured that we will succeed. Failure could mean spiritual death of the planet.

According to esotericism, the great world religions were all founded by humans who achieved Self-Realization in that incarnation. It should be noted that, according to these systems, not all or even most of the souls who have started Self-Realization work in the field of religion or even dwell on "spirituality" at all. They may contribute to art, science, industry, government, or whatever, as part of the human group realization.

After the final human step is achieved and the cycle of birth and death is transcended, some choose to "stay" as Bodhisattvas, Adepts, or spiritual Masters. The question arises, then, where are these guys (gender inclusive)?

Esotericists say that we are nearing the end of a Dark Age, or Kali Yuga. In the Dark Age it was counterproductive for spiritual Masters to function openly in a world of extreme separativeness, deluded intent, and inability to respond to higher wisdom. The Vedantic calendrical system, which predates the current age, for instance, of various periods and time cycles is based on the astronomical fact of the precession of the equinoxes (precession of the Earth's spin axis) which takes about 26,000 years.

The evolved spiritual beings are said, especially by Theosophists and Sufis, to be slowly starting to emerge, now, as teachers (*not* as controllers or authorities) for humanity in this time of crisis and opportunity. The Theosophical works of Alice A. Bailey (written in the 1920s, 1930s, and 1940s), for instance, even refer to these beings as "Elder Brothers," and says that they remain mostly hidden, except to selected individuals, for specific purposes, in "the Himalayas, and other remote places." The similarity of the Esoteric message to the message of the Kogi Mama "Elder Brothers" is striking, and apparently they are independent of each other.

13: Intelligence—Allowing Spirit into Matter

Tales and legends of Himalayan reclusive sages with apparently superhuman spiritual development are well known. Could some of the stories contain some literal truth? As previously mentioned, Paramahansa Yogananda, and his teachers Sri Yukteswar and Lahiri Mahasay—all highly respected teachers from a respected Indian Vedantic lineage—wrote about meeting one of those Himalayan recluses, called Mahamouni Babaji, or just Babaji.

More recently, a series of books that also contain a ring of authenticity—complete with documentation that the author was asked, and refused, to lead both the current branches of the above-mentioned lineage, and with endorsements from Indian High Court jurists, and university professors—describes having spent long periods in the Himalayas with the same Babaji, and with other sages. That author says he was sent to the West to teach a form of yoga, specifically on Babaji's instructions (and, as he writes, even though he preferred to stay in seclusion).[239]

A Canadian immigrant from Abkhazia, Murat Yagan, claims to have studied with, and left, unable to complete the training, a similar group of reclusive sages in a very remote region of the Caucasus Mountains. Yagan says:

> "People talk in vague terms about the 'New Age' in which we are living. But what distinguishes this New Age from any age before is that it marks the marriage of positive science with mysticism. We are just now celebrating the wedding festivity of this union of mysticism and science. They have yet to go to bed together and produce offspring, but eventually they will. It is in the light of this New Age that I am trying to tell you about my tradition ..."

Yagan says that the "Source" of all Sufism (and Islam, including the Prophet Mohammed) is a group of highly developed reclusive sages in remote places in the Caucasus. Yagan says (before the emergence of the Kogi and their message), "The Source I am speaking of can be traced back some 26,000 years through Caucasian legends, fairy tales, and folk songs.

According to these legends, there are three places where people survived the Flood: [A flood that he associates with the Flood of

Noah, and places 8,000 or 12,000 years ago. It is not clear whether he means a metaphorical spiritual flood, or actual climate and ecological changes associated with the end of the last Quaternary ice age.] the occidental skirts of the Himalayas called the Hindu Kush; the Andes Mountains of South America; and the heights of the Caucasus Mountains. People in these three regions have played a primary role in the spiritual development of the world."[240]

More Western Sufi orders, such as the Shadiliyeh mentioned in Chapter 11, also speak of the Central Asian region (the Caucasus) as a powerful spiritual source.

The Kogi people live in the northernmost region of the Andes, consistent with the Caucasian legends. Could the Kogi Mamas, the Babaji Group, and the Caucasian Sufi schools be not entirely mythical? Could they be elite representatives, or in touch with representatives, of a "union of mysticism and science" that will in time guide the development of society as a whole?

In Ereira's book about the Kogi Mamas, he also notes that they mention that they are not the only beings working on the spiritual planes and that they "meet" others in the "mind"—that is, traveling in the nonmaterial, but real, components of the emotional, or mental, or spiritual bodies. A coherent model seems to be emerging that goes as follows. The great world religions, be they "Eastern" or "Western" or "Native American," have related and ultimately common sources.

Which of the legends of these sources are closer to literal, and which are metaphorical (or plain wrong), is slowly emerging, along with increasing concrete knowledge of world history—both geophysical and cultural. The present world period may be entering a new phase of spiritual and material integration that builds on the scientific revolution and the democratization of spiritual and religious experience, and is informed by increasingly direct influence from the original religious sources.

A Plausible Avatar

The Ageless Wisdom may be percolating to the surface again, now, with new meanings and new developments for the present scientific culture. A problem with discussing distant and past spiritual masters is distinguishing between the metaphorical and the

13: Intelligence—Allowing Spirit into Matter

literal, and the accompanying tendency to dismiss it all as overblown myth, if not actual fabrication, or simply to accept only that part which reinforces one's preexisting belief structures.

Living great yogis are said to express "yogic powers" like telepathic rapport and more astonishing feats, which would provide direct evidence for hylozoic functioning. The respected teachers and teachings also say, though, that such powers, if authentic, should not be displayed (for important spiritual reasons), and that the greatest yogis usually remain in seclusion.

But many ageless wisdom followers indicate that this is slowly changing. According to many people, for instance, at least one extraordinarily rare being is functioning in full public view, now. These followers believe that a full avatar is now acting openly in human form. His believers include a former president of India, the present president of India, Dr. Shankar Dayal Sharma; the prime minister of India, Narasimha Rao; the former prime minister of Italy, Bettino Craxi; the former president of Sri Lanka, J.R. Jayewardene,[241] and many other government leaders, scientists, and ordinary people. This is the living Indian saint Sathya Sai Baba.

The Western press has largely ignored Sai Baba (perhaps partly because he does not seek publicity). In India, the widely circulated, largely conservative and secular Indian news publication, *India Today*, estimates that Sai Baba's followers number fifty million around the world, including countless poor and ordinary people as well as major public figures. Such numbers would qualify them as a major world religion, except that Sai Baba emphasizes that devotees should follow their own major religious tradition, whichever it may be. They should just become aware that all the major religions have a common spiritual source.

While Sai Baba himself lives simply and accepts no personal gifts, his followers have created an estimated fifteen billion rupees of charitable and educational works.[242] These include a major university, hundreds of colleges and schools, and an enormous modern hospital, free for the poor in southern India, designed by British architect Keith Critchlow, partly with funds from Hard Rock Cafe and House of Blues businessman and Sai Baba devotee Isaac Tigrett.[243]

Sai Baba's Education in Human Values program for including moral values and a spiritual basis in education has been the focus of a doctoral dissertation at Columbia University.[244] The Minister of Education of Thailand, Dr. Armstrong Jumsai, a Sai Baba devotee, has formally introduced the EHV into Thailand's educational system.[245] According to Jumsai, while Mikhail Gorbachev was leader of Soviet Russia, he persuaded Gorbachev to order the inclusion of Sai Baba's EHV in Russian schools. The education department of Singapore has implemented Sai Baba's EHV in over 1,500 secondary and primary schools, and Japan has launched a pilot EHV program, as has India.[246]

The more I research Sai Baba and his influence, the more impressed I become. Remember that this is the "subjective" part of this book. A full length "objective" study of the news reports, devotional literature and controversies related to Sai Baba and his followers is not possible here. He does have detractors. My own impression is influenced by my personal dreams, and meditation experiences, some of which are described below. One reader of a preliminary version of this chapter said that it was "subjectively weighted hearsay," that "undercut" my scientific objectivity, and "didn't prove" anything. Those claims miss the point. We are done with the objective scientific part of the book! This is the human part. The scientific part showed us that science as it stands now is *inconclusive* on whether the world is hylozoic or hylostochastic.

In this time of flux, personal experience necessarily plays a role in orienting our perspective, and in the individual it seems to be the key factor in really shifting to a hylozoic perspective. Sometimes the experiences involve a human figure like Sathya Sai Baba (and other great teachers living and past), and sometimes the experience is of the inner teacher, or of both inner and outer.

The following pages focus on Sai Baba because he is part of my personal experience, and because he is a public figure readily investigated by anyone, and because he seems to demonstrate direct evidence for the hylozoic nature of the world. This section suggests that he is one (perhaps important) representative of the universally relevant ageless wisdom teachings, of which there are many teachers.

13: Intelligence—Allowing Spirit into Matter

Sai Baba seems to be emerging as unique in the magnitude of his influence. M. K. Rasgotra, India's High Commissioner to the United Kingdom, and former Foreign Secretary in the Indian Government, and long time devotee of Sai Baba, seems still astonished at his own devotion. Rasgotra said in a public speech at Sai Baba's ashram:

> "Divinity is supposed to be airy stuff and not the province of politicians and businessmen. And yet here they come, all of them—heads of state, ministers, high government officials and top executives. All kneel down at the feet of Baba."[247]

Sai Baba has said that his first task is to heal the ills of India, before he will travel abroad. Given the enormity of that task, it is astonishing that he, and those affected by his influence seem to be making progress. His mission is essentially universal though, "... to carry out the supreme mission of spiritually regenerating and uniting mankind," he says.[248]

The keys to his teachings are the underlying universal and unitive natures of all the world religious and spiritual traditions, and the direct realization and experience of the reality of the spiritual aspect of man and nature. He says:

> "The world today is in the grip of a supreme moral and spiritual crisis ... While science has overcome the barriers of time, distance, and nationality, it has done little to promote better understanding between man and man, and nation and nation. ... The oneness of all creation, affirmed by the ancient seers and sages must be expressed in a transcendental love which embraces all humanity, regardless of creed, community, or language."

Sai Baba's followers include a number of significant scientists, most eminently, Dr. S. Bhagavantam, a prominent nuclear physicist and former director of the prestigious Indian Institute of Science in Bangalore, and former adviser to India's Defense Ministry and past-president of the Indian Science Congress Association.[249]

I mention all of the above, first, because of the difficult-to-accept nature of what else Sai Baba is famous for—what are commonly called "miracles." Sai Baba has routinely been observed, for decades, materializing vibhuti (sacred ash), rings, statues, out-of-season fruits, apparent hybrid fruits, even hot foods and liquids, apparently out of thin air. Large numbers of people claim to have witnessed Sai Baba apparently manifesting other "miracles" associated with great holy men of the past—"miracles" which are often asserted to have been merely mythical, such as those ascribed to Jesus Christ and Krishna. He has, according to the witnesses, instantaneously moved from place to place, predicted future events, known of distant events instantaneously, healed many people, multiplied food for crowds, and in one case, at least, resurrected someone from death.

Significantly, though, the miracles are not the focus of his life and teaching. The spiritual uplift of mankind is the focus. He calls the materializations his "calling cards," and he says their only purpose is to motivate people to investigate their own true nature, which he says is potentially divine.

He is believed by his followers to be a full avatar. In Vedantic tradition, an avatar is the embodiment of a Divine (spiritual) principle in a (material) human form. While all humans are considered to be, at core, sparks of the Divine, and we are each striving to realize that divinity, an avatar is fully identified with the divine throughout his (or her, and there have been female avatars) incarnation. An avatar is a special descent of divinity into human form, in order to fill some world purpose.

All the major religions contain the concept of avatars, in some form. In Christianity, Jesus was a sort of avatar. Of course the Fundamentalist Christians assert that Jesus was the only avatar who ever was and ever will be. In Buddhism, Buddha was an avatar, and Bodhisattvas are nearly avatars (though perhaps technically not because they started out as human, but the idea is similar). Vedanta doesn't get hung-up on exclusive authority posturing. In Vedanta, there have been (and are believed to be now) many avatars, and even several degrees and types of avatar. This complicates, but does not contradict, the fact that Vedanta is also the most monistic spiritual tradition.

Sai Baba is believed by many people to be not only an avatar, but an "integral avatar," a very high avatar indeed. Whatever the theological details, if this avataric incarnation is a truth, as increasingly numerous and credible observers believe, it is clearly evidence that the world is strongly hylozoic and not hylostochastic.

To form an opinion on whether it may indeed be a truth, one first has to decide whether, in principle, avatars may exist, ever. The hylozoic paradigm opens up the possibility, in principle, of avatars. The "miracles" themselves are a more specific occurrence, that create a different conceptual difficulty, which we'll discuss later. The possibility of a spiritual entity inhabiting an emergent material body, however, is consistent with the hylozoic paradigm. In fact, that's what the ageless wisdom and the avataric teachers say that humans are, too (spiritual entities inhabiting and co-creating material bodies). An avatar is just an embodiment of a different degree. Given that avatars may occur, it seems to me that Sathya Sai Baba is, in fact, a plausible avatar in human body.

I am not unaware that there is tremendous resistance to a concept like this, whether the figure in question is a living Sai Baba, or a recently passed Ramakrishna, or a reclusive Mahamouni Babaji, or a historical Jesus Christ, Krishna, or Buddha. But these are the resistances that need to be faced head on in a shift to the hylozoic paradigm. The spiritual realities pointed to by the metaphors of the great spiritual traditions need to be faced again with renewed strength in the light of contemporary science.

While there has been little mention of Sai Baba in the Western press, that which exists has been amazingly positive, given the unusualness of the phenomena reported about Sai Baba. *The Economist* magazine (not known for expressing wild spiritual fantasies) wrote, "[the child Sai Baba's] hands began to drip ash and he was declared the incarnation of a holy figure who has lived earlier this century.[250]

Many more miracles followed. Over the years dozens of implacable rationalists and other mischief-makers have tried to discredit him, but never successfully. ... He is also a philanthropist, running more than 100 colleges, schools and an enormous hospital for the poor. Judges, politicians, bureaucrats and film stars ... crave an audience ..."[251]

The staid *London Times* called Sai Baba, "the most impressive holy man in centuries."[252]

Typical of the scientifically-minded among Sai Baba followers is the case of an American psychiatrist. Dr. Samuel H. Sandweiss

(M.D. board certified psychiatrist and clinical professor in psychiatry at the University of California in San Diego) heard about Sai Baba and his miracles and large numbers of believers. Sandweiss saw this as an interesting opportunity. He decided to travel to Sai Baba's ashram to study first hand what was clearly either hypnosis, mass delusion, hallucination, hysteria, an effect of cultural shock or drug intoxication, and perhaps write a few academic papers about it. On his first visit, he was thwarted from close contact with Sai Baba for days because of the huge crowds. Then, just before he was about to leave disappointed, a brief encounter with Sai Baba transformed his opinion. Essentially, the brief encounter triggered a profoundly joyous inner experience that left Sandweiss "no doubt in my mind that Sai Baba is divine. I astound myself to say such a thing."[253]

Sandweiss returned to his psychiatric practice and teaching to try and include the spiritual aspect more directly in the field. He was careful to include spirituality in a universalistic sense, and not focus on the personal figure of Sai Baba (his teaching is strongly universalistic, and emphasizes the God within, which can be thought of by any of the names of the religious tradtions). Sandweiss did make the mistake of telling his friends and colleagues, all at the same time in a gathering in his house, that he believed he had met a true avatar in India. Immediately thereafter, he says, "Psychiatric residents I taught in medical school were contacted to see if I had gone crazy. It was then that I began to realize how hot this issue was."[254]

On three occasions, he was prohibited even from presenting a research paper about Sai Baba at psychiatric professional conferences. Nevertheless, over the years he has seen some of his colleagues slowly start acknowledging the relevance of spiritual realities, and a few even suddenly transforming as he did.[255] And his expanded perspective has enhanced his own practice.

We seem to have created an utterly schizophrenic culture. Presidents can't get elected if they don't at least claim some sort of belief in God. And yet a fully qualified psychiatrist who simply describes a living experience of transcendence is immediately suspected of insanity. Apparently it is fully respectable to believe in an ossified God that is somehow both dead and authoritarian at the same time. Yet it is insane to believe in a living avatar of divinity.

13: Intelligence—Allowing Spirit into Matter

In recent years, many charismatic leaders with small bands of followers have been willing to believe that their leader is a god of whatever sort one would want. Such leaders have sometimes proved tragically dangerous, and will be discussed briefly in the next chapter. As Sandweiss himself notes: "Serious students of the scriptures know that warnings have been voiced by tried and true spiritual masters about being spiritually deceived. They rightfully warn us to avoid being gullible and overly accepting where such an important dimension of life is concerned, without serious inquiry and study."[256]

Another initially skeptical inquirer, who has written about his personal reversal in spiritual belief, on the basis of serious inquiry and personal transformative experience, is R.K. Karanjia. At the time, Karanjia was editor-in-chief of the weekly magazine *Blitz*, printed in Bombay, with a circulation in the millions. He was an avowed Marxist, and considered himself a sophisticated atheist, with no use or regard for the spiritual traditions of his country.

Blitz magazine reflected Karanjia's attitude editorially. A colleague challenged him by saying that it was inconsistent to form an opinion of Sai Baba without ever having seen or met him. Karanjia agreed. He visited Sai Baba's ashram and, while there, was granted Sai Baba's first major interview with the press, in August 1976. The interview, which was published in *Blitz*, and his experience and observation of Sai Baba, transformed Karanjia into a devoted believer and spiritual seeker.[257]

Dr. Bhagavantam (mentioned previously) also describes such a process. Bhagavantam says that he was very skeptical with regard to all holy men, but that circumstances created a meeting with Sai Baba, walking outdoors. According to Bhagavantam, Sai Baba initiated a discussion about the relevance of spirituality and the ignorance of it among scientists. Bhagavantam felt defensive and noted that American scientist Robert Openheimer, for instance, often quoted the Bhagavad-Gita. At this, Baba said, "Do you believe in the Bhagavad-Gita? Would you read Gita if I gave you one?"

Bhagavantam said, "I would not make a fetish of reading it today but I would certainly treasure it."

"Well stretch out your hand," Sai Baba said, and then picked up a handful of sand and poured it into Bhagavantam's hand. The sand,

Bhagavantam claims, changed into a small text of the Bhagavad-Gita."[258]

Bhagavantam says that witnessing numerous similar occurrences, and his own inner searchings, over years, finally convinced him that he was witnessing evidence of realities beyond those accepted by contemporary physics.

Another scientist, Dr. Y. J. Rao, head of the Geology Department of Osmania University in Hyderabad, has related a similar experience. According to Rao:

> "One day, Baba picked up a rough piece of broken granite and, handing it to Dr. Rao, asked him what it contained. The geologist mentioned a few of the minerals in the rock.
> Baba: 'I don't mean those—something deeper.'
> Dr. Rao: 'Well, molecules, atoms, electrons, protons.'
> Baba: 'No, no—deeper still!'
> Dr. Rao: 'I don't know, Swami.'
> Baba took the lump of granite from the geologist and, holding it up with his fingers, blew on it. Dr. Rao says that although it was never out of his sight, when Baba gave it back, its irregular shape had changed to a statue of Lord Krishna playing his flute. The surprised geologist noted also a difference in color and a slight change in composition of the rock.
> Baba: 'You see? Beyond your molecules and atoms, God is in the rock. And God is sweetness and joy. Break off and taste it.'
> Dr. Rao found no difficulty breaking off the 'granite' foot of the little statue. Putting it in his mouth, he discovered, he says, that it was candy."[259]

The lesson is clear and specific. Beyond the microphysics of protons and electrons are deeper spiritual realities associated with the great spiritual and religious traditions—the world is hylozoic.

Sai Baba's miracles are not performed as magic shows. They only manifest at moments when an important spiritual lesson can be learned, although they do also occur before enormous gatherings. As a full avatar, if indeed he is, the public display of these events does not violate the spiritual traditions that say that "yogic powers," if a seeker happens to acquire them, should not be displayed in public, or even used consciously at all.

Two researchers, Karlis Osis (Ph.D. and Research Fellow at the American Society for Psychical Research), and Erlendur Haraldsson (professor of psychology at the University of Iceland), studied Sai Baba and his followers for ten years.[260] In his extensively researched 1987 book, Haraldsson discusses the miracles associated with Sai Baba.[261] Haraldsson concludes that, although they could not convince Sai Baba into partaking in laboratory experiments, there is significant evidence to suggest that his miracles are genuine. Haraldsson and Osis witnessed many materializations first hand, and interviewed large numbers of other witnesses and also interviewed skeptics.

Osis says in a foreword to Haraldsson's book:

"India, the land of guru worship, abounds with holy men who are often called 'babas.' Sathya Sai Baba is a unique individual—a kind of genius towering over the whole landscape. ... I was present when a person holding one of the highest elected offices in India [the Vice President], escorted by a three-star general, approached him. They both got down on the floor and touched Baba's feet with bare foreheads [This is a traditional way to greet a revered holy man and so may not be as strange as it seems to Westerners.] ... Indian journalists are as aggressive as their counterparts anywhere in the world, but no one has been able to find tricks behind his reported phenomena. ... Sleight of hand and other arts of the magician are well developed in India, and some famous swamis don't mind resorting to them, as I have personally observed. Haraldsson is acutely aware of these 'other explanations.' ... with vigour [Haraldsson] cuts through the jungle of storytelling and candidly reports the outcome of his quest. ... *It would have been cowardly simply to ignore* what so many witnesses have said and *what our own eyes have observed, just because it is so out of the ordinary.*" [Emphasis mine.]

Haraldsson documents that numerous witnesses, including non-devotees and ex-devotees, attest that "there has been a continuous flow of objects from him for over [fifty] years, since he was in his teens in the early 1940's."[262]

Haraldsson notes that one of Sai Baba's predictions which came true is that he "is frequently visited by the highest officials of the land; ministers of the state and central governments, governors, members of the supreme court, generals and chiefs of the armed forces"—which Sai Baba predicted 40-50 years ago in his youth.[263]

Another prediction made by Sai Baba, which we can all test, is that he will live to be 94 years of age, dying in the year 2020 or 2021. And, he has predicted that he will then take rebirth only one year later. He has predicted the approximate location of that birth, and even has created a partial image of what that incarnation will look like as a man.[264]

The credibility of Sai Baba's believers seems high, so those who wish to debunk him are left to asserting sophisticated trickery. Regardless of the quality of the witnesses, and even of the films and videos, because Sai Baba has refused to submit to controlled laboratory experiments, fraud cannot be disproved, and so some will always assert fraud. It is questionable, though, whether laboratory experiments would be accepted, or appropriate. From Sai Baba's perspective, his mission is the spiritual regeneration of individuals and groups, not drawing attention to unusual tricks. He is doing quite well in his task without laboratory experiments.

An analogous situation may be the role of prayer and other nonlocal (necessarily hylozoic) effects in medicine and healing. Many people believe that they know from experience that this sort of thing happens conclusively. Also, many laboratory experiments have been conducted. Physician Larry Dossey, in an extensive review of these studies, presents a strong case that the experiments have been of very high scientific quality (higher quality, according to an independent expert, than many well-accepted medical studies), and high credibility, and that their collective results are overwhelmingly positive that prayer and other nonlocal methods do sometimes play a clinically verifiable role in healing.[265] And yet, Dossey reports, the orthodox medical community ignores, or continually disbelieves, the results.

If Sai Baba were to start engaging in laboratory experiments, he would likely have to do so repeatedly for every disbeliever who

13: Intelligence—Allowing Spirit into Matter

would not trust the other experimenters. Also, experiments would overemphasize the importance of such "powers," countrary to the true spiritual message. In practice, Sai Baba is achieving his results more efficiently through receiving countless visitors directly, and sometimes remotely through dream and meditation experience.

If the materializations are true, though, are they consistent with the hylozoic paradigm? Why do I bring them up in the context of this book? The answers to these questions are a little complicated. Consider a piece of granite turning into a statue of Krishna made of candy. In order for this to happen, the atoms and molecules of granite need to be replaced by the atoms and molecules of candy. The atomic content of candy is different from the atomic content of granite, so we can't simply rearrange the molecular bonds. The protons, neutrons, and electrons, however, may be the same. So all we need to do is transmute the elements, and the molecular bonds.

In the case of a single molecule, a shift to a different molecular structure of the same total energy would have some nonzero quantum probability of occurring per unit time. But such probabilities are very, very small. And the probabilities of the atomic numbers shifting around (to other configurations of the same total energy) are even smaller. We can safely estimate that, in the entire history of the universe, even if all stars have planets with granite surfaces, no hunks of granite ever spontaneously transmute (by pure random chance) into statues of Krishna made of candy.

At first this would seem, then, to be even beyond the scope of the hylozoic paradigm. But in our analysis we assumed that the quantum possibilities were eventuated randomly, and that is the old hylostochastic paradigm. If we first assume that there is another, spiritual, nonmaterial component of reality, the analysis could be different. We have to know how the spiritual reality works in detail before we can make such a judgment.

The hylozoic paradigm says that the present laws of physics are essentially the correct description of matter, and those laws have little quantum gaps in them because that is how matter actually is. Something in the spiritual reality may know how to work in those gaps to make things happen that wouldn't happen otherwise, while maintaining the detailed balance of the apparent "laws" of physics.

Human conscious living itself is arguably miraculous in ways that we don't understand. That we seem to observe beings, avatars, spiritual scientists, Masters, etc. in ways that we can't understand, can't be dismissed on the basis of "physics." In other words, the materializations are certainly not consistent with the hylostatic or hylostochastic paradigms. They seem to stretch even the hylozoic paradigm, but at least the hylozoic paradigm is closer to including both what we know about physics and what we seem to be observing in our environment (like the phenomena associated with Sai Baba, nonlocal effects and prayer in healing, etc.).

A Sublime Dream

A step in deciding whether this sort of thing is possible can be to look into ourselves to see if we think there is anything, at all, beyond those gaps in matter. If we think there is something there, then a next step may be looking around to see who knows more about it, and that is what leads us to the spiritual masters and sages.

Since we are in the midst of shifting paradigms, questions like these require a mix of "subjective" inner experience and rational and empirical analysis. In this section, I discuss the role of dream and meditation experience in shaping my own thinking about Sai Baba. It should be emphasized that the important point here is not the personal figure of Sai Baba. He is an example of one of many types of evidence for the universe being hylozoic, and for our own essentially divine spiritual potential.

Americans are conditioned to have an inability to discriminate among issues of a spiritual and religious nature. Some popular American religions use fear, and the requirement of slavish belief in clearly irrational dogmas as primary tools—effectively extinguishing clarity of intellect and the ability to discriminate. American textbook manufacturers prohibit any serious discussion of spirituality at all, for fear of lawsuits and controversies that might reduce sales. (They also prohibit serious discussion of science, in some cases such as evolution, for the same reasons.) American "high brow" and elite press likewise shun serious analysis of spiritual issues.

When my own personal events and life situation made me feel that I had to start functioning in a discriminating manner with regard to spirituality, I felt I had to start from square one, even though it

13: Intelligence—Allowing Spirit into Matter

was part of a long-standing "intellectual" interest. As part of that process, along with reopening to traditional scriptures and their sources, I decided to look into what living people, today, are doing and saying along these lines.

As part of that process, I decided to view essentially all of the videos available at a metaphysical bookstore in the city where I was living (Tokyo). These included the fantastic adventures of Shirley MacLaine, the antics of well-known antinomian buffoon-gurus like Bhagwan Rajneesh, serious attempts to investigate the life of Jesus the man,[266] and the pristine intelligence and razor-sharp intellect of J. Krishnamurti.

A short video that I would not have been inclined to watch, except for my campaign to look at them all, introduced me to Sathya Sai Baba. In that video, a small black-skinned Indian man with fuzzy hair and a simple close-fitting orange robe was shown walking amongst thousands of quietly seated people, all in rapt attention. As he walked, he casually waved his hand, palm down, and caught vibhuti as it materialized apparently out of thin air, and gave it to someone with outstretched hand. He did this many times, almost nonchalantly, as he walked and collected letters and notes, and spoke with people. My first reaction was incredulous. A video, of course, cannot be proof of authenticity. I very much doubted the authenticity. Having some experience with sleight-of-hand stage magic, I slowed down and repeated the tape but couldn't make any judgments that way. But I was impressed by the presence of the figure of Sai Baba.

Gradually, over many months, along with many unrelated studies, I read books about Sai Baba by his followers. These had a ring of clarity, authenticity, and credibility. Sai Baba's teachings are clear, uplifting, and moral. He is definitely, as *The Times* newspaper put it, not a guru "of the fleet-of-rollers 'n' bimbo variety." But the materializations were a barrier for me that I couldn't accept.

Then I had a dream in which I found myself taking a walk with Sai Baba. It was a sublime experience. He radiated clarity and unaffected love, and made me feel my own connection to divinity. After a short walk, Sai Baba indicated, nonverbally, that it "was time for him to go back to work." His manner was unassuming and direct, almost as if among equals.

We turned around and walked back into an institutional-looking building. We walked down a corridor to an opened door. Inside the room, men and women in white laboratory coats were waiting for him. I stood at the door and watched Sai Baba enter the room and lie down on a gurney. Still radiating love, Sai Baba allowed the lab-coated people to strap him down. He opened his mouth and they began examining him with instruments. I felt an intense compassion for this incarnation of divinity performing his "job" of submitting himself to the primitive examinations of humanity.

Of course, we have all manner of dreams. Some are clearly important and meaningful. Others are less meaningful fleeting imaginings. That dream was a doosey. For months, I couldn't think of the dream without feeling the intense compassion. In 1865, the German chemist F.A. Kekule visualized in a dream one night the important chemical ring formula of benzene. About inner learning, Kekule said, "Let us learn to dream … then perhaps we shall find the truth … but let us beware of publishing our dreams before they have been put to the proof by the waking understanding." I don't think I can "prove" my dream, but I've tried to verify it by waking research.

Another experience deepened the initial impression of the dream. I was attending part of an interfaith meditation retreat jointly led by Christian, Buddhist, and Jewish leaders. On a Buddhist day led by Jack Engman,[267] well-known American Zen Buddhist leader Bernard Glassman was also present. As the morning began, I was sitting in Zen meditation posture, next to a woman in Buddhist robes who was obviously associated with Bernard Glassman:

> I was feeling rather disgruntled because it was earlier than is usual for me and I was a little uncertain about sitting out there with these sorts of characters. Also, there were few people in attendance for what I felt should be an important interfaith dialogue, and especially there were few unattached young women while it was a socially lonely period for me. (Yes, these are the sorts of pristine thoughts that often inhabit me when I go to meditations.) Nevertheless, when Jack Engman began a series of simple meditation exercises, I tried to apply myself.

In the first part we were to enter deep silent meditation and then visualize forgiving ourselves and wishing ourselves to be joyful and happy and loving. Not much happened for me, but I noticed that tears were streaming down the face of the woman next to me.

In my foolish self-centered state, I actually thought that she must be putting on a show to impress her teacher. In the second part of the exercise, we were told to envision someone who had helped, or guided, or unconditionally loved us, and to wish for them also to be happy and truly joyful. I was uncertain whom to imagine.

I remembered my Sai Baba dream and decided to try him. My thinking mind said that if he really is an avatar he wouldn't need any well-wishing from me, but I went ahead with the exercise anyway. Almost immediately, an intense wave of compassion and gratitude flowed into me. It was as if the avatar truly appreciated the wish for his joy and happiness, and reciprocated. I was astonished, tears were streaming down my face, and I was quite repentant about having judged my neighbor.

When I shared the experience with the group, and my surprise at the way it worked, Jack Engman said, simply, "That's how Sai Baba works."

The rest of the exercises were to extend the same blessings to an acquaintance, and then to an enemy or someone who's harmed you (this was difficult but enlightening for many of us). The exercise seemed to be part of a general series of Theravadan Buddhist exercises that end up similarly to the seventh makham of Sufism mentioned in an earlier chapter. I later found out that the woman next to me was a Ph.D. biochemist, as well as a sanctioned "dharma holder" of the Zen lineage (that is, a teacher herself—a rare thing, especially for an American).

These dream experiences, of course, can't be conclusive; but they are indicative of the way people seem to actually shift to the hylozoic perspective. All the theoretical studies, and books, and science theories may help to point the way (I hope anyhow), but it seems that only some sort of personal experience (be it of an outer or inner teacher, or another sort of event) really re-orients individual perspectives. There are indications though that the frequency of this sort of experience is increasing. Possibly, a collective experience, or series of experiences will initiate a true cultural shift.

Two Different Masters

Another interesting case is that of D. Rajagopalacharya and Krishnamurti. Rajagopal was, for fifty years, the most constant companion, affairs manager, and editor, for J. Krishnamurti (the well known spiritual teacher and philosopher mentioned several times already).[268]

In his early teens, the poor Indian boy Krishnamurti was "discovered" by the Theosophical Society, raised, groomed and prepared to be the vehicle for a "World Teacher." Gradually two things happened, one expected and the other not.

First, a profound spiritual energy did start flowing though Krishnamurti and he began giving inspiring public discourses and writings. But also he became disaffected with the Theosophical Society. It was a heady time in the Theosophical Society and certain senior members began "verifying" absurdly inflated degrees of divinity on each other and their friends. Finally, in 1929 at the age of 34, Krishnamurti severed all ties with the organization that had been set up to propagate his teachings, and he washed his hands of the whole lot except for a few close associates like Annie Besant who had essentially been a mother to him, and Rajagopal whom Besant asked to take care of Krishnamurti. From then on, Krishnamurti's teachings emphasized direct inner experience, detachment from self-serving religious organizations and detachment from self-agrandizing gurus. Krishnamurti never accepted disciples or devotees.

In the 1960s, Rajagopal and Krishnamurti separated for still unclear personal reasons. In a recent book, Rajagopal's stepdaughter Diana Baskin (the daughter of Rajagopal's second wife whom he married in 1962, and was still with in 1990 at the time of Baskin's book), documents extensive correspondence of a devotional nature between Sai Baba and Rajagopal during the last decades of Rajagopal's life. Baskin and her mother, Rajagopal's wife, have been close devotees of Sai Baba since the 1960s. Baskin claims that Krishnamurti himself sought Sai Baba's company:

"Secretly and unknown to the public, Krishnamurti asked to meet Swami and have His darshan [sight of a holy man] while both were in Madras. Swami gave details of the meeting to Mother and introduced her to a teacher in his college who was present at the meeting. I am sure the meeting, in which Krishnamurti presented a rose to Swami, had a great impact on him and perhaps marked the beginning of the return."[269]

Even if what Baskin says is true, I do not see it as hypocritical of Krishnamurti (as some do see it, because he rejected "gurus"). I see both Krishnamurti's and Sai Baba's teachings as extremely valuable. Sai Baba, when questioned about his divinity, usually responds with something like "*you* are god"—meaning that we are all sparks of the divine and that it is our job, through inner Self-realization, to actualize that. Those Krishnamurti followers who want to believe that he was the one and only disseminator of truth seem unwittingly to be caught in the sort of idol worship that Krishnamurti tried to liberate them from. Sai Baba and J. Krishnamurti seem to me to both embody the same ageless wisdom teachings in different vehicles, as do many other teachers past and present.[270]

Hylozoic What?

The above sections are offered as partial description of my own investigations of where the hylozoic paradigm might lead. It will undoubtedly lead farther than we expect. The avatars, sages and ageless wisdom teachers of past and present indicate that the two great realms—spirit and matter—are in the process of reuniting in human beings, and that process has planetary and cosmic significance in *both* realms.

The recent explosion of knowledge of the one realm of matter, through science, can only aid in the process. Rediscovery and reintegration of the more serious of the metaphysical traditions is the other part of the process. That our potential may be so vast as the ageless wisdom teachers describe and exhibit, is difficult to comprehend even with the aid of the hylozoic paradigm. Any productive new development in science usually leads to whole new fields of inquiry, instead of closing off inquiry.

The specific personalities I have discussed are meant to be representative of the ageless wisdom, and should not be overemphasized. I included some detail on Sathya Sai Baba for two reasons—my personal experiences, and his public openness and ease of investigation for anyone interested. There are ageless wisdom teachings abundantly available, and with a little paying of attention, many teachers can be found. Careful discrimination is essential, and the finding of a true ageless wisdom teacher is a problem that I am not qualified to expound upon here.

Collectively, the marriage of science and esoteric spirituality (a marriage which we are calling the hylozoic paradigm) is beginning. All we have to do to take part is to release our belief structure from the old paradigm and *investigate* the new. If what the Kogi Mamas (and other native peoples, like the Hopi) say, from their extensive inner experience and long study of ecology, is right, then the need for that marriage is terribly great, even essential. Many physical scientists are concluding that continuing our present course of global influence, knowing that our actions do have major global consequence but not knowing just what that consequences are, is a quite dangerous experiment.

The problem for scientists is that predictions cannot be made precisely. In fact, in many cases, old paradigm-style prediction is fully impossible because the future is emergent. What to do? The Kogis say "learn the way things really are"—learn that there is spirit as well as matter. If this is right, as I believe it is, we are fortunate that there are models like the ageless wisdom, and teachers past and present to help us learn. A century of war shows that the interpersonal aspects of our present crises are just as great as the ecological problems.

Are the human crises unrelated to the ecological ones, with totally different causes? If the human body-mind is purely mechanical matter, then maybe self-destruction and community destruction is inevitable. If the body-mind is spiritual as well as material, and if the problem is inability to allow harmony between the two aspects of the one universe, then just knowing that the universe is hylozoic is an important start.

How can just knowing that the universe is hylozoic start to effect change? Typical self-aware, egoic, active thought may, in fact, be a product of the purely material processes discussed in Chapter 10. This type of thought collects and analyzes data, chooses between options based on past experience, assembles a coherent image of the external world and responds to stimuli. This type of thought can be labeled intellect. It is conceivable that intellect is an essentially deterministic material process.

Computers are becoming very proficient at intellect. Truly creative thought, intuitive thought, telepathic rapport with another, and transcendent experience, represent other mind processes. These—call them collectively intuition—do not seem to be active thought at all. They sort of occur "out of the blue" and then active thought (intellect) interprets and stores them. The esoteric ageless wisdom model is that intuition is the friction between spirit and matter—the filling of the openness of matter.

It is not surprising that intellect can distrust, ignore even fear intuition, and hence create ridiculous theories of a universe in which intuition cannot exist. Such denial of spirit, by matter, will make the friction between the two more painful. The allowance of a coherent interplay between intellect and intuition, between spirit and matter, is obviously more productive. The allowance of spirit into matter, intuition into intellect, may be a better definition of intelligence than a score on a test.

In mythological terms, the tendency to confuse intellect with intelligence can be seen as an overabundance of the immature masculine archetype in our culture. The opening of intellect to intuition requires a receptive, feminine, opening of matter to spirit, not denying the masculine archetype but integrating the two.

To investigate the truths of metaphysics, as well as physics, because they affect each other, is immensely practical. All the great sages have indicated that there are serious pitfalls and dangers along the way to developing intuition and on the spiritual paths. If human culture as a whole is moving onto a spiritual path, new methods of discrimination and rigor for opening to the mystical are needed. How to look at the world hylozoically, with discrimination, is the subject of the next chapter.

14. Frauds, Fools, Magicians, Messiahs, and Us

> *"The foundations have been all undermined, and modern man, whatever he may say in public, knows in the privacy of his heart that he can no more 'believe.' Believing certain things because an organized body of priests tells him to believe, believing because it is written in certain books, believing because his people like him to believe, the modern man knows to be impossible for him. There are, of course, a number of people who seem to acquiesce in the so-called popular faith, but we also know for certain that they do not think. ...*
>
> *Not only will [spiritual investigation] be made scientific—as scientific, at least, as any of the conclusions of physics or chemistry—but it will have greater strength, because physics or chemistry has no internal mandate to vouch for its truth which religion has. ...*
>
> *Religion deals with the truths of the metaphysical world, just as chemistry and the other natural sciences deal with the truths of the physical world. ... The sage is often ignorant of physical science because he reads the wrong book—the book within; and the scientist is too often ignorant of religion, because he, too, reads from the wrong book—the book without."*[271]
>
> — Vivekananda, in England, 1896.

Vivekananda's message of a century ago is amazingly fresh today—even more fresh because of the recent breakdown in the scientific belief structure. Vivekananda was describing the breakdown of the religious belief structures. Western culture tried to replace the loss of religious certainty with scientific certainty. We now seem terrified to acknowledge the failure of scientific certainty as well. We have yet to make spirituality scientific (not on a broad cultural scale anyway), but that must be our course. The breakdown of the encompassing certainty, though not the content, of the scientific belief structure is a prerequisite to an inclusive synthesis—a synthesis not here yet, but perhaps on the horizon. The breakdown of false certainties only prepares the way.

The identification of representatives of the new myths representing the underlying spiritual realities is needed. Some of these representatives may already be popping up in the world culture and environment. The application of discrimination in spiritual matters is needed to convincingly identify those that will inform the new paradigm—and methods of discrimination can be learned from the methods of science. Some of my own clearly limited ideas about the contemporary relevance of the spiritual traditions and Ageless Wisdom teachings were given in the preceding chapters. This chapter presents some thoughts and observations on being discriminating in identifying informative representatives of the new hylozoic paradigm.

Time Travel As Example

First, an example from the old scientific paradigm reminds us of how many basic things we really know very little about. The old "grandfather paradox" proves that time travel is impossible. The paradox goes like this. You travel back in time, and encounter your grandfather. He is having dinner with his fiancée, your future grandmother. Being a young version of your own genetic material, you find her attractive. Your grandfather notices. He becomes insanely jealous, stomps out of the restaurant, and marries someone else. Now, your parents will never be born, and neither will you, and so you could not have been there to travel back in time in the first place.

That is just one example of the general paradox. Any visit to the past would cause some small change, of some sort, in the sequence of events leading up to the future from which the traveler needed to have come. And so, time travel is proven to be impossible—right? Wrong.

Physicists have traditionally invoked concepts like the "grandfather paradox," called a "chronology principle," to rule out the possibility of travel into the past. And yet, no known physical laws or principles actually do rule out such possibilities. Two physicists (David Deutsch and Michael Lockwood) who have carefully analyzed the relevant physics, emphasize that, because of the fundamental quantum openness of the way matter works, travel to the past is, in theory, possible.[272]

Of course, we have no idea about how any conceivable technology could actually transport us, or anything, to different times and back. Deutsch and Lockwood's point is that it is not, in theory, impossible.

Deutsch and Lockwood employ the "many worlds" interpretation of quantum mechanics for their argument. The many worlds interpretation is just one of the whole class of possible hylozoic interpretations of quantum mechanics, as noted in Part II of this book. The many worlds interpretation says that, at each progressive instant in time, the universe branches into a huge class of possible future universes. Something determines, in each instant, which of the possible universes we remain aware of and are "in."

What the something that causes the branching is—whether it is a consciousness principle, or a spiritual entity, or whatever—we don't know. As you can imagine, the range of possible universes that have come and gone throughout history is absolutely enormous. Deutsch and Lockwood show that, in the many worlds interpretation of quantum mechanics, natural avenues for time travel which they call "closed timeline curves" (CTC's) exist. They argue that CTC's could be used for time travel without violating any paradox principles.

Obviously, it is tempting to use concepts like CTC's to "explain" miracles like Sai Baba's materializations and apports (see previous chapter). Could Sai Baba be in touch with spiritual realities that allow him to move us into an adjacent parallel universe in which most everything is the same, except for the presence of the hot food or whatever it is that has been "materialized"?

That sort of "explanation" would also be consistent with the fact that avatars, while not bound by what we think of as the old paradigm laws of mechanistic materialism, *are* bound by more encompassing laws like the Law of Karma (the Law of Cause and Effect) , and the Law of Free Will. In Vedantic tradition, avatars themselves are bound by the principle that they cannot interfere with human free will.

A lot of caution should be used with such "explanations," for they are not explanations at all. They are possible descriptions of how our observations of the world may not be completely inconsistent with the truths of old paradigm science. Concepts like CTC's are broad theoretical speculations about the nature of space-time, and are far divorced from knowledge of what an avatar is or how it functions. What concepts like CTC's should do is keep us from using not-fully-analyzed and overinterpreted concepts of "the laws of physics" to apply a dismissive and closed attitude to not observing and comprehending the events in the world around us.

Deutsch and Lockwood make no mention of the relevance of CTC's for a spiritual or hylozoic understanding of nature. They are analyzing purely in terms of the standard mathematics of quantum theory. If they did think about making such connections, they were probably scared away from doing so by the great mass of hucksters, charlatans, delusionary, unscrupulous, and irrational individuals that can be encountered in such waters. I argue, though, that it is the refusal of "mainstream" scientists and intellectuals to make the appropriate analyses, and their equally emotional, dismissive, and ridiculous attitude, that allows the deluded and the charlatans to flourish.

Spiritual Abduction?

A case in point may be the so-called "alien abduction" phenomenon. Whitley Strieber, a fiction writer, in his 1987 nonfiction book *Communion*, starts with the statement "this is the story of one man's attempt to deal with a shattering assault from the unknown. It is a true story ..." He continues, "What happened to me was terrifying. There has been a lot of scoffing ... It has been falsely claimed that [these] memories are a side-effect of hypnosis. This is not true ... Scoffing at [people who experience this] is as ugly as laughing at rape victims." To emphasize his seriousness, Strieber included the results of a polygraph test of himself and an endorsement from the Director of Research of New York State Psychiatric Institute—who had examined Strieber.

14: Frauds, Fools, Magicians, Messiahs, and Us

Strieber's story was of being "abducted," and otherwise encountering, alien nonhuman beings that seemed to coexist with us here on Earth. In his book, Strieber emphasized that his experiences (and those of at least some other "abductees") were in some sense real. He left open the interpretation of just what the nature of the phenomenon he encountered was, but the book strongly hinted that he felt the alien beings and their craft were materially real in some sense, technologically superior to us.

I had a short conversation with Strieber while he was working on his second book on the topic.[273] I said that I found his story very interesting, but that, as a physicist, I suspected that only physical evidence (photographs or artifacts) would stop the scoffing of skeptics. Strieber, who seemed slightly agitated from his experiences, explained that he agreed. He said that a number of physicist friends (and others) were working closely with him to produce such evidence. At his upstate New York home, where some of the encounters occurred, they set up video and infrared cameras, ultraviolet and motion sensors, and sound recorders.

On some occasions when the encounters occurred, the recording equipment was in place. But always something would interfere with the gathering of evidence. The cameras would mysteriously stop, or the action would happen out of view, or one of the people would get frightened and botch the recording. Some of the investigators themselves had alien encounter experiences. But no "hard" evidence was ever produced.

In his subsequent book *Transformation*, Strieber started to lean toward the view that the phenomenon was not material—and so, the usual type of "hard" evidence could never be produced. He also leaned more toward the opinion that the phenomenon had important spiritual meanings. Apparently now, his opinion has moved even more toward this direction, and he has stopped writing about the subject.

The expert psychiatric opinion on the alien encounter experiences of Strieber and others is equally inconclusive. Representative of the "skeptical" camp, one researcher has concluded:

> "Six adults who had recently experienced sudden recall of preschool memories of sex abuse or alien abduction/visitation

were given the complete Halstead-Reitan Neuropsychological Test Battery (HRNB). Memories emerged when hypnosis was used within a context of sex abuse therapy groups or New Age religion and were followed by a reduction in anxiety. Subjects displayed significant elevations of childhood imaginings, complex partial epileptic-like signs, and suggestibility. Right frontotemporal anomalies and reduced access to the right parietal lobe were found. MMPI profiles were normal. Results support the hypothesis that a history of anxiety, complex-partial epileptic-like signs, and suggestibility may facilitate the creation of images whose content is determined by social context or expectancy. If these images reduce existential anxiety, they may be reinforced and perceived as memories."[274]

Studies like these are essentially a sophisticated description of the subjects and an hypothesis that their memories were "created." Such an argument is hardly conclusive. Apparently, for example, exactly what epilepsy is, why it occurs in detail, why many people seem to have only one epileptic-like occurrence without recurrence, is not understood.

To use "complex-partial epileptic-like signs" as an "explanation" for a mysterious psychological experience is not entirely convincing. Sure, the hypothesis that the memories are "created" is plausible. But is the plausibility of that hypothesis evidence that sexual abuse never occurs? Is the hypothesis evidence that encounter with transcendent entities (aliens) never happens?

The stuff about different brain regions being more or less active cannot be definitive either. Sure, their brains behaved differently than other people's brains behave because other people don't think they've encountered aliens, and those people did. If I don't have a head, I won't experience the world. This does not prove that all experience originates in my head. The same goes for more specific types of experience and more localized regions of the brain.

The researcher quoted above (Michael Persinger) is a neuroscientist. He argues that unexplained UFO sightings are actually sightings of glowing plasma balls that are supported by radio frequency electromagnetic fields, created from stressed rocks in the earth, before earthquakes.[275]

He says that the hippocampal region of the temporal lobes of the brain is an especially "electrically unstable" mass of neurons. When that brain region is stimulated artificially (with an electrode), he says, dreamlike experiences occur. He says such experiences can seem very meaningful, and can have a cosmic quality "very similar to a type of religious experience." He speculates that an electric discharge from the UFO plasma ball to a person's head can cause partial amnesia and stimulate the temporal lobe of the brain, causing an experience that the experiencer later interprets as abduction by aliens.

Persinger also argues that the unusual events in Fatima, Portugal, in the early years of this century—when large numbers of people saw a bright light that they experienced as a spiritual being—were caused by the same process.

There are immediate problems with Persinger's model. First, it is not generally accepted by geophysicists that the sorts of electromagnetic fields needed to produce the described lights actually are produced from stresses in the earth. In the case of Fatima, for instance, the phenomenon recurred several times, in the same place, for long periods of time.

The geophysical problems are not the major problem though. What I want to point out is an unstated assumption of Persinger's model. A region of the brain that is associated with "religious experience" may well exist, as identified by Persinger. Just because we can identify such a brain area, and perhaps even artificially stimulate some sort of false religious experience, does that mean that true religious experience (or spiritual experience) does not also occur? We can artificially stimulate the taste of bananas by stimulating a portion of the brain—does that mean that real bananas do not exist?

In contrast to Persinger, a distinguished psychiatrist believes that some abductees experienced something quite real. John E. Mack, Professor of Psychiatry at Cambridge Hospital, Harvard Medical School, and author of a Pulitzer Prize-winning biography of T. E. Lawrence, studied 76 alleged UFO abductees.[276]

Mack concludes that his patients—including an electronics technician, a fine arts professor, an accountant, a business executive, and others—underwent authentic experiences not based on delusion or hallucination.

Mack also emphasizes the spiritual significance of the "abduction" experiences. One of Mack's patients prefers to call them [space] "brothers" rather than "aliens," and many experiencers are at least partially willing participants in the experiences. It may be better to call them "brother encounters" rather that "alien abductions." Mack's patients reported deep personal growth, profound spiritual insights, and heightened awareness of Earth's ecological crisis, as a result of their encounters. Some of them re-experienced events from former incarnations, and some encountered powerful spiritual teachers.

Mack accepts the experiences as evidence that a higher intelligence is trying to aid human awareness. Mack also suggests that many other psychiatrists treat these profound, essentially religious, experiences of their patients with a degree of disbelief and ridicule that they would not feel appropriate for a therapist reacting to more prosaic experiences—confusing and alienating, rather than aiding, the patients.

Importantly, Mack reports that his studies of his patients had profound influences on his own worldview. He says:

> "I have come to see that the abduction phenomenon has important philosophical, spiritual, and social implications. ... The abduction phenomenon has led me ... to see ... that we participate in a universe or universes that are filled with intelligences from which we have cut ourselves off, having lost the senses by which we might know them. ... The contemporary Western tenet that we are alone in the universe, conversant only with ourselves, is, in fact, a minority perspective, an anomaly."

Mack believes that the aliens are "beings from another dimension." He says that Tibetans, for instance, "have long believed that humans could separate from the 'etheric' or 'subtle' body and go traveling in an 'out of body' capacity for hours or days at a time."[277]

In the old hylostochastic and hylostatic paradigms, if we wanted to accept that some UFO and alien encounters are real, we'd have to conclude that they are material craft and material beings. In that model, the continuing lack of physical evidence for such craft becomes an unresolveable paradox. In the hylozoic paradigm, UFO/alien encounters may be quite real—as Mack concludes they are. They may also be quite nonmaterial in origin. The strength that the old materialist paradigms have over our belief structures creates some of the sorts of confabulations that Persinger postulates.

People ("abductees") experience something that they are quite certain is real. Their culture says that anything real must be material, and so they are caught in a bind in which they must assert that the encounters were material, or else they must concede that they are gullible and foolish "believers," if not liars. Of course, the UFO subculture also contains wild claims and fabrications—some motivated by profit or desire for attention.

The UFO subculture is kept fertile for the more absurd stories, and is kept with an inability to discriminate as to what is usefully relevant, by the primitive adherence of mainstream culture and science to outdated materialism.

Serious analysis of things such as apparent alien encounter experiences, from the hylozoic perspective, does introduce further complications. Things cannot be black or white. The accounts cannot be either complete fabrication, or else materially true in every detail. We need new hylozoic language to describe hylozoic events.

In the model of the hylozoic perspective that I am presenting, the "abduction" experience happens like this. The brain—probably the temporal lobes as Persinger says—is sitting there all primed to do a tremendously large range of things. It is highly sensitive—a material "bell" waiting to be "rung" by nonmaterial spiritual happenings, and spiritual entities (the "aliens"). The physical brain enters into various sleep states, meditative states, and hypnotic states, that make it sensitive to the etheric body—the etheric body being the activity of the pranic lifetrons (see Part III).

The conscious awareness of the person identifies more with the etheric (nonmaterial) counterpart of the material physical brain. The etheric counterpart of the person then encounters the "alien" beings whose primary existence and awareness is normally in the nonmaterial etheric body. Given our exclusively material language structures, the closest the experiencer can come to describing it, even under hypnosis, is as a gross physical alien encounter.

The encounters often contain self-contradictions, odd quirky happenings, and general bizarreness. In the hylozoic perspective, we need to try to understand the material plane interpretations of the experiences in terms of the spiritual realities described by the spiritual traditions (the "Ageless Wisdom"). As described in the previous chapter, the perennial philosophy says that there are various types and qualities of spiritual planes and entities associated with our various material bodies—physical, emotional, mental, etc.

The spiritual traditions say that the emotional or "astral" planes of spirit cause the odd quirks and contradictions of spiritual experiences. The traditions say that our emotional selves (both material and nonmaterial) are what we most often (almost exclusively) associate with. Just watch some TV and the emotional emphasis of our culture is apparent.

The traditions also say that the emotional-astral planes are the most full of illusion, miasma, and "junk." This is why we often dismiss things as "emotional" and therefore untrustworthy. The error in such dismissals is the implication that an emotional-astral, nonmaterial, experience cannot be an actual real experience. The correct hylozoic attitude is that it may be unreliable, not lastingly true, and not helpful, but it might at the same time be as real as the chair you are sitting on. (Of course there are also very powerful and positive types of emotional experience—emotions are neither inherently "bad" nor "good.")

The further error is associating all spiritual experience with unreliable "emotional" experience. *Some* spiritual experience is unreliable emotional experience.

Fundamentalist Christians call this a "soulish" experience, and distinguish between. illusory and useless "soulish" experience, and enlightening "spiritual" experience. This is one area where the Fundamentalists and the Ageless (and New Age) Wisdom agree. Alice Bailey called it "lower psychism." Lower psychism manifests in seances, and much of what passes as "astrology," "psychic readings," and "channeling." The ageless wisdom spiritual traditions say that beyond such "lower" aspects are higher, true, and importantly meaningful spirit-influenced experiences—as professor Mack concluded he found in some of his "abductees."

The coexistence, in deep meditation experiences as well as in "alien encounters," of "lower psychic" quirks, bizarreness, and emotional fantasy, together with profound insights and meaningful information, gives fodder to the "scientific skeptics." These skeptics question the character of anyone who would even study the subject. A senior writer for *Scientific American* magazine bluntly states, "His [a certain government scientist's] 'interest' in alien abductions and paranormal phenomena, about which most scientists are deeply skeptical, raises questions about his judgment."[278]

The writer is arguing that the scientist's interest in alien abductions calls into question his ability to work on other *unrelated* subjects. The justification for this sort of upside-down witch hunt seems to be simple association with the quirkiness and bizarre nature that accompanies the meaningful component of the subject. (This must be the writer's justification because there is no scientific evidence that physics proves that inner experience cannot be meaningful.) Such dismissal may be akin to dismissing anyone who watches TV, because the *Beavis and Butthead* show is on TV, while ignoring that Shakespeare's plays are also on TV.

All the contemplative spiritual traditions have a concept similar to "lower psychism." For instance in Zen practice, the phantasmagoria of lower psychism is called "makyo," and is supposed to be ignored as it is a hindrance to true insight. In Christianity, Jesus endured the temptations of "demons" in his desert meditation practice, as did Gautama Buddha.

The "scientific" mindset dismisses the experiences of the time-honored inner traditions by asserting that they are metaphorical descriptions of hallucinations caused by mechanical chemical disturbances in the brain. The hylozoic paradigm says that, while chemistry certainly plays an important role, both the makyo and the deep insights are the result of the interplay of real spiritual stuff, and real material stuff. It is important to learn to discriminate amongst the chafe and the wheat. The alien abduction experiences investigated and described by Mack contain elements of both, just as all the contemplative traditions tell us that deep meditative experiences also contain both.

Plant Behavior?

Another case of old paradigm thought prohibiting meaningful analysis may be the "crop circle" phenomenon. In the early 1980s, some attention was brought to seemingly mysterious occurrences in Southern England cereal crop fields. Circles of plants, within farm fields, were found to be flattened. According to reports, usually the plants were bent and not broken. The phenomenon continued annually. A small number of serious investigators steadily studied the phenomenon. A larger number of people became interested out of a feeling that the circles had a spiritual significance. The phenomenon was discovered in many other places in England, and worldwide. The media reported sporadically on the circles, usually noting meteorologist Terence Meaden's whirlwind theory for the circles' formation.

In 1990, the circle designs evolved into more complicated patterns. The more complicated patterns could not possibly be formed by standard meteorological phenomena, and these patterns further inspired those who found spiritual meaning in the crop circle phenomenon. (Most meteorologists don't think even the plain circles could be formed by standard meteorological phenomena.) In 1991, a British tabloid newspaper reported that two elderly artists (Doug and Dave) said they hoaxed all the circles and patterns.[279]

This tabloid "hoax explanation" was widely reported by the major media around the world. "Mainstream" media that normally ignore the wild claims of the tabloids reported this "explanation" without investigating its source or reliability, and without investigating the serious studies that had accompanied the phenomenon for years.

In 1991, British filmmaker John Macnish made a documentary on the phenomenon, "Crop Circle Communiqué," that emphasized the mystery of the phenomena and leaned toward the position that at least some of them were "genuine." Because of inconsistencies in Doug and Dave's stories, Macnish and others questioned whether they had made any circles, much less all of them.

In 1992 and 1993, Macnish, who says he was "obsessed" with finding out how the circles formed, went "underground." He employed sophisticated night vision equipment and long hours in the English countryside in the middle of the night. He secretly collaborated with Doug and Dave, to photograph them making circles and patterns. Macnish also discovered and surveillanced other "hoaxer" groups. He commissioned and photographed the making of patterns without telling the "believer" groups and the "expert" investigators. Macnish claims that the "experts" pronounced as "genuine" many of his documented hoaxes. But Macnish seems to have been undiscriminating in who he accepted as "experts."

A primary source of his "expert" pronouncements was a dowser who relied solely on his dowsing feelings, and continued to assert that the hoaxed patterns had unusual energies even after Macnish revealed photographs of their construction. Macnish reversed his "believer" stance and concluded, in his book, that all of the circles and patterns ever reported were hoaxes. But Macnish does not even consider the more standard scientific evidence in favor of the genuineness of some of the phenomena, relying on his observation of the fallibility of self-described "experts."[280]

Thinking about the possibility that some crop circles are genuine is especially interesting because they seem to be "on the edge" of paradigms in many ways. For one thing, the simple circles were, as Meaden argued, almost plausibly createable by unusual but "normal" wind phenomena. Also, even if a wind explanation cannot work (and assuming that some of them are not hoaxes), then it is still not clear how far out of the old paradigm these patterns are. Mature sunflowers follow the sun across the sky during the day, illustrating that plants can easily bend "if they want to" in a short period of time. Indeed, the early eyewitness reports described the crop circle plants as just bending over in about thirty seconds—no exotic flashing lights or UFO landing gear involved.[281]

Could the crop circles be a sort of "plant behavior"? The many worlds interpretation of quantum mechanics says, basically, that anything that can happen does happen—some place in the enormous range of different branching universes. Plants can bend, and so, in some universes it seems that circles of plants will bend together. So perhaps the circles are within the old paradigm—a form of "plant behavior." But the observed patterns would occur only in an extremely unlikely group of universes—so unlikely that we would expect never to see a spontaneous crop circle—leading us back to a necessarily hylozoic "explanation."

On an occasion when a circle appeared, overnight, in a field that was under photographic surveillance, nothing discernible was detected on the films. Maybe there was nothing to detect. Maybe the plants just "decided" to bend over. It is the old materialist paradigm that makes us expect to see some huge machine descend and crush the plants. The patterns and pictograms lead even further into the hylozoic paradigm.

But a tabloid newspaper said that they are all hoaxes, and so the mainstream now believes. Wouldn't investigation be warranted before we conclude? Old paradigm science says, "no," crop circles are impossible and so they are not worth investigating. Hylozoic paradigm science says, investigate! And certainly, if others have conducted serious investigations, at least consider what they've done. Such consideration, in this case, seems to deepen the mystery.

Gerald Hawkins, professor of astronomy at Boston University, after studying the patterns, proposed that some crop circle formations illustrate previously unknown geometric theorems (*Science News*, February 2, 1992). Archie Roy, professor of physics at Glasgow University, "was convinced humanity was encountering an advanced intelligence," after investigating the circles.[282]

Roy says, "Since 1980, scientific hypotheses have been framed (about the formations) and then scrapped. Other, stranger, guesses have multiplied as fast as the circles themselves. Several books have been written about them; and an international conference has been held, and its proceedings published. Scores of television programs have covered them. Thousands of photographs have been taken. Reports and articles published in the local and national press have now passed well beyond counting. Yet the mystery, far from being solved continues to grow."[283]

An obvious step in the investigation is to determine whether a clear distinction can be made between the "hoaxed" (that is, man-made) circles and the genuine ones. There are, of course, scientific professionals who specialize in cereal crop biological development studies. One of them, biophysicist W.C. Levengood of Pinelandia Biophysical Lab in Michigan, has studied samples of the affected plants. Levengood is author of many peer-reviewed scientific papers, on biochemical energetics in plants and plant-tissue structures. He is also the inventor of an 'automatic seed analyzer,' based on an electronic system for examining the tissue integrity and membrane breakdown in seeds, which is used world-wide.[284]

Levengood is studying the morphological development of plants growing within the circles. He was initially interested because, "If some form of electromagnetic energy is involved in the formation of these circles, then (based on what I am finding in recent research) there is a good chance that the intracellular spatial associations between organelles would be quite different in plant tissues from the circle regions than from tissues from the normal growing plants."[285]

Levengood's first investigation of plants suspected to be from a "genuine" pattern found a condition he felt was very unusual. He reported the glumes of the plants were empty of seeds, a condition called "polyembryony." To obtain perspective on the probability of the condition he observed, he consulted with an agronomist and a plant breeder. He says, "Without giving them any details, I posed the question, 'What is the probability of randomly removing a single, normal appearing wheathead in a field and finding it completely empty?' In essence their answer was, 'About as likely as winning a lottery three times in a row.' "[286]

Levengood found similar abnormalities in plants from other formations. He has also found unusual enlargement of plant cell wall pits (small holes allowing fluid to flow in the plant). Levengood thinks these enlargements are indicative of rapid heat, such as in a microwave oven. Stepping on plants increases pressure in the cells and so also can enlarge cell wall pits, but Levengood finds the formation plant cell pit enlargements occur in regular patterns, and with gradual gradations in size that indicate a nonmechanical cause.[287]

Many believers in the authenticity of some of the crop circles would "explain" them as being created by UFO's. But that is putting the cart before the horse. We don't know what UFO's are in the first place. I am arguing that pigheaded adherence to long outdated old paradigm belief structures hinders serious study of interesting crop circle phenomena.

On the other end of the spectrum from serious investigators, the many clearly delusionary individuals that show up at the circles and in the circle study groups do not help. For instance, about a circle that appeared in Illinois, the *Chicago Tribune* reported that the busloads of interested people who showed up included numerous "kooks, goofs, and squirrels," including a delusionary individual who claimed to be a "government man" who "identified" footprints as alien because "spacemen walk backwards."[288]

Almost understandably, that kind of stuff makes serious scientists run for the hills. And so it is left—a lot of "squirrelly ideas" and irrational assertions, some interesting phenomena, and little serious detailed investigation.

The fact that a lot of ordinary people (and also a lot of people with wishful and not-carefully-analyzed ideas) are interested in crop circles is not evidence that there is no truly interesting phenomena there. Huge numbers of reporters and ordinary folk always showed up at the NASA Voyager spacecraft planetary encounter press conferences at the Jet Propulsion Laboratory in Pasadena—because they were interested. If one talked to these people, one would find a lot of bizarre ideas about what they were looking at in the photos and data that Voyager was sending back from other planets. Popular public interest in a topic should not be taken as evidence for scientific contempt of the topic. Arrogant dismissal of new observations, like crop circles, by scientists, only fuels the conspiracy nuts and other wild ideas.

So, first noting that I haven't found any reports of "drop-dead conclusive" evidence, and that I might be wrong, I should state how I feel about the crop circles and patterns. My intuition is that, while most are manmade, somewhere in the crop circles and patterns there is a very interesting and important natural phenomenon that should be investigated. I say "natural phenomenon" not in the old paradigm sense of strictly mechanistic and mechanical, but in the hylozoic sense of an interplay between spirit and matter. The "genuine" crop circles, if they exist, are best classified as unusual plant behavior. Until there is documented evidence of something mechanical ("UFO" landing gear or whirlwinds) making the circles, they should be viewed as something that plants "do"—a sort of plant spiritual experience.

If the circles *are* a sort of plant spiritual experience, what might they mean? Native American spiritual leaders who have studied the patterns say that the circles are a message from the plant kingdom—a sad message that the Earth's ecosystem is seriously ill. The patterns may also be an enlivening message—a message that the world is far more sublime, and far more alive, than we have hitherto noticed.

Macnish believes that our "fear of being alone" in the universe caused many "believers" to believe that hoaxed crop circles are a message from an unknown intelligence.

Psychiatry professor John Mack concludes the exact opposite. Mack suggests that our fear of admitting that our limited intellects are neither alone nor supreme in the universe causes "mainstream" psychiatrists to disbelieve the reports by their patients of encountering other intelligences. In the emerging view of transpersonal psychology, both views may be partially correct. In the case of infantile and not fully individuated psyches, Macnish's type of fear supports an inability to rationally consider the truth about the world. Macnish reports, for instance, that public meetings, in which crop circle hoaxers tried to present their evidence of hoaxing, were disrupted by shouting and even "screeching" from the audience.

However, the more sober "believers" also report that their presentations are disrupted by the same sorts of incontinence from "skeptics." In this case, transpersonal psychology would say, individuated psyches are trying to prevent the release of evidence that they are not the ultimate controlling authority of their world.

Oddly, Macnish suggests that the Native American spiritual leaders' interpretation of the message of the crop circles is accurate even though the circles are hoaxes. Macnish posits that Doug and Dave are unwittingly "Western shamans"—creating meaningful images, from their subconscious, in the crops.

If the crop circles are messages from beyond our intellects (whether from the plants themselves or from Doug and Dave's unconscious), are we ready to receive the messages? The prevalence and degree of shenanigans surrounding the circles and patterns is not encouraging. Obviously most crop circles are manmade and have sometimes fooled even the most serious investigators. It would do no good to show the secrets of the universe to a troop of baboons. If crop circles are messages from an advanced intelligence, the source must believe that we are at least close to being ready or it would not send the messages. All we can do is apply dispassionate investigation, and lay off the ridicule, hoaxing, and shenanigans.[289]

Debunking Debunkers

A group of stage magicians, rationalists, and scientists has organized themselves into a "paranormal" debunking organization called Committee for the Scientific Investigation of Claims Of the Paranormal (CSICOP). The acronym is designed to rhyme with "psi cop"—"psi" having been a popular term for "psychic" in the 1970's. The CSICOP journal publishes opinions and debunking studies of psychics and "paranormal" phenomena. CSICOP emphasizes the gullible nature of "believers" and the blatant manipulation of that gullibility by charlatans. As such, studies like CSICOP's could be valuable to a serious investigator of the hylozoic paradigm.

The problem with debunkers arises when they imply that selected cases of fraud and abuse mean that all of religion, all of spirituality, is similarly fraudulent. They further imply that such an opinion is the only correct "scientific" opinion—while there is no scientific basis for this assertion. As such, the studies become repetitive, often supplying innuendo where serious study is lacking—no positive result of a CSICOP-like study is possible because the fact that anyone is a "believer" (in religion, or spirituality, or mystery) is held as evidence that he is untrustworthy.

Many of CSICOP's subjects have been quite fraudulent, and quite worthy of their debunking. One of CSICOP's favorite subjects is the famous spoon-bender and stage magician Uri Geller. This is a good example of CSICOP's "beating of dead horses." I was a boy when I saw Uri Geller on the *Johny Carson Show*. I watched very carefully, and it was apparent to me even then that he was trying to pass off standard stage magic as psychic phenomena. This is what CSICOPers, with their professional magicians, specialize in debunking, and they love bashing Uri Geller. Perhaps the continued attention on Geller by CSICOP was partly justified because Geller continued to fool some academic researchers.

In 1988, I attended a panel discussion called something like "Science and the Paranormal." At that time, a well-known California University research psychologist brought up Uri Geller as an example of genuine paranormal phenomena. I mentioned my disappointment. He replied that in his opinion Geller "was too psychologically agitated" to be only a charlatan—the implication being that some of Geller's tricks were probably genuine, judging on the basis of his agitated psychological state. Such reasoning seems unconvincing, but it does have a history in parapsychological studies.

Colin Wilson, in his book *The Occult*, studies a number of cases of what he believes is the standard model of occult magicians—a meteoric rise in esteem and success (financial and otherwise) followed by an equally rapid fall. Wilson concludes that such paranormalists are of three types:

1. Those who were frauds all along, and whose fall is from exposure of the truth;
2. Those who had some sort of genuine paranormal experience, usually in adolescence or childhood. Being convinced of genuineness themselves, they were able to convince others. Usually though, the powers or phenomena abandoned them, and they often resort to trickery to reproduce them. This explains why some of them strenuously and convincingly argue that they are not fakes, and might fit a psychological profile of genuineness, and yet are caught in blatant fakery. Probably some of the mischievous gurus in India fall into this category—with the added miasma that the fakery is OK because it helps people turn toward "spirituality." One of our points is that such antics are wrong in the extreme, and for them, CSICOP's are a great service;
3. Genuine individuals who do not deceive, but who inevitably lose their abilities after making shows of them.

Wilson's basic conclusion is that there is overwhelming evidence that something "paranormal" or "psychic" is associated with what humans are, but those who make professional or self-agrandizing use of it are in for a great fall. Obviously, if Wilson is right, there is a sort of catch-22 with regard to trying to study such phenomena.

That dichotomy is not new, however. The ancient spiritual traditions describe exactly the same issue. In Vedanta (and the other spiritual traditions), "yogic powers" are said to naturally occur as part of any serious spiritual discipline—from physical yoga, to true devotional spirituality, to simple nonviolent living. But yogic powers are not to be used, and certainly not displayed for their own sake. If they are used without complete detachment, an enormous karmic debt is incurred—a debt that often manifests in what Wilson describes as a meteoric fall.

Another difficulty arises in that avatars and certain masters are said to be exceptions to the rule—perhaps having sufficiently dispatched their karmic debts so as to consciously use their powers without mucking everything up—Jesus turning water into wine, for instance.

Anyway, debunking of bunk is quite useful, but overzealous beliefs that all of religion and spirituality are bunk lead to inexcusable defamations on the basis of little or no evidence. Consider an example.

Example: A Rumor of Fraud

As already noted, there is little written about Sathya Sai Baba by "outside experts." There are many books by devotees, and the book by Haraldsson and Osis, and a couple of others by academic sociologists. Some of Sai Baba's "devotees" have very impressive credentials. It is not clear how established a movement must become before everyone associated with it is no longer considered suspect simply by reason of being associated with it. Should we dismiss the observations of anyone who has been associated with Catholicism, Protestantism, or Judaism, because all these religions believe in some pretty wild and nonrational stuff?

Most people are not scientists; the relevance of comments by an "outside expert" about a complex scientific argument would be questionable. In any case, the few comments by outside experts about the Sai Baba phenomenon have a disproportionate impact.

In a book by a well-known writer on psychic phenomena (Rogo, 1982)—that is part debunking, and part attempt to validate some (mostly Roman Catholic) miracles, like weeping statues—a short statement appeared to discredit Sai Baba:

> "There is ... some indication that Sai Baba often deliberately fakes his purported miracles. (When films taken of some of his exhibitions are slowed down, it is clear that he is quite an expert at sleight-of-hand.)"[290]

Haraldsson (writer of the extensively researched book on Sai Baba discussed in Chapter 13) was surprised to read Rogo's statement, and so Haraldsson tried to clarify Rogo's claim by investigating further. Haraldsson describes:

> "In a letter to Rogo, I asked for further details, particularly which films he was referring to. He answered in a letter that he had had several conversations in 1975 with Dr. Edwin C. May, a physicist at the prestigious SRI Institute near San Francisco, and that Dr. May had told him that he had filmed Sai Baba producing objects. According to Rogo, Dr. May had told him that when the films were slowed down and examined frame-by-frame, sleight-of-hand was evident. Rogo himself, however, had never seen Dr. May's films but had taken his word for this. He suggested that I write to Dr. May.
>
> Furthermore, Rogo said that he had seen some films at Sai Baba's headquarters in Los Angeles, which to him had shown clear evidence of fraud. Rogo concluded that some of Baba's materializations had been hidden in his Afro-style hair, since it seemed to Rogo that Baba had 'touched his hair with passing motions on several occasions before producing his little objects.'
>
> I wrote to Dr. May, who rang me up a few days later and told me that he had never met Sai Baba; hence he had never taken films of him and had never even seen any film of Baba. He had filmed a woman in Bombay, alleged by a small flock of followers to produce kumkum paranormally, and he had found her clearly engaged in fraud. Rogo might have been referring to this film."[291]

In spite of Haraldsson's detailed evidence that Rogo's claim to have found Sai Baba as fraudulent was based on no facts whatsoever, another book again cites Rogo's claim as "evidence" that Sai Baba is a fake. Debunker Joe Nickell, who is often cited by CSICOP, devotes a half page to discrediting Sai Baba (*Looking for a Miracle*, 1993). The only mention of any evidence of fakery by Sai Baba, noted by Nickell, is Rogo's statement:

"Actually, as Scott Rogo has pointed out, there is evidence that Sai Baba 'often deliberately fakes his purported miracles.' According to Rogo, 'When films taken of some of his exhibitions are slowed down, it is clear that he is quite an expert at sleight-of-hand.' "

Nickell's debunking method is to put this "evidence" in a section called "Apport Production," following three paragraphs about blatant frauds, including: "During the heyday of spiritualism, mediums usually claimed spirits delivered the apports ... many mediums were exposed as tricksters. ..." Nickell then says "Other apport producers may be found among the Sufis of Islam and the holy men of the Hindus." He does mention that *Harper's Encyclopedia of Mystical and Paranormal Experiences* says, "others, such as Sai Baba of India, have never been exposed as frauds." But then Nickell cites the above "evidence" from Rogo as his exposure. Case closed—Nickell has debunked Sathya Sai Baba.

We could use Nickell's debunking technique, similar to that of many CSICOP "skeptics," to discredit the life and works of Albert Einstein as follows. First we could note that throughout the history of science, there have been outright frauds perpetrated, some at the highest levels of professional scientific authority ("others of Einstein's ilk"). Examples of these can be found in *Stealing Into Print*, by Marcel C. Lafollette (1992). Lafollette, the editor of the respected peer-reviewed journal *Science, Technology, and Human Values*, classifies a long list of unethical scientific conduct, including:

- Describing imaginary data, artifacts, or subjects
- Describing forgeries or faked data
- Misrepresenting authentic data
- Plagiarism and deliberate violation of copyright
- Misrepresenting authorship
- Misrepresenting publication status
- Lying in a professional review
- Forging or fabricating reviews
- Stealing from unpublished manuscripts.

Lafollette cites cases from the time of Leonardo da Vinci (the 15th century Sienese architect Francesco di Giorgio was reluctant to publish his inventions because he was convinced they would be stolen by "ignoramuses [who seek to] adorn themselves with the labours of others") to the present time. He documents fraud cases involving the highest influence levels: Nobel Laureates, and university presidents.

Lafollette also suggests that the incidence of fraud in science has been increasing, and the exposure of fraud is strongly discouraged. Lafollette notes, "a congressional staff member who has investigated scientific fraud has stated that for 'every one of the cases we looked at, there was hardly a single person you could point to that ever raised a question [about the fraudulent practices of a superior] and survived [in the scientific community]."[292]

Thus, in our hypothetical and ludicrous debunking of Einstein, we could note that, "besides, people have said that Einstein was wrong about quantum mechanics," and note that Einstein had a falling-out with Niels Bohr over the matter. End of story—Einstein debunked. We won't do such a debunking of course, because Einstein *was* a great scientist.

The point is that debunkers, to be of value, have to be open to dispassionate observation of reality, and not assert guilt by rumor and innuendo whenever one thinks the subject is "unscientific." Can we really dismiss all the great religious figures of history by associating them with 19th century charlatan "spiritualists"?

Of course, there is a difference in degree of fraudulent activity in the divergent camps of science and religion. Perhaps those involved with spirituality have been victimized by a higher rate of fraud than has science. On the side of CSICOP, as Carl Sagan notes, "extraordinary claims require extraordinary proof." Sure, but which is more extraordinary?

1. To claim that Jesus and all his chief disciples, the distinguished Paul and the rest, were all psychotic charlatans, or,
2. To claim there seems to have been at least some truth to the miracles they witnessed and experienced.

I submit history indicates (1) is the more extraordinary claim. As Einstein argued (see quote before Chapter 13), the likes of Jesus, Moses, Buddha, Krishna, Mohammed and others have created far greater good than have the impressive intellectual feats of scientists.

Anti Antinomian Authorities (The Inflationary Guru Problem)

*"While it is unnecessary to awaken a person already awake
and easy to awaken a person who is asleep,
we cannot awaken, however much we try,
a person pretending to be asleep!"*[293]

As long as our cultural leaders insist on pretending to be asleep (if not actually snoozing), new leaders will be looked for. Many imperfect ones have been found. A class of spiritual leaders that were popular in the West in the 1960s, 70s, and 80s produced a number of examples. They have been called "crazy-wisdom" teachers, and more technically, teachers of Left-hand Tantrism. These "gurus" and many of their disciples can be seen as the organized religious counterparts of the nondiscriminating individuals surrounding ("fringe") phenomena discussed in this chapter.

The failure of mainstream religion to seriously address the true relevance of spirituality directly in terms of our scientific culture fosters an environment in which dangerous cult gurus can attract disaffected people. A tragic example was the Branch Davidian cult of Waco, Texas, led by David Koresh.

George Fuerstein, a former devotee of one Left-hand Tantric guru, describes some of their antics.[294] Though clearly disillusioned, he does not condemn these teachers outright, but argues that their followers and readers often are not as aware as they should be of what their gurus are really up to.

At the same time as these antinomian gurus were functioning, many gurus and teachers from traditions that include moral values were also functioning, as always. But, in the West, the wildest and most bizarre antinomian gurus got the most press, and for a time attracted many followers. This short section is not meant as a full study of gurus, in any sense. In spite of their indiscretions, many of the followers of these gurus may have received some positive influences from them. But the harm done is also significant, and needs to be aired properly in any shift to the hylozoic paradigm.

The harmful influence of these gurus arises from an explosive mixture of an antinomian moral stance, secretive "advanced" practices, organizations, elite "inner circles," and authoritarian control. Arguing that antinomian sages have existed throughout history, Fuerstein keenly describes the "crazy-wise," or antinomian, saints and sages of the Great Religions, including Christianity. But Fuerstein overlooks the key point that the antinomian sages of history (and many great sages were neither antinomian nor "crazy-wise") rejected all authority, especially their own. Lao Tsu for instance, whose teaching was clearly to transcend all cultural norms and can therefore possibly be called antinomian, was reluctant even to voice his philosophy, and did so briefly, only once, before disappearing into the mountains, for good.

None of the respected antinomian sages of history (in my opinion) set themselves up as despots warding over organized groups of devotees. The essence of the antinomian stance is that any manifested moral authority is necessarily corrupt because, being manifested at all, it is dualistic, whereas God is monistic. This is akin to the basic Kabbalistic idea that nothing (or no one) manifest can ever be perfect. It is the same as the Zen concept of "no-mind," i.e., that all thoughts, be they about morality or whatever, are limitations on acting directly from the Buddha-nature. Obviously, an antinomian belief structure, coupled with the placing of ultimate authority over others, in the personality of a guru, is fraught with peril.

I attended a lecture by a certain college teacher and self-professed follower of the antinomian way. His lecture contained some interesting intellectual ideas, and sophisticated historical allusions, but there was something subtle troubling me that I tried to discuss with him afterwards. Aside from the fact that he immediately started questioning my credentials (which seems odd for an anarchist to do), my sense of conflict increased as I tried to pin down his idea on a fundamental point. Finally he summarized his position with, "I can be a shit if I want to be!" That is, in fact, a self-empowering attitude, and probably a needed antidote for an overly puritanical and controlling culture, especially for those with alternative or unusual lifestyles. But the marrying of such an attitude with an authoritarian guru-centric social organization just makes no sense to me.

According to Fuerstein's book, and numerous other accounts from inner circle members and from outside observers, many of the antinomian guru-centric communities suffered from just the sorts of abuse—sexual, financial and emotional—that one might expect of any such isolated community.

My point is that the denial, by advocates of the hylostatic and hylostochastic paradigms, of spiritual realities, makes those people who feel a need to turn to spiritual traditions prone to the attitude that "anyone who exhibits unusual spiritual, psychic, or emotional abilities is extraordinary and should be given authority over my own inadequate self." And there are numerous individuals, of varying degrees of enlightenment, ignorance, saintliness and debauchery, willing to take on the role.

A member of the inner circle of one famous "guru," and the editor of his most widely translated books noted, after she became disaffected:

> "His ability to manipulate sexual energy to bring large groups of people to peaks of ecstasy I took as proof of his enlightenment. It's unquestionably a remarkable talent, but probably no more indicative of Buddhahood than any other power: psychic, learned, or intuitive."[295]

If we had an adequate hylozoic worldview, we would be more able to apply discrimination from the start, and to avoid the dangers of self-inflated cult leaders. Indeed in India, the source of many gurus, the society in general is quite aware of the shenanigans of some types of "guru," and people are generally more discriminating than are the newly-seeking Westerners.

In a similar vein is the popularity of fictional, or semi-fictional, accounts written by Western devotees of secretive native "shamans." Serious anthropologists (like Michael Harner) have pointed out that (regardless of the veracity of the reported exotic experiences), many of these stories are essentially of sorcery only, and not of true shamanism. True shamanism, Harner describes, is focused on healing work, and ecological balancing, and cultural leadership, as well as magic; whereas many of the popular, secretive-fictional, accounts are only of magic: sorcery.

Western seekers who sense that spiritual realities are important, and yet have no serious context for developing that sense, are easily drawn to the first sorcerer or mass-hypnotist, or novel about such, that they hear about. And since these experiential realms involve nonintellectual realities, even many highly intellectual people are easily swayed.

All of these movements have overemphasized the importance of Left-hand Tantrism and moral antinomianism. The positive aspect of such movements is that they are part of the general spiritual re-awakening of the West. The great damage is that the Western general public's view of Eastern religions has been warped.

That the shenanigan-gurus were popular in the West at the same time as the rise of Hugh Hefner's "Playboy Philosophy," suggests they may have been simply profiting from dressing-up existing cultural tendencies in politically correct sophisiticated religious garb.

Left-hand Tantrism is only one branch of Tantrism, which is only one of twelve major spiritual paths, as described, for instance, by Satyeswarananda. These paths include; Jnana yoga, the path of knowledge; Hatha yoga, popular in the West and often mistakenly just called "yoga"; Kriya yoga, introduced to the West by Paramahansa Yogananda; Bhakti yoga, the devotional path (much of Christianity might fall into this category); Mantra yoga, concentration on the names of God; and others.[296]

Left-hand Tantra is also the most difficult to distinguish from (because it is the closest to) self-serving sorcery; the line between amoral transcendent states and ordinary immoral dysfunction is dangerously thin and blurry.

Each path, like Tantra, in turn has many branches. Left-hand Tantra is antinomian, and employs physical sexual exercises and the indulging in meat and alcohol. There is also right hand or "pure" Tantra that takes the indulgences only symbolically. All the twelve types of yoga can be valid paths. (Yoga just means spiritual "path"—others divide the yoga categories differently, but all the major historical Teachers have agreed there are many paths.)

While all the paths are valid, each person only has one path valid for himself, which he must find. True Left-hand Tantra may only be valid in rare instances when a person is naturally disposed to an austere life and when he or she becomes attached to the austerity—the attachment being a hindrance; I suggest it may never be valid in an organized authoritarian guru-centric context.

An instance of valid Left-hand Tantric-like development may be the case of a late Japanese Zen Buddhist Roshi (awakened teacher) known as "Bobo Roshi." Bobo Roshi entered a traditional Zen monastery in his teens. For twenty years, he adhered strictly to the austerities of the monastery—abstinence, a sparse vegetarian diet, a severe daily meditation regime, little sleep, and koan practice. A few of the other monks made real progress and had actual awakenings, but Bobo Roshi made little progress despite the encouragement of his teacher, and despite his dedication.

Finally in despair, Bobo Roshi left the monastery. Completely naive, he wandered into a high-class geisha house. He was fed, bathed, elegantly served sake, and given a beautiful and skillful geisha. His twenty years of strict austerity and painful Zen meditation prepared him for the rare and deep awakening that he experienced instantaneously in his first sexual encounter.

The other spiritual paths, besides Left-hand Tantra, mostly have strong moral codes, some of them very strict. The moral codes of most of the great Eastern spiritual traditions are very similar to the "Judeo-Christian" moral codes.

While the attraction of many Westerners to the antinomian gurus may be explained by the lack of serious indigenous spiritual leadership, such an explanation is not an excuse. The fact that many of the indiscretions of these gurus involve sexual abuse cannot be dismissed by facile arguments that Westerners are "too puritanical."

The Eastern societies, from which many of the authoritarian traditions come, often have far more strict social mores than does the West. Rather, it is likely that one can be very advanced spiritually, so as to appear as a charismatic teacher, and still not have fully "solved" the issues of sexuality; and so should never be in the position of an authoritarian guru.

In fact, the spiritual traditions and the Ageless Wisdom teachings describe a series of levels of spiritual evolution. They say there is a certain intermediate level that is characterized by profound creative illumination. Many important artists, philosophers, scientists and spiritual teachers of history can be modeled as being at that level. But the traditions say that this level is also characterized by a profound danger of "stepping off the path" into precisely the sorts of abuses of (or inability to handle properly) psychic and spiritual powers described in Fuerstein's book. Such abuses can be extremely damaging to all involved.

The Ageless Wisdom says, also, that this level, while a great achievement, is far below the level of attainment of the Great Teachers of history (Krishna, Christ, Buddha, etc.), and also below the level that can safely function as a true "guru" (which should be distinguished from a teacher) in the traditional sense.[297]

The model that, in recent centuries, these "Great Ones" have, with very few exceptions, worked entirely behind the scenes without contacting the public at all[298] might explain why society creates its own "gurus" out of unqualified, if extraordinary, individuals whose proper function might be "teacher."

History will judge the proper perspective on the various teachers. In the meantime, common sense, careful discernment and conventional morality should never be dispensed with, certainly not because someone else tells you to do so.

The problem of developing right sexual relations is obviously one of the primary, and most difficult, cultural problems of our time. Regardless, sexual abuse is always inappropriate whether the perpetrator calls himself a "guru" or not. Many highly respected teachers indicate that physical sexual relations between guru and disciple are never appropriate, except in the case of husband and wife. Undoubtedly sexual exploration can be a growthful process for many people. But one could simply read the novels of Henry Miller rather than couching the issues of sexual liberation in inflated religious contexts.

The rise and fall of the antinomian gurus in the West has done a disservice to the gradual coming together of serious Eastern and Western spiritual traditions, which is a part of the shift to the hylozoic paradigm. The overeager brand of Left-hand Tantrics created a dangerous tendency to confuse amorality (moral antinomianism) with the core of all spirituality.

The worst extremes of that tendency have empowered truly evil individuals like mass murderers Charlie Manson and Jim Jones. According to the serious spiritual traditions, amorality (not immorality) is a very subtle aspect of high levels of spiritual attainment—a level that occurs *after* one has thoroughly integrated, practiced and become deeply moral. Then, through difficult spiritual practice, if all opposites are transcended, amorality—beyond good and evil—may also be experienced (the teachings say). Such glimpses of unitive consciousness are effects of rare meditative states. In everyday life, in interacting with people, which is necessarily in the realm of dualism, moral behavior is always necessary.

The antinomian "guru" problem is relevant to the scientific shift to the hylozoic paradigm as follows. The descent into what we are calling "Fundamentalism" has so hindered the ability to discriminate as to empower the confusion of immorality with spirituality, just as scientific Fundamentalism impedes the shift to the hylozoic paradigm.

Religious Fundamentalism is organized dogmas and practices devoid of living spirituality, and creates an environment in which people are unable to discriminate among types and paths of true spirituality. Scientific Fundamentalism also destroys the ability to discriminate, and destroys the ability to observe the world, and oneself, dispassionately. The placing of rigid dogmatic belief structures above direct experience of the world, and above personal verification and discrimination, sets people up for brain-washing.

We should note that the sorts of secretive shenanigans described above are not confined to the gurus and followers of Eastern religions. American culture, since its inception, has been plagued by hypocritical, evangelical Fundamentalist preachers who, guru-like, develop and then fleece, financially or emotionally, cult followers, in the name of Jesus. It is well known that the private lives of some of these preachers might do a "bimbos n'rollers"-type antinomian guru proud. These have always coexisted with more serious Christian spiritual teachers.

In early 19th century America, revivalist Presbyterian, Methodist, and Baptist preachers were using fire-and-brimstone tactics against each other. Out of that milieu, a young Joseph Smith Jr. founded a new religion complete with a semi-deified powerful inner circle, and secret inner circle practices, including the taking of many wives in order to "spiritualize" them. The circumstances of the end of Smith's life are almost similar to that of Rajneesh, both centered in the deserts of the American West.

According to *Harper's Encyclopedia of Mystical and Paranormal Experience*, "In 1844 Smith declared his candidacy for President of the United States, meanwhile selecting a secret Council of Fifty within the church as his erstwhile cabinet. News of the moves leaked to an opposition newspaper, and Smith reacted by destroying the press. Smith and his brother Hyrum were arrested for treason and held in jail in Carthage, where an angry mob assassinated them both on June 27, 1844. Even after his death, several Mormon women entered into 'celestial marriage' with Joseph Smith's spirit." In spite of apparent indiscretions, the Mormonism that Smith founded is now a respected, nearly mainstream, religion. Other similar guru-preacher cult events date back to even the pre-Revolutionary United States. Some of the recent "Eastern" spirituality movements, in the US anyway, seem to be applying Eastern names onto the working out of repeating indigenous patterns.

In the lack of a hylozoic perspective to integrate the spiritual traditions with the scientific worldview, these problems will only increase.

De-Glamourized Teachers, Intuition, and Four Signs of Ego Inflation

Given our existing primitive belief structures, and the lack of accepted guidelines for the new hylozoic ideas, openness to spirituality clearly leaves us vulnerable to charismatic false gurus and the like. That vulnerability is reason for more discrimination and careful analysis, not for an assertion that spiritual realities don't exist.

A guide might be that, if one is drawn to the guru-disciple type path (and there are other valid paths), then the guru, his (or her) tradition, his disciples, his teachers, his words and his practices should be carefully studied, and those of other gurus studied, for comparison, for a long time—twenty years might be reasonable—before giving him guru-like authority over yourself (if that is ever appropriate).

Also consider: do the guru's long-term followers live balanced, creative and service-oriented lives connected with the rest of society? Are the long-term followers individualized personalities in their own right, "self-propelled," not pale copies of the guru, and are they inspiring role models?

Now, a profound suspicion of leaders, spiritual and otherwise, "seems to be in the air" as President Clinton has noted. This suspicion may be obscuring recognition of a now emerging group of significant spiritual leaders—leaders who might be in touch with the transcendent in a way that can inform us how to live consciously, nonviolently, and effectively in the world.

Inevitably, when people voice their suspicion of leaders, they mention Hitler. Why not also consider Winston Churchill? Hitler was clearly as evil an individual as we have known in modern times, and he was also mystical in his outlook. But that does not mean that all mysticism, especially the discriminatingly careful mysticism which is esoteric spirituality, is also evil. The universe also gave us Winston Churchill, without whom Hitler probably would not have been defeated.

Churchill, in his way, was also mystical. The young Churchill, for instance, fearlessly disregarded self-protection in impossibly dangerous battles, because he had come to "know" that he would have an indispensable "role to play" in world affairs—which he did, decades later—and so Providence would not allow him to be killed.[299]

Interestingly, Churchill was also highly emotionally sensitive in an unusual sort of way. Spotted coming out of a theater playing a sappy film, sobbing as he often would, Churchill said, "Yes, I'm a blubberer." In the midst of his wartime leadership, surrounded by assistants and impossibly busy, he would notice an insect on his desk. He would instruct his "man servant" to take the offending bug outside and release it, on strict orders not to harm it. A couple of hours later, he might look up and ask if she got off all right—meaning the bug.[300]

Another major political leader whose mystical inclinations are well known is US President Abraham Lincoln. His most famous speeches are peppered with sincere references to the importance of the transcendent. Yet Lincoln was quite effective in his leadership of an inevitable war that, on balance, diminished the evil of slavery.

Lincoln was not a fool or a hypocrite. He meant it when he spoke of the relevance of the transcendent.

It is irrational to ascribe the evil of a Hitler to his mysticism and to ignore the mystical insight of a Churchill, or a Lincoln, and, on an even larger scale, a Krishna, or a Christ. It is rational to hypothesize that there is something very important, pointed-to in the transcendent rhetoric of these powerful forces for good—something that should inform our worldview.

It is interesting to note, also, that up to the level of major regional political and cultural leaders, there have been both extraordinarily good and extraordinarily evil individuals (e.g. Lincoln and Mandela versus Hitler and Stalin), while at the larger scale of lastingly major world-influencing individuals (such as Christ, Krishna, Abraham, Confucius, and Mohammed), those on the side of good have been historically real figures whereas those on the side of evil have been only mythical (e.g. "Satan").

This chapter argues that the myriad psychics, magicians, and gurus run the gamut from cynical frauds, and well-meaning but deluded individuals, to true saints and actual avatars. A successful shift to the hylozoic paradigm will require the extension of the discriminating and rigorous methods of old paradigm science to the major spiritual traditions as well. It will require the inclusion of the two ways of knowing (empirical science and mystical intuition) into a single encompassing worldview.

One method for applying that discrimination is to use the most sophisticated apparatus known—our human physical body-minds—as tools for intuitive discrimination. What the Great Spiritual traditions offer (both East and West, especially their esoteric cores which contain explicit and direct systems rather than mere metaphorical platitudes) are systems for developing intuition. Intuition, in this sense, is the contact of the physical (material) mind and body, with metaphysical (spiritual) realities, *and* the ability to glean relevant truths and information from that contact.[301]

An obstacle to applying discernment in this area is the trap of thinking that anything truly psychic, or occult, or magical, is necessarily good, or useful, or relevant. That trap is prepared by the inculcation in us by the supposedly "scientific" secular worldview of anti-spiritual attitudes. When personal experience, or truly clear rationality, opens us to accepting spiritual relevance, we are open to spiritual junk as well as spiritual enlightenment.

A unique capacity for developing—and evolving because of—individual spiritual intuition is what distinguishes the human kingdom (if anything does so distinguish it) from the animal kingdom. As such, spirituality is supremely democratic—it is part of what humans *are*. No one has a special claim to spirituality. But, as in any endeavor, there may be some from whom we can learn.

How can we distinguish valid spiritual teachers? One way is to apply the same criteria that one would apply to one's own intuitive development. That is, distinguish useful, relevant, and good intuitions from mistaken intuitions, fantasies, and lower-emotional desires. As we've noted, once we accept that real nonmaterial planes do exist and interrelate with the material world, then we also need to accept that there is a lot of garbage in the nonmaterial realities, just as there is a lot of garbage on the material plane. Wrong intuitions add to the garbage on the intuitional planes. Wrong intuitions become "mistaken wild ideas," or more technically, "illusion," "glamour," and "maya." For instance, if I have made serious mistakes in interpreting the intuitions on which this book is based, and if you accept the ideas undiscriminatingly, a whole new series of traps on the spiritual path will be put "out there" into the mind belt, accessible in the form of mistaken intuitions by others.

There are many ways wrong intuitions can develop, including: wrong perception; wrong interpretation; wrong appropriation; wrong direction; wrong integration; wrong embodiment; and wrong application.[302] These errors lead the person—seeker, scientist, guru, teacher—to ego inflation, that is, being enthralled with one's own illusions and glamours.

One spiritual tradition lists four signs for noticing when one is in the presence of illusion, glamour, and ego inflation. The signs are:

1. Criticism, when careful analysis would show that no criticism is really warranted;
2. Criticism where there is no personal responsibility involved—where it is not the place or duty of one to criticize;

3. Pride in achievement or satisfaction that one is spiritually evolved—the belief that one is on (or leader of) *the* only right path;
4. Any sense of superiority, separative tendency, or tendency to abuse authority.[303]

Clearly, if devotees had applied these criteria, some of the gurus mentioned before might have been spared the burden of many of their gullible flocks. By applying these criteria, we may finally be able to ferret-out some valid de-glamourized spiritual leaders. The same criteria can be applied to spiritual paths, and to oneself on a path. The next chapter considers whether science itself might be a spiritual path.

As the materialist paradigm crumbles and the hylozoic paradigm emerges, we will search for new spiritual teachings and teachers. We don't know yet who and what they are. We have a good idea of the qualities they will and will not express. They are not authoritarian. They are not unduly critical and prone to ridicule others. They are not full of self-pride and separativeness. The new spiritual teachers are universalistic and inclusive, and foster open questioning and penetrating rational inquiry. They may be people. They may be things that happen, in our environment, and in our presence, right now.

Most importantly, the new teachers and teachings show us that the world is stunningly alive.

15. Freedom from the Known—Science as Partner

"The body without the spirit is dead, so faith [spirituality] without work [science] is dead also."
— James 2:26

"Knowledge should beget wisdom like the cloud begets lightning."
— Sathya Sai Baba[304]

"The Kingdom of [Heaven] is spread upon the Earth and men do not see it."
— Jesus[305]

The previous three chapters discussed evidence that the world is hylozoic. People who experience those events gain spiritual and or religious insight. Old paradigm science has always claimed to be separate from spiritual and religious concerns. Of course, it really hasn't been separate; the tension between religious dogma and direct observation of the world spawned modern science in the first place.

The present movement to the hylozoic paradigm continues the process. In fact, I believe it will make a circle of it, reuniting science with spirituality and eventually with religion. This need for relating science and spirit is also a barrier, because we are emotionally unsettled by the prospect of submitting our spiritual and religious lives to the klieg lights of science.

But the integration of the scientific and spiritual traditions is necessary and one key linking mechanism is personal experience. Writing this last part of this book is very difficult because the integration has clearly only begun. There is no catechism or fixed dogma that I can puff my chest out about and say, "That's the final answer."

Transformations require a period of ambiguity, polarization and vulnerability; I think our whole culture is in such a period now. But if we postpone action until the new forms appear with certainty, we will miss the journey. The personal shift to spiritual awareness cannot occur in isolation; one of the truths of the spiritual realities is that everything, especially humanity, is connected in a very real sense. The ageless wisdom says that, while individual effort and individual advancement are essential, one of the effects of spiritual advancement is further integration of the individual into the human and planetary organism. The wisdom traditions indicate that any personal advancement in awareness must actually be put into practice in one's life and community before further personal advance.

In Part II, I described how the generally accepted scientific facts show that matter functions as an open system because of the indeterminacy of quantum mechanics and the sensitivity of chaotic dynamics; matter is fundamentally self-connected across space and time.

In Part III, we saw that the fundamental openness of matter leaves two possibilities:

1. The openness of the "no-things-in-themselves" quantum indeterminacy of matter (the property of "emergence") is filled only by randomness—the hylostochastic paradigm;
2. The emergent possibilities are chosen among partly by the influence of a spiritual component of the world—the hylozoic paradigm.

We discussed how highly complex systems—weather, climate, formation of solar systems, functioning of human minds and biogeochemical evolution of the planets—are very sensitive to nonmaterial spiritual influences, if such influences exist. Complex events are rigorously mysterious.

The scientific orthodoxy assumes the world is hylostochastic: spiritually dead. Part III showed there is no evidence that the world is hylostochastic; the generally accepted facts of science are equally consistent with a hylozoic world. Part IV argues the hylozoic paradigm agrees with an "ageless wisdom" that underlies all the great spiritual traditions and explains experience; it is simpler to explain our experience hylozoically than hylostochastically. Occam's razor is on the side of the hylozoic view.

In Part II, we investigated how "little details" that didn't fit into the existing paradigms sometimes led to vast new horizons for science. A "little detail" that, I believe, will lead to the vast new horizons of the hylozoic paradigm is the spiritual experience of human beings. The ageless wisdom says the special place of the human being is as a link between pure matter and pure spirit—a link with a special role in the cosmic process of spiritualizing matter.

Experimental Certainty?

Why can't we just design a direct experiment to prove once and for all that things are hylozoic, and then get on with investigating the new paradigm? Someone may still figure out how to do that, but I doubt it. It can't be a standard physics experiment; the hylostochastic interpretation of quantum experiments speaks only about the probability distribution of large numbers of repeated identical experiments, and says that any single event, no matter how strange, proves nothing. The hylozoic paradigm however allows for meaning in the unique single event that is the unfolding universe. (The universe is a unique event by the way, so one could argue that, rigorously considered, quantum mechanics can say nothing about it.)

Only highly complex phenomena lend themselves to hylozoic effects, and highly complex single events can always be doubted because they are not repeatable in exact detail. For example, many people (people are highly complex phenomena) believe that they *know* they were healed of cancer, or recovered from near death because of the influence of a spiritual force. For them, the world is clearly hylozoic. Onlookers who want to assert a secular-materialist paradigm can claim such healings are meaningless "random remission." Medical experiments and trials can be performed that would constitute strong clinical evidence that a spiritual process plays a role; such experiments have been performed and will be described in a little more detail later; yet these results are dismissed because they cannot be "explained" by a reductionistic hylostochastic mechanism.

Mystical Physiology

The ageless wisdom tells us that experience of spirituality arises from the fact that our bodies and brains function hylozoically. If we ourselves don't function in a hylozoic way, then we may as well describe the world as hylostochastic. There is a subtle but important point here. A stone for instance can act as our quintessential hunk of matter. Physics tells us that a lot is actually happening, all the time, even in an ordinary stone. The stone has a temperature and temperature fluctuations; it has a complex set of crystalline structures all vibrating and subtly shifting; sound waves, phonons and low intensity electromagnetic currents infuse the stone; the atoms and molecules vibrate, rotate and occasionally shift.

All of that may be subtly hylozoic, but the stone does not consciously co-create the universe. Human beings can. Human beings have a choice. We can essentially remain stones—matter unconsciously buffeted by spirit. In that case, even though the world around us may be hylozoic, we could not distinguish it from being hylostochastic. If we become aware of the spiritual nature of our own selves, then we can identify with it in our environment too, while remaining highly rational and reality-based.

This is what Plato's cave analogy was about. Plato said we are like cave dwellers observing our shadows on the cave wall. The shadows move and interact, and much of what they do and how they function is mysterious. When the cave dweller sees that the shadows are actually the creation of a bright sun shining past active shadow-makers, he realizes that he creates his own shadow. If the cave dweller doesn't realize this, then the shadows will remain the ultimate reality for him; the way the shadows move will remain mysteriously random and seemingly not connected to himself. Someone telling him that the shadows are actually the result of a deeper reality will make little difference to him, unless he sees for himself.

The shift to the "technologies" of prana, or lifetrons, or Planckian butterflies will be just as large as was the shift to the contemporary material technologies and it will be different in quality. The clues for making this shift are what we get from the ageless wisdom of the spiritual and religious traditions. These traditions have all said that, coexisting with the physical human body, is a "mystical physiology" that allows the individual to act spiritually.

Just as there are material organs of the body such as liver, spleen, heart and brain, the spiritual traditions say there are spiritual organs that interact very subtly but very effectively with the material body. The organs of the mystical physiology can be thought of as the intermediaries between the immortal spiritual soul and the ephemeral material body. (Remember that intellect and thought, for instance, are functions of the material brain and are not necessarily spiritual at all, as discussed in Chapter 11.)

Joseph Campbell and other mythologists show that many of the descriptions of the human "mystical physiology" are the same in the major spiritual traditions, including Native American, and (Gnostic) Christian, as well as "Eastern."

The human mystical physiology begins to develop a coherence of spirit and matter in the body-mind. When this happens, the human being begins to co-create the hylozoic world. If we, by design or by will, remain completely separated from our spiritual selves, then the world will appear to be the same as hylostochastic. The larger spiritual-material entity of the planet as a whole, with its own cosmic mystical physiology, may make its own hylozoic evolutions. But such changes would probably not be auspicious for us if we do not bring ourselves up to speed. A hylozoic universe is a participatory universe.

The Self-realizing evolution of the consciousness of the human body-mind-spirit is the key to the shift to the hylozoic paradigm. This is what the ageless wisdom tells us. From the standpoint of fully living, isn't it also what makes sense?

Suppose the world were indeed full of spirits, gods, demons and angels, while humans are stuck only in our lower physico-mechanical, aspiritual, egoic selves; human life would be completely a Hobbesian existentialist sociobiological struggle for accumulation of matter and sensation, absolutely nothing else. Without connection to our own mystical-physiological higher selves, trying to understand the spiritual universe would be as fruitful as a troop of lemurs looking at differential equations.

An early Western-academic researcher of the Eastern approach to mystical-physiological awakening was Mircea Eliade.[306] According to the ageless wisdom, the mystical physiology is active in a wide range of human experience, from romantic love, to "kundalini energy" movements as discussed in Part I, to transcendental love, to very extreme "yogic powers" or "sidhis." Some of the latter are discussed by Eliade, based on the Yoga-Sutras of Patanjali.

The following examples are extremes hinting at the vastness of the human spiritual potential. Discussing the extremes that the spiritual teachings say occur on the path to Self-realization or Soul-connection requires discrimination because inflated claims are all too often the tools of hucksters, charlatans and deluded individuals. I discuss the extremes, here, for two reasons:

1. Apart from the hucksters and charlatans, those spiritual teachers and masters past and present whom I trust do acknowledge that such extremes are part of the human potential;
2. A standard tool of physics for assessing the importance of a new hypothesis or idea is to consider the logical extremes of the idea.

That so many of the great spiritual figures of history have described such extremes suggests that the shift to the hylozoic paradigm will be more than just a new little wiggle on our world view. Eliade writes:

"In his list of siddhis, Patanjali mentions all the legendary 'powers' that obsess Indian mythology, folklore, and metaphysics with equal intensity. Unlike the folklore texts, Patanjali gives some very brief elucidations of them. Thus, wishing to explain why samyama [a yogic technique] concerning the form of the body can make him who practices it invisible, Patanjali says that samyama makes the body imperceptible to other men, and 'a direct contact with the light of the eyes no longer existing, the body disappears.' This is the explanation he gives for the disappearances and appearances of yogis, a miracle mentioned by countless Indian religious, alchemical, and folklore texts.

[another yogi-scholar] comments: 'The body is formed from five essences [tattva]. It becomes an object perceptible to the eye by virtue of the fact that it possesses a form [rupa, which also means color]. It is through this rupa that the body and its form become objects of perception. When the yogin practices samyama on the form of the body, he destroys the perceptibility of the color [rupa] that is the cause of perception of the body. Thus, when the possibility of perception is suspended, the yogin becomes invisible. The light engendered in the eye of another person no longer comes into contact with the body that has disappeared. In other words, the yogin's body is not an object of knowledge for any other man. The yogin disappears when he wishes not to be seen by anyone.'

This passage ... attempts to explain a yogic phenomenon through the theory of perception, without recourse to miracle. Indeed, the general tendency of the more important yogic texts is to explain any parapsychological and occult phenomenon in terms of the 'powers' acquired by the practitioner and to exclude any supernatural intervention.

Patanjali also mentions the other "powers" that can be obtained through samyama, such as the power of knowing the moment one is to die, or extraordinary physical powers, or knowledge of 'subtle' things, etc. ... By virtue of renunciation, of asceticism (tapas), men, demons, or gods can become powerful to the point of threatening the economy of the entire universe. ... The yogin must reject these 'magical hallucinations,' these 'false sensory objects that are of the nature of dreams,' 'desirable only for the ignorant,' and persevere in his task of gaining final emancipation. ... Only a new renunciation and a victorious struggle against the temptation of magic bring the ascetic a new spiritual enrichment. ...

And yet ... nostalgia for the 'divine condition' conquered by force, magically, has never ceased to obsess ascetics and yogins."[307]

The point is that the great spiritual realizers of history have experienced that extreme yogic powers are a reality; but they have also experienced that any attachment to, or use of them for personal gain, is regressive. So, while we should not dwell on these things either, the fact that the religious and spiritual traditions accept yogic or saintly powers as verified is evidence in favor of the hylozoic model of matter. Another significant yogi, now living, relates a recent experience of similar events and interprets them similarly.

Satyeswarananda (mentioned previously) seems highly credible because of his background in Western-style education as a law professor, and as the leader of two highly respected spiritual traditions (though rejecting official office in them because of the well known perils of creating religious organizations), and because his books are aimed at restoring complete integrity to the spiritual path, and are technically illuminating but clearly not meant to garner income or devotees by appealing to a mass audience. Once, walking in the Himalayas with the rarely seen but widely regarded yogi Mahamouni Babaji and a handful of other disciples, Satyeswarananda relates:

"One day, a strange thing happened as we were walking on the track. Two pilgrims were returning from Badrinath. They greeted us in the traditional way. Pilgrims: 'Om Namo Narayana Babaji!' ["Babaji" is a common high honorific appellation.] [I] thought they saw [Mahamouni] Babaji and recognized him and greeted him. [I] was startled to learn that the greeting was meant for [me] only. [I] silently acknowledged their greeting with folded hands. Then one of the pilgrims asked [me], addressing [me] as Babaji, why [I] was walking alone in the dangerous forest. It then became clear to [me] that [Mahamouni] Babaji could not be seen by [the pilgrims], as it was not always possible to see his body or other members of the group. A curtain of invisibility had been drawn around them so that people might not "see" or "hear" them. [I] did not concern [myself] about these yogic techniques."[308]

According to these yogis, development of the mystical physiology enters one into realms in which the conscious perception of the world, by others, is affected. That is, if we accept Satyeswarananda's account, then his companions either altered the passers-by so that they thought they couldn't see them or they altered their own bodies so that they actually were not seen. If this in fact occurs, as so many great teachers have indicated, it may not be "miraculous" because the ageless wisdom yogic texts do "explain" it, but it sure means that the world is hylozoic.

Eliade maintains his academic respectability by noting that the "more important" yogic texts refrain from reference to "miracles" and explain such yogic feats through "the theory of perception" and other details of the mystical physiology. In any case, yogic powers are evidence for a hylozoic world but they are only experienced when one begins functioning hylozoically oneself—Satyeswarananda saw his teacher but the pilgrims didn't.

As Satyeswarananda indicates by "not concerning" himself, such yogic techniques should never be a goal or a desire of spiritual growth. They are, probably rarely, an effect of spiritual growth when certain sorts of development of the mystical physiology occur. Dwelling on them is either foolish or wrong. A favorite story of esoteric Buddhists illustrates the foolishness:

> The Buddha once was walking in the forest and deigned to give a local ferryman some teachings while the man ferried the Buddha across the river. The novice ferryman was so impressed by the Buddha that he dedicated his life to developing a yogic technique.
>
> Thirty years later the Buddha happened by again. The proud ferryman said to the Buddha, "Look I've spent thirty years practicing and now I can walk across the river!" And he illustrated his feat.
>
> The Buddha said, "I'm sorry you've wasted so much time when it is so easy to cross on the boat!"

The spiritual traditions also tell us that there are real dangers involved with premature, or improperly prepared contacts with our mystical physiologies. A great mystic has noted that saints and the insane find themselves awash in the same ocean; the difference is that the saints learn how, or know how, to swim and the insane do not. The ocean is the realization and experience of the presence of the spiritual dimensions. The esoteric spiritual traditions tell us that separating the material and spiritual aspects or "planes" of reality are semi-permeable "veils."

The veils exist individually for each human, collectively for groups, for the whole planet, and possibly for the solar system and beyond. In the case of an individual, the tearing or premature removal of a veil before the individual is prepared and able to function in an expanded environment can be disastrous. This is why some types of meditation and "energetic exercises" can actually be very dangerous if done without expert guidance. The spiritual oceans are not the boring little ponds one might imagine from Sunday lectures. They are vast, horrific, sublime, ecstatic and probably incomprehensible. Sogyal Rinpoche's story about a Tibetan frog illustrates the point:

> An old frog lived all his life isolated in a puddle in the bottom of a small dark well. One day, a young frog fell in, by accident. The old frog asked the other, "Where'd you come from"? The second frog replied, "From the ocean," and he told of the vastness and the brilliance and the activity of the ocean. The old frog understood the words and sensed they might be true, but he was skeptical. The young frog decided to show him. They crawled out of the well and made their way toward the ocean. When the old frog came over a dune, and saw the roaring ocean, his head exploded.[309]

It is my observation that many Westerners are shifting to a re-spiritualized view of the way the world works—a view that is not contradictory to science but is inclusive of it. For many people even, the shift seems far too slow. But there may be a good reason why it happens slowly; if the veil were rent open too quickly, our collective heads might explode.

Above, we went right to extreme cases of yogic powers. More mundane examples happen all the time, to all of us, usually without notice. We may be drawn to turn toward the telephone before it rings. We may think of an acquaintance, and then it is she on the phone. We may look at the back of a distant stranger, and he turns to return our stare. These, according to the ageless wisdom, are fleeting occurrences of rapport with the spiritual reality that connects us all.

An Historical "Pack of Tricks," Benignly

Bearing in mind Voltaire ("history is a pack of tricks that we play on those who are dead"), we can identify a lot of historical momentum for the shift to the hylozoic paradigm. The following examples trace the development of the Western Christian church, but I believe that similar traces could be made for other religions, East and West.

One classic example of experiential transformation is, of course, St. Paul on the road to Damascus. This zealous persecutor of the Christian heresy (as he viewed it) was mystically seized, blinded, painfully physically reorganized from within (the regeneration of his mystical and material physiology), and given inner visions all during the broad daylight observation of two baffled Roman guards. He emerged an absolutely convinced believer and teacher in Jesus as an embodiment of the Christ principle. I agree with Campbell's interpretation of just what it was that Paul realized. Campbell says, "It is my opinion that the realization of St. Paul on the Road to Damascus was that the death of [Jesus] on the Cross could be identified with the [initiations] of the ancient [pagan and Greek] mystery schools."

Paul's later explanatory teaching, and integration of Christianity with existing Roman social ideas, was the key to the success of the early Christian Church. The Greek mystery schools continued to thrive for the first three centuries A.D., in parallel with the Christian expansion. Then, in the fourth century, the concept of direct nonrational experience of a transcendent God was officially proclaimed heresy by the "Christian" Church-State authorities.

In the place of discriminating personal gnostic experience was forced the unquestioning belief in the historicity of the personality of Jesus as the exclusive, *only* incarnation of God. Officially outlawed was the interpretation of Jesus Christ as an example of the potential within each individual and the emphasis on individual experience and individual reason that went with it.

The following and perhaps partially resulting European Dark Ages continued for eight centuries until the bubbling up (in 1150 – 1250) of the "Grail Quest" myths—the rebirth of the concept of individual romantic love as a metaphor for, and initial path to, God-realization (Self-realization). The individual experiential component reemerged in the Grail Quest as the individual being seized by the transcendent quality of romantic love. The enforced authority of the Church Inquisition soon efficiently squelched that rebirth of the Self-realization quest. The Inquisition told people what to think, what God thinks, and enforced it militarily for centuries.[310]

Then, in the European Renaissance, the Corpus Hermeticum of the forgotten pagan Greek mystery schools was translated from the Greek into the standard Latin, making it accessible to the ordinary reader of the time. The Renaissance mind realized again that the teachings of the ancient mystery schools (the ageless wisdom) were entirely consistent with a mystical reading of the life and teaching of Jesus Christ. This initiated, according to Campbell and others, an explosion of Renaissance art illuminated by that fact.

As described in Chapter 2, many of the founders of modern science were similarly motivated by the Renaissance reacceptance of personal experience—finding out for oneself—which became formalized as scientific experimentation and observation. They realized that Church-State authorities may assert whatever they like, but if the authorities are at odds with verifiable empirical fact and personal observation, illumined by mathematical reason, then they are wrong. This is essentially the mystical stance in its highest form—*not* anti-rational but fully rational in being conscious of the limits of rationality.

The two conflicting strains in our pack of historical tricks, thus, are:

1. The experience-based ageless wisdom esoteric perennial philosophy, exemplified by questioning, application of reason, mystical insight, attention to the mystical physiology of the body and continual evolution, with the primary intention to penetrate to the truth of the world whatever that truth may be;

2. The Fundamentalist, Fanatical, fixed-religious stance, characterized by enforcement of authority-imposed belief structure, rejection of contrary evidence and devaluation of individual reason, questioning and experience with the intention to maintain authority and control.

The European Dark Age can be thought of as materialism devoid even of basis in rational thought. In this model, the Renaissance was the reintroduction of rationalism. The scientific-industrial revolution was the concretization, in matter, of that rationalism pioneered in the Renaissance.

Marxist authoritarian Communism and primitive market forces worshipping accumulative capitalism are the dual politicizations of rational materialism. They are now seen to be incomplete—neither inherently evil nor the utopian panacea, just incomplete. The coming period will be the inclusion of the spiritual with the rational and the material—all three on equal footing. I believe the great role of modern science will be to facilitate an unprecedentedly complete involvement of the spiritual realities with the material plane. This requires a hylozoic understanding of science.

Today, the purveyors of the contemporary Western materialistic paradigm have managed to bring us back to the unquestioning acceptance of dogmatic authority over experience, reason and personal discrimination. Francis Crick, winner of the Nobel prize for 1950's work co-discovering the DNA molecule, proposes, in a recent book, his "astonishing hypothesis" that all human existence, inner and outer, including all thought, emotion, mystical and religious experience, is entirely self-contained material process devoid of any contact with transcendent or spiritual realities.[311]

As this book has already described, Crick's hypothesis is neither astonishing nor new to scientists. From a hundred years ago, we read, "... in a lecture recently delivered before the Anthropological Society of Washington ... [it was shown] that protoplasm is not merely the physical basis of life, but is the physical basis of mind also ... mind is no more a mystery than matter."[312]

In fact, Crick's "astonishing [materialistic] hypothesis" is the standard reference—the hylostochastic paradigm. The most irksome aspect of Crick's book is that he claims to be bringing the study of consciousness within the authority of experimental materialist paradigm science. But in fact he does not propose a single test or observation that could disprove his hypothesis—such a test being a fundamental criterion for a valid scientific hypothesis. The tests he does suggest apply only to distinguishing among various sub-models of the same materialist hypothesis. None of Crick's tests address the basic "astonishing" hypothesis.

Of course, among eminent scientists, there are major exceptions to the supporters of Crick's hypothesis. Roger Penrose, Nobel winning physicist, asserts that mind must exploit nondeterministic effects that rest on quantum mechanics. (I don't know if Penrose would agree but I view his as a hylozoic perspective.) Penrose even ventures a possible location for the connection: "microtubules," tiny tunnel-shaped proteins serving as structural supports in living cells.[313] Plausible theories like Penrose's, and even experimental evidence like that described in the next section, though, are ignored by much of the scientific community.

Experimental Tests Exist But Are Not Accepted

I criticized Crick for not presenting real tests for his hypothesis. But can we test our own hylozoic hypothesis? In fact there have been many experiments designed explicitly to test it. These range from the mind-machine coupling experiments of Princeton engineering professor Robert Jahn (mentioned in Part I), to the medical remote healing experiments reviewed by physician Larry Dossey discussed below and in Chapter 12. Jahn's results are positive for a hylozoic effect. They are ignored, however, probably because the results are positive. Some scientists even call experiments like Jahn's "bad science" because positive results would mean the old paradigm is in error.

Dean Radin, as director of the Consciousness Research Laboratory at the University of Nevada, reviews Jahn's results as well as many others on psychokinesis and telepathy in his recent *The Conscious Universe*. Radin's careful meta-analyses of many studies indicate further that there may, in fact, be a small repeatably measurable hylozoic effect.

The medical and biological experiments reviewed by Dossey are even more convincing. Dossey considers the experimental evidence in favor of nonlocal hylozoic effects such as from prayer and intention as, "so impressive that I have come to regard them as among the best-kept secrets in medical science." Dossey says these are ignored by the bulk of the medical community. Dossey reports, for instance, that the US National Research Council (the NRC, a major government science body) commissioned Harvard University psychologist Robert Rosenthal, one of the world's experts in evaluating controversial research claims, to evaluate several research areas, including parapsychology.

Rosenthal and his co-author found that the research quality of the parapsychology research was "the best of all the areas under scrutiny." The NRC committee chairman asked Rosenthal to withdraw the parapsychology section of his report. Rosenthal refused. The final NRC report referenced the Rosenthal study only in regard to the nonparapsychological topics.[314]

Even so, those experiments cannot be viewed as absolute proof either. The experiments reviewed by Dossey often give inconsistent results. For instance an experiment involving praying for heart disease patients, with double blind controls and all, may give statistically significant results that would seem to prove a hylozoic effect. Later, an apparently identical experiment might yield negative results.

These apparent inconsistencies might be explainable. Such experiments are actually identical only as viewed in the materialist paradigms in which there can be no spiritual effect. Viewed hylozoically, there may be extreme differences. The mystical physiological state of the individuals, groups and locations involved may be different in the materially identical experiments. Most of us are not even aware of, much less able to control, our mystical physiology. Hylozoic experiments must take into account the spiritual, just as rigorously as old paradigm experiments take into account the material.

The past three centuries have given many examples of experimental and observational breakthroughs that were ridiculed and not accepted by the scientific authorities of the time. In Part I, we mentioned the ridicule, in the 18th and 19th centuries, of people who reported that "rocks fall from the sky." They are now known as meteorites. The view that large craters on Earth and other planets are created by large meteoroids, asteroids and comets, was not accepted until this century. As if to punctuate the point, as I write this, the pieces of an enormous comet are sloughing into the planet Jupiter.

In 1912, A. L. Wegener observed geophysical evidence and proposed that the continents move. The ridicule from his eminent colleagues caused him to give up pushing the idea. After his death, Wegener's idea of continental drift became the standard concept.

In 1847, the young Viennese doctor Ignaz Philipp Semmelweis proposed that his colleagues wash their hands with disinfectant after dissection, before they delivered babies. His program cut the death rate of mothers in his hospital ward from 16 percent to less than 2 percent. Semmelweis—the equivalent of an intern—was hounded out of Vienna by his superiors. After repeating his success in a provincial city, he died from a dissection wound and the puerperal fever he had shown how to avoid.

When Carl Anderson of Cal Tech discovered the positron in 1932, both Bohr and Rutherford dismissed the new finding "out of hand."[315]

What the above examples lacked was an understandable physical mechanism to explain how the observations came about, so the observations were rejected. (The positron is an exception to this.) Wegener was correct *that* the continents drift; his idea for the physical mechanism of *how* they drift turned out to be wrong.

Bronowski notes: "Charles Darwin did not invent the theory of evolution: that was known to his grandfather. What he thought of was a machinery for evolution: the mechanism of natural selection ... Once Darwin had proposed this [mechanism], the theory of evolution was accepted by every one; and it was thought the most natural thing in the world to call it Darwin's theory."[316]

We are in an analogous situation now with hylozoic observations and experiments. The ageless wisdom esoteric teachings contain clues, even explicit details, on how the hylozoic spiritual mechanisms work. They also tell us, though, that we will not fully understand those mechanisms until we begin to connect with our own mystical physiology, and that's not easy.

There are hints that the scientific community is starting to get a whiff of major shifts. For instance Edward Lorenz, whose pioneering work applying chaos theory to predicting climate we discussed in Part II, recently received a medal honoring his contributions. The presenter noted, "... [about Lorenz's work, the] more powerful effect this revolution [of knowing the prevalence of chaos in natural systems] is bound to have [is] on the way people think about themselves." Lorenz himself suggested that an unusually broad reassessment of much of science is needed:

> "It is apparent that chaos poses a scientific challenge in any field where it arises, but in a less obvious manner it can also pose a moral challenge. All of us have run across studies that have been sloppily performed, and we may even have witnessed instances of willful falsification of data. ... Where chaos is dominant and duplication is not to be expected in any case, unjustified claims can ... easily gain the status of established facts. If we perform an experiment several times and obtain several different results, and if, without so stating, we choose to publish only the one case that fortifies a previously conceived hypothesis, we can do so without falsifying any data but our action will not be entirely honest.
>
> Closer to the borderline would be an instance where, perhaps because of lack of more time, we perform an experiment only once and obtain and publish favorable results even though we suspect that a second case would not agree with the first. If instead we are quite unaware that chaos could cause future experiments to differ from the present one, dishonesty is not involved, but are we performing good science?"[317]

Lorenz was saying that the extent to which scientists present their work as supporting "previously conceived hypotheses," when other interpretations are equally valid, is underestimated.

Some movement toward acceptance of a hylozoic view in medicine and psychiatry may be occurring, too. In 1992, the U.S. Congress authorized the U.S. National Institute of Health (NIH) to spend $2 million to organize an Office of Alternative Medicine (OAM) to provide research grants to investigate nonconventional medical practices. Originally the NIH announced 30 OAM grants, each of about $30,000.

Many people assumed that the OAM's purpose was to investigate spiritually-oriented medical practices. According to an independent watchdog group, though, only one of the original 30 projects was designed to actually test for hylozoic effect.[318]

The whole OAM budget is less than one 10,000th of the NIH's $10.9 billion budget, the rest of which is vested in "conventional" paradigm studies. For another comparison, the U.S. Congress spent $3 billion, including termination costs, on the superconducting supercollider, essentially a single elementary particle experiment, before deciding not to finish the project—100,000 times the OAM grants.

Luckily, because of the experiential nature of the hylozoic shift, numbers of dollars may not be very important. Recent advances in psychiatric understanding illustrate this. A new entry appeared in the second edition of the American Psychiatric Association's Diagnostic and Statistical Manual of Mental Disorders (DSM II). The entry read "Religious or Spiritual Problem." It is categorized in a section that includes problems of living rather than psychiatric illness. By recognizing problems involving religion or spirituality, the psychiatric community may be inching slightly away from a view of religion as a comforting illusion and a means of escapism or immaturity.

San Francisco psychiatrist Dr. Francis Lu and two other mental health professionals proposed the addition because they recognized that some unusual states of consciousness and experiences were being misdiagnosed as symptoms of mental disorder. Dr. Lu considers this proposal as the living out of his own "epiphany" experienced during a five-day seminar in 1978 with Joseph Campbell.

Another sponsor, psychiatrist Dr. Robert Turner, cited "near-death" and "after-death" experiences by cardiac patients and other peak, transcendent experiences as real events that people had trouble integrating into their everyday lives. These were previously viewed as signs of mental disorder or regression. The new entry in the manual is intended to imply that these experiences could be validated and understood within a framework including a religious or spiritual perspective, actually leading to a higher level of functioning.

The 200 members of the Assembly of the American Psychiatric Association approved the revision. In the past such changes in the manual have had a major impact on social attitudes, even though the manual serves mainly to provide a common terminology.[319]

The key to these advances was direct personal experience, in Lu's case, and the credible personal experience of others in Turner's case.

Waking Up

> We were a group of physicists, astronomers, and postgraduate students, required to attend weekly public seminars. Sitting in a large, sloping lecture hall, we filled only about a quarter of the 500 seats, most of us with empty chairs in between us. The speaker was a primadonna research professor from a famous technical university. He was introduced with anecdotes about his athletic and romantic prowess as well as about his intellectual feats. He was delivering a lively and arrogant lecture about the physics of the Sun.
>
> A classmate of mine was sitting one empty seat away from me. He was sitting upright, head slightly lolled, asleep. Like students in most professional training, we were overworked so that we would feel like we deserved the rewards of the profession when we were finished. My classmate would catch up on his sleep during lectures, but he hadn't quite mastered the technique of sleeping quietly upright.
>
> The snoring began very softly and gradually increased in volume. Due to the wonderful acoustics in the hall, most people became aware of the snoring when it was only slightly audible and not a distraction. Because the volume increased slowly, eventually everyone was aware of it without there having been any discernible starting point. To nudge him, anyone would have had to reach across empty seats, drawing attention, so no one did. Besides, I hadn't really thought of waking him. My attention was focused outward on the whole event. In that perspective, he seemed to be making an elegantly spontaneous somatic commentary on the whole lot of us. I was all for him.
>
> By brief snorts, the volume became quite loud until a handful of those professors who were not themselves snoozing had focused all their attention on my friend and not on the famous lecturer. Then, a fateful loll of the head coincided with a very

loud snort, conspiring to awaken him in the midst of it, in such a way that his waking self heard the end of his own sleeping snort, so that he realized what had been going on. The lecturer paused. A few people glared at my classmate, and then the lecture continued. My friend immediately glared at me. He was quite angry with me for not waking him. I realized that from the perspective of friendship, I should have nudged him in the ribs to wake him and reduce his embarrassment, rather than let the telling somatic commentary run its course.

This book is meant as a nudge in the collective ribs. It is quite apparent to many people that the snores of our "scientific" culture are growing in volume. In this cultural metaphor though, many of us are both arrogant lecturers and snoring sleepers. Do we want to continue happily as before—broadcasting our snores louder and louder until finally one loud snort thoroughly embarrasses our whole culture? Or should we wake up now and start playing a vital part in an emerging living culture?

It is becoming more apparent that the world is in a moral and spiritual crisis. This is reflected in the malaise in the "scientific communities." That one could be very successful at old paradigm science without any experience with inner work was shown by a tragic recent example. Noted astrophysicist, accomplished physics teacher and president of American University, Richard Berendzen, had a monumentally disturbed inner life of which, he claims, he was normally not even aware. In his (brave) book, he describes how he was arrested and convicted of making obscene phone calls from his presidential office. The obscene calls were the product of his disturbed inner life, which he had separated from his outer life of physics and administration. He described how he had structured his life since childhood so that he wouldn't confront his painful inner life: "my field was astrophysics, and, you know, we don't deal with those touchy-feeling things."[320]

Only the revivifying effects of reintegrating science with a serious spiritual perspective can remedy the crises in the scientific communities. This requires acceptance of, and some education in, the inner traditions: meditation, prayer, yoga or spiritual practice.

If Berendzen is representative of a larger trend, what inner spiritual cauldrons of our culture have been brewing beneath the too-long-imposed materialist paradigms? To be sure, the purely material physics will always be useful, as engineering is useful. But the hylozoic forefront sciences of the future will require experience of the inner as well as of the outer. Hands-on experience with physics experiments is indispensable for a complete understanding of physics; direct inner experience of the spiritual and material dual identities of humanity will be needed for full understanding of the spiritual and material interrelationship.

Hylozoic Astronomy

The spiritual traditions tell us that we may be getting a little help, now, from cosmic spiritual sources. One undisputed fact links the myths of astrology with the science of astronomy—the precession of the equinoxes. The Earth spins on an axis that is tilted with respect to the plane of its orbit about the Sun. The tidal force of the Sun on the spinning Earth causes the Earth's axis to wobble, or "precess," very slowly, 360 degrees around the normal (perpendicular direction) to its orbital plane. This precession completes one full circle regularly every 25,800 years. Thus the apparent position of the Sun in its background of distant stars on the day of the vernal equinox moves each year, completing a full circuit of the heavens in 25,800 years. Likewise the north pole, and "polar star" closest to the spin axis direction of the Earth, are constantly changing on a 25,800 year cycle.

The ancients divided the circular zodiac into twelve portions, and so the apparent position of the Sun (the actual direction of the Earth's spin axis) moves through one zodiacal region or "sign" about every 2,150 years. About 2,000 years ago (plus or minus 100 years or so), the Sun appeared to move into the region called "Pisces"— the fish. The early Christians saw Jesus Christ as the teacher for their new age of Pisces. Thus the symbol of the fish dominated the early Christian symbology and is still a common symbol of Christianity. Now 2,000 years later, the Sun is moving into the region called Aquarius.

The "dawning of the Age of Aquarius" is not only a song or fantasy. It is an astronomical fact (as long as one recognizes the ancient divisions of the zodiac). The interesting question is whether this fact can have any meaning beyond the verification of the physics of torque on rotating bodies. (The torque makes the equinoxes precess, much as a spinning top precesses.) The hylozoic paradigm says, "Yes it can have meaning and it is our job to figure out whether it actually does, and if so what the meaning is." The hylostochastic paradigm says, "No, it cannot have meaning."

The hylozoic paradigm does not say that it means this dogma or that dogma, this fantasy or that fantasy. It does say it may mean something real, verifiable and knowable, and a discriminating contemporary reading of the ancient spiritual traditions may help in the knowing. The hylostochastic paradigm assumes the dogma of meaninglessness, and it does so on the basis of no evidence or verifiable theory. The hylozoic paradigm is consistent with an unbiased, dispassionate and empirical understanding of modern physics.

The hylozoic model is, of course, that there are two basic components in the universe: matter and spirit. Matter is everything explained, and explainable, by the presently accepted laws and equations of physics. The spiritual realities affect, direct, and are affected by the material possibilities. As the material planetary, solar and galactic systems exist in an oriented space, so might their spiritual components exist. As the physical galaxy has different qualities in different regions, so might the spiritual galaxy. Perhaps the ancients intuited, observed or somehow learned some of these different qualities and named the regions of the zodiac after them.

The conventional view would have it that the ancients simply fantasized about shapes that they imagined seeing in the constellations and that all the different qualities of the different signs are also fantasy. But it is at least possible that, as the Earth's spin axis physically moves through different angles, different spiritual qualities impact the planet. (Another possibility is that there are periodic temporal spiritual cycles that conveniently coincide with the regular precession of the equinoxes.)

The ancient sages and religious giants said that astronomical ages of Aquarius are different in spiritual quality than ages of Pisces, consistent with a contemporary (hylozoic) understanding of astrophysics. The traditions say that Piscean Ages are colored by spiritual influences emphasizing authority and the importance of belief and ideology. They say that Aquarian Ages are colored by direct knowledge, emphasis on individual understanding and collective harmony.

Also, Swami Sri Yukteswar, in his 1894 book *The Holy Science* unified the Vedic calendar of four cyclical "yugas" with the precession of the equinoxes and with the western zodiac cycles. In that system, the spiritual influences for the Earth cycle twice through four basic yugas during one equinoctal cycle. According to Yukteswar's count, around 500 A.D. was the darkest part of the Kali Yuga, Kali Yugas being the darkest spiritual periods characterized by gross materiality and insensitivity. And according to Yukteswar, approximately 1600 marked the passage into a Dwepara Yuga, Dwepara Yugas being characterized by increasing sensitivity to more subtle aspects of reality.

Arguing that the possibility of spiritual influences should inform our world-view as we continue to do astronomy and physics is not "dangerous" to science. To the contrary: the space exploration programs of the world are floundering without purpose, having lost their basis in (Cold) war. What better way to recapture the cultural imagination than to inform the space exploration program with deeper spiritual meaning? The public is galvanized by an exploratory search for the *truth* about the way the universe really is, in the deepest metaphysical as well as physical senses. People are repulsed by arrogant assertions that we are servo-mechanical consumers incapable of spiritual insight and development.

I believe the hylozoic sciences of the Aquarian age will be motivated by a partnership of mathematical physical science and a profoundly spiritual orientation, informed by the empirical facts of the world, the ageless wisdom teachings, and direct personal inner experience. There will be need for those who emphasize the "outer" physical and mathematical skills, and for those talented with inner spiritual discrimination, and for those who work with both.

"New Science" Is Reconnection with the Ageless Wisdom

The stubborn rejection of reintegration of the two components of reality has effects beyond our personal selves. Global change is affected, from ozone depletion and greenhouse warming, deforestation and species depletion, to political and economic interdependence.

Many aspects of these complex problems are beyond the scope of traditional science; they are emergent processes, open to the influence of spiritual realities. To continue rejecting hylozoic investigation, with closed intellect walled off from an undeveloped intuition, can only lead to degeneration. The development of intuition as partner of intellect, science as partner to being, can only lead to hope and to freedom.

Perhaps we reject evidence because we are not capable of understanding what we cannot create. This is a reason for the experiential component of the "New Science" of hylozoism. Our experience may precede our ability to create. And like the concept of the "New World Order," the concept of "New Science" is not very new. The early post-Renaissance mythic philosopher and judge, Giambattista Vico (1668-1744) was probably the first to publish a book by the title (*New Science*). Vico, sometimes called the first modern historian, argued that man could understand only what he could create. Vico's was a science of the stages and cycles of human consciousness. History, according to Vico, was the story of unfolding human consciousness. As such, Vico's stages and cycles of human consciousness were even then not new; they were the ageless wisdom. The newness of Vico's "New Science" was the application of modern European Renaissance methods of reason, experience, test and verification to the stages of human consciousness.[321]

Like the threads of the ageless wisdom that always suffused and countered the "Christian" Church authoritarianism, Vico's influence is more strongly with us than we may notice. James Joyce was a student of Vico. Joyce apparently based his whole colossal epic *Finnegans Wake* on Vico's New Science.[322]

Heavily influenced by Joyce, and an early interpreter of the difficult *Finnegans Wake*, was Joseph Campbell. Campbell's popular teachings on mythology, religion and spiritual traditions, based on the ageless wisdom teachings, have done much to dispel the illusion that the great spiritual and religious traditions are incompatible with each other. Campbell, Joyce, Vico, and others such as Jung were able to present inspiring visions of life inclusive of the transcendent and inclusive of the spiritual because they knew of its relevance from personal creative experience.

If the ancients knew all of this stuff anyway, then in the long run, how relevant have the past two hundred years of science been? Many esotericists indicate the following. The basic theme of all mythology (and religion) is that coexisting with, infusing and vivifying the physical plane is a spiritual reality. What is the basic theme of the scientific revolution? It is not, as so many would have it, that all of mythology and religion was wrong. It is that direct physical plane experience—observation, experiment and ratiocination—is a very good way (in fact, the best way) to get information on, and interact with, the physical plane. A next step, as Swami Vivekananda eloquently advocated a century ago, is to apply the basic theme of the scientific revolution (direct experience, experiment, verification) to spiritual growth. This entails a great awakening.

Sure, the ancients (the avatars, sages and saints of the past) did know this stuff. But they did not know it in the way and detail that we can know it now. Also, in the past, only an elite few knew it.

The scientific revolution has physically overcome the barrier of distance among peoples; it has created a body of universally knowable knowledge. This paves the way for a planetary, democratically accessible, awakening—as the saints, sages and yogis of the past were awakened by transformations of the mystical physiology, and then the physical physiology, of their bodies. The scientific revolution is preparing the mystical physiology of the planetary demos (the human "nosphere," as Tielhard de Chardin called it) for a transformation of being.

The hylozoic shift now will finally complete the awakening begun in the Renaissance.

Endnotes

1. The interpretation is called the Copenhagen interpretation because it was initially advocated by Niels Bohr's group of theoretical physicists, located there. It is discussed in Chapter 3, and Part II. There is evidence, discussed later in this book, that Bohr himself would not have agreed with the extreme uses to which this interpretation has since been put.
2. If you're not familiar with concepts of three and four dimensions, this type of description will be made in more detail in Part II.
3. In fact, in terms of our normal three-dimensional thinking, the hylostatic world's time evolution is deterministic. But in four dimensions, it doesn't change at all! Talk about a recipe for existential despair.
4. Actually, this sort of thing was hotly debated during the time of Bohr's Copenhagen institute, but since World War II, consideration of this issue has been relegated to a fringe, subspecialty working on the "foundations of quantum theory," and regarded as irrelevant to the mainstream science.
5. I don't say *the* truth, because there may be no single truth. I don't define truth—the common sense definition will be good enough.
6. I am always astonished when this word is used about maverick scientific ideas. For example, an anonymous "peer review," on a federal grant proposal of mine that was rejected, actually wrote that my idea that solids and gases in the solar nebula might have separated somewhat *before* the planets formed was "dangerous"—apparently because it was different from the premises of well-known theorists.
7. Art Hobson, Editor of *Physics and Society*, quarterly of the Forum on Physics and Society of the American Physical Society, Vol. 22, No. 1, Jan., 1993. This "gloom" has also been documented by Nobel laureate physicist Leon M. Lederman in a report "Science: The End of a Frontier?" to the Board of Directors of the American Association for the Advancement of Science, January, 1991.
8. David Ruelle, writing in *Chance and Chaos*, Princeton Univ. Press, 1992.
9. See the discussions of the Baltimore case in *Nature* magazine in 1991 and 1992.
10. Interview in *The New York Times*, 1990.
11. See, "E-Mail Links Science's Young and Frustrated," *Science*, Vol. 256, p.606, May 1, 1992.

[12] Emeritus professor of physics, at the Cavendish Laboratory, in the University of Cambridge, writing in *Nature*, Vol. 357, p.29, May 7, 1992.
[13] See *Physics Today*, October, 1991, p.14-.
[14] Picador, 1992. Published in the United States by Doubleday.
[15] Emeritus professor of physics, at the Cavendish Laboratory, in the University of Cambridge, writing in *Nature*, Vol. 357, p.29, May 7, 1992.
[16] Vol. 356, p. 729-730, April 30, 1992.
[17] *Physics and Society*, Vol. 22, No.1, p.14, January, 1993.
[18] *Science*, Vol. 258, p.200-201, October 9, 1992.
[19] *American Journal of Physics*, September, 1992, 779-781.
[20] See, e.g., *Coming to Our Senses: Body and Spirit in the Hidden History of the West*, by Morris Berman, 1989, Simon and Schuster, 1990, Bantam.
[21] Kepler (1571 - 1630) founded the modern science of celestial mechanics—which is still used in astronomy and in the space program.
[22] Sir Isaac Newton (1642 - 1727) is generally credited with founding modern physics (especially the science of Mechanics), and the invention of the mathematics of Calculus (though Leibniz may be equally deserving of this credit). Newton investigated the spectral nature of sunlight, and discovered the law of Universal Gravitation. Newton pursued theology and alchemy in the second half of his career. It is often asserted that Newton was doing chemistry, instead of alchemy, because they "didn't know the difference back then." An examination of Newton's writings makes it quite clear that Newton knew the difference, and he was pursuing alchemy.
[23] Girolamo Cardano (Jerome Cardan), (1501-76), was a crucial figure in the history of mathematics and a founder of probability theory. (See Berman, p. 233).
[24] *Coming to Our Senses: Body and Spirit in the Hidden History of the West*, by Morris Berman, 1989, Simon and Schuster, 1990, Bantam.
[25] Ibid.
[26] At least the consciousness of those of us still around to experience it. In Berman's model the implication is that complete consciousness has always been attainable through direct somatic experience. So, civilizations and individuals of the distant past may have realized everything including that of which science is only an incomplete part. But we rather insensitive and thick types have needed the lessons of science and the modern crises in order to awaken.
[27] Christian Huygens (1629–95) Dutch mathematician, physicist, and

astronomer. Son of influential diplomat Constantine Huygens. Christian Huygens discovered Titan—Saturn's largest moon, and he figured out the true nature of Saturn's rings. He was a student of Rene Descartes, and a colleague and friend of Anton van Leeuwenhoek (1632–1723) pivotal biologist and pioneer in microscopy.

[28] Quoted in Carl Sagan's *Cosmos*.
[29] See Chapter 1, and Morris Berman.
[30] Abraham H. Maslow, 1970, *Religions, Values, and Peak Experiences*. Viking/Penguin.
[31] I am quoting from memory of a video taped lecture, but I'm sure I have the essence of his words correct.
[32] Gopi Krishna, with commentary by James Hillman, 1967, *Kundalini: The Evolutionary Energy in Man*, Shambhala Publications.
[33] "Manic depression"
[34] Gopi Krishna, with commentary by James Hillman, 1967, *Kundalini: The Evolutionary Energy in Man*, Shambhala Publications.
[35] Ibid.
[36] Richard Moss, 1986, *The Black Butterfly*, Celestial Arts.
[37] Paul Pearsall, Ph.D., 1992, *Making Miracles*, Avon Books.
[38] Ibid. And references therein.
[39] Mary Lutyens, 1976, *Krishnamurti: The Years of Awakening*, Avon Books.
[40] David Bohm was Professor of Physics at Birkbeck College, London University. He was a significant contributor to quantum theory, and he was a friend and colleague of Albert Einstein at Princeton for a time.
[41] Grof, S., *Beyond the Brain*, Albany: State University of New York Press, 1985.
[42] Ibid. Grof is careful not to imply that all psychosis is experience of nonordinary reality, but that some is, and therefore should not be labeled "psychosis" at all.
[43] Ibid.
[44] This in turn seems to be a reinvention of ancient Yogic and meditative practices, described in numerous books on these subjects.
[45] *Spiritual Emergency: When Personal Transformation Becomes a Crisis,* Edited by S. Grof, and C. Grof, 1989, Jeremy P. Tarcher.
[46] Ibid.
[47] Ibid.
[48] Stanislav Grof, private communication.
[49] For example, *Autobiography of a Yogi*, by Paramahansa Yogananda.
[50] Stanislav Grof, private communication.
[51] For example, *River's Way*, by Arnold Mindell, 1989, Arkana.

[52] *Journal of Humanistic Psychology*, Vol. 22, No. 1, Winter 1982.
[53] From a Gallup poll reported in *The Atlantic* magazine.
[54] Paul Boyer, professor of history at the University of Wisconsin, author of *When Time Shall Be No More: Prophecy Belief in Modern American Culture*—Harvard Univ. Press, writing in *The New Republic*, May 17, 1993.
[55] S. Chandrasekhar (another eminent astrophysicist) wrote a book with that title, Cambridge University Press, 1983.
[56] Ibid.
[57] I heard this from a graduate professor. It may not be exactly correct, but in any case de Broglie's thesis was short.
[58] See *Quantum Questions*, edited by Ken Wilber.
[59] From, *The Physicists*, by Daniel J. Kevles, Harvard University Press, 1987.
[60] Ibid.
[61] Quoted in Wilber.
[62] Quoted in Kevles.
[63] Ibid.
[64] Pauli's "Der Einfluss archetypischer Vorstellungen auf die Bildung naturwissenschaftlicher Theorien bei Kepler," together with Jung's "Synchronizitat als ein Prinzip akausater Zusammenhange," formed the volume *Naturerklarunf und Psyche* (Studien aus dem C.G. Jung-Institute, IV; Zurich, 1952). This volume was translated as *The Interpretation of Nature and the Psyche*, (New York [Bollingen Series LI] and London, 1955).
[65] Quoted in Wilber.
[66] Ibid., from Heisenberg's own accounts.
[67] Quoted in Wilber.
[68] See e.g., *Autobiography of a Yogi*, by Paramahansa Yogananda. Interestingly, Kali Yuga is often translated "epoch of materialism" with "materialism" meant in the literal sense because Kali is the Goddess of matter. And here we are, coming out of the materialist paradigm—the religious belief that only matter exists!
[69] From, *Looking Glass Universe*, by John P. Briggs, and F. David Peat.
[70] Bohr *was* known for spending much of his lectures trying to light his pipe and mumbling.
[71] Quoted in Wilber.
[72] Or about a hundred and thirty thousand in the case of this book.
[73] Quoted in Wilber.
[74] Ibid.
[75] Quoted in Briggs and Peat.

[76] "The Creation of the Universe," PBS show, May 16, 1993.
[77] To be fair, elsewhere, when pressed, Feynman has said that there are things "like love" that were not included in such statements. So perhaps Feynman the man was more complex than such quotes imply, but we take the quotes at face value.
[78] This will be discussed in more detail in a later chapter.
[79] Charles Tart is professor of psychology at the University of California.
[80] There are theorists, like Roger Penrose who argues in *The Emperor's New Mind* that the synthesis of gravity and quantum mechanics will reveal an entirely new level of causality in the quantum realm, on size scales very relevant to every day phenomena—but that is not a consensus idea.
[81] Renee Weber, *Dialogues with Scientists and Sages: The Search for Unity in Science and Mysticism*, New York, Methuen, 1986, p.210.
[82] e.g., public lecture delivered at the University of Tokyo, Summer 1991.
[83] *Larry King Live*, TV show, sometime in 1992.
[84] The Charlie Rose Show, 1992.
[85] Quoted in *Scientific American*, December, 1992.
[86] Some of CSICOP's shenanigans, and internal political squabbles, indicate less than an objective perspective. These are noted in Chapter 14.
[87] Isaac Asimov, "Science and the Mountain Peak," in Frazier, p. 299.
[88] From an interview with Fritjof Capra in *The Holographic Paradigm*. Rabindranath Tagore was a very important mystical poet in his own right, and he was, incidentally, the son of a very influential spiritual teacher who is regarded, in the Vedantic traditions, as a member of a line of avatars.
[89] Ibid.
[90] It is interesting that Feynman's son's great desire was to become a philosopher. [I believe he now is a philosopher.]
[91] The annual meetings of the Division for Planetary Sciences of the American Astronomical Society.
[92] *Science with a Vengeance: How the Military Created the US Space Sciences After World War II*, David H. De Vokin, New York, Springer-Verlag, 1992.
[93] Harvard University Press, 1987.
[94] A number of SSC proponents did argue that the engineering problem of building the SSC would result in technological advancements, but I am not aware of any scientist who argues that the actual results of the experiment would have practical applications.
[95] Government estimates predicted $11 billion for construction and $20

billion total project costs.
[96] Interview with John Bell in C. W. Davies and J. R. Brown, eds., *The Ghost in the Atom*, Cambridge: Cambridge University Press, 1986, p. 51.
[97] Giordano Bruno, 1548?-1600. Taken from a lecture by Jean Achterberg.
[98] Galileo's punishment may have been more severe if he hadn't capitulated somewhat to authorities. But facts are facts.
[99] See, for instance, a number of articles in *Nature* magazine.
[100] In the process of the historical review, I mention a number of famous names in relation to significant ideas and advances. Though these individuals invariably had a great deal to do with those ideas and advances, our historical fixation on a single name in relation to such advances is often out of proportion, and always ignores many individuals who contributed greatly. In a few cases, the individual is nearly deserving of his hagiolatry. In a few cases, the individual actually engaged a shameless, and successful, campaign to advance his name and reputation at any cost, including the names of deserving but less ruthless other scientists.
[101] So called because many of them are found on Celtic beaches.
[102] See, e.g., "lunar tidal effects are the main cause of error in determining the mass of the Z boson. Scientists at the CERN laboratory in Geneva, Switzerland, with help from workers at SLAC and the University of Lausanne, have found that the Moon's gravitational pull warps the LEP (Large Electron Positron) collider by as much as a millimeter (out of a total circumference of 27 km). This blurs the Z mass estimates by about 10 MeV. Hereafter, calibrations of the beam energy will take into account the phase of the Moon." (CERN Press Release, 23 Nov. 1992.) Then scale to human or planet size.
[103] Isaac Newton (1642–1727), English philosopher and founder of modern physics. Newton is too large a figure to do justice to in any note (probably even in any book). If there had been Nobel Prizes then, Newton would have qualified for at least half a dozen. Almost predictably, he also had trouble interacting with his contemporaries. Like most geniuses, the true nature of Newton's character is enigmatic. He has been interpreted as a noble and beneficent figure. He has also been reviled as a "coward" for holding and acting on sentiments such as "... I refrain from publishing books [and he did indeed not publish huge portions of his discoveries] for fear that disputes and controversies may be raised against me by ignoramuses." Others have argued that Newton actually witheld his discoveries out of a mystical understanding that his culture wasn't ready for them. As mentioned elsewhere in this book, Newton

concerned himself as much with metaphysics as he did with physics. (Quote taken from George Simmons, *Differential Equations with Applications and Historical Notes*, McGraw Hill, 1972.)

[104] A coincidence of possible interest to haiku poets is that, on the other side of the planet, another interesting thing was happening. The most famous haiku poet of all time, Basho, was born in Japan in 1644, just two years after Newton was born in England. At the height of his career, just about the time that Newton ogled that apple, Basho wrote the most famous haiku poem of all time. This poem is known by more than a hundred million people today (many more people than know about the Law of Universal Gravitation). The poem is said to capture the moment of Basho's deepest enlightenment—his unification with the essence of poetry. It was composed during a very quiet sit in a garden. The poem goes: Furu ike ya. Kawazu tobiko mu. Mizu no oto. It means: An old pond. A frog jumps in. The sound of water. The coincidence seems somehow worthy of note. Basho is sitting there in his garden, and plop, a frog *falls* into the water, and bam! a glimpse of enlightenment. Almost simultaneously, Newton is sitting there in his garden, and plunk, an apple falls, and bam! a glimpse of the Law of Universal Gravitation. Viewed externally these are very similar events. Internally (to Newton and Basho), the Easterner connected with the great immeasurable field of enlightenment. The Westerner connected with an intuition of the great measurable field of science.

[105] The size of an atomic nucleus is about $10^{(-15)}$ meters, or one one-hundred-thousandths of the size of an atom. The size of an atom is about one ten billionth the size of a meter (which is about half the size of you).

[106] See, for instance, Ruelle's book.

[107] Maxwell (1831 – 79), Scottish physicist. A seminal figure in electromagnetism and statistical physics.

[108] See, e.g., *Maxwell on Saturn's Rings*, eds. Brush et al., (1983).

[109] Some science historians might argue with the interpretation that it was Maxwell's Saturn's rings studies that led him into the kinetic theory of gases. We do know that the former preceded the later chronologically (and that Maxwell's studies of Saturn's rings are much less well known than are his works on the kinetic theory of gases, which again are less well known than his tremendously important unification of electromagnetism). The assumption of causal relation is mine.

[110] Ludwig Boltzmann (1844 – 1906), Austrian physicist.

[111] See, e.g., *Looking Glass Universe*, by John P. Briggs and F. David Peat, for discussion of Prigogine.

[112] From Kevles.
[113] From Kevles, p.4.
[114] Some readers will recognize that this is an adaptation of a Sufi story, in which the main character is the famous Sufi mystic and rascal "Nasrudin."
[115] See e.g., *Crucial Experiments in Modern Physics*, by George L. Trigg, Crane, Russel and Company, Inc. New York, 1971, p.37.
[116] Ibid.
[117] This description draws from a very good description of the development of our understanding of black-body radiation, in Trigg.
[118] Quoted in Kevles.
[119] Einstein, "Concerning a Heuristic Point of View about the Creation and Transformation of Light," reprinted in Henry A. Boorse and Lloyd Motz, eds., *The World of the Atom* (2 vols., New York, 1966), I, 553.
[120] Noted in Kevles.
[121] Briggs and Peat, p. 44,45.
[122] Noted in *Quantum Reality*, by Nick Herbert.
[123] Quoted in Kevles, p.164.
[124] Ibid., p.164.
[125] Ibid., p.166.
[126] Quoted in Briggs and Peat, p.54.
[127] N. Bohr, *Nature* 121, 580, 1928.
[128] Quoted in Kevles, p.167.
[129] Quoted in Herbert, p.45.
[130] Briggs and Peat, p.97.
[131] Herbert, p.120, criterion 5, of his characterization of the "orthodox ontology's opposition" is, "Quons in the same state show measurable differences because they were physically different before measurement."
[132] In, *The Character of Physical Law*, by Richard Feynman.
[133] Phrase from the book of that title by J.C. Pearce.
[134] A detailed description, with minimal and readable mathematics, is given for instance by Roger Penrose, *The Emperor's New Mind*.
[135] Bell, J.S., 1987. *Speakable and Unspeakable in Quantum Mechanics*. Cambridge Univ. Press.
[136] Aspect, A. and Grangier, P., 1986, Experiments on Einstein-Podolsky-Rosen-type correlations with pairs of visible photons. In *Quantum Concepts in Space and Time* (ed. R. Penrose and C. J. Isham), Oxford University Press.
[137] This actually violates the relativistic speed limit (the speed of light) only in spirit. There is some sort of nonlocal instantaneous connection

between events. But it cannot be used to send messages from one place to the other faster than the speed of light. This is because, in the Aspect experiment for instance, the *results* from the two detectors need to be physically brought together and compared in order to show that the nonlocal correlation actually occur. There is no way to tell the orientation of the other detector, or whether that orientation has been changed, until the results from the two detectors are compared. Ways to use quantum mechanical nonlocality to send faster than light signals have been extensively investigated, and as far as I know it has always been shown to be impossible. Occasionally rumors that the military is spending money on trying to do so sparks interest. Even if the rumors are true it doesn't mean much. The military spends a lot of money on a lot of other goofy things too.

[138] In technical physics language, inelastic means bounces without losing energy, like a perfect "super-ball" would be, and is what we have been using all along for our model air molecules. In common usage (as Ruelle used) elastic (which means deformable and therefore perhaps bouncy but bouncy with some energy loss) is often used to mean inelastic.

[139] Ruelle, pp.76, 77.

[140] This is also why the Chinese-originated game called Go, which is played on a 19 by 19 board (with 361 locations) with white and black stones and rules much simpler than chess, has not been successfully played by a computer. The best computer Go program is barely equal to a novice human player. The computer Chess programs however are now rivaling, and will probably soon surpass, the best professional human chess players.

[141] Ruelle, p.64.

[142] Ruelle, p.8.

[143] Ruelle, p.71.

[144] Waldrop, p.80.

[145] Waldrop, p.35.

[146] *Turbulent Mirror*, p. 202.

[147] This is based on an actual account of an educator who thought she was looking for bright young children who would answer "Columbus!" The one reticent gifted child transformed the perspective of the *educator*.

[148] Hamlet, after an encounter with a spirit (from Shakespeare).

[149] Paramahansa Yogananda, *Autobiography of a Yogi*, p.415.

[150] Paramahansa Yogananda, *Autobiography of a Yogi*, p.564.

[151] Paramahansa Yogananda, *Autobiography of a Yogi*, p.57.

[152] Ibid., p.477, 8.

[153] Ibid., p.485.
[154] Some philosophers and theologians would argue that I use the term Gnostic too broadly. As far as I can tell, though, Gnostic is always an imprecise term (see discussions in the magazine *Gnosis*). So, the reader may understand "Gnostic," for now, as it is described by the context in which it is used here.
[155] There is now a quarterly journal called the *Teilhard Review*. Followers of Teilhard de Chardin's view include popular New York state governor Mario Cuomo. Teilhard de Chardin's influence, though still large, was probably decreased by the fact that his Church superiors forbade his major and most explicit works to be published until after his death. According to Julian Huxley, the knowledge that his work would at least be published after his death kept him going.
[156] *The Phenomenon of Man*, first published in French, 1955, published in English, 1959, Harper and Row, New York.
[157] Joel Kramer and Diana Alstad, North Atlantic Books/Frog Ltd. Berkeley, California, 1993.
[158] This does not necessarily exclude the true Bhakti, or devotional, path, if it is done with full self-involvement.
[159] Sai Baba is, in fact, a devotional teacher. And so, my use of his teachings at first glance might seem to contradict the view of The Guru Papers. I look at this (apparent self contradiction) as an indication that the new paradigm is *not* some sort of simple formula or authority.
[160] *The Embers and the Stars*, University of Chicago Press, 1984.
[161] Clearly, nonduality could not be experienced. It could only be become.
[162] A central tenet of Vedanta is of course nonduality. And since that small part of Vedanta that I think I understand seems to me entirely correct, I'd bet that it is right about much of the other stuff too. And the Vedantists themselves, despite their ultimate nondualism, find it important to articulate detailed and sophisticated models of matter, prana, finer levels of prana, and all their interrelations. Are they "being dualistic" and thus self-contradictory? Sure. Any utterance or action is "dualistic" in that sense.
[163] Little, Brown, and Company, Boston, 1991.
[164] I used this word several times before I realized that it is not in my dictionary. I hope the reader will forgive me for deciding, rather than to change it, to argue that it *should* be in dictionaries. Mentation means all actions of or pertaining to the functioning of the mind. The word 'thinking' has too small a connotation for this purpose. 'Thinking' does not include, for instance, dreaming, or hallucinating, or meditating, or experiencing creativity, or forgetting—'mentation' does.

[165] *A Physicist's Guide to Skepticism*, Prometheus Books, Buffalo, NY., 1988. p. 193.

[166] If the previous chapters of this book did not convince you, see Bell, J.S., 1987, *Speakable and Unspeakable in Quantum Mechanics*, Cambridge Univ. Press.

[167] Except a 1949 reference to the originator of the modern use of the term "information theory" related to electronic computers—Claude Shannon.

[168] C.H. Bennett, IBM J. Res. Dev. 17, 525 (1973); C.H. Bennett, "Time/space Trade-Offs for Reversible Computation," SIAM J. on Computation, Aug, 1, V18, N4, (1989); C.H. Bennet, "Notes on the History of Reversible Computation," IBM J. Res. Dev. (1988); J. Berger, Int. J. Theor. Phys. V.29, p985, (1990); R. Landauer, Phys. Scr. V.35, 88 (1987); R. Landauer, "Information is Physical," *Physics Today*, May (1991). Also *Physics Today*, letters on pp. 98-100, March (1992).

[169] From a 1985 lecture, "Life and Mind in the Universe" by Dr. George Wald. [quoted in HPB by Sylvia Cranston Jeremy P. Tarcher/Putnam, New York, 1993.]

[170] This is noted by Ruelle, p. 181.

[171] Ibid.

[172] Ibid.

[173] This is not to imply that I think that the detailed models of brain function, such as those presented by Dennett, are irrelevant. I think they are especially relevant because they could help us appreciate how spirit and matter work together to produce human functioning—if the models would allow the spiritual dimension to exist.

[174] See, *Infinite in All Directions*, by Freeman J. Dyson, Bessie/Harper and Row, 1988.

[175] See, for example, *Man and Transformation*, edited by Joseph Campbell, 1964, Princeton University Press.

[176] See, especially, the essays in *Spiritual Emergency* (see note 2 above). Also *The Collected Works of Carl Jung*, especially *Civilization in Transition*, and *Psychology and Alchemy*, Princeton University Press.

[177] "Shake-up for Earthquake Prediction," by Robert J. Geller, *Nature*, 1991, Vol. 352, p. 275.

[178] The Tokai district is the area along the Pacific coast just south of Tokyo. Based on past seismicity, this area is due soon for a major quake which could affect major metropolitan areas including Tokyo. The Kanto district which includes Tokyo, based on past seismicity, is due in the next few decades for a quake similar to the 1923 Great Kanto Earthquake, which killed 140,000 people.

[179] See, *Sixty Seconds That Will Change the World: The Coming Tokyo Earthquake*, by Peter Hadfield, Charles E. Tuttle, 1992. Also, *The Anticipated Tokai Earthquake: Japanese Prediction and Preparedness Activities* / Prepared by the EERI Committee on the Anticipated Tokai Earthquake, Earthquake Engineering Research Institute, Berkeley, CA, 1984.

[180] A technical analysis of synchronicity and coincidence from the psychological standpoint is given by Carl Jung, in "Synchronicity: An Acausal Connecting Principle." In: *The Structure and Dynamics of the Psyche*, Collected Works, 8, Translated by R.F.C. Hull, Princeton University Press, 1977. An essay on the topic from the physical science standpoint, by Nobel prize winning physicist Wolfgang Pauli, was published together with a version of Jung's "Synchronicity" essay in a volume translated as *The Interpretation of Nature and the Psyche* (New York, Bollingen Series LI, and London, 1955). A moving account of the meaning of coincidences and synchronicity in medicine and personal healing is given by Paul Pearsall, in *Making Miracles*, Avon Books, 1993.

[181] The first reference was replied to by Kazuo Hamada, "Unpredictable Earthquakes" *Nature*, 1991,Vol. 353, p.611, and Hamada was rebutted by Robert Geller on p. 612. These were commented on by David Swinbanks, "Earthquake Prediction: Trying to Shake Japan's Faith in Forecasts," *Nature*, 1992, Vol. 356, p. 464, and "Japanese Report Shows Cracks in Predicting Earthquakes," Vol. 358, p. 361. The debate was also covered in newspapers in the U.S. and Japan and in the Far East Economic Review (Hong Kong).

[182] "Self-Organized Criticality" by Per Bak and Kan Chen, in *Scientific American,* January, 1991, and the references therein.

[183] *Chaos: Making a New Science*, by James Gleick, Penguin Books, 1988.

[184] A few hours estimate is based on analogy with the Ruelle (*Chance and Chaos*, by David Ruelle, Princeton University Press, 1992.) turbulence calculations. A more refined calculation would take into account that the purely turbulent system considered by Ruelle is somewhat more chaotic than the actual weather, and would yield a longer time possibly on the order of a few days. The exact amount of time is irrelevant to the essential point here.

[185] The 1991 annual meeting of the Division for Planetary Sciences of the American Astronomical Society. Short Lecture by Jack Wisdom, referenced in *Bulletin of the American Astronomical Society*, Vol. 23, No. 3, 1991. See also, "Chaotic Evolution of the Solar System," by G.J. Sussman and J. Wisdom, in *Science*, Vol. 257, N. 5066, 1992.

[186] The standard model of solar system formation is described by George W. Wetherill in "Formation of the Earth" in *Annual Reviews of Earth and Planetary Science*, Vol. 18, 1990. The formation of the Oort Cloud of comets is described by Paul R. Weissman in "The Oort Cloud" in *Nature*, Vol. 344, p. 825-830, 1990. These are both described in my papers "Does Debris from the Formation of Other Planetary Systems Impact Earth?" in *Icarus*, Vol. 94, p. 250-254, 1991, and "Motes in the Solar System's Eye," due in a summer 1993 issue of *Astronomy*.

[187] Quoted in "The New Challenges," by John Horgan, in *Scientific American*, Dec., 1992.

[188] Thomas Jefferson is rumored to have said, of a reported meteorite fall in 1808, "I would rather believe that two Yankee professors would lie than that rocks could fall from heaven." But the only documentable quote is Jefferson's written words, "(the meteorite's) descent from the atmosphere presents so much difficulty as to require careful examination." The histories of both quotes are discussed in *Meteorites and Their Parent Planets*, by H. Y. McSween Jr., Cambridge University Press, 1987.

[189] Discussed in *Meteorites and Their Parent Planets*, by H. Y. McSween Jr., Cambridge University Press, 1987.

[190] Ibid.

[191] I have heard this quote attributed variously to Nobel prize winning physicist Richard Feynman, and to California Institute of Technology astrophysicist Peter Goldreich. The true origin of the quote is uncertain, but physicists seem to like it.

[192] Estimate, for instance, from Thinking Machines Corp. founder (Hillis) in *Omni Magazine* interview.

[193] See, for instance, *Scientific American* circa 1994.

[194] Reference available.

[195] Interview, in *Venture Inward* (Virginia Beach, Va.), Vol. 4, 1990, pp. 16-19, 36-7.

[196] For instance, the Nag Hammadi Library, and the Dead Sea Scrolls, and the recent scholarly interpretations of them.

[197] Lest anyone doubt my credibility—this crow (called kaa-chan by the children) was reported on by the international press in November, 1993. The American television network CNN aired footage of kaa-chan behaving exactly as described.

[198] Autobiography of Millikan (referenced in previous chapter).

[199] Udana, p. 80-81. Trans. by Frank Lee Woodward. Pali Text Society, 1926—as quoted in *Human Being in Depth: A Scientific Approach to Religion*, by Swami Ranganathananda, State Univ. of New York Press,

1991, p.54. I slightly altered Woodward's English translation, in the interest of clarity. His exact translation was, "There is, brethren, an unborn, a not-become, a not-made, a not-compounded. If there were not, brethren, this that is unborn, not become, not made, not compounded, there could not be made any escape from what is born, become, made, compounded. But since, brethren, there is this unborn, not-become, not-made, not-compounded, therefore is there made known an escape from what is born, become, made, compounded."

[200] Lovelock, J.E., "Gaia as seen through the atmosphere," *Atmospheric Environment*, V. 6, 1972, 579-80, Lovelock, J.E., and Margulis L., "Biological Modulation of the Earth's Atmosphere, *Icarus*, V. 21, 1974.

[201] Lovelock, *Healing Gaia: Practical Medicine for the Planet*, Harmony Books, New York, 1991.

[202] A not so technical description of this is given in Ibid. also in *Earth Shock*, by Andrew Robinson, Thames and Hudson Ltd., London, 1993. More detailed descriptions can be found in the papers in *Global Climate Change and Life on Earth*, Richard L. Wyman (ed.), 1991.

[203] A technical, but readable, description of the solar system formation standard model can be found in "Formation of the Earth," in *Annual Reviews of Earth and Planetary Science*, V.18, p. 205-256, by George W. Wetherill. A brief, nontechnical description, related to detecting interstellar debris, is given in "Motes in the Solar System's Eye: How can tiny, high-speed meteorites help give astronomers the big picture on how solar systems form?," in *Astronomy*, May, 1993, p. 34-39, by Thomas Brophy.

[204] Meaning baryonic atomic nuclei, as opposed to neutrinos and other "exotic" particles.

[205] Astronomers often call any atom heavier than helium a "metal," because of this fundamental difference between the original gaseous stuff, hydrogen and helium, and the heavier elements that had to be formed later. So argon or oxygen for instance is a "metal" to this sort of astronomer.

[206] See *Protostars and Planets III*, eds. E.H. Levy and J.I. Lunine, Univ. of Arizona Press, Tucson, 1993.

[207] There are some ideas for how the gas was dissipated. See, "Photo-evaporation of the Solar Nebula and the Formation of the Giant Planets," by F.H. Shu, D. Johnstone, and D. Hollenback, *Icarus*, Nov.1, 1993, V.106, N1, p.92, and references therein.

[208] Chyba, C.F., "Impact Delivery and Erosion of Planetary Oceans in the Early Inner Solar System," *Nature*, Jan.11, 1991, V343, N6254, p.129.

Chyba and Sagan also believe that comets may have "seeded and then destroyed life many times" on the early Earth, *Nature*, Jan. 9, 1992, V355, N6356, p.125, and *Astronomy*, Nov.1, 1992, V20, p.28.

[209] For example, *Protostars and Planets III*, eds. E.H. Levy, and J.I. Lunine, Univ. of Arizona Press, Tucson, 1993; *Protostars and Planets II*, eds. D.C. Black, and M.S. Matthews, Univ. of Arizona Press, Tucson, 1985; *Protostars and Planets: Studies of Star Formation and of the Origin of the Solar System*, ed. T. Gehrels, Univ. of Arizona Press, 1978.

[210] The precise details of the dynamics in the asteroid belt is still not entirely understood. Some other factor may have also led to the formation of the asteroid belt. Whatever the exact case is, is unimportant to the point of the story of this chapter.

[211] In scientific notation, a trillion is 10(12). 10(12) is a big number, but not as big as other numbers. The number of atoms in your body for instance is about 10(29)—much much bigger than 10(12).

[212] All of these times are guesses. The fact of emergence, though, as defined in previous chapters has been established.

[213] For more technical studies, one could start with, "Understanding and Predicting Atmospheric Chemical Change—An Imperative for the US Global Change Research Program," US National Research Council, 1993.

[214] Ibid.

[215] Swami Ranganathananda, p.50.

[216] The same goes for the esoteric core of all the religions, as I've already mentioned.

[217] A very large city park in Tokyo.

[218] As already mentioned, by Babaji, and Sri Yukteswar, Lahiri Mahasay in the 1800's (as described in Yogananda's *Autobiography of a Yogi*, and in the recent books by Swami Satyeswarananda), by the Dalai Lama (see Part I of this book), J. Krishnamurti (as described, for instance, by David Bohm, and by Fritjof Capra in his later interviews), and Swami Vivekananda's lucid analyses from the late 1800's, recently synopsized by Swami Ranganathananda in *Human Being in Depth: A Scientific Approach to Religion*, and of course by Trelihard de Chardin, and in the first part of this century in the books by Alice A. Bailey (for instance *A Treatise on Cosmic Fire*), and by many others.

[219] The Shadhiliyyah order—described in "Sufism Comes to America," by Jay Kinney, in *Gnosis Magazine*, Winter 1994, p.18-23, and references therein. There are many orders of Sufism, with a wide range of practices. This order is considered more "sober" and perhaps closer to

mainstream Islam.
[220] I feel that I should note here that I am not asserting that all scientists must meditate in order to be productive. Similarly, I do not argue that all spiritual teachers must do mathematical physics in order to be effective. I do argue that there is a need, that is especially acute now, for information to flow between both camps, and a mostly unrecognized need for some who would try a little of each.
[221] Sixth to eighth century B.C. spiritual poems.
[222] From *Freedom in Exile: The Autobiography of the Dalai Lama*, p. 99, 100, Harper Perennial, 1990.
[223] Ibid.
[224] J. Krishnamurti stated it in these terms.
[225] See *The Autobiography of the Dalai Lama*.
[226] "The End of the Modern Era," in *The New York Times*, on 1 March 1992.
[227] Daniel Kleppner, of MIT, in *Physics Today*, August, 1993.
[228] See, for instance, Yogananda's *Autobiography of a Yogi*.
[229] These are described in Joe Pearce's 1992 book.
[230] *T.A.Z. Temporary Autonomous Zone*, Autonomedia, Brooklyn.
[231] *Healing Words: The Power of Prayer and the Practice of Medicine*, by Larry Dossey, Harper San Francisco, 1993.
[232] This is an account of a conversation as it occurred. The things the monk related may or may not be true. The stories themselves are not the point. The point is the relevance of them to my psychological state at the time.
[233] [It is interesting to note, in the context of this story that if Roosevelt had been around for the decision whether to use the atomic bombs, he might have decided differently than did President Truman.] This is an account of the monk's conversation, and is not necessarily my interpretation of the events of World War II.
[234] Omar Nelson Bradley, 1893–1981. Called "one of the ablest US generals of World War II," *American Academic Encyclopedia*. Chairman of the United States Joint Chiefs of Staff (1949–53).
[235] From *A Treatise on Cosmic Fire*, by Alice A. Bailey, Lucis Press.
[236] Ranganathananda, p.66.
[237] He specifically argues that there is a place for divination in decision making, in his book *The Autobiography of the Dalai Lama*.
[238] The Miami Herald, Sun., Oct. 18, 1987, 10J, by Bob MacGregor and Trish Janeshutz.
[239] See, *Babaji: Vol. 1*, and other Volumes, by Swami Satyeswarananda.
[240] From, *Gnosis Magazine*, Winter, 1994, p. 41-47.
[241] *The Economist*, December 25th, 1993 - January 7th, 1994, p.26.

[242] *India Today*, July 15, 1993, p. 35-37. (Fifteen billion rupees is about 500 million dollars, as of February, 1994.)

[243] *The Sunday Times*, June 27, 1993.

[244] *An Analysis of the Implementation of a Curriculum Innovation for Character Development: Sathya Sai Education in Human Values*, Marantz, Ronne Diane, ED.D, 1991, Columbia University Teachers College (0055).

[245] Described in, *Glimpses of the Divine*, by Brigitte Rodriguez, Samuel Weiser, York Beach, Maine, 1993.

[246] *South China Morning Post*, August 9, 1992.

[247] Rodriguez, p.31.

[248] Ibid. p. 58.

[249] Bhagavantam is quoted extensively in the books and articles about Sai Baba, referenced here. Other scientists quoted as devotees include Dr. P. K. Bhattacharya, the head of the Department of Chemistry in the same institute, who received his doctoral degree from the University of Illinois; the physicist Dr. K. Venkatessan of the same institute, who received his training at Oxford University and in Geneva; and Dr. V.K. Gokak, a former president of Bangalore University.

[250] Shirdi Sai Baba, a revered saint who had both Moselm and Hindu followers, and who also exhibited miracles.

[251] *The Economist*, January 7th, 1994, p.26.

[252] Times reference available.

[253] *Sai Baba: The Holy Man and the Psychiatrist*, Birth Day Publishing Co., San Diego, CA, USA, 1975.

[254] *Spirit and the Mind*, Sandweiss, p.41.

[255] Described in the Sandweiss books.

[256] Ibid., p.xii.

[257] The interview, from September of 1976 in *Blitz* magazine, is reprinted in *Spirit and the Mind*, by Samuel H. Sandweiss.

[258] Sandweiss, p.46. Bhagavantam is also quoted about this story in the books by Murphet, Hislop, and Osis, referenced herein.

[259] Ibid., p.22. Same events also related in Howard Murphet, *Sai Baba—Man of Miracles*, Fredrick Muller, Ltd., London, 1971, p. 156.

[260] Osis and Haraldsson would not fit the term "skeptic" as some would prefer it—meaning rabid and unthinkingly dogmatic materialists—but they do fit "skeptic" as in one who applies critical analysis.

[261] *Modern Miracles: An Investigative Report on Psychic Phenomena Associated with Sathya Sai Baba*, by Erlendur Haraldsson, Ph.D., Fawcett Columbine, New York, 1987. Correspondence: Dr. Erlendur Haraldsson, Department of Psychology, University of Iceland, 101

Reykjavik, Iceland.
[262] Ibid., p. 52,53.
[263] Ibid., p.287-288.
[264] Described in *My Baba and I*, by John S. Hislop, Ed.D., Birth Day Publishing Company, San Diego, CA, 1985. (Sathya Sai Baba is believed to be the middle of a triple incarnation of the avatar, the first being the Hindu and Moslem saint Shirdi Sai Baba, who reportedly also predicted reincarnation eight years after his death—Sathya Sai Baba's birth year. See, for instance, *The Life and Teachings of Sai Baba of Shirdi*, by Antonio Rigopoulos, State University of New York Press, 1993. Book evolved out of a 1987 doctoral dissertation at the University of Venice, Italy, by the same author.)
[265] *Healing Words*, by Larry Dossey, Harper San Francisco, 1993.
[266] Film, *The Lost Years of Jesus*, by Richard Bock.
[267] Harvard Professor and Theravada Buddhist teacher.
[268] See, *Krishnamurti: The Early Year*, and *Krishnamurti: The Years of Fulfillment*, by Mary Lutyens.
[269] Ibid., p. 284.
[270] Howard Murphet, in his book, also argues eloquently for this view.
[271] Swami Vivekananda, lecturing in England, in 1896. As quoted by Swami Ranganathananda, pages 6 and 7.
[272] A nontechnical description is given in "The Quantum Physics of Time Travel," by David Deutsch and Michael Lockwood, in *Scientific American*, March, 1994.
[273] *Transformation*.
[274] "Neuropsychological profiles of adults who report sudden remembering of early childhood memories: Implications for claims of sex abuse and alien visitation/abduction experiences." Persinger, M. A., Laurentian U. of Sudbury, Behavioral Neuroscience Lab, ON, Canada, In *Perceptual & Motor Skills*, 1992, Aug., Vol 75(1), p. 259-266.
[275] From interview on *Nova* television show, "UFO's: Are We Alone?"
[276] "*Abduction: Human Encounters with Aliens*," by John E. Mack, Scribners, 1994.
[277] Ibid., pages, 3-7.
[278] *Scientific American*, July, 1994, p. 10.
[279] British tabloid newspaper *Today*, September 9, 1991. I use term "hired" as in using the services of. It is not clear if any money was involved.
[280] *Crop Circle Apocalypse*, by John Macnish, Circlevision Publications, 1993.
[281] Ibid. Macnish reports one of these accounts, which apparently has not been retracted or shown to be from an unreliable observer. Macnish

also reports another account of a circle being found, and a teenage boy coming forward to report he "observed" the formation. The boy told a fantastic story of lights and UFO's and space beings. Later he admitted that he had fabricated the story and in fact hoaxed the circle himself.

[282] Reported by Linda Moulton Howe (Pulitzer Prize-winning documentary film maker), in *Share International* magazine, May 1993, p.19.
[283] Ibid.. p.21.
[284] *Crop Circles: Conclusive Evidence?*, by Pat Delgado, Bloomsbury Publishing Limited, 2 Soho Square, London W1V 5DE, 1992.
[285] Ibid.
[286] Ibid.
[287] Ibid., and same as note 9 above.
[288] "Unidentified Farm Object shakes state," *Chicago Tribune*, Sunday, October 28, 1990, by Wes Smith.
[289] This book is finally going to press about four years after this section was drafted. In the interim, stronger evidence has emerged that the vast majority of crop circles are hoaxes. My opinion that possibly some small number of circles are genuine has weakened some, but otherwise I stand by the logic of this section.
[290] Rogo, p. 90.
[291] Haraldsson, p. 213-214.
[292] Lafollette, p.148.
[293] Sathya Sai Baba [from Sandweiss, (2), p. 232]
[294] In his book *Holy Madness: The Shock Tactics and Radical Teachings of Crazy-wise Adepts, Holy Fools, and Rascal Gurus*, Arkana, 1990.
[295] Ibid., p. 131.
[296] Satyeswarananda, pages 154-.
[297] Described, for instance, in *A Treatise on Cosmic Fire*, by Alice Bailey.
[298] This "behind the scenes" perspective is described, for instance, by Yogananda, both his teachers (Sri Yukteswar, and Lahiri Mahasay), Alice Bailey, and by H.P. Blavatsky and the Theosophical Society. More recently, also, by Satyeswarananda, Torkom Saraydarian (*The Ageless Wisdom*, and references therein), several recent Sufi teachers, and others.
[299] See *The Young Lion*, biography of Winston Churchill.
[300] Ibid.
[301] A rather technical, but very specific, description of intuition and its development is given in *From Intellect to Intuition*, by Alice A. Bailey, and in Bailey's other works.
[302] From *Glamour: A World Problem*, Alice Bailey, p. 65.
[303] Adapted from Ibid., p. 84.

[304] From, *Sanathana Sarathi*, Prasanthi Nilayam newsletter, December 1993.
[305] From, *The Gospel According to Thomas*.
[306] Mircea Eliade, a native of Romania, lectured in the Ecole des Hautes-Etudes of the Sorbonne and was chairman of the Department of History of Religions at the University of Chicago.
[307] *Yoga*, by Mircea Eliade, p. 86, 87.
[308] *Babaji, Vol. 1*, by Satyeswarananda, p. 119.
[309] Paraphrased from, *The Tibetan Book of Living and Dying*, by Sogyal Rinpoche, Harper San Francisco, 1992.
[310] The concepts in this paragraph, and the two flanking it, are heavily influenced by the (very accessible) publications of Joseph Campbell.
[311] The title of his book, *The Astonishing Hypothesis*.
[312] *Scientific American* magazine, April, 1894, reprinted 100 years later.
[313] See, *The Emperor's New Mind*, by Roger Penrose, and *Scientific American*, July, 1994, p. 93.
[314] *Healing Words: The Power of Prayer and the Practice of Medicine*, by Larry Dossey, page 247.
[315] From Daniel J. Kevles, *The Physicists*, New York, Knopf, 1977, p.233.
[316] From Bronowski, *Common Sense*, p.61.
[317] *EOS, The Journal of the American Geophysical Union*, July 6, 1993, p. 301.
[318] Noted in *Nexus* Magazine, Boulder, CO., Feb., 1994, p. 10, 11.
[319] From, *The New York Times*, Feb. 10, 1994, Sec. A, p.16. (As this book goes to press, DSM IV is out and still contains the addition.)
[320] From *Larry King Live* interview.
[321] Described in *The Creators*, by Daniel J. Boorstin (former Librarian of Congress), p. 713.
[322] Ibid., presents this view. *Finnegans Wake* begins, "Riverrum, past Eve and Adam's, from swerve of shore to bend of bay, brings us by a commodious vicus of recirculation back to Howth Castle and Environs." Which completes the final incomplete sentence, "A way a lone a last a loved a long the." "Vicus," Boorstin points out, is the Latin form of the Italian name Vico.

Index

Age of Aquarius, 331
Ageless Wisdom, 248, 254, 276, 284, 302-303, 333
American Physical Society, 6, 338
Anderson, Philip W., 6-7
Appleyard, Bryan, 7-8, 10
Artaud, Antonin, 25
Asimov, Isaac, 49-50
Assaggioli, Roberto, 24

Babaji, 136, 253-254, 259, 318
Bak, Per, 159
Baltimore, David, 5, 338
Bartok, 25
Bergson, Henri, 34
Berman, Morris, 11-12, 50, 228
Big Bang cosmology, 48, 169, 172, 200, 202
Black Elk, 137
Bohm, David, 23, 94-95, 142
Bohr, Niels, 32-49, 87-101, 130, 142, 182, 297, 326, 338
Boltzmann, Ludwig, 65-70, 83-85, 100-103, 106, 110
Boltzmann's equation, 67-70, 100, 106, 110
Boyer, Paul, 32, 88-89
Brown, George E., Jr, 9-10, 18
Brownian motion, 81
Buchner, 25
Buddha, 29, 137, 197, 215, 223, 228, 237, 258-259, 285, 298-299, 303, 319
Butterfly Effect, 103, 113

Campbell, Joseph, 17, 29, 153, 250, 315, 321-322, 328, 334
Cantor, 116
Cardan, Jerome, 11-12

Chaos theory, 106, 113-118, 166
Chardin, Teilhard de, 137-138, 147, 184, 335
Christ, 29, 136, 258-259, 303, 307, 321-322, 331
Christianity, Esoteric, 227
Christianity, Gnostic, 137, 250
Churchill, Winston, 306-307
Clare, John, 25
Classical Mechanics, 59-66
Classical Physics, 80
Closed timelike curve (CTC), 277-278
Cold War, 10, 52-54, 121
Committee for the Scientific Investigation of Claims Of the Paranormal (CSICOP), 49, 143, 292-297
Complementarity, 91
Consciousness, 141, 175, 195, 324
Copenhagen interpretation, 40-44, 93-94, 97, 103, 338
Corpus Hermeticum, 322
Cowan, George, 121
Creative Universe, 129

Dalai Lama, 23, 223-226, 247
DaVinci, Leonardo, 53
De Broglie, Louis, 33, 88, 94
Dead Sea Scrolls, 50
Dennett, 141-144, 176-185, 195, 198
Descartes, Renee, 11-12, 16-19, 23, 59, 228, 230
Dualism, 140
Dyson, Freeman, 149

Earthquakes, 150, 154, 158
Eddington, Arthur, 32-33, 142, 144-145

Einstein, Albert, 32-34, 40-43, 74, 78, 85-97, 103, 142, 228, 237, 296-298
Eisenhower, President, 9, 16, 18
Electricity, 71
Eliade, 316, 319
EPR experiments, 43, 97-98, 131

Feynman, Richard, 45-51, 95-96, 239
Fitzeau, 74
Fractal, 116-117
Franklin, Benjamin, 71
Freud, Sigmund, 25-27

Galileo, 12, 15-16, 55-56, 138, 227
Gandhi, Indira, 23, 134
Gibbs, J. Willard, 68
Giordano Bruno, 55, 227
Glass Bead Game, 195
Great Dark Spot, 212-213
Great Tokyo earthquake, 154
Grof, Stanislav, 23-26, 153

Havel, Vaclav, 9-10, 18, 225-226, 250
Hawking, Stephen, 47, 49
Heisenberg, 32, 36-43, 49, 87-93, 130
Henry, Joseph, 72
Hesse, Herman, 195-196
Hillman, James, 18, 20
Hitler, Adolf, 196, 306-307
Holderlin, 25
Huxley, Aldous, 23, 248
Huygens, Christian, 6, 15-16
Hylostatism, xii, 44, 54, 59, 75 78-79, 95, 100, 103-104, 109 129-130, 189, 224, 266, 282, 300

Hylostochastism, 94-95, 100-105, 130-132, 138, 147-152, 173, 177, 213, 224, 240, 256, 259, 265-266, 282, 300, 311-314, 323, 331
Hylozoism, xi, 9-10, 14, 16-21, 27, 31-32, 43, 48, 55, 68-71, 75, 100-101, 124, 132-141, 147-153, 163-166, 170-173, 177-184, 188-192, 198-202, 205-207, 212, 215-218, 221-224, 227-240, 247, 255-259, 262-266, 270-278, 283-290, 299-305, 309-327, 330-334

Inflationary Guru Problem, 298
International Astronomical Union, 3
Intuition, 221, 227, 234, 305-307

Jahn, Robert, 6-7, 324
Jung, Carl, 20, 24-26, 35, 151-153, 230, 334

Kepler, Johann, 11-12, 63, 166
Kevles, Daniel J., 53
Kogi Indians, xv, 240-248, 253-254, 272
Kolmogorov theory, 108, 119-120
Krishna, Gopi, 18-20, 21, 23, 26, 137, 230, 258-259, 262, 265, 298, 303, 307
Kuhn, Thomas, x
Kyoto, 3

Laing, R.D., 24-25, 29
Lao Tze, 29
Law of Universal Gravitation, 63, 65, 71

Lederman, Leon, 48, 338
Leibniz, 6
Lorentz, 74, 78

Magnetism, 71
Mandelbrot set, 114, 116
Mao Tse Tung, 223
Maslow, Abraham, 17-18, 24
Maxwell, James Clerk, 65-76, 80, 83, 85, 87, 100, 103
Michelson, 73-74
Mindell, Arnold, 24, 26
Mohammed, 29, 137, 253, 298, 307
Morley, 73-74
Moses, 29, 137, 237, 298
Moss, Richard, 20-21, 23, 26, 230
Munch, 25

Nag Hammadi Library, 50
NASA, viii, 15, 48, 52, 224, 290
Nature magazine, 6, 8, 338
NCAR, 163
Nehru, Jawaharlal, 23
New Science, 333-334
Newton, Sir Isaac, 6, 11-12, 63, 65, 67-71, 74-76, 86-87, 103, 106-107, 110, 166, 228
Nietzsche, 25
Nonlocality, 97

Occam's razor, 313
Oppenheimer, Robert, 49

Patanjali, 29, 316-317
Pauli, 35-38, 40, 97
Pearsall, Paul, 21-23, 26
Persinger, Michael, 280-281, 283
Physics Today, 6
Pippard, Brian, 6-8, 10

Planck, Max, 34-35, 54, 83-89, 92, 97, 130, 132-133, 149
Planckian butterfly effect, 132
Pound, Ezra, 25
Prana, 133-134
Pribram, Karl, xiii
Prigogine, Ilya, 68
Quantum theory, 103

Rajagopal, 270
Rank, Otto, 24-25
Rayleigh, Lord, 82-83
Relativity, 59, 71, 90
Rimbaud, 25
Ruelle, David, 106-108, 113-121, 124, 146, 160-161, 164-165, 168, 207, 338
Rutherford, Lord, 86-87, 326

Sai Baba, 139, 255-272, 277, 294-296, 311
Sandweiss, 260-261
Saturn's rings, 6, 66-67, 71
Schrodinger, 38-40, 88-89, 91, 95-96
Schumann, 25
Shaw, George Bernard, 23
Shingon, 233-235
Solvay Brussels conference, 33, 40, 93
Soviet Communism, 10, 52, 119, 196, 225, 227, 250, 256, 323
Strieber, Whitley, 278-279
Strindberg, 25
Sufis, 137, 140, 217, 252, 296
Superconducting Super Collider, 48, 53
Synchronicity, 35

Tagore, Rabrindranath, 49, 56
Theory of Everything, 8

Tibetan Pali manuscripts, 50
Tides, lunar, 61, 63
Tornadoes, 169
Turbulence, 115, 204

UFOs, 4, 280-283, 287-290

Van Gogh, Vincent, 25
Vedantic, xv, 39, 134, 137, 139, 252-253, 258, 277
Vivekananda, 275, 335
Volcanoes, 161
Voyager, 15, 52, 212-213, 290

Walden, George, 8, 10, 18
Waldrop, M. Mitchell, 120-124
Weather, 109, 163
Weiss, Brian L., 185-187, 190, 192, 196
Wilber, Ken, xiii, xiv, 27, 31, 38, 248, 251

Yogananda, Paramahansa, 133-138, 253, 301
Yukteswar, 134, 136, 253, 333